INDEX TO ALABAMA WILLS
1808 - 1870

Compiled

by

ALABAMA SOCIETY
DAUGHTERS OF THE AMERICAN REVOLUTION

CLEARFIELD

1955

Reprinted with the permission of
the Alabama Society,
Daughters of the American Revolution

Genealogical Publishing Co., Inc.
Baltimore, 1977

Reprinted for
Clearfield Company, Inc. by
Genealogical Publishing Co., Inc.
Baltimore, Maryland
1998, 1999, 2005

Library of Congress Catalogue Card Number 77-72078
International Standard Book Number: 0-8063-0765-X

Made in the United States of America

Copyright © 1955
Alabama Society
Daughters of the American Revolution
All Rights Reserved

TO

MARIE BANKHEAD OWEN

whose breadth of vision is exceeded only by
her love for Alabama, and in grateful appre-
ciation for her having made this work possible, this book is affectionately dedicated
by the Alabama Society, Daughters of the
American Revolution.

FOREWORD

This index is the outgrowth of a wish by the State Regent of the Alabama Society, Daughters of the American Revolution, Mrs. John Oden Luttrell, for a project for the Genealogical Records Committees which would be statewide in its scope, which could be done by women untrained in research, and which would be of value when completed. When asked for suggestions, the Department of Archives and History of the State of Alabama suggested the compilation of an index of all the wills probated prior to 1871 throughout Alabama. This suggestion appealed to the State Regent, who secured from Mrs. Marie Bankhead Owen, the Director of the State Department of Archives and History, the co-operation of that Department on the project, and especially the Department's Historical Materials Collector, Miss Maud McLure Kelly, to serve as the chairman of the Genealogical Records committee, of the Alabama Society, D.A.R.

The actual compilation has been done by the chapter committees named below, or by the members of the State Committee working with the chapter committees. A suggested quota was prepared and each chapter was requested to compile a specified part of the whole, with awards of gold, silver, blue or green starred certificates for completion of these quotas by deadline dates. Most of the chapters did all that was asked of them, and a number did more and won additional "stars" after completion of their original quotas. The "Lieutenant Joseph M. Wilcox" Chapter was the first to send in its completed quota, followed by "Bigbee Valley" and "Tuscaloosa" soon thereafter.

The chapters with location and committee, who made this compilation and stars won, are as follows:

"Alamance", Florence, Mrs. G. C. Cash; silver
"Andrew Jackson", Talladega, Miss Ruth Hamner, silver
"Anne Phillips", Montgomery, Miss Elizabeth Banks Pickett
"Bienville", Anniston, Mrs. Robert Bowie, Mrs. Otto Seyforth,
    gold and silver
"Bigbee Valley", Livingston, Mrs. Alex Horn, gold
"Cahawba", Birmingham, Mrs. Willard McCall, Mrs. S. G. Fallaw,
    Mrs. Pauline Pattberg, gold
"Canebrake", Uniontown, Mrs. Val Taylor, Mrs. E. R. White,
    Mrs. Wirt Naugher, silver and blue
"Captain William Bibb", Mount Meigs, Miss Frances Hails, blue
"Choctaw", Greensboro, Mrs. J. B. Stickney, Sr., Mrs. W. T. Dale,
    silver
"Colbert", Tuscumbia, Mrs. William Haden Wood, silver
"Conecuh", Evergreen, Mrs. Marie W. McCreary, gold and blue
"David Lindsay", Montevallo, Mrs. A. W. Vaughan, gold
"Elijah Pugh", Jackson, Mrs. W. W. Andrews, silver
"Elizabeth Bradford", Grove Hill, Miss Minnie Mae Pugh, silver
"Fort Conde", Mobile, Mrs. Robert Woods, Mrs. R. E. Porter, gold
"Fort Mims", Stockton, Mrs. T. J. Morgan, green
"Fort Strother", Oxford, Mrs. Hemphill Whiteside,
    Mrs. T. W. Coleman, gold and silver

"Francis Marion", Montgomery, Miss Lucharlle Wilson, silver
"General Sumter", Birmingham, Mrs. T. F. Farrell, gold
"Heroes of King's Mountain", Guntersville, Mrs. James N. Jacobs,
    silver
"John Parke Custis", Birmingham, Mrs. David Adams III, Mrs. Theodore
    Swann, Mrs. Bert Meadows, Mrs. Paul Bowron, Mrs. George F.
    Miller, gold
"John Wade Keyes", Athens, Mrs. George W. Smith, silver
"Jones Valley", Bessemer, Mrs. L. W. Greiner, Mrs. Rose Huey,
    Mrs. H. P. Lipscomb, gold
"Joseph McDonald", Sylacauga, Mrs. E. J. Prather, gold and silver
"Lewis", Eufaula, Mrs. E. W. Norton
"Lt. Joseph M. Wilcox", Camden, Mrs. E. M. Curtis, Mrs. William Cook,
    Mrs. D. Sadler,.Jr., gold
"Light Horse Harry Lee", Auburn, Miss Dana Gatchell, green
"Luxapalilla", Fayette, Mrs. W. R. Martin, Mrs. A. M. Grimsley,
    silver and green
"Margaret Lee Houston", Marion, Miss Eunice Fuller, silver
"Martha Wayles Jefferson", Opelika, Mrs. C. P. Stowe, Mrs. H. N.
    Segrest, gold and silver
"Mobile", Mobile, Miss Willie Mae Discher, gold
"Old Elyton", Birmingham, Mrs. H. L. Jackson, silver
"Oliver Wiley", Troy, Mrs. Wyche G. Pruitt, Miss Catherine Gardner,
    silver
"Ozark", Ozark, Mrs. A. D. Matthews, Mrs. H. H. Herndon, silver
"Peter Forney", Montgomery, Mrs. E. J. McManus, silver
"Pickett", Birmingham, Mrs. E. T. Glass, Mrs. H. E. Cross,
    Mrs. G. L. Martin, silver
"Princess Sehoy", Birmingham, Miss Nettie Edwards, Mrs. John B.
    Privett, Mrs. Kenneth McDonald, Mrs. Howard Langston,
    Mrs. F. G. Koenig, Mrs. E. A. Richey, gold and silver
"Robert Grierson", Headland, Mrs. Marvin Scott, Mrs. R. E. Solomon,
    silver
"Stephens", Decatur, Mrs. C. M. Graham, Mrs. Phil Pointer, gold
    and silver
"Sunset Rock", Birmingham, Mrs. F. A. Shelton, Mrs. C. M. Gray, gold
"Sylacauga", Sylacauga, Mrs. J. M. Peters, gold and silver
"Tidence Lane", Scottsboro, Mrs. Rutledge Larkin, two green
"Tuscaloosa", Tuscaloosa, Mrs. J. H. Hoit, Mrs. B. G. Gandrud,
    Mrs. Louis Weatherford, Mrs. Chester Knight, gold
"Twickenham Town", Huntsville, Miss Martha Lou Houston, Miss
    Minnie A. Rodgers, Mrs. R. P. Geron, Mrs. W. A. Estes,
    Mrs. W. F. Eigenbrod, Mrs. T. J. Young, gold
"William Rufus King", Selma, Mrs. S. E. Lott, gold
"William Speer", Birmingham, Mrs. W J. Flanigan, Mrs. E. L.
    Martin, green
"William Weatherford", Atmore, Mrs. Murray Greer, silver

No doubt others, both members and nonmembers, aided these committees
in some instances. To all who made this compilation will go the
grateful thanks of whoever, through the years, finds this index
of service.

In using this index, it should be remembered that the original records were old, many badly faded and poorly written, and that they were often difficult to read. It is realized that "David" and "Daniel" are frequently hard to distinguish in the old faded handwriting, as are the initials "J" and "I", "S" and "L", and the letters "v" and "u". Be charitable, therefore, in your judgment.

Wills were found recorded in surprising places, as well as loose and not recorded at all. Some counties recorded some wills among the deeds even while recording other wills in other records. Occasionally the same will is found recorded in more than one place and without explanation for this double recording. While great effort has been made to make this index both accurate and complete, it has not been possible for the State Committee to re-check all county records and it is possible that there are errors in the compilations as sent in by the chapter committees, and that some wills have been overlooked which should have been included. If so, the Alabama State Department of Archives and History, at Montgomery, will appreciate being so informed.

This has been a pleasant task, made easier by the almost unanimous support of the membership, but it would have been impossible of completion but for the complete and sympathetic co-operation of our State Regent, Mrs. John Oden Luttrell, and of the Director of our State Department of Archives and History, Mrs. Marie Bankhead Owen. To them, the Committee gives this completed report with both pride and personal affection.

    Maribel Bartee Adams (Mrs. David III)

    Lillian Pugh Andrews (Mrs. Walter W.)

    Frances Morgan Coleman (Mrs. Thomas W.)

    Bernice Robbins Estes (Mrs. William A.)

    Clyde Stovall Scott (Mrs. Marvin)

    Dixie Mays Jones (Mrs. Blair) Vice-Chairman

    Maud McLure Kelly, Chairman

    Genealogical Records Committee, A.S.D.A.R.

C O P I E S

For copy of any will listed herein, except those shown as being in the Department of Archives and History, or in the office of a Register in Chancery, apply to the Judge of Probate, at the county seat of the county in which the will is recorded, giving the testator's name, with the name and dates of the book and the page where the will is recorded. He may be addressed simply as "The Judge of Probate of _____ County" at the county seat, as shown on the table of counties elsewhere in this book.

For copy of any will listed herein as being in the office of a Register in Chancery, apply to him at the county seat of the county where the will is recorded, giving the title and number (or letter) of the book and the page where the will is recorded. This officer may be addressed as "The Register in Chancery of _____ County", at the county seat.

For copy of any will listed herein as being in the Department of Archives and History, address the request to "The Director, Department of Archives and History, Montgomery, Alabama."

The fee for copies of records is fixed by law, depending upon the length of the document. Inquiry must be made in each instance as to the charge for the copy. There is an additional fee for certification, but most counties, and the State Department of Archives and History have photostatic service. Usually, certification of photostatic copies is not necessary.

COUNTIES OF ALABAMA

CREATED	COUNTY	COUNTY SEAT	REMARKS
1818	Autauga	Prattville	
1808	Baldwin	Bay Minette	Location changed 1820
1832	Barbour	Clayton	
1818	Bibb*	Centerville	Originally Cahawba County
1818	Blount*	Oneonta	
1866	Bullock	Union Springs	
1819	Butler*	Greenville	Courthouse burned 1852
1832	Calhoun*	Anniston	Originally Benton
1832	Chambers	LaFayette	
1836	Cherokee**	Centre	
1868	Chilton	Clanton	
1847	Choctaw**	Butler	
1812	Clarke	Grove Hill	
1866	Clay**	Ashland	
1866	Cleburne	Heflin	
1841	Coffee**	Elba	
1867	Colbert*	Tuscumbia	
1818	Conecuh*	Evergreen	
1832	Coosa	Rockford	
1821	Covington**	Andalusia	
1866	Crenshaw**	Luverne	
1877	Cullman	Cullman	
1824	Dale**	Ozark	
1818	Dallas	Selma	
1837	DeKalb	Fort Payne	
1866	Elmore	Wetumpka	
1868	Escambia	Brewton	
1866	Etowah	Gadsden	Originally Baine County
1824	Fayette**	Fayette	
1818	Franklin**	Russellville	
1868	Geneva**	Geneva	
1819	Greene	Eutaw	
1867	Hale	Greensboro	
1819	Henry	Abbeville	
1903	Houston	Dothan	
1819	Jackson*	Scottsboro	
1819	Jefferson	Birmingham	
1867	Lamar	Vernon	Originally Jones then Sanford
1818	Lauderdale	Florence	
1818	Lawrence	Moulton	
1866	Lee	Opelika	
1818	Limestone*	Athens	
1830	Lowndes	Hayneville	
1832	Macon	Tuskegee	
1808	Madison	Huntsville	

* Will records prior to 1871 partially lost
** Will records prior to 1871 totally lost

CREATED	COUNTY	COUNTY SEAT	REMARKS
1818	Marengo	Linden	
1818	Marion**	Hamilton	
1836	Marshall	Guntersville	
1812	Mobile	Mobile	
1815	Monroe*	Monroeville	
1816	Montgomery	Montgomery	
1818	Morgan	Decatur	Originally Cotaco County
1819	Perry	Marion	
1820	Pickens**	Carrollton	
1821	Pike*	Troy	
1832	Randolph**	Wedowee	
1832	Russell	Phenix City	
1818	Saint Clair	Ashville	
1818	Shelby	Columbiana	
1832	Sumter	Livingston	
1832	Talladega	Talladega	
1832	Tallapoosa	Dadeville	
1818	Tuscaloosa	Tuscaloosa	
1823	Walker**	Jasper	
1800	Washington*	Chatom	
1819	Wilcox	Camden	
1850	Winston**	Double Springs	Originally Hancock

* Will records prior to 1871 partially lost
** Will records prior to 1871 totally lost

SYMBOLS AND ABBREVIATIONS

∅	- In the State Department of Archives and History, Montgomery, Alabama
##	- In the Office of the Register in Chancery in the County Courthouse
Admr. R	- Administration Records
Deeds	- Deed Book, Register of Deeds
DMR	- Deeds, Mortgage & Reports
FR	- Final Record, Orphans Court Final Record
GE & W	- Guardians Estates & Wills
INV.	- Inventories, Inventories of Estates
I & W	- Inventories & Wills, Inventory & Will Records
OB.	- Order Book, Orphans Court Order Book, Probate Court Order Book
OCM	- Orphans Court Minutes
OCR	- Orphans Court Records
PM	- Probate Minutes, Probate Court Minutes
PR	- Probate Court Records, Probate Court Final Records
Reports	- Reports, Final Reports
RE	- Record of Estates
Wills	- Will Book, Will Record, Register of Wills
WAC & A	- Wills, Accounts Current & Administrations
W & A	- Wills & Administrations
W & D	- Wills & Deeds
WG & A	- Wills, Guardianships & Administrations
W & I	- Wills & Inventories
W & OCR	- Wills & Orphans Court Records
W & PM	- Wills & Probate Minutes

TESTATOR	COUNTY	WHERE FOUND		PAGE
Aaron, Samuel	Baldwin	Wills A	1811-1881	40
Abbercrombie, Abner	Montgomery	Wills 2	1820-1845	11
Abbot, Jacob	Madison	PR 2&5	1818-1826	58
Abbott, David	Mobile	Wills I	1813-1837	210
Abercrombie, Albert G.	Montgomery	Wills 3	1840-1854	111
Abercrombie, Charles	Russell	Wills 1	1838-1849	46
Abercrombie, Isaac	Perry	Wills A	1821-1855	20
Abercrombie, Isaac	Perry	W & I	1823-1833	91
Abercrombie, Mary	Montgomery	Wills 4	1853-1869	354
Abercrombie, Milo B.	Montgomery	Wills 4	1853-1869	315
Abercrombie, Sally	Macon	Records 3	1845-1850	374
Abernathy, Claton D.	Marshall	FR 1	1840-1844	90
Abney, Gilley	Russell	Wills I	1838-1849	144
Abney, Hardie	Sumter	Wills I	1828-1851	255
Abston, Elijah	Tuscaloosa	Wills I	1821-1855	227
Acklin, Edward	Madison	PR 8	1831-1839	626
Acklin, Louisa	Madison	Wills I	1853-1875	301
Acklin, William	Madison	Wills I	1853-1875	479
Acre, Samuel	Baldwin	Wills A	1811-1881	43
Acre, Samuel	Mobile	Wills 2	1837-1857	24
Adair, Hiram	Lawrence	I&W A	1850-1857	179
Adair, James W.	Tallapoosa	Wills I	1838-1866	73
Adair, William	Perry	Wills A	1821-1855	259
Adam, Samuel	Butler	Wills I	1853-1864	250
Adams, Absolam	Chambers	Wills 1-2	1833-1856	201
Adams, Colson	Pike	Wills A	1845-1862	154
Adams, George W.	Lauderdale	Wills B	1859-1870	50
Adams, Green W.	Coosa	W&OCR 2	1843-1883	209
Adams, Hardy	Montgomery	Wills 3	1840-1854	164
Adams, James	Talladega	Wills C	1845-1853	282
Adams, James R.	Sumter	Wills I	1828-1851	194
Adams, James S.	Lowndes	Wills C	1861-1899	170
Adams, Joel	Lowndes	Wills B	1830-1859	156
Adams, John	Chambers	Wills 1-2	1833-1856	288
Adams, John, Sr.	Dallas	Wills B	1850-1871	237
Adams, John	Lowndes	Wills B	1830-1859	37
Adams, John	Montgomery	Wills 2	1820-1845	252
Adams, Joseph	Madison	PR 8	1831-1839	278
Adams, Joseph	Madison	PR 15	1850-1853	278
Adams, Joshua	Chambers	Wills 3	1856-1899	176
Adams, Littleberry	Madison	PR 4	1826-1829	166
Adams, Lucy A.	Sumter	Wills 2	1851-1872	292
Adams, Nathaniel L.	Autauga	Wills I	1862-1925	8
Adams, Sarah	Dallas	Wills B	1850-1871	110
Adams, Spencer	Dallas	Wills A	1821-1849	74
Adams, Thomas	Mobile	Wills 3	1857-1870	70
Adams, William	Clarke	PR K	1858-1861	267
Adams, William	Limestone	Wills 7	1844-1847	290
Adams, William	Tallapoosa	Wills I	1838-1866	119
Adams, William L.	Tuscaloosa	Wills I	1821-1855	37
Adams, William F. L.	Sumter	Wills 2	1851-1872	88

TESTATOR	COUNTY	WHERE FOUND		PAGE
Adams, William H.	Pike	Wills B	1862-1879	1
Aday, Mary M.	Madison	PR 2&5	1818-1826	400
Adcock, John D.	Monroe	W&D D	1850-1856	309
Aderson ?, William	Sumter	Wills 1	1828-1851	249
Adkins, Burell	Elmore	Wills A	1866-1906	10
Adkins, Charles	Limestone	Wills 12	1866-1872	130
Agee, N. J. Kitrell	Monroe	W&D D	1833-1870	273
Aiken, Esther	Tuscaloosa	Wills 1	1821-1855	116
Aikens, James L. G.	Tuscaloosa	Wills 1	1821-1855	234
Aikin, Mary	Perry	Wills A	1821-1855	28
Akers, A.	Lauderdale	Wills A	1835-1858	29
Akin, William	Greene	Wills C	1840-1864	764
Albright, John	Talladega	WI D	1867-1880	5
Albritton, Allen	Wilcox	Wills 4	1847-1862	212
Albritton, P. I.?	Lowndes	Wills C	1861-1899	81
Aldridge, Nathan	Russell	Wills 2	1850-1873	344
Aldridge, Reuben	Russell	Wills 1	1838-1849	154
Aldridge, Reubin	Autauga	Reports E-B	1841-1845	1
Alexander, William, Jr.	Russell	Wills 2	1850-1873	153
Alderson, Mary	Mobile	Wills 3	1857-1870	414
Alderson, William	Mobile	Wills 3	1857-1870	127
Aleck, Cecile Krebs	Mobile	Wills 3	1857-1870	222
Alexander, Elizabeth	Lauderdale	Wills B	1859-1870	37
Alexander, Franklin	Marshall	PR 2	1857-1888	522
Alexander, J.? W.	Calhoun	Loose	Probated 1849	
Alexander, James F.	Cleburne	WG&A	1866-1884	20
Alexander, James R.	Lauderdale	Wills A	1835-1858	248
Alexander, John D.	Dallas	Wills A	1821-1849	163
Alexander, Love	Calhoun	PR A-2	1856-1866	445
Alexander, Lucy P.	Lauderdale	Wills B	1859-1870	71
Alexander, Mathew	Cleburne	WG&A	1866-1884	283
Alexander, Moses	Henry	Deeds C	1840-1846	404
Alford, Asenath	Chambers	Wills 1-2	1833-1856	227
Alford, Julius C.	Montgomery	Wills 4	1853-1869	392
Alfrey, J. D.	Lauderdale	Wills 4	1821-1825	114
Alison, Margaret	Dallas	Wills A	1821-1849	352
Allaire, Peter	Mobile	Wills 1	1813-1837	138
Allan, John	Madison	PR 11	1842-1849	46
Allen, Andrew	Montgomery	Wills 2	1820-1845	294
Allen, Asa	Limestone	Wills 6	1841-1846	110
Allen, Benjamin	Limestone	Wills 3	1826-1831	379
Allen, Benjamin H.	Limestone	Wills 3	1826-1831	382
Allen, David	Talladega	Wills A	1833-1839	193
Allen, Dennis ?	Montgomery	Wills 4	1853-1869	412
Allen, Drewery	Clarke	PR J	1856-1858	198
Allen, Henry	Autauga	Reports C	1834-1839	551
Allen, Henry J.	Lauderdale	Wills B	1859-1870	120
Allen, Hezekiah	Coosa	W&OCR 2	1843-1883	271
Allen, Ignatius F.	Coosa	W&OCR 2	1843-1883	125
Allen, James	Lawrence	I&W D	1835-1840	10
Allen, James	Montgomery	Wills 2	1820-1845	56

TESTATOR	COUNTY	WHERE FOUND		PAGE
Allen, James	Pike	Wills B	1862-1879	18
Allen, James	Russell	Wills 2	1850-1873	38
Allen, John W.	Montgomery	Wills 4	1853-1869	268
Allen, John W.	St. Clair	RE C	1852-1859	115
Allen, Joseph	Sumter	Wills 1	1828-1851	264
Allen, Joseph	Washington	Wills 1 ∅	1827-1888	117
Allen, Joseph	Washington	Wills B	1827-	75
Allen, Josiah	Talladega	W&I C	1852-1857	454
Allen, Mary L.	Wilcox	Wills 5	1855-1870	425
Allen, Orsamus	Baldwin	Wills A	1811-1881	30
Allen, Rebecca	Shelby	Wills L	1838-1858	735
Allen, Robert	Dallas	Wills A	1821-1849	333
Allen, Robert	Montgomery	Wills 2	1820-1845	77
Allen, Robert	Perry	Wills A	1821-1855	162
Allen, Sarah R.	Talladega	Wills A	1833-1839	116
Allen, Thomas	Chambers	Wills 3	1856-1899	20
Allen, Wade	Montgomery	Wills 3	1840-1854	169
Allen, Wade H.	Montgomery	Wills 4	1853-1869	335
Allen, William	Madison	Deeds S	1840-1842	575
Allen, William	Tallapoosa	Wills 1	1838-1866	194
Allen, William B.	Tuscaloosa	Wills 1	1821-1855	151
Allison, John	Limestone	Wills 5	1836-1841	182
Allison, John	Madison	PR 9	1839-1841	537
Allison, John	Madison	Wills 1	1853-1875	336
Allison, Nancy	Madison	Wills 1	1853-1875	485
Allison, Robert G.	Sumter	Wills 1	1828-1851	368
Allison, William J.	Madison	PR 7	1834-1837	92
Allman, Warden	Montgomery	Wills 3	1840-1854	294
Allmond, Hezekiah	Lauderdale	Wills A	1835-1858	295
Allsup, Randolph	Calhoun	Loose	Probated 1856	
Allsup, Thomas	Lauderdale	Wills B	1859-1870	318
Alston ?, Elijah	Tuscaloosa	Wills 1	1821-1855	227
Altman, Henry	Sumter	Wills 2	1851-1872	387
Amason, Elbert	Sumter	Wills 2	1851-1872	402
Amason, Uriah	Montgomery	Wills 3	1840-1854	101
Amonet, John	Madison	PR 6	1832-1834	308
Anderson, A.	Monroe	WD E	1856-1861	58
Anderson, Edward	Montgomery	Wills 4	1853-1869	123
Anderson, Elijah	Lowndes	Wills C	1861-1899	105
Anderson, Elisha	Montgomery	Wills 2	1820-1845	107
Anderson, Elizabeth	Lowndes	Wills B	1830-1859	408
Anderson, Elizabeth G.	Perry	Wills C	1862-1895	106
Anderson, Francis	Madison	PR 3	1823-1826	95
Anderson, Hannah W.	Sumter	Wills 2	1851-1872	207
Anderson, J.	Monroe	WD 8	1870-1871	178
Anderson, James	Sumter	Wills 1	1828-1851	286
Anderson, James A.	Greene	Wills D	1851-1888	183
Anderson, Jane	Greene	Wills C	1840-1864	567
Anderson, Joe A.	Greene	Wills C	1840-1864	506
Anderson, John	Perry	Wills A	1821-1855	295
Anderson, Jonathan	Marengo	Wills A	1820-1864	189

TESTATOR	COUNTY	WHERE FOUND		PAGE
Anderson, Jordan, Jr.	Marengo	Wills A	1820-1864	276
Anderson, Jordan, Sr.	Marengo	Wills A	1820-1864	191
Anderson, Lewis	Henry	Deeds C	1840-1846	250
Anderson, Margaret	Jefferson	OCR	1841-1844	300
Anderson, Mary	Madison	PR 10	1842-1842	146
Anderson, Nancy	Madison	Wills 1	1853-1875	368
Anderson, Rich'd. Paulding	Wilcox	Wills 4	1847-1862	154
Anderson, Samuel	Mobile	Wills 2	1837-1857	373
Anderson, William	Madison	Wills 1	1853-1875	399
Anderson, William	Marengo	Wills A	1820-1864	38
Anderson, William	Sumter	Wills 1	1828-1851	249
Andoe, Lucinda	Clarke	PR J	1856-1858	416
Andress, Lowry	Madison	PR 2	1818-1823	267
Andress, Martha	Monroe	W&D D	1850-1856	136
Andress, Rebecca Y.	Chambers	Wills 1-2	1833-1856	474
Andrew, Francis	Baldwin	Wills A	1811-1881	38
: Andrews, Allen	Calhoun	PR A-2	1856-1866	453
Andrews, Benjamin	Madison	PR 4	1826-1829	216
Andrews, James C.	Dallas	Wills B	1850-1871	454
Andrews, John	Wilcox	Wills 3	1826-1858	266
Andrews, Mary	Coosa	WOCR 2	1843-1883	214
Andrews, Mark	Chambers	Wills 3	1856-1899	3
Andrews, May	Lowndes	Wills B	1830-1859	33
Andrews, Milton	Chambers	Wills 3	1856-1899	98
Andrews, Moses	Lowndes	Wills B	1830-1859	33
Andrews, P. H.	Greene	Wills C	1840-1864	475
Andrews, Robert	Lauderdale	Wills A	1835-1858	154
Anglin, Nancy	Barbour	OCR 6	1854-1856	576
Ansley, Samuel	Lowndes	Wills B	1830-1859	108
Anthony, David R.	Greene	Wills D	1851-1888	224
Antimes,? Joseph	Mobile	Wills 3	1857-1870	475
Antumes,? Joseph	Mobile	Wills 3	1857-1870	475
Anyan, George	Madison	PR 6	1832-1834	320
Appling, Joel	St. Clair	RE C	1852-1859	179
Archer, John M.	Lowndes	Wills B	1830-1859	32
Archibald, E. A.	Greene	Wills D	1851-1888	200
Archibald, James Hall	Greene	Wills C	1840-1864	751
Archibald, Robert	Greene	Wills C	1840-1864	100
Archibald, Thomas	Tuscaloosa	Wills 3	1858-1865	174
Ard, Abraham	Lauderdale	Wills B	1859-1870	290
Armistead, Fannie	Lauderdale	Wills A	1835-1858	157
Armistead, Robert B.	Mobile	Wills 3	1857-1870	336
Armistead, William	Montgomery	Wills 4	1853-1869	106
Armstead, William	Clarke	PR E	1840-1846	148
Armour, Sarah Ann	Montgomery	Wills 3	1840-1854	128
Armstrong, Addison S.	Montgomery	Wills 4	1853-1869	328
Armstrong, Fleming H.	Autauga	Wills 1	1862-1925	2
Armstrong, James M.	Lowndes	Wills B	1830-1859	165
Armstrong, Jonathan	Madison	Deeds C	1816-1818	100
Armstrong, Joseph T.	Montgomery	Wills 2	1820-1845	293
Armstrong, Sally	Pike	Wills A	1845-1862	108

TESTATOR	COUNTY	WHERE FOUND		PAGE
Armstrong, Thomas C.	Montgomery	Wills 4	1853-1869	157
Armstrong, William T.	Montgomery	Wills 4	1853-1869	6
Arnet, James	Madison	PR 3	1823-1826	368
Arnett, Thomas	Shelby	Wills E	1845-1850	352
Arnold, Absolam W.	Dallas	Wills B	1850-1871	322
Arnold, Edmund H.	Wilcox	Wills 4	1847-1862	219
Arnold, Thomas	Dallas	Wills A	1821-1849	245
Arnold, Wyatt	Bibb	Adm.R J	1865-1876	80
Arrington, Halman	Barbour	OCR 3	1847-1851	519
Arrington, Joseph W.	Montgomery	Wills 4	1853-1869	305
Arrington, Mary M.	Sumter	Wills 2	1851-1872	296
Arrington, Mary T.	Sumter	Wills 2	1851-1872	306
Arrington, William	Barbour	OCR 4	1850-1852	98
Arrington, Samuel J.	Sumter	Wills 2	1851-1872	341
Arterberry, Archelis	Dallas	Wills A	1821-1849	97
Ashe, Elizabeth	Greene	Wills B	1817-1841	220
Asher, John	Lauderdale	Wills A	1835-1858	51
Asher, John	Lauderdale	Wills 3	1821-1825	78
Ashley, Elizabeth G.	Montgomery	Wills 2	1820-1845	282
Ashley, William, Sr.	Montgomery	Wills 2	1820-1845	68
Ashley, William R.	Greene	Wills C	1840-1864	306
Ashley, Wilson	Conecuh	OB A	1865-1870	97
Ashurst, Francis	Montgomery	Wills 2	1820-1845	161
Ashurst, John	Montgomery	Wills 2	1820-1845	87
Askew, Benjamin	Henry	OCR M	1861-1862	222
Askew, James	Chambers	Wills 3	1856-1899	244
Atcherson, Bennett	Bibb	Adm.R I	1858-1865	11
Atcheson, James	Bibb	Adm.R E	1838-1846	380
Atkins, John	Chambers	Wills 3	1856-1899	194
Atkins, John	Chambers	Wills 3	1856-1899	352
Atkins, Willie	Montgomery	Wills 2	1820-1845	261
Atkinson, Eli	Lowndes	Wills C	1861-1899	68
Atkinson, Stephen	Talladega	Wills C	1845-1853	87
Atkinson, Uriah	Monroe	W&D E	1833-1870	314
Atwood, Henry	Wilcox	Wills 3	1826-1858	120
Audrey, Simon	Baldwin	Wills A	1811-1881	13
Audry, Euphrosine	Mobile	Wills 1	1813-1837	164
Audry, Romeo	Mobile	Wills 3	1857-1870	641
Auerbach, Edward	Mobile	Wills 3	1857-1870	513
Augustin, Lucy	Autauga	Reports F	1845-1850	485
Auld, Ann	Coosa	W&PM	1834-1842	111
Auld, Michael	Montgomery	Wills 2	1820-1845	183
Austill, Sarah	Wilcox	Wills 1	1821-1844	253
Austin, Alexander	Lawrence	I&W D	1835-1840	7
Austin, John	Lauderdale	Wills B	1859-1870	114
Austin, Margaret B.	Marengo	Wills A	1820-1864	340
Autrey, A. B.	Conecuh	OB A	1865-1870	262
Autrey, Adam	Talladega	Wills C	1845-1853	95
Autrey, Frederick	Wilcox	Wills 1	1821-1844	261
Autry, William	Monroe	W&D D	1833-1870	100
Auze, Joseph	Mobile	Wills 2	1837-1857	32

TESTATOR	COUNTY	WHERE FOUND		PAGE
Avent, Mason	Marengo	Wills A	1820-1864	117
Averett, Benjamin	Autauga	Deeds A		107
Averett, Benjamin	Talladega	W&I D	1867-1880	712
Averhart, James P.	Lowndes	Wills C	1861-1899	50
Averhart, Patrick H.	Lowndes	Wills C	1861-1899	94
Avert, Jonathan	Dallas	Wills A	1821-1849	239
Avery, Allen	St. Clair	RE B	1834-1859	53
Avery, Bryant	Hale	Wills A	1867-1923	47
Avery, Henry	Bibb	Adm.R. J	1865-1876	540
Avery, Thomas	Chambers	Wills 1-2	1833-1856	333
Axum, Robert	Marengo	Wills A	1820-1864	303
Aycock, Henry	Morgan	Records A	1820-1828	238
Aymon, Paul	Mobile	Wills 2	1837-1857	230
Ayers, Moses, Sr.	Jefferson	OCR	1824-1831	482
Ayers, Samuel	Madison	PR 4	1826-1829	168
Ayres, Andrew	Mobile	Wills 1	1813-1837	233
Ayres, William	Jefferson	Wills I	1818-1840	301
Babe, Andrew	Mobile	Wills 1	1813-1837	265
Bacon, Ann	Limestone	Wills 4	1831-1837	125
Bacon, Eliza R.	Russell	Wills 1	1838-1849	95
Bacon, Joseph	Chambers	Wills 1-2	1833-1856	440
Baggett, Abram	Wilcox	Wills 3	1826-1858	117
Bagley, James C.	Jefferson	Wills A	1856-1880	186
Bagley, Josiah	Talladega	Wills A	1833-1839	559
Bagshaw, Amelia	Greene	Wills C	1840-1864	412
Bailey, Charles C.	Mobile	Wills 2	1837-1857	93
Bailey, Enoch	Marengo	Wills A	1820-1864	50
Bailey, Henry B.	Coosa	WOCR 2	1843-1883	1
Bailey, Hezekiah	Madison	PR 13	1838-1848	564
Bailey, James	Madison	PR 10	1842-1842	264
Bailey, James	Coosa	W&OCR 2	1843-1883	296
Bailey, Joel	Shelby	Wills D	1841-1846	172
Bailey, John G.	Perry	Wills A	1821-1855	175
Bailey, Michael	Lauderdale	Wills 3	1821-1825	137
Bailey, Moses P.	Shelby	Wills H	1847-1866	316
Baily, Moses	Madison	PR 7	1834-1837	50
Bailey, Sarah H.	Mobile	Wills 3	1857-1870	426
Bailey, Urbin C.	Macon	Records 4	1850-1852	60
Baine, David W.	Lowndes	Wills C	1861-1899	24
Baird, Alexander	Jefferson	OCR	1831-1832	82
Baird, Alexander	Jefferson	PM	1831-1832	82
Baird, Alexander	Talladega	Wills A	1833-1839	108
Baird, Sarah	Jefferson	Deeds 1	1818-1828	208
Baird, Tabitha	Tallapoosa	Wills 2	1864-1907	62
Baker, Abner	Tallapoosa	Wills 1	1838-1868	176
Baker, Alpheus	Barbour	OCR 9	1858-1859	425
Baker, Benjamin H.	Russell	Wills 2	1850-1873	344
Baker, Catherine	Montgomery	Wills 3	1840-1854	211

TESTATOR	COUNTY	WHERE FOUND		PAGE
Baker, Charles	Russell	Wills 2	1850-1873	276
Baker, Elijah	Coosa	W&OCR 2	1843-1883	178 ?
Baker, Elisha O.	Montgomery	Wills 4	1853-1869	422
Baker, Eliza H.	Barbour	OCR 16	1866-1868	891
Baker, Elizabeth	Madison	PR 11	1842-1849	541
Baker, Hans	Mobile	Wills 3	1857-1870	25
Baker, J. G.	Lauderdale	Wills 4	1821-1825	62
Baker, James	Barbour	OCR 3	1847-1851	54
Baker, John	Washington	Wills B	1827-	53
Baker, John	Washington	Wills 1 ∅	1827-1888	82
Baker, John M. B.	Pike	Wills A	1845-1862	152
Baker, Johanna	Mobile	Wills 3	1857-1870	657
Baker, Lucretia	Greene	Wills C	1840-1864	491
Baker, Nicholas	Tuscaloosa	Deeds 1	18	12
Baker, Neill H.	Coosa	W&OCR 2	1843-1883	288
Baker, Obed	Tuscaloosa	Wills 1	1821-1855	2
Baker, Robert A.	Mobile	Wills 3	1857-1870	482
Baker, Stephen	Autauga	Wills 1	1862-1925	17
Baker, Tabitha	Russell	Wills 2	1850-1873	150
Baker, William	Madison	Wills 1	1853-1875	261
Baker, William	Russell	Wills 2	1850-1873	148
Baker, William	Shelby	Wills H	1847-1866	310
Baker, William	Shelby	Wills H	1847-1866	312
Baker, William	Tallapoosa	Wills 1	1838-1866	78
Baker, William	Tuscaloosa	Wills 3	1858-1865	156
Baker, William	Tuscaloosa	Wills 4	1868-1897	127
Baker, William A.	Washington	Wills 1 ∅	1827-1888	113
Baker, William A.	Washington	Wills B	1827-	72
Baker, William W.	Limestone	Wills 3	1826-1831	387
Baldwin, Celia	Montgomery	Wills 2	1820-1845	211
Baldwin, Henry C.	Baldwin	Wills A	1811-1881	233
Baldwin, Martha Ann	Bullock	Wills A	1868-1902	9
Balfour, John Oswald	Talladega	Wills B	1839-1845	305
Balfour, Regina	Talladega	Wills B	1839-1845	324
Ballard, Ann	Dallas	Wills A	1821-1849	17
Ballard, Ann	Dallas	Wills A	1821-1849	95
Ballard, James	Talladega	W&I A	1852-1857	531
Ballantine, William	Mobile	Wills 3	1857-1870	585
Ballinger, John	Mobile	Wills 1	1813-1837	201
Bandy, James	Autauga	Reports C	1834-1838	508
Bandy, William C.	Lee	Wills A	1867-1898	3
Banks, Mary	Bibb	Loose	1858	
Banks, Mary	Tuscaloosa	Wills 1	1821-1855	145
Banks, Willis	Tuscaloosa	Wills 1	1821-1855	310
Banner, Benjamin	Monroe	W&D D	1850-1856	339
Barbee, Mark	Jackson	Records	1861-1881	615
Barber, David W.	Greene	Wills D	1851-1888	34
Barclay, Henry A.	Mobile	Wills 2	1837-1857	109
Barclay, J. J.	Monroe	W&D E	1856-1861	233
Barfield, James	Marengo	Wills A	1820-1864	85
Barfield, Sarah	Tallapoosa	Wills 1	1838-1866	133

TESTATOR	COUNTY	WHERE FOUND		PAGE
Bargainer, John	Lowndes	Wills C	1861-1899	77
Barge, Abel	Wilcox	Wills 4	1847-1862	215
Barge, John	Butler	Wills 1	1853-1864	219
Barker, Elizabeth	Tuscaloosa	Wills 1	1821-1855	73
Barkman, Jacob	Madison	PR 2&5	1818-1826	57
Barlow, Branson	Clarke	GE&W	1832-1839	424
Barlow, John	Dallas	Wills B	1850-1871	57
Barlow, Lewis	Clarke	OCR F	1846-1850	335
Barnaby, George W.	Baldwin	Wills A	1811-1881	153
Barnard, Elisha S.	Henry	OCR P	1864-1866	298
Barnes, Ann R.	Marengo	Wills A	1820-1864	534
Barnes, Jeremiah	Lauderdale	Wills 3	1821-1825	23
Barnes, John F.	Marengo	Wills A	1820-1864	248
Barnes, John Thomas	Sumter	Wills 2	1851-1872	380
Barnes, Rodman	Mobile	Wills 1	1813-1837	208
Barnes, Sarah	Mobile	Wills 2	1837-1857	340
Barnes, Samuel Thomas	Clarke	OCR F	1846-1850	359
Barnett, Asa	Pike	Wills B	1862-1879	132
Barnett, David	Dallas	Wills A	1821-1849	60
Barnett, Ezekiel	Lauderdale	Wills B	1859-1870	105
Barnett, Francis M.	Montgomery	Wills 4	1853-1869	102
Barnett, Hugh	Greene	Wills A	1821-1827	9
Barnett, Margaret H.	Tallapoosa	Wills 1	1838-1866	120
Barnett, Margaret H.	Tallapoosa	Wills 1	1838-1866	144
Barnett, Michael	Montgomery	Wills 2	1820-1845	154
Barnett, Nathaniel	Montgomery	Wills 2	1820-1845	12
Barnett, Sally S.	Montgomery	Wills 2	1820-1845	44
Barnett, Thomas	Lauderdale	Wills A	1835-1858	308
Barnett, William	Montgomery	Wills 2	1820-1845	153
Barnett, William H.	Chambers	Wills 1-2	1833-1856	502
Barnette, George	Monroe	W&D A	1833-1841	13
Barney, Daniel, Jr.	Mobile	Wills 1	1813-1837	168
Barney, George W.	Marengo	Wills A	1820-1864	468
Barney, Hindman	Mobile	Wills 2	1837-1857	298
Barnhill, John	Perry	Wills A	1821-1855	15
Barnhill, John	Perry	W&I	1823-1833	50
Barnum, Augustus	Dallas	Wills B	1850-1871	144
Barr, Robert, Sr.	Marengo	Wills A	1820-1864	521
Barr, William	Calhoun	Loose	Prob. 1855	
Barreal, Joseph	Mobile	Wills 3	1857-1870	403
Barrell, Charles	Montgomery	Wills 4	1853-1869	441
Barrell, George	Montgomery	Wills 5	1863-1887	72
Barrett, Caroline M.	Sumter	Wills 2	1851-1872	427
Barrett, Curtis	Coosa	W&OCR 2	1843-1883	306
Barrett, Michael E.	Montgomery	Wills 4	1853-1869	485
Barrett, William	Madison	PR 2	1818-1823	145
Barren, G. W.	Lauderdale	Wills 4	1821-1825	1
Barrentine, William	Tallapoosa	Wills 1	1838-1866	49
Barretts, John	Montgomery	Wills 2	1820-1845	124
Barron, Elias Jefferson	Perry	Wills B	1858-1873	3
Barron, Elizabeth V.	Perry	Wills B	1858-1873	374

TESTATOR	COUNTY	WHERE FOUND		PAGE
Barron, Mrs. Jane	Perry	Wills A	1821-1855	349
Barron, Nancy Jane	Perry	Wills B	1858-1873	398
Barron, Thomas C.	Perry	Wills A	1821-1855	196
Barry, Charles M.	Greene	Wills C	1840-1864	94
Barry, Jane	Greene	Wills C	1840-1864	439
Barry, Samuel D. C.	Mobile	Wills 3	1857-1870	330
Bartee, A. M.	Tallapoosa	Wills 2	1864-1907	105
Bartee, James H.	Sumter	Wills 2	1851-1872	349
Bartee, Thomas J?	Macon	Record 10	1863-1865	1
Bartlett, John	Mobile	Wills 2	1837-1857	97
Barton, David	Perry	Wills A	1821-1855	228
Barton, Elizabeth	Dallas	Wills A	1821-1849	200
Barton, Sarah	Montgomery	Wills 2	1820-1845	308
Barton, Thomas	Jefferson	Wills A	1856-1880	73
Barton, Thomas	Montgomery	Wills 2	1820-1845	38
Barton, Willoughby	Mobile	Wills 1	1813-1837	147
Basham, Jonathan	Morgan	OCR 6	1831-1837	556
Baskin, Henry W.	Talladega	Wills C	1845-1853	422
Baskin, James R.	Talladega	W&I A	1852-1857	298
Bass, Allen	Barbour	OCR 6	1854-1856	9
Bass, Andrew	Jefferson	Wills A	1856-1880	6
Bass, Ezekiel H.	Washington	Wills 1 ∅	1827-1888	135
Bass, Ezekiel H.	Washington	Wills 1 ∅	1827-1888	1-8
Bass, E. W.	Washington	Wills B	1827-	138
Bass, Hartwell	Russell	Wills 1	1838-1849	113
Bass, Mary	Madison	W&I	1810-1820	207
Bass, Richard	Madison	PR 6	1832-1834	695
Bass, Samuel	Barbour	OCR 16	1866-1868	972
Bass, Sterling, Jr.	Russell	Wills 2	1850-1873	108
Bass, Temperance	Limestone	Wills 5	1836-1841	497
Bass, Thomas J.	Barbour	OCR 14	1863-1865	17
Bass, Uriah	Madison	W&I	1810-1820	144
Bassett, John Y.	Madison	PR 15	1850-1853	613
Bassett, Sarah	Washington	Wills B	1827-	60
Bassett, Sarah	Washington	Wills 1 ∅	1827-1888	93
Bateman, Harry	Mobile	Wills 2	1837-1857	178
Bates, Albert	Perry	Wills A	1821-1855	52
Bates, James	Montgomery	Wills 2	1820-1845	23
Bates, James F.	Washington	Wills B	1827-	120
Bates, James F.	Washington	Wills 1 ∅	1827-1888	196
Bates, John	Perry	Wills B	1858-1873	327
Bates, Joseph	Baldwin	Wills A	1811-1881	164
Bates, Joseph, Sr.	Baldwin	Wills A	1811-1881	21
Bates, Joseph, Sr.	Clarke	GE&W	1832-1839	507
Bates, Lydia	Mobile	Wills 2	1837-1857	71
Bates, Robert	Perry	Wills B	1858-1873	366
Bates, Thomas	Baldwin	Wills A	1811-1881	25
Batre, Charles	Mobile	Wills 2	1837-1857	18
Battelle, John A.	Mobile	Wills 2	1837-1857	363
Battie, William A.	Dallas	Wills B	1850-1871	189
Battle, Davis	Madison	PR 3	1823-1826	159

TESTATOR	COUNTY	WHERE FOUND		PAGE
Battle, Elizabeth	Macon	Record 7	1857-1859	651
Battle, Fleming H.	Marengo	Wills A	1820-1864	232
Battle, Jacob W.	Madison	PR 12	1845-1849	546
Battle, James	Mobile	Wills 2	1837-1857	464
Battle, John A. M.	Mobile	Wills 3	1857-1870	549
Battle, John M.	Pike	Wills B	1862-1879	22
Battle, John W.	Montgomery	Wills 4	1853-1869	482
Battle, Littleberry	Calhoun	Loose	Prob. 1846	
Battle, Mary E.	Madison	Wills 1	1810-1820	477
Battle, Nancy	Montgomery	Wills 4	1853-1869	419
Battle, Thomas, Sr.	Marengo	Wills A	1820-1864	544
Battles, Nelson	St. Clair	Deeds B	1831-1849	298
Battles, Noah	St. Clair	Deeds B	1831-1849	693
Baty, William	Sumter	Wills 2	1851-1872	40
Baugh, Elizabeth	Chambers	Wills 3	1856-1899	7
Baugh, Elizabeth	Lauderdale	Wills B	1859-1870	64
Baugh, Richard	Chambers	Wills 1-2	1833-1856	39
Baugh, Richard	Lauderdale	Wills A	1835-1858	113
Bayless, Jane	Madison	PR 8	1831-1839	355
Baylis, George L.	Jefferson	Wills A	1856-1880	5
Bayne, Charles V.	Russell	Wills 2	1850-1873	107
Bayol, Honorie	Greene	Wills B	1817-1841	161
Baxley, Mary M.	Coosa	W&OCR 2	1843-1883	150
Baxter, James	Montgomery	Wills 2	1820-1845	63
Bazile, Marseline	Mobile	Wills 1	1813-1837	140
Beadle, Abraham	Madison	Wills 1	1853-1875	182
Beadle, Elizabeth	Madison	Wills 1	1853-1875	197
Bealle, Charles S.	Tuscaloosa	Wills 3	1858-1865	228
Beall, John S.	Tuscaloosa	Wills 4	1868-1897	18
Beall, Thaddeus	Chambers	Wills 3	1856-1899	191
Beaman, Abraham	Pike	Wills A	1845-1862	25
Bean, Alexander	Pike	Wills A	1845-1862	133
Bean, Dorcas	Pike	Wills A	1845-1862	133
Bean, James F.	Pike	Wills B	1862-1879	17
Bean, William	Morgan	OCR 7	1837-1843	505
Beard, Andrew	Madison	Wills 1	1853-1875	410
Beard, Jabez	Lauderdale	Wills A	1835-1858	244
Beard, James A.	Montgomery	Wills 4	1853-1869	405
Beard, James A.	Montgomery	Wills 5	1863-1887	22
Beard, Thomas (Miss)	Mobile	Wills 3	1857-1870	351
Beasley, Alston H.	Macon	Record 10	1863-1865	3
Beasley, John	Dallas	Wills A	1821-1849	264
Beasley, John G.	Barbour	OCR 14	1863-1865	110
Beasley, Nancy	Marengo	Wills A	1820-1864	407
Beasley, Peter R.	Madison	PR 11	1842-1849	541
Beaty, James	Chambers	Wills 3	1856-1899	204
Beavers, James	Sumter	Wills 2	1851-1872	244
Beazley, Dillard	Greene	Wills A	1821-1827	20
Beazley, John W.	Sumter	Wills 1	1828-1851	45
Beazly, William N.	Sumter	Wills 1	1828-1851	312
Bebe, Andrew	Mobile	Wills 1	1813-1837	265

TESTATOR	COUNTY	WHERE FOUND		PAGE
Bebivo, Ramon	Mobile	Wills 2	1837-1857	70
Beck, Alfred J.	Wilcox	Wills 4	1847-1862	204
Beck, Franklin K.	Wilcox	Wills 5	1855-1870	150
Beck, Thomas R.	Wilcox	Wills 5	1855-1870	14
Becket, James	Tallapoosa	Wills 1	1838-1866	68
Beckham, Albert G.	Elmore	Wills A	1866-1906	12
Beckham, John	Clarke	OCR F	1846-1850	178
Beckham, Julius	Coosa	W&OCR 2	1843-1883	59
Beckham, Levi S.	Clarke	GE&W	1832-1839	344
Beckham, Philemon	Madison	PR 2	1818-1823	381
Beckler, Jacob	Lowndes	Wills B	1830-1859	182
Beckwith, Virginia B.	Lauderdale	Wills B	1859-1870	172
Becton, Frederick I.	Dallas	Wills B	1850-1871	340
Becton, Sarah E. M.	Dallas	Wills A	1821-1849	358
Bedell, Joseph Robert	Macon	Record 4	1850-1852	233
Beebe, Asa	Dallas	Wills A	1821-1849	202
Beebe, Asa	Sumter	Wills 1	1828-1851	178
Beene, Jesse	Dallas	Wills A	1821-1849	248
Beers, George	Lowndes	Wills B	1830-1859	183
Beeson, Vestal	Blount	Records A	1837-1845	133
Beeson, Vestal	Blount	OB	1829-1841	513
Bell, Arther	Lowndes	Wills B	1830-1859	125
Bell, Calhoun	Dallas	Wills A	1821-1849	343
Bell, E. R.	Greene	Wills C	1840-1864	664
Bell, Elisha	Morgan	OCR 7	1837-1843	24
Bell, Elizabeth	Morgan	OCR 7	1837-1843	267
Bell, Enoch	Dallas	Wills B	1850-1871	10
Bell, Francis	Madison	Wills 1	1853-1875	180
Bell, Frederick	Sumter	Wills 2	1851-1872	180
Bell, James	Dallas	Wills B	1850-1871	63
Bell, John	Greene	Wills B	1817-1841	191
Bell, John	Mobile	Wills 3	1857-1870	574
Bell, John D.	Coosa	W&OCR 2	1843-1883	158
Bell, John N.	Madison	W&I	1810-1820	109
Bell, John R.	Dallas	Wills B	1850-1871	138
Bell, John T.	Talladega	W&I B	1858-1864	591
Bell, Jonathan	Wilcox	Wills 1	1821-1844	397
Bell, Joseph	Lowndes	Wills B	1830-1859	410
Bell, Joseph G.	Mobile	Wills 3	1857-1870	706
Bell, Pamelia	Sumter	Wills 1	1828-1851	252
Bell, Rachel	Dallas	Wills A	1821-1849	261
Bell, Rebecca	Greene	Wills C	1840-1864	46
Bell, Thomas	Perry	Wills B	1858-1873	129
Bell, Thomas	St. Clair	Deeds B	1831-1849	828
Bell, William	Dallas	Wills A	1821-1849	74
Bell, Will	Greene	Wills B	1817-1841	153
Bell, William A.	Greene	Wills C	1840-1864	147
Bell, William H.	Madison	PR 2&5	1818-1826	213
Bell, Williams M.	Cleburne	Wills 1	1866-1884	77
Bellah, Samuel S.	Henry	OCR P	1864-1866	488
Belser, James E.	Montgomery	Wills 4	1853-1869	193

TESTATOR	COUNTY	WHERE FOUND		PAGE
Belvin, Lorenzo D.	Russell	Wills 2	1850-1873	247
Belzer, John	Mobile	Wills 2	1837-1857	10
Benbow, Ann E.	Pike	Wills A	1845-1862	175
Benbow, Edward	Montgomery	Wills 4	1853-1869	70
Benbow, Gershom	Montgomery	Wills 2	1820-1845	192
Bendall, Jesse	Madison	PR 11	1842-1849	548
Benerley, Robert B.	Greene	Wills C	1840-1864	208
Bennett, Anthony	Sumter	Wills 1	1828-1851	257
Bennett, Benjamin	Perry	Wills A	1821-1855	16
Bennett, Benjamin	Perry	W & I	1823-1851	87
Bennett, Burwell B.	Wilcox	Wills 3	1826-1858	313
Bennett, George	Greene	Wills B	1817-1841	143
Bennett, James	Barbour	OCR 4	1850-1852	683
Bennett, James	Henry	OCR L	1860-1861	433
Bennett, James	Henry	OCR M	1861-1862	185
Bennett, Jeremiah, Sr.	Russell	Wills 2	1850-1873	104 ?
Bennett, Mitchell	Russell	Wills 2	1850-1873	181
Bennett, Rhoda	Wilcox	Wills 1	1821-1844	291
Bennett, Samuel	Colbert	Wills A	1861-1903	60
Bennett, Vincent	St. Clair	Deeds B	1831-1849	139
Bennett, William	Greene	Wills C	1840-1864	57
Bennett, William L.	Greene	Wills B	1817-1841	301
Benning, William	Lowndes	Wills B	1830-1859	18
Benson, Gabriel	Perry	Wills A	1821-1855	83
Benson, James	Tallapoosa	Wills 1	1838-1866	193
Benson, Nathaniel W.	Morgan	PR 22	1865-1866	87
Bentley, James B.	Montgomery	Wills 2	1820-1845	188
Bently, John	Chambers	Wills 1-2	1833-1856	296
Bentley, William A.	Macon	Record 10	1863-1865	8
Benton, Archer	Lowndes	Wills B	1830-1859	20
Beny, James	Marshall	PR 9	1867-1869	550
Bernard, John H.	Greene	Wills D	1851-1888	98
Bernody, Regis (Negro)	Mobile	Wills 1	1813-1837	170
Berry, Daniel P.	Mobile	Wills 3	1857-1870	662
Berry, Sarah Catherine	Dallas	Wills A	1821-1849	350
Berry, Thomas	Tallapoosa	Wills 2	1864-1907	4
Best, Lavinia	Madison	Wills 1	1853-1875	32
Beten, John	Madison	W&I	1810-1820	114
Bethea, Celia	Mobile	Wills 2	1837-1857	345
Bethea, Davis	Wilcox	Wills 2	1832-1850	106
Bethea, Tristram	Lowndes	Wills B	1830-1859	245
Bethune, John	Pike	Inv A	1845-1862	412
Betsell, William O.	Autauga	Reports L	1862-1863	54
Bettis, Francis	Clarke	PR G	1850-1854	26
Bettis, John	Clarke	PR G	1850-1854	362
Bettis, Matthew	Clarke	GE&W	1832-1839	33
Bettis, Sarah A.	Clarke	PRN	1866-1870	167
Betts, Joshua	Wilcox	Wills 3	1826-1858	241
Bevel, Joseph	Marengo	Wills A	1820-1864	257
Bevell, William	Shelby	Wills B	1818-1840	170
Beverley, Lovley	Tuscaloosa	Wills 1	1821-1855	246

TESTATOR	COUNTY	WHERE FOUND		PAGE
Bevill, William	Shelby	Wills D	1841-1846	36
Bevill, Woodliff	Greene	Wills B	1817-1841	187
Beyelle, Joseph	Greene	Wills B	1817-1841	105
Bibb, James H.	Madison	Wills 1	1853-1875	429
Bibb, John H.	Morgan	OCR 7	1837-1843	367
Bibb, Joseph B.	Montgomery	Wills 5	1863-1887	25
Bibb, Joseph W.	Montgomery	Wills 2	1820-1845	94
Bibb, Mary A.	Dallas	Wills B	1850-1871	140
Bibb, Peyton	Montgomery	Wills 2	1820-1845	229
Bibb, Thomas	Limestone	Wills 5	1836-1841	439
Bibby, John L.	Coosa	W&OCR 2	1843-1883	103
Bickerstaff, R. H.	Russell	Wills 2	1850-1873	46
Bickley, William H.	Marengo	Wills A	1820-1864	438
Bidie, John	Marshall	FR 1	1840-1844	63
Bigeon, ? Henry	Mobile	Wills 1	1813-1837	105
Bigger, Joseph	Lauderdale	Wills A	1835-1858	176
Biggers, Robert C.	Lowndes	Wills C	1861-1899	19
Biggs, Michel	Monroe	W&D D	1850-1856	6
Biggs, John	Monroe	W&D A	1833-1841	197
Biggs, Tully	Monroe	W&D F	1861-1867	52
Bilbro, Thomas	Chambers	Wills 1-2	1833-1856	127
Billingsley, Clement	Autauga	Reports E-B	1841-1845	49
Billups, Joseph	Coosa	W&OCR 2	1843-1883	31
Binford, Elizabeth	Limestone	Wills 12	1866-1872	124
Binford, Hugh	Madison	Wills 1	1853-1875	247
Binford, John M.	Madison	PR 3	1823-1826	365
Binford, John M.	Limestone	Wills 4	1831-1837	534
Binford, Peter	Madison	Wills 1	1853-1875	265
Binford, Peter	Madison	PR 8	1831-1839	434
Binion, William	Tuscaloosa	Wills 1	1821-1865	165
Binnard, Michael	Montgomery	Wills 4	1853-1869	76
Bird, Charles	Russell	Wills 2	1850-1873	1
Bird, Henry G.	Lowndes	Wills B	1830-1859	202
Bird, Hugh	Lowndes	Wills C	1861-1899	57
Bird, Jesse J. J.	Sumter	Wills 1	1828-1851	232
Bird, Joseph L.	Greene	Wills C	1840-1864	309
Bird, Richard	Bibb	Loose	Probated 1822	
Bishop, Amanda	St. Clair	Deeds B	1831-1849	317
Bishop, Asa	Marengo	Wills A	1820-1864	212
Bishop, Elizabeth	Sumter	Wills 1	1828-1851	280
Bishop, John	Jefferson	Wills 1	1818-1840	283
Bishop, John	Perry	Wills A	1821-1855	198
Bishop, William	Barbour	OCR 2	1842-1847	54
Bivens, Valentine	Jefferson	Wills A	1856-1880	66
Black, F. P.	Calhoun	PR A-2	1856-1866	10
Black, John	Limestone	Wills 11	1865-1866	19
Black, Margaret	Lowndes	Wills B	1830-1859	226
Black, Peter	Calhoun	PR A-2	1856-1866	150
Black, Samuel	Tallapoosa	Wills 1	1838-1866	146
Blackburn, Ashley	Madison	PR 3	1823-1826	161
Blackburn, Benjamin	Tuscaloosa	Wills 1	1821-1855	77

TESTATOR	COUNTY	WHERE FOUND		PAGE
Blackburn, Clement	Limestone	Wills 6	1841-1846	314
Blackburn, David	Madison	Wills 1	1853-1895	270
Blackburn, Greenberry M.	Jefferson	Wills A	1856-1880	160
Blackburn, John D.	Tuscaloosa	Wills 1	1821-1855	218
Blacker, Peter	Jackson	Records	1861-1881	309
Blackman, James	Macon	Records 5	1853-1855	609
Blackshear, Martha	Montgomery	Wills 4	1853-1869	497
Blackshear, Randolph	Henry	OCR O	1864-1865	81
Blacksher, David	Sumter	Wills 2	1851-1872	385
Blackwell, Francis M.	Dallas	Wills B	1850-1871	243
Blackwell, John B.	Montgomery	Wills 2	1820-1845	66
Blackwell, Robert	Mobile	Wills 1	1813-1837	158
Blackwell, Thorogood	Autauga	Reports B	1829-1833	287
Blackwood, James	Limestone	Wills 3	1826-1831	102
Blair, David	Mobile	Wills 2	1837-1857	238
Blake, Caroline V.	Shelby	Wills H	1847-1866	566
Blake, Thomas, Jr.	Mobile	Wills 1	1813-1837	65
Blake, William	Coosa	W&OCR 2	1843-1883	168
Blakley, Joseph A.	Bibb	Loose	Probated 1858	
Blakeley, Joseph A.	Perry	Wills B	1858-1873	78
Blakely, Mary E. C.	Chambers	Wills 3	1856-1899	106
Blakeley, Thomas	Greene	Wills C	1840-1864	735
Blakeney, John	Marengo	Wills A	1820-1864	551
Blakeney, James A.	Wilcox	Wills 5	1855-1870	179
Blakey, James C.	Montgomery	Wills 4	1853-1869	246
Blalock, Harden	Russell	Wills 2	1850-1873	66
Blalock, Martha	Dallas	Wills A	1821-1849	344
Blankenship, Edmond	Madison	PR 6	1832-1834	361
Blankenship, Hannah	Madison	PR 16	1831-1861	318
Blankenship, Wylie	Madison	PR 10	1842-1842	71
Blankinship, John ?	Wilcox	Wills 1	1821-1844	380
Blanks, A. S.	Marengo	Wills A	1820-1864	314
Blann, Silas	Dallas	Wills B	1850-1871	169
Blanton, John	Lauderdale	Wills A	1835-1858	250
Blassingame, John W. M.	Perry	Wills A	1821-1855	73A
Blassingame, Will E.	Perry	Wills A	1821-1855	117
Bledsoe, Allen	Madison	PR 4	1826-1829	20
Bledsoe, Benjamin	Talladega	Wills C	1845-1853	137
Bledsoe, William	Pike	Wills A	1845-1862	123
Blevins, George P.	Dallas	Wills B	1850-1871	175
Blevens, John C.	Dallas	Wills B	1850-1871	131
Blevins, William	Dallas	Wills A	1821-1849	314
Bloodgood, John	Mobile	Wills 3	1857-1870	174
Blount, Emily J. ?	Mobile	Wills 3	1857-1870	663
Blount, Frederick	Washington	Wills 1 ∅	1827-1888	62
Blount, Frederick	Washington	Wills B	1827-	41
Blount, James K.	Washington	Wills B	1827-	132
Blount, James K.	Washington	Wills 1 ∅	1827-1888	221
Blount, William	Chambers	Wills 1-2	1833-1856	468
Blue, Mary	Wilcox	Wills 1	1821-1844	423
Blue, John	Pike	Wills A	1845-1862	27

14

TESTATOR	COUNTY	WHERE FOUND		PAGE
Blunt, Benjamin B.	Dallas	Wills	A	1821-1849	164
Blunt, Margaret	Dallas	Wills	A	1821-1849	187
Blunt, William	Montgomery	Wills	4	1853-1869	456
Blythe, Temperance	St. Clair	RE	G	1866-1870	702
Blythe, William	St. Clair	RE	G	1866-1870	101
Boans, Col. Joseph	Sumter	Wills	1	1828-1851	118
Bobbitt, Corintha	Montgomery	Wills	3	1840-1854	247
Bobo, Lucy Robuck	Lawrence	I&W	D	1835-1840	572
Bodan, Alexander	Baldwin	Wills	A	1811-1881	76
Boddie, John E.	Marengo	Wills	A	1820-1864	218
Boddie, O. B.	Marengo	Wills	A	1820-1864	477
Boddie, Sidney S.	Marengo	Wills	A	1820-1864	483
Boddie, Thomas H.	Madison	PR	4	1826-1829	81
Boens, Lavinia	Madison	Wills	1	1853-1875	32
Boggan, Jonathan	Butler	Wills	1	1853-1864	101
Boggan, Jonathan	Butler	Wills	1	1853-1864	1
Boggess, Bennett	Madison	PR	10	1842-1842	130
Bohannon, Milledge	Lowndes	Wills	B	1830-1859	242
Bohannon, Richard	Madison	Deeds	NNN	1887-1887	624
Bohannon, Young	Sumter	Wills	1	1828-1851	185
Bowhannon, Archibald M.	Madison	Wills	1	1853-1875	107
Boisseau, William E.	Montgomery	Wills	3	1840-1854	285
Bolckom, Alexander	Henry	OCR	D	1842-1846	437
Boldan, Stephen	Dallas	Wills	B	1850-1871	418
Boles, Richard R.	Calhoun	Loose		Probated 1855	
Boling, Elisha	Madison	Wills	1	1853-1875	58
Boling, J. M.	Lowndes	Wills	B	1830-1859	269
Boling, William R.	Sumter	Wills	2	1851-1872	189
Bolling, Samuel	Perry	Wills	B	1858-1873	202
Bolling, William M.	Montgomery	Wills	4	1853-1869	206
Bolton, Benjamin	Greene	Wills	D	1851-1888	173
Bolton, Vira C.	Madison	Wills	1	1853-1875	415
Bolton, William	Sumter	Wills	2	1851-1872	4
Boltz, Henry	Wilcox	Wills	6	1862-1870	45
Bond, Alfred C.	Pike	Wills	B	1862-1879	109
Bond, N. P.	Limestone	Wills	4	1831-1837	123
Bonds, Jesse	Chambers	Wills	1-2	1833-1856	432
Bonds, Richard	Calhoun	Loose		Probated 1834	
Bondurant, Frences E.	Mobile	Wills	3	1857-1870	5
Boner ? M. F.	Dallas,	Wills	A	1821-1849	342
Bones, Elizabeth	Wilcox	Wills	1	1821-1844	273
Bones, Sarah M.	Wilcox	Wills	1	1821-1844	116
Boney, Nancy	Sumter	Wills	2	1851-1872	59
Bonham, George W.	Montgomery	Wills	4	1853-1869	144
Bonham, Nathaniel	Montgomery	Wills	4	1853-1869	364
Bonham, Simeon Smith	Wilcox	Wills	1	1821-1844	267
Bonifay, Madeline G.	Mobile	Wills	1	1813-1837	216
Bonivitt, Elizabeth	Marengo	Wills	A	1820-1864	338
Bonn, Philip	Mobile	Wills	3	1857-1870	58
Bonnell, John A.	Lowndes	Wills	B	1830-1859	43
Bonnell, Mary	Lowndes	Wills	B	1830-1859	264

TESTATOR	COUNTY	WHERE FOUND		PAGE
Bonner, Ahab	Clarke	OCR F	1846-1850	246
Bonner, Jordan	Washington	Wills B	1827-	61
Bonner, Jordan	Washington	Wills 1 ∅	1827-1888	95
Bonner, Samuel	Wilcox	Wills 1	1821-1844	104
Booker, (Mrs.) Pernecy	Perry	Wills A	1821-1855	327
Booker, Peter R.	Lauderdale	Wills B	1859-1870	85
Boothe, Charles	Limestone	Wills 7	1844-1847	71
Booth, Elihu J.	Dallas	Wills B	1850-1871	39
Booth, Harriett J.	Lauderdale	Wills B	1850-1870	99
Booth, Joseph, Sr.	Baldwin	Wills A	1811-1881	168
Booth, Judith	Lauderdale	Wills 3	1821-1825	31
Booth, Henry H.	Montgomery	Wills 3	1840-1854	287
Booth, Redding S.	Perry	Wills A	1821-1855	344
Boozer, William	Marengo	Wills A	1820-1864	549
Borden, Elizabeth	Calhoun	Loose	Probated 1859	
Borom, James D.	Macon	Records 3	1845-1850	128
Bosage, John Baptiste	Mobile	Wills 1	1813-1837	267
Boss, Jesse	Dallas	Wills A	1821-1849	67
Bostick, Hampton	Dallas	Wills A	1821-1849	71
Bostic, Henry H.	Montgomery	Wills 2	1820-1845	15
Bostwick, James	Mobile	Wills 1	1813-1837	268
Boswell, John	Pike	Wills A	1845-1862	79
Boswell, Thomas C.	Pike	Wills A	1845-1862	24
Bosworth, Cyrus	Mobile	Wills 2	1837-1857	448
Boteler, Elizabeth	Morgan	OCR 11	1850-1852	233
Bothwell, Ebenezer W.	St. Clair	RE F	1862-1867	179
Boudre, Thomas	Russell	Wills 1	1838-1849	158
Boulware, James	Tallapoosa	Wills 1	1838-1866	227
Boulware, Spencer	Tallapoosa	Wills 1	1838-1866	55
Bowdon, Elizabeth	Shelby	Wills E	1845-1850	350
Bowdon, Samuel Will	Shelby	Wills D	1841-1846	1
Bowen, Averius	Montgomery	Wills 4	1853-1869	438
Bowen, Daniel	Russell	Wills 2	1850-1873	175
Bowen, Jacob	Dallas	Wills A	1821-1849	116
Bower, Benjamin	Pike	Wills B	1862-1879	175
Bowers, Elizabeth J. ?	Dallas	Wills A	1821-1849	273
Bowie, Alexander	Talladega	W&I D	1867-1880	365
Bowles, Henry H.	Madison	PR 2&5	1818-1826	55
Bowling, Aseneth	Washington	Wills 1 ∅	1827-1888	258
Bowling, Aseneth	Washington	Wills B	1827-	148
Bowling, Barbara	Washington	Wills B	1827-	64
Bowling, Barbara	Washington	Wills 1 ∅	1827-1888	100
Bowling, John H.	Macon	Records 10	1863-1865	650
Bowling, Frederick S.	Chambers	Wills 3	1856-1899	157
Bowling, Smith	Chambers	Wills 1-2	1833-1856	290
Box, George	Calhoun	Loose	Probated 1840	
Boyd, Casper W.	Pike	Wills A	1845-1862	249
Boyd, David	Wilcox	Wills 3	1826-1858	303
Boyd, James F.	Chambers	Wills 1-2	1833-1856	499
Boyd, John	Chambers	Wills 3	1856-1899	69
Boyd, John	Sumter	Wills 1	1828-1851	291

TESTATOR	COUNTY	WHERE FOUND		PAGE
Boyd, John	Sumter	Wills	2	1851-1872	50
Boyd, John P.	Dallas	Wills	B	1850-1871	190
Boyd, Margaret	Montgomery	Wills	4	1853-1869	378
Boyd, Richard	Chambers	Wills	3	1856-1899	18
Boyd, Richard H.	Chambers	Wills	3	1856-1899	105
Boyd, Robert	Montgomery	Wills	5	1863-1887	5
Boyd, Samuel	Montgomery	Wills	3	1840-1854	152
Boyd, Sam B.	Sumter	Wills	2	1851-1872	77
Boyd, Thomas	Montgomery	Wills	2	1820-1845	194
Boyd, William	Montgomery	Wills	2	1820-1845	292
Boyett, Ellen	Sumter	Wills	2	1851-1872	114
Boyett, Lock	Sumter	Wills	1	1828-1851	89
Boyett, Robert	Sumter	Wills	1	1828-1851	64
Boyett, Sarah	Sumter	Wills	1	1828-1851	225
Boyetts, Missouri	Sumter	Wills	1	1828-1851	349
Boying, Henry	Sumter	Wills	1	1828-1851	210
Boykin, Francis	Barbour	OCR	13	1863-1864	228
Boykin, Francis	Dallas	Wills	A	1821-1849	171
Boykin, F. H.	Montgomery	Wills	4	1853-1869	479
Boykin, John, Jr.	Washington	Wills	B	1827-	10
Boykin, John, Jr.	Washington	Wills	1 ∅	1827-1888	16
Boykin, Mary	Lawrence	I&W	D	1835-1840	311
Boykin, Samuel	Russell	Wills	1	1838-1849	168
Boyle, George R.	Marengo	Wills	A	1820-1864	474
Boyle, James	Montgomery	Wills	3	1840-1854	206
Boyles, Jane	Marshall	FR	10	1869-1871	798
Boyls, James A.	Perry	Wills	B	1858-1873	251
Boylston, Joseph C.	Barbour	OCR	11	1860-1861	427
Boynton, Moses	Macon	Records	5	1853-1855	121
Bozeman, Agnes	Dallas	Wills	A	1821-1849	51
Bozeman, Chapman	Blount	PM	B	1852-1856	155
Bozeman, Nathan	Coosa	W&OCR	2	1843-1883	22
Brack, Elizabeth	Montgomery	Wills	4	1853-1869	65
Brack, Gaius	Montgomery	Wills	2	1820-1845	288
Braden, William	St. Clair	Deeds	A	1824-1832	625
Bradford, Eaves	Montgomery	Wills	4	1853-1869	522
Bradford, Henry	St. Clair	Deeds	B	1831-1849	725
Bradford, John J.	Sumter	Wills	1	1828-1851	23
Bradford, Philemon	St. Clair	RE	B	1834-1859	16
Bradford, Robert R.	Perry	Wills	B	1858-1873	248
Bradford, Samuel	Monroe	W&D	B	1841-1845	178
Bradford, Sarah	Perry	Wills	A	1821-1855	53
Bradford, Warren J.	Marengo	Wills	A	1820-1864	272
Bradley, Charles L.	Monroe	W&D	D	1850-1856	519
Bradley, Gospo ?	Monroe	W&D	E	1856-1861	297
Bradley, Mary C.	Pike	Wills	A	1845-1862	188
Bradley, Thomas	Clarke	OCR	F	1846-1850	423
Bradshaw, John	Pike	Wills	A	1845-1862	77
Bradshaw, John H.	Pike	Wills	B	1862-1879	148
Bradshaw, Robert	Sumter	Wills	2	1851-1872	416
Brady, Francis W.	St. Clair	Deeds	B	1831-1849	618

TESTATOR	COUNTY	WHERE FOUND		PAGE
Bragg, Luna W.	Madison	Wills 1	1853-1875	497
Bragg, Thomas	Madison	PR 6	1832-1834	275
Bragg, William T.	Sumter	Wills 1	1828-1851	295
Bragg, Zebulon D.	Russell	Wills 2	1850-1873	74
Brainard, James M.	Mobile	Wills 3	1857-1870	628
Brame, George W., Sr.	Perry	Wills A	1821-1855	177
Brame, Marcus G.	Perry	Wills A	1821-1855	173
Bramlett, Lunsford M.	Talladega	W&I B	1858-1864	415
Branbridge, James	Marengo	Wills A	1820-1864	315
Brand, Blaney	Greene	Wills B	1817-1841	301
Brandon, Byrd	Madison	PR 8	1831-1839	416
Brandon, J. H.	Lauderdale	Wills B	1859-1870	132
Brandon, Josiah S.	Lauderdale	Wills 4	1821-1825	94
Brandon, Sara Eliza ?	Lauderdale	Wills B	1859-1870	440
Brandon, William	Madison	PR 14	1846-1850	98
Brannick, John	Mobile	Wills 3	1857-1870	429
Brannon, Rosier	Henry	OCR R	1866-1867	775
Bransford, Abram	Madison	Wills 1	1853-1875	141
Bransford, Elizabeth H.	Madison	Wills 1	1853-1875	111
Branson, Nathan	Clarke	OCR B	1818-1824	105
Brantley, Ely	Conecuh	OB A	1865-1870	407
Brantley, George R.	Dallas	Wills B	1850-1871	392
Brantley, James	Montgomery	Wills 2	1820-1845	269
Brantley, James B.	Dallas	Wills A	1821-1849	273
Brantley, Mary	Conecuh	OB A	1865-1870	403
Brantley, Thomas	Dallas	Wills A	1821-1849	2
Brantly, Green D.	Chambers	Wills 1-2	1833-1856	304
Brasell, Allen	Bibb	Loose	Recorded 1858	
Brasfield, A. W.	Greene	Wills C	1840-1864	713
Brasfield, George D.	Greene	Wills C	1840-1864	556
Brasfield, M. R.	Greene	Wills D	1851-1888	97
Brassfield, William F.	Greene	Wills C	1840-1864	341
Brasheans, ? Ellen S.	Sumter	Wills 1	1828-1851	170
Brashear, Dennis Payne	Mobile	Wills 3	1857-1870	321
Braswell, James W.	Pike	Wills A	1845-1862	90
Brassell, Jacob	Montgomery	Wills 4	1853-1869	263
Brassell, William	Coosa	W&OCR 2	1843-1883	249
Bratton, W. B.	Greene	Wills C	1840-1864	669
Brazell, James	Marshall	PR 2	1857-1888	436
Brazeal, Joel	Tuscaloosa	Wills 1	1821-1855	47
Brazeal, William	Tuscaloosa	Wills 1	1821-1855	291
Breathwait, James	Greene	Wills D	1851-1888	91
Breedlove, John	Montgomery	Wills 2	1820-1845	97
Breitling, Gottleib	Marengo	Wills A	1820-1864	517
Breittling, Joseph	Mobile	Wills 3	1857-1870	49
Brevard, Ephraim A.	Montgomery	Wills 4	1853-1869	31
Brevards, Joseph A. M.	Tallapoosa	Wills 1	1838-1866	23
Brewer, Elizabeth	Madison	PR 2&5	1818-1826	171
Brewer, George	Washington	Wills 1 ∅	1827-1888	85
Brewer, George	Washington	Wills B	1827-	55
Brewer, Matthew	Marengo	Wills A	1820-1864	154

TESTATOR	COUNTY	WHERE FOUND		PAGE
Brewer, William	Dallas	Wills A	1821-1849	114
Brewer, William	Macon	Records 7	1857-1859	642
Brewer, William	Sumter	Wills 2	1851-1872	20
Brewton, James	Madison	Deeds B	1810-1816	121
Brewton, James	Madison	Deeds NNN	1887-1887	219
Briant, Elizabeth	Clarke	PR J	1856-1858	391
Bridgeman, Wiley	Macon	Records 10	1863-1865	530
Bridges, Billings	Calhoun	Loose	Probated 1849	
Bridges, John W.	Wilcox	Wills 4	1847-1862	23
Bridges, Peter	Washington	Wills 1 Ø	1827-1888	194
Bridges, Peter	Washington	Wills B	1827-	118
Bridy, Thomas	Mobile	Wills 2	1837-1857	232
Bright, Nathan G.	Macon	Records 2	1838-1842	137
Brights, Alexander	Montgomery	Wills 2	1820-1845	106
Briggs, Amos	Tuscaloosa	Wills 1	1821-1855	337
Briggs, E. E.	Montgomery	Wills 3	1840-1854	163
Briggs, Elkanah	Butler	Wills 1	1853-1864	56
Briggs, Melinda	Greene	Wills D	1851-1888	65
Briggs, Sarah	Autauga	Reports E-B	1841-1845	83
Briggs, Zebediah	Autauga	Reports C	1834-1838	1
Briscoe, Caroline Matilda	Marshall	FR 6	1859-1867	434
Brim, William G.	Lauderdale	Wills B	1857-1870	124
Britt, Mather	Barbour	OCR 4	1850-1852	530
Britt, Priscilla	Russell	Wills 2	1850-1873	72
Brittingham, Isaac	Wilcox	Wills 2	1832-1850	299
Britton, Sarah	Wilcox	Wills 4	1847-1862	123
Brock, James	Calhoun	Loose	Probated 1839	
Brock, James	Calhoun	PR A-2	1856-1866	236
Brock, James	Talladega	Wills B	1839-1845	1
Brock, John	Calhoun	PR A-2	1856-1866	61
Brock, John	Calhoun	PR A-2	1856-1866	62
Brock, John	Montgomery	Wills 2	1820-1845	128
Brock, Lawrence	Calhoun	PCR B	1856-1865	235
Brock, Ward	Montgomery	Wills 4	1853-1869	220
Broiles, Jacob	Madison	PR 10	1842-1842	65
Bronaugh, James B.	Madison	Wills 1	1853-1875	112
Brooks, John E.	Mobile	Wills 1	1813-1837	50
Brooks, John S.	Blount	PM B-1	1844-1851	153
Brooks, M.	Limestone	Wills 9	1847-1850	106
Brooks, Posey P.	Russell	Wills 2	1850-1873	250
Brooks, Robert	Pike	Wills A	1845-1862	20
Brooks, Thomas	Morgan	OCR 7	1837-1843	134
Brooks, William	Coosa	W&OCR 2	1843-1883	301
Brooks, William T. H.	Madison	Wills 1	1853-1875	437
Brooking, Edward B.	Russell	Wills 1	1838-1849	89
Bross, Ellen M.	Coosa	W&OCR 2	1843-1883	257
Brothers, Caleb F.	St. Clair	RE F	1862-1867	118
Brothers, Philip	St. Clair	Deeds B	1831-1849	734
Broughton, Nathaniel	Monroe	W&D E	1856-1861	263
Broutin, Narcisse	Mobile	Wills 2	1837-1857	54
Browder, Mary M.	Barbour	OCR 11	1860-1861	43

TESTATOR	COUNTY	WHERE FOUND		PAGE
Browder, Milton A.	Barbour	OCR 10	1859-1860	408
Brown, Alanson	Sumter	Wills 1	1828-1851	27
Brown, Allen D.	Greene	Wills C	1840-1864	325
Brown, Ann M.	Wilcox	Wills 1	1821-1844	343
Brown, Archibald	Mobile	Wills 3	1857-1870	344
Brown, Benjamin G.	Pike	Wills B	1862-1879	67
Brown, Betheda	Dallas	Wills A	1821-1849	119
Brown, Burrell B.	Lowndes	Wills C	1861-1899	16
Brown, Catherine	Monroe	W&D A	1833-1841	204
Brown, Daniel	Lauderdale	Wills A	1835-1858	300
Brown, Edward	Mobile	Wills 2	1837-1857	242
Brown, Elijah	Jefferson	Wills A	1856-1880	125
Brown, Elizabeth	Tuscaloosa	Wills 1	1821-1855	140
Brown, Elizabeth	Tuscaloosa	Wills 1	1821-1855	165
Brown, Elizabeth	Tuscaloosa	Deeds R		81
Brown, Ephraim	Russell	Wills 2	1850-1873	15
Brown, F. H.	Marengo	Wills A	1820-1864	319
Brown, Frances	Mobile	Wills 3	1857-1870	480
Brown, Francis	Mobile	Wills 2	1837-1857	34
Brown, George M.	Madison	W&I	1810-1820	2
Brown, George P.	Talladega	Wills B	1839-1845	32
Brown, Hamilton	Greene	Wills C	1840-1864	65
Brown, Henry	Madison	PR 7	1834-1837	293
Brown, Isaac	Greene	Wills B	1817-1841	176
Brown, Jacob L.	Chambers	Wills 3	1856-1899	117
Brown, James F.	Macon	Records 10	1863-1865	584
Brown, James P.	Perry	Wills A	1821-1855	39
Brown, James P.	Lauderdale	Wills A	1835-1858	63
Brown, James R.	Montgomery	Wills 3	1840-1854	137
Brown, Jeremiah	Jackson	Wills L	1865-1866	464
Brown, John	Barbour	OCR 1	1833-1843	196
Brown, John	Henry	OCR F	1848-1853	41
Brown, John	Mobile	Wills 3	1857-1870	302
Brown, John B.	Talladega	W&I B	1858-1864	516
Brown, John S.	Dallas	Wills A	1821-1849	114
Brown, Jonas	Mobile	Wills 1	1813-1837	228
Brown, Jonas	Mobile	Wills 1	1813-1837	231
Brown, Julana	Sumter	Wills 1	1828-1851	30
Brown, Margaret K.	Dallas	Wills B	1850-1871	235
Brown, Mary	Limestone	Wills 3	1826-1831	171
Brown, Marion	St. Clair	RE F	1862-1867	195
Brown, Milton A.	Montgomery	Wills 4	1853-1869	429
Brown, Nancy	Greene	Wills C	1840-1864	655
Brown, Noel	Lauderdale	Wills 4	1821-1825	59
Brown, Robert A.	Sumter	Wills 2	1851-1872	284
Brown, Robert L.	Sumter	Wills 2	1851-1872	351
Brown, Samuel	Madison	PR 2&5	1818-1826	176
Brown, (Mrs.) Sibby	Perry	Wills A	1821-1855	112
Brown, Thomas	Montgomery	Wills 2	1820-1845	277
Brown, Thomas B.	Montgomery	Wills 4	1853-1869	373
Brown, Thornton	Baldwin	Wills A	1811-1881	33

TESTATOR	COUNTY	WHERE FOUND		PAGE
Brown, Venus	Lowndes	Wills B	1830-1859	170
Brown, William	Marshall	FR 10	1869-1871	127
Brown, William	Perry	Wills A	1821-1855	199
Brown, William	Tallapoosa	Wills 1	1838-1866	22
Brown, William L.	Tuscaloosa	Wills 1	1821-1855	290
Brown, William P.	Tuscaloosa	Wills 1	1821-1855	335
Browning, James M.	Lowndes	Wills B	1830-1859	73
Browning, John F.	Lowndes	Wills B	1830-1859	82
Browning, Joseph A.	Talladega	Wills B	1839-1846	5
Browning, Nelson	Marengo	Wills A	1820-1864	271
Browning, William	Lowndes	Wills B	1830-1859	18
Brownings, John W.	Montgomery	Wills 2	1820-1845	86
Broxton, Isaac I. ?	Pike	Wills B	1862-1879	127
Bruce, Eleanor	Madison	PR 9	1839-1841	16
Bruce, John B.	Madison	PR 4	1826-1829	24
Bruce, John B.	Marengo	Wills A	1820-1864	354
Bruce, Lemuel	Limestone	Wills 3	1826-1831	487
Brumbelow, Edward	Chambers	Wills 1-2	1833-1856	276
Brundidge, David	Bullock	Wills A	1868-1902	21
Brundidge, William	Limestone	Wills 4	1831-1837	212
Brunson, Leman C.	Sumter	Wills 2	1851-1872	85
Brunson, Marion A.	Barbour	OCR 16	1866-1868	217
Brunson, Nathan	Clarke	OCR B	1818-1824	105
Bryan, David H.	Perry	Wills B	1858-1873	161
Bryan, Edward	Clarke	PCR L	1861-1864	95
Bryan, John, Sr.	Barbour	OCR 2	1842-1847	177
Bryan, John M.	Hale	Wills A	1867-1923	49
Bryan, Nancy	Wilcox	Wills 4	1847-1862	169
Bryan, Nathan	Marengo	Wills A	1820-1864	456
Bryan, Needham	Talladega	W&I B	1858-1864	744
Bryan, Susan	Marengo	Wills A	1820-1864	309
Bryant, Marshall	St. Clair	RE C	1852-1859	290
Bryant, Martha	Baldwin	Wills A	1811-1881	103
Bryant, Richard	Jefferson	OCR	1824-1831	1
Buchanan, Abner	Macon	Records 10	1863-1865	547
Buchanan, Margaret	Greene	Wills B	1817-1841	184
Buchner, Charlotte	Butler	Wills 1	1853-1864	163
Buck, Ellen	Mobile	Wills 3	1857-1870	266
Buck, John	Lowndes	Wills B	1830-1859	394
Buckanan, May	Sumter	Wills 2	1851-1872	183
Buckholts, William H.	Sumter	Wills 1	1828-1851	41
Buckley, Dennis	Mobile	Wills 3	1857-1870	253
Buckley, Maurice	Mobile	Wills 2	1837-1857	303
Buckner, Charlotte	Russell	Wills 2	1850-1873	102
Buckner, Charles B.	Coosa	W&OCR 2	1843-1883	259
Buffalizza, John	Mobile	Wills 2	1837-1857	51
Buffington, R.	Lowndes	Wills B	1830-1859	269
Buffington, Susan	Lowndes	Wills B	1830-1859	338
Buffler, Joseph T.	Lauderdale	Wills B	1859-1870	171
Buford, Duncastle S.	Madison	Wills 1	1853-1875	22
Buford, Edward Burrell	Lowndes	Wills C	1861-1899	192

TESTATOR	COUNTY	WHERE FOUND		PAGE
Buford, John	Montgomery	Wills 3	1840-1854	240
Buford, Thomas	Mobile	Wills 3	1857-1870	511
Buford, William K.	Montgomery	Wills 3	1840-1854	82
Bugg, Samuel	Autauga	Reports C	1834-1838	515
Buice, John	Tallapoosa	Wills 1	1838-1866	103
Bull, Alexander	Coosa	W&OCR 2	1843-1883	15
Bull, William P.	Talladega	W&I B	1858-1864	232
Bullard, Ann B.	Montgomery	Wills 3	1840-1854	100
Bullard, Certf?	Montgomery	Wills 2	1820-1845	160
Bullington, John W.	Lauderdale	Wills B	1859-1870	436
Bullock, Ann	Montgomery	Wills 4	1853-1869	9
Bullock, Edward C.	Barbour	OCR 12	1861-1863	226
Bullock, Elizabeth C.	Greene	Wills C	1840-1864	425
Bullock, John M.	Greene	Wills C	1840-1864	343
Bumes, Basil M.	Wilcox	Wills 3	1826-1858	299
Bunker, Eliza Ann	Mobile	Wills 2	1837-1857	400
Burch, John	Montgomery	Wills 2	1820-1845	164
Burchfield, Thomas	Jefferson	Wills A	1856-1880	147
Burdick, Isaac	Dallas	Wills B	1850-1871	274
Burdick, Sarah	Macon	Records 5	1853-1855	409
Burdin, J. W.	Marengo	Wills A	1820-1864	533
Burdine, Jeremiah	Madison	PR 16	1831-1861	314
Burdine, Richard	Madison	PR 3	1823-1826	362
Burgess, Celia	Tuscaloosa	Wills 1	1821-1855	320
Burgess, James M.	Monroe	W&D F	1861-1867	621
Burgess, Jane	Monroe	W&D 8	1870-1871	436
Burgess, Joseph	Monroe	W&D G	1868-1870	757
Burgess, W. E.	Monroe	W&D F	1861-1867	180
Burget, Henry	Mobile	Wills 2	1837-1857	105
Burke, Mary W.	Perry	Wills B	1858-1873	416
Burke, William	Mobile	Wills 2	1837-1857	292
Burks, J?. M.	Tallapoosa	Wills 1	1838-1866	91
Burks, Narcissa J?	Tallapoosa	Wills 1	1838-1866	142
Burleson, William B.	Morgan	FR 22	1865-1866	205
Burnes, Stephen	Blount	Record	1852-1856	227
Burnett, Lewis	Shelby	Wills H	1847-1866	567
Burnett, Mary H.	Perry	Wills B	1858-1873	46
Burnett, William	Monroe	W&D D	1833-1870	224
Burns, Catherine	Mobile	Wills 3	1857-1870	256
Burns, G. L.	Lamar	Wills 1	1844-1910	3
Burns, Isabella	Calhoun	Loose	Exec. 1840	
Burns, Margaret	Tallapoosa	Wills 1	1838-1866	157
Burns, Stephen	Blount	PM B	1852-1856	227
Burpo, Thomas	Wilcox	Wills 3	1826-1858	324
Burns, William	Calhoun	Loose	1830	
Burrill, J. W.	Wilcox	Wills 5	1855-1870	239
Burroughs, Benjamin	Tuscaloosa	Wills 1	1821-1855	190
Burroughs, Raymond	Tuscaloosa	Wills 1	1821-1855	97
Burrow, Elizabeth	Lauderdale	Wills B	1859-1870	57
Burrow, Jack	Lauderdale	Wills B	1859-1870	418
Burrows, Joel	Lauderdale	Wills 4	1821-1825	65

TESTATOR	COUNTY	WHERE FOUND		PAGE
Burrows, Russel	Mobile	Wills	2	1837-1857 255
Burson, Enoch	Wilcox	Wills	1	1821-1844 409
Burt, James	Morgan	OCR	6	1831-1837 423
Burt, Martin R.	Autauga	Wills	1	1862-1925 10
Burt, Mathew	Lowndes	Wills	B	1830-1859 178
Burton? Archer	Lowndes	Wills	B	1830-1859 20
Burton, Drury L.	Sumter	Wills	1	1828-1851 344
Burton, Jacob	Chambers	Wills	3	1856-1899 179
Burton, John B.	Marengo	Wills	A	1820-1864 224
Burton, John G.	Marengo	Wills	A	1820-1864 248
Burton, Martha J.	Chambers	Wills	3	1856-1899 53
Burton, Thomas B.	Montgomery	Wills	4	1853-1869 288
Burton, Thomas O.	Madison	Wills	1	1853-1875 228
Burwell, James William	Madison	Wills	1	1853-1875 464
Busby, Elisha	Cleburne	Wills	1	1866-1884 170
Busby, William M.	Montgomery	Wills	3	1840-1854 175
Bush, Charles D.	Barbour	OCR	5	1852-1853 280
Bush, David	Morgan	OCR	8	1844-1848 303
Bush, John	Calhoun	Loose		Probated 1847
Bush, Mary	Morgan	OCR	11	1850-1852 30
Bush, Mary E.	Marengo	Wills	A	1820-1864 399
Bush, Moses E.	Barbour	OCR	3	1847-1851 41
Bush, N. B.	Marengo	Wills	A	1820-1864 252
Bush, William	Washington	Wills	1 ∅	1827-1888 88
Bush, William	Washington	Wills	B	1827- 57
Bussey, Zadock	Montgomery	Wills	2	1820-1845 217
Buston, Charles	Clarke	OCR	F	1846-1850 3
Butler, Edmund	Dallas	Wills	A	1821-1849 93
Butler, Gabriel	Lauderdale	Wills	A	1835-1858 262
Butler, Hiram	Talladega	W&I	D	1867-1880 390
Butler, Isaac	Greene	Wills	A	1821-1827 64
Butler, Isaac	Lowndes	Wills	B	1830-1859 44
Butler, Jesse T.	Greene	Wills	C	1840-1864 513
Butler, Thomas	Lowndes	Wills	C	1861-1899 18
Butler, Thomas	Montgomery	Wills	4	1853-1869 29
Butler, William	Lawrence	I&W	D	1835-1840 250
Butts, Henrietta	Russell	Wills	2	1850-1873 323
Butts, John	Greene	Wills	C	1840-1864 71
Butts, Thomas	Butler	Wills	1	1853-1864 44
Buycke, Ann	Coosa	W&OCR	2	1843-1883 70
Buys, Jeremiah	Limestone	Wills	12	1866-1872 664
Byard, Garrett Hamilton	Mobile	Wills	2	1837-1857 87
Byars, John	Talladega	Wills	A	1833-1839 573
Byars, Striplin	Jefferson	OCR		1831-1832 248
Byars, Stripling	Jefferson	PM		1831-1832 249
Bynum, Drew S.	Lawrence	I&W	D	1835-1840 337
Bynum, Tapley	Blount	OCR		1829-1841 482
Byrd, Edward	Henry	OCR	L	1860-1861 287
Byrd, M.	Monroe	W&D	8	1870-1871 587
Byrd, Octavius	Lawrence	I&W	A	1850-1857 407
Byrd, Pleasant	Limestone	Wills	7	1844-1847 138

TESTATOR	COUNTY	WHERE FOUND		PAGE
Byrd, Thomas	Mobile	Wills 2	1837-1857	89
Byrd, William, Sr.	Russell	Wills 2	1850-1873	728
Byrd, William	Sumter	Wills 1	1828-1851	75
Byrne, Gerald	Mobile	Wills 1	1813-1837	17
Byrne, John	Mobile	Wills 3	1857-1870	637
Byrne, Michael	Mobile	Wills 3	1857-1870	380
Byrne, Thomas, Sr.	Baldwin	Wills A	1811-1881	183
Byrnes, Charles H.	Lauderdale	Wills 4	1821-1825	51
Byrnes, Thomas	Mobile	Wills 1	1813-1837	200
Cabaniss, Charles	Madison	PR 3	1823-1826	306
Cabell, Alice W.	Tuscaloosa	Wills 3	1858-1865	43
Cabiness, William	Tuscaloosa	Wills 1	1821-1855	19
Caddel, M. B.	Etowah	Wills A	1866-1870	7
Cade, Drury B.	Greene	Wills A	1821-1827	63
Cade, Ervin C?	Dallas	Wills B	1850-1871	203
Cade, Ignatius	Pike	Wills B	1862-1879	28
Cade, William	Marengo	Wills A	1820-1864	311
Caffey, Avington B.	Montgomery	Wills 4	1853-1869	165
Caffey, Dr. John P.	Montgomery	Wills 4	1853-1869	1
Caffey, John, Sr.	Montgomery	Wills 2	1820-1845	35
Caffey, Michal J.	Montgomery	Wills 4	1853-1869	204
Cage, Jesse	Sumter	Wills 1	1828-1851	263
Cain, Elisha	Autauga	Reports G	1850-1853	238
Cain, George	Tuscaloosa	Wills 1	1821-1855	274
Cain, Jacob T.	Russell	Wills 2	1850-1873	77
Cain, Joseph	Mobile	Wills 2	1837-1857	398
Cain, William	Marengo	Wills A	1820-1864	417
Calahan, Elizabeth	Lauderdale	Wills A	1835-1858	146
Calderon, Simon	Mobile	Wills 1	1813-1837	227
Caldwell, David F.	Lowndes	Wills C	1861-1899	120
Caldwell, Elizabeth	Tuscaloosa	Wills 1	1821-1855	193
Caldwell, James H.	Mobile	Wills 3	1857-1870	446
Caldwell, James H.	Mobile	Wills 3	1857-1870	736
Caldwell, John	Chambers	Wills 1-2	1833-1856	159
Caldwell, Joshua	Chambers	Wills 1-2	1833-1856	413
Caldwell, Mary	Chambers	Wills 3	1856-1899	17
Caldwell, Nancy	Macon	Records 10	1863-1865	494
Caldwell, Samuel, Sr.	Autauga	Reports E-A	1838-1841	239
Caldwell, Thomas G.	Marengo	Wills A	1820-1864	221
Caldwell, William	Tuscaloosa	Wills 1	1821-1855	26
Caldwell, William H.	Talladega	W&I A	1852-1857	142
Calhoun, Charles	Chambers	Wills 1-2	1833-1856	321
Calhoun, Christian	Tallapoosa	Wills 1	1838-1866	21
Calhoun, John L.	Russell	Wills 1	1838-1849	173
Calhoun, Mildred	Lee	Wills A	1867-1898	38
Calhoun, Patricia	Russell	Wills 2	1850-1873	362
Calhoun, Patrick	Montgomery	Wills 4	1853-1869	500
Calhoun, Robert	Montgomery	Wills 4	1853-1869	196

TESTATOR	COUNTY	WHERE FOUND		PAGE
Callaway, David	Montgomery	Wills 3	1840-1854	217
Callaway, Edward	Macon	Records 7	1857-1859	57
Callaway, Henry Armstrong	Lowndes	Wills C	1861-1899	199
Callen, James	Dallas	Wills A	1821-1849	199
Callen, James C.	Dallas	Wills B	1850-1871	269
Callen, John K.	Dallas	Wills B	1850-1871	337
Callen, William	Dallas	Wills B	1850-1871	206
Caller, Green D.	Mobile	Wills 2	1837-1857	138
Caller, Winny	Clarke	OCR F	1840-1845	281
Calloway, Christopher C.	Hale	Wills A	1867-1923	21
Calloway, Francis	Chambers	Wills 3	1856-1899	152
Calloway, James Madison	Barbour	OCR 3	1847-1851	252
Calloway, Mary E.	Montgomery	Wills 4	1853-1869	380
Calloway, Ralph C.	Montgomery	Wills 4	1853-1869	431
Calom, Mary A.	Limestone	Wills 4	1831-1837	158
Camak, David	Tuscaloosa	Wills 1	1821-1855	350
Cameron, Loughlan	Barbour	OCR 7	1854-1857	530
Cameron, Mary	Barbour	OCR 13	1863-1864	167
Cameron, Nancy	Barbour	OCR 13	1863-1864	167
Cammack, David	Clarke	PR G	1850-1854	18
Cammell, Owen	Madison	PR 3	1823-1826	97
Camness, Anthony	Madison	Deeds A	1810-1816	48
Camp, Abishai	Bibb	Loose	dated 1841	
Camp, Anna N.	Butler	Wills 1	1853-1864	229
Camp, Thomas	St. Clair	Deeds C	1846-1855	191
Campbell, Aron	Bibb	Loose	dated 1857	
Campbell, Benjamin W.	Pike	Wills A	1845-1862	242
Campbell, Daniel D.	Chambers	Wills 1-2	1833-1856	289
Campbell, David	Greene	Wills C	1840-1864	119
Campbell, Donald	Montgomery	Wills 3	1840-1854	26
Campbell, Drucilla	Clarke	PR J	1856-1858	255
Campbell, Duncan	Clarke	OCR	1825-1832	1
Campbell, Elizabeth	Dallas	Wills A	1821-1849	50
Campbell, Georgia Ann	Macon	Records 10	1863-1865	115
Campbell, James	Baldwin	Wills A	1811-1881	149
Campbell, James	Jefferson	OCR	1831-1832	86
Campbell, James C.	Dallas	Wills A	1821-1849	241
Campbell, James M.	Lowndes	Wills B	1830-1859	194
Campbell, John	Dallas	Wills A	1821-1849	312
Campbell, John K.	Dallas	Wills B	1850-1871	38
Campbell, John M.	Talladega	W&I A	1852-1857	336
Campbell, Lucinda	Greene	Wills C	1840-1864	426
Campbell, Mary	Lowndes	Wills B	1830-1859	349
Campbell, R. W.	Sumter	Wills 2	1851-1872	119
Campbell, Robert	Marengo	Wills A	1820-1864	196
Campbell, William	Madison	PR 2&5	1818-1826	565
Campbell, William B.	Madison	Wills 1	1853-1875	246
Campbell, William H.	Marengo	Wills A	1820-1864	391
Cander, Archibald	Mobile	Wills 1	1813-1837	208
Cannon, Barbary	Calhoun	Loose	Probated 1846	
Cannon, David	Lauderdale	Wills A	1835-1858	114

TESTATOR	COUNTY	WHERE FOUND		PAGE
Cannon, David, Jr.	Mobile	Wills 2	1837-1857	364
Cannon, David R.	Montgomery	Wills 4	1853-1869	385
Cannon, Elinor M.	Mobile	Wills 3	1857-1870	515
Cannon, Everit	Tallapoosa	Wills 1	1838-1866	212
Cannon ?, James	Jefferson	OCR	1824-1831	4
Cannon, Minos	Madison	Wills 1	1853-1875	37
Canter, John S.	Montgomery	Wills 3	1840-1854	93
Canterberry, Jeremiah	Madison	PR 12	1845-1849	29
Cantrell, John	Lauderdale	Wills A	1835-1858	26
Canty, William R.	Montgomery	Wills 4	1853-1869	346
Capehart, Nancy	Wilcox	Wills 5	1855-1870	416
Capehart, Nancy	Wilcox	Wills 5	1855-1870	445
Capell, Charles	Wilcox	Wills 1	1821-1844	98
Capellas, John	Baldwin	Wills A	1811-1881	120
Capers, William W.	Tuscaloosa	Wills 1	1821-1855	120
Capps, Adam	Montgomery	Wills 3	1840-1854	299
Cardwell, James	Tuscaloosa	Wills 1	1821-1855	295
Carey, Charles W.	Macon	Records 10	1863-1865	459
Cargile, Jason	Pike	Wills A	1845-1862	181
Cargill, John	Macon	Records 8	1859-1860	685
Carithers, Robert G.	Russell	Wills 2	1850-1873	204
Carlen, Michael	Mobile	Wills 3	1857-1870	281
Carleton, Ambrose	Clarke	OCR B	1818-1824	61
Carleton, Warren	Sumter	Wills 1	1828-1851	28
Carlile, John	Tuscaloosa	Wills 1	1821-1855	46
Carlisle, E. K., Sr.	Perry	Wills B	1858-1873	431
Carlisle, Elizabeth	Chambers	Wills 1-2	1833-1856	436
Carlisle, Mrs. Susanna	Perry	Wills A	1821-1855	265
Carloss, William C?	Montgomery	Wills 3	1840-1854	280
Carlton, Ira	Greene	Wills C	1840-1864	172
Carmichael, Daniel	Madison	PR 8	1831-1839	467
Carmichael, George W.	Madison	Wills 1	1853-1875	320
Carnathan, John F.	Greene	Wills B	1817-1841	154
Carnes, John W.	Greene	Wills B	1817-1841	291
Carnes, William D.	Russell	Wills 2	1850-1873	9
Carney, Joshua	Baldwin	Wills A	1811-1881	24
Carney, Sarah	Clarke	GE&W	1832-1839	107
Carnley, Lewis	Pike	Wills A	1845-1862	11
Carpenter, Daniel	Montgomery	Wills 2	1820-1845	175
Carpenter, John B.	Montgomery	Wills 4	1853-1869	343
Carpenter, John C.	Madison	Wills 1	1853-1875	525
Carpenter, Lucy S.	Montgomery	Wills 5	1863-1887	57
Carr, Josiah	Montgomery	Wills 2	1820-1845	137
Carr, Kintchen	Talladega	Wills C	1845-1853	172
Carr, Robert E.	Lauderdale	Wills B	1859-1870	32
Carrall, Thomas B.	Dallas	Wills A	1821-1849	173
Carrington, William E.	Perry	Wills A	1821-1855	312
Carroll, Ansley	Autauga	Reports G	1850-1853	437
Carroll, Dennis	Lauderdale	Wills A	1835-1858	180
Carroll, Grief	Lauderdale	Wills A	1835-1858	11
Carroll, James	Montgomery	Wills 4	1853-1869	345

TESTATOR	COUNTY	WHERE FOUND		PAGE
Carroll, John	Autauga	Reports H	1853-1857	226
Carroll, Wilson	Lauderdale	Wills B	1859-1870	74
Carson, David W.	Dallas	Wills A	1821-1849	27
Carson, H. John	Greene	Wills A	1821-1827	27
Carson, Hugh	Greene	Wills A	1821-1827	72
Carson, Hugh	Greene	Wills B	1817-1841	5
Carson, James	Jefferson	OCR	1824-1831	4
Carson, Robert S.	Dallas	Wills A	1821-1849	185
Carson, Samuel W.	DeKalb	W&D	1837-1863	36
Carter, Anderson	Madison	Wills 1	1853-1875	267
Carter, Charles	Bibb	Admr.R. I	1858-1865	742
Carter, Claiborne	Clarke	PCR K	1858-1861	624
Carter, David	Tallapoosa	Wills 1	1838-1866	209
Carter, Giles	Henry	OCR O	1864-1864	132
Carter, James F.	Macon	WAC & A 11	1862-1870	104
Carter, John M.	Marshall	OCR 1	1836-1837	7
Carter, John W.	Butler	Wills 1	1853-1864	217
Carter, Lacy	Tallapoosa	Wills 2	1864-1907	41
Carter, Lazarus	Conecuh	OB A	1865-1870	398
Carter, R. C.	Marengo	Wills A	1820-1864	267
Carter, Stith M.	Lowndes	Wills B	1830-1859	172
Carter, Thomas	Wilcox	Wills 2	1832-1850	202
Cartilege, Euphemia	Barbour	OCR 9	1858-1859	908
Cartledge, Edmund	Barbour	OCR 14	1863-1865	611
Cartright, H. B.	Limestone	Wills 12	1866-1872	710
Cartwright, John	Madison	PR 9	1839-1841	28
Carwile, David	Autauga	Reports F	1845-1850	254
Carwile, John T.	Autauga	Reports H	1853-1857	433
Cary, Edward	Lauderdale	Wills B	1859-1870	154
Cary, George	Madison	Wills 1	1853-1875	126
Cary, J. F.	Lowndes	Wills B	1830-1859	256
Casban, Emanuel	Tallapoosa	Wills 1	1838-1866	179
Case, Adam	Wilcox	Wills 1	1821-1844	406
Casey, Eliza	Mobile	Wills 2	1837-1857	53
Casey, Elizabeth	Lauderdale	Wills A	1835-1858	70
Casey, John	Barbour	OCR 11	1860-1861	781
Casey,? Rebecca	Montgomery	Wills 3	1840-1854	251
Casey, Thomas	Mobile	Wills 1	1813-1837	211
Casey, Thomas	Mobile	Wills 2	1837-1857	152
Cash, Abi	Barbour	OCR 12	1861-1863	126
Cashaden, Mary	Greene	Wills B	1817-1841	294
Caskaden, George	Washington	Wills 1 Ø	1827-1888	1
Caskaden, George	Washington	Wills B	1827-	3
Cassity, Levi	Lauderdale	Wills A	1835-1858	172
Castel, Charles	Mobile	Wills 2	1837-1857	404
Catching, Nathaniel	Tallapoosa	Wills 1	1838-1866	139
Cates, Thomas	Tuscaloosa	Wills 3	1858-1865	233
Cathey, A. C.	Marengo	Wills A	1820-1864	227
Catlin, John D.	Marengo	Wills A	1820-1864	391
Cato, Anderson F.	Washington	Wills B	1827-	71
Cato, Anderson F.	Washington	Wills 1 Ø	1827-1888	111

TESTATOR	COUNTY	WHERE FOUND		PAGE
Cato, Burrell P.	Washington	Wills B	1827-	45
Cato, Burrell P.	Washington	Wills 1 Ø	1827-1888	68
Cato, Green T.	Washington	Wills B	1827-	66
Cato, Green Tatum	Washington	Wills 1 Ø	1827-1888	102
Cato, Lewis	Washington	Wills B	1827-	26
Cato, Lewis	Washington	Wills 1 Ø	1827-1888	40
Cato, William	Monroe	W&D A	1833-1841	202
Cato, William M.	Dallas	Wills A	1821-1849	131
Catta, Bennett	Mobile	Wills 3	1857-1870	359
Caulfield, Edwin	Greene	Wills D	1851-1888	1
Caulfield, James	Monroe	W&D B	1841-1845	60
Causey, Cullen	Washington	Wills B	1827-	128
Causey, Cullen	Washington	Wills 1 Ø	1827-1888	212
Cautey, John	Russell	Wills 2	1850-1873	168
Cavette, Richard	Madison	PR 11	1842-1849	308
Cavitt, Richard	Madison	W&I	1810-1820	208
Center, Henry	Mobile	Wills 2	1837-1857	73
Centerro, Manuella Sorancia	Mobile	Wills 2	1837-1857	131
Chadwick, Asa, Sr.	Mobile	Wills 3	1857-1870	124
Chaffin, John	Chambers	Wills 1-2	1833-1856	138
Chamberlain, Henry J.	Mobile	Wills 4	1857-1878	51
Chamberlain, Robert T.	Mobile	Wills 3	1857-1870	390
Chamberlayne, William	Sumter	Wills 1	1828-1851	159
Chambers, A.	Lauderdale	Wills B	1859-1870	369
Chambers, David	Dallas	Wills A	1821-1849	188
Chambers, Elizabeth	Sumter	Wills 1	1828-1851	113
Chambers, George A.	Mobile	Wills 2	1837-1857	460
Chambers, James, Sr.	Montgomery	Wills 3	1840-1854	234
Chambers, Jane J.	Perry	Wills A	1821-1855	148
Chambers, John	Dallas	Wills A	1821-1849	265
Chambers, Joseph Boyd	Perry	Wills A	1821-1855	332
Chambers, Robert B.	Perry	Wills A	1821-1855	42
Chambers, Robert W.	Perry	Wills A	1821-1855	184
Chambers, Samuel C.	Calhoun	Loose	dated 1840	
Chambers, William	Lowndes	Wills B	1830-1859	212
Chambers, William C.	Lauderdale	Wills 3	1821-1825	97
Chambless, Stephen	Madison	PR 10	1842-1842	10
Chambliss, David	Montgomery	Wills 4	1853-1869	262
Champion, Robert	Lowndes	Wills B	1830-1859	251
Champion, William	Barbour	OCR 14	1863-1865	108
Champion, William	Lowndes	Wills C	1861-1899	35
Chance, Jesse	Dallas	Wills A	1821-1849	153
Chanceller, Gilbert	Butler	Wills 1	1853-1864	131
Chancellor, John	Tuscaloosa	Wills 3	1858-1865	56
Chancey, Thomas	Henry	OCR L	1860-1861	316
Chandler, Allen	Calhoun	Loose	Probated 1856	
Chandler, Joel	St. Clair	Deeds B	1831-1849	615
Chandler, John	Mobile	Wills 2	1837-1857	7
Chandler, Robert	Lauderdale	Wills 3	1821-1825	86
Chandler, Robert	Lauderdale	Wills B	1859-1870	102
Chandler, William G.	Mobile	Wills 3	1857-1870	298

TESTATOR	COUNTY	WHERE FOUND		PAGE
Chaney, Peyton	Sumter	Wills	1	1828-1851	84
Chapman, B. T.	Russell	Wills	2	1850-1873	427
Chapman, Benjamin	Montgomery	Wills	2	1820-1845	47
Chapman, Catherine L.	Talladega	W&I	D	1867-1880	620
Chapman, Elijah	Clarke	OCR	F	1846-1850	259
Chapman, Giles	Clarke	PR	N	1866-1870	220
Chapman, James A.	Russell	Wills	2	1850-1873	415
Chapman, John	Clarke	PR	N	1866-1870	148
Chapman, John M.	Hale	Wills	A	1867-1923	31
Chapman, Lemuel	Montgomery	Wills	2	1820-1845	53
Chapman, Mrs. Mary	Talladega	W&I	B	1858-1864	531
Chapman, Samuel	Dallas	Wills	B	1850-1871	286
Chapman, William	Perry	Wills	B	1858-1873	59
Chappell, George	Macon	Records	5	1853-1855	123
Chappell, Thomas M.	Macon	OCM	2	1835-1842	153
Charles, Ann W.	Perry	Wills	A	1821-1855	65
Charles, John S.	Hale	Wills	A	1867-1923	25
Charles, Nancy Ann	Mobile	Wills	1	1813-1837	271
Charles, Nanette ?	Mobile	Wills	2	1837-1857	74
Chastang, Bazile	Mobile	Wills	1	1813-1837	177
Chastang, Edward	Mobile	Wills	2	1837-1857	79
Chastang, Francoise	Mobile	Wills	2	1837-1857	22
Chastang, Francoise	Mobile	Wills	2	1837-1857	111
Chastang, Isabel	Mobile	Wills	2	1837-1857	59
Chastang, John	Mobile	Wills	2	1837-1857	112
Chastang, Margueritte	Mobile	Wills	1	1813-1837	10
Chastang, Philip	Mobile	Wills	3	1857-1870	275
Chastang, Soustin	Mobile	Wills	2	1837-1857	141
Chastang, Zenon	Mobile	Wills	3	1857-1870	241
Chatham, Charles N. B.	Coosa	W&OCR	2	1843-1883	273
Chaudron, Simon	Mobile	Wills	2	1837-1857	158
Chavanna, Jean	Mobile	Wills	1	1813-1837	94
Cheatham, John	Lowndes	Wills	B	1830-1859	128
Cheatham, William	Limestone	Wills	9	1847-1850	322
Cheatham, William B.	Madison	PR	2&5	1818-1826	73
Cheesbrough, Hiram	Mobile	Wills	1	1813-1837	273
Chennault, Stephen	Madison	W&I		1810-1820	137
Cherry, Israel	Sumter	Wills	2	1851-1872	411
Cherry, Penelope	Greene	Wills	B	1817-1841	178
Cherry, Samuel T.	Greene	Wills	C	1840-1864	63
Cheshire, James	Lowndes	Wills	C	1861-1899	52
Chesson, Uriah	Macon	Records	3	1845-1850	695
Chestang, John	Baldwin	Wills	A	1811-1881	3
Chestang, Pierre	Mobile	Wills	2	1837-1857	180
Chestang, Solidele	Mobile	Wills	2	1837-1857	202
Chester, Ezekiel	Tallapoosa	Wills	1	1836-1866	104
Chighizola, G.	Mobile	Wills	2	1837-1857	205
Childers, David	Madison	PR	2	1818-1823	137
Childers, George	Dallas	Wills	B	1850-1871	76
Childre, William	Montgomery	Wills	3	1840-1854	278
Childress, Elizabeth	Lauderdale	Wills	B	1859-1870	4

TESTATOR	COUNTY	WHERE FOUND		PAGE
Childress, James	Tuscaloosa	Wills 1	1821-1855	86
Childress, Mary	Tuscaloosa	Wills 3	1858-1865	89
Childress, Thomas	Lauderdale	Wills A	1835-1858	123
Chiles, Jonathan	Greene	Wills A	1821-1827	49
Chiles, Thomas	Greene	Wills C	1840-1864	28
Chiles, Walter	Sumter	Wills 1	1828-1851	316
Chiles, William	Greene	Wills B	1817-1841	39
Chilton, Mary	Calhoun	Loose	Probated 1849	
Chisolm, John	Lauderdale	Wills A	1835-1858	149
Chisholm, William R.	Lauderdale	Wills B	1859-1870	169
Chisolm, Robert J.	Henry	OCR P	1864-1866	152
Chittenden, W. H.	Lauderdale	Wills A	1835-1858	234
Chivers, Henry T.	Chambers	Wills 1-2	1833-1856	150
Choak-Chos-hadjo	Coosa	W&PM A	1834-1842	1
Chotard, Sarah	Tuscaloosa	Wills 1	1821-1855	22
Chreistberg, Jane	Mobile	Wills 2	1837-1857	431
Christian, Allen, Sr.	Madison	PR 7	1834-1837	531
Christian, Dorotha	Tuscaloosa	Wills 4	1868-1897	30
Christian, George	Wilcox	Wills 1	1821-1844	111
Christian, James	Chambers	Wills 1-2	1833-1856	171
Christian, James	Tuscaloosa	Wills 1	1821-1855	314
Christian, John M.	Henry	OCR S	1867-1868	713
Christian, John W.	Madison	PR 4	1826-1829	406
Christian, Lucy P.	Wilcox	Wills 1	1821-1844	400
Christian, Margaret	Madison	PR 10	1842-1842	126
Christian, Thomas	Chambers	Wills 1-2	1833-1856	262
Christian, W. W.	Dallas	Wills A	1821-1849	327
Christmas, Henry M.	Henry	OCR O	1864-1864	159
Christmas, Henry M.	Henry	OCR O	1864-1864	261
Christopher, R. S.	Sumter	Wills 1	1828-1851	65
Cicley, Mrs. C. S.	Lowndes	Wills B	1830-1859	285
Clannahan, William H.	Chambers	Wills 1-2	1833-1856	467
Clanton, Francis A.	Greene	Wills D	1851-1888	479
Clanton, George	Sumter	Wills 1	1828-1851	70
Clanton, Harriett R.	Sumter	Wills 1	1828-1851	364
Clanton, John J.	St. Clair	RED	1859-1867	20
Clanton, N. H.	Macon	Records 5	1853-1855	692
Clanton, Nathaniel H.	Macon	Records 8	1859-1860	441
Clanton, Richard	Tuscaloosa	Wills 3	1858-1865	90
Clanton, Sandon	Sumter	Wills 1	1828-1851	56
Clappe, Edmund B.	Clarke	GE&W	1832-1839	406
Clarey, Wiley S.	Pike	Wills B	1851-1872	89
Clark, D. W.	Sumter	Wills 2	1851-1872	55
Clark, Daniel N.	Tuscaloosa	Wills 4	1868-1897	21
Clark, Elizabeth	Autauga	Reports C	1834-1838	614
Clark, Elizabeth D.	Dallas	Wills A	1821-1849	10
Clark, Henry C.	Dallas	Wills B	1850-1871	408
Clark, Isham J.	Clarke	PCR M	1864-1866	425
Clark, James D.	Wilcox	Wills 4	1847-1862	238
Clark, John	Bibb	Admr. R	1858-1865	796
Clark, John B.	Dallas	Wills B	1850-1871	312

TESTATOR	COUNTY	WHERE FOUND		PAGE
Clark, John P.	Sumter	Wills 1	1828-1851	92
Clark, Nathaniel	Perry	Wills A	1821-1855	1
Clark, Samuel	Calhoun	Loose	Probated 1838	
Clark, William	Chambers	Wills 3	1856-1899	37
Clark, Zachariah	Calhoun	Loose	Probated 1853	
Clarke, Alexander	Bibb	Loose	Probated 1851	
Clarke, Charles	Madison	PR 6	1832-1834	52
Clarke, Cornelius	Madison	PR 4	1826-1829	318
Clarke, Eli	Russell	Wills 2	1850-1873	103
Clarke, Henrietta M. H.	Perry	Wills B	1858-1873	61
Clarke, James E.	Madison	PR 13	1838-1848	398
Clarke, John	Madison	PR 7	1834-1837	221
Clarke, John	Pike	Wills A	1845-1862	237
Clarke, Lucy	Madison	PR 13	1838-1848	400
Clarke, Mary	Lauderdale	Wills B	1859-1870	107
Clarke, Robert, Sr.	Madison	PR 8	1831-1839	197
Clausell, Martha W.	Monroe	W&D E	1856-1861	216
Clay, Clement C., Sr.	Madison	Wills 1	1853-1875	357
Clay, Samuel M.	Limestone	Wills 6	1841-1846	606
Clayton, George R.	Montgomery	Wills 3	1840-1854	35
Clayton, Nelson	Lee	Wills A	1867-1898	23
Cleckley, John L.	Macon	Records 6	1855-1858	258
Cleere, Thomas	Lawrence	I&W D	1835-1840	127
Clem, Adam	Madison	PR 2	1818-1823	39
Clemens, James	Madison	Wills 1	1850-1875	299
Clemens, Jeremiah	Madison	Wills 1	1853-1875	312
Clement, Joseph	Mobile	Wills 1	1813-1837	203
Clements, Elizabeth	Madison	PR 7	1834-1837	86
Clements, Hardy	Tuscaloosa	Wills 3	1858-1865	207
Clements, Israel	Tuscaloosa	Wills 4	1868-1897	12
Clements, Jacob	Tuscaloosa	Wills 1	1821-1855	224
Clements, Nancy	Chambers	Wills 1-2	1833-1856	437
Clements, Reuben	Tuscaloosa	Wills 1	1821-1855	24
Clemons, Henry	Lauderdale	Wills B	1859-1870	117
Clemons, Henry	Montgomery	Wills 3	1840-1854	229
Cleveland, Benjamin F.	Coosa	W&OCR 2	1843-1883	34
Cleveland, Carter H.	Dallas	Wills B	1850-1871	290
Cleveland, Fanney	Dallas	Wills A	1821-1849	121
Cleveland, George	Mobile	Wills 3	1857-1870	588
Cleveland, George A.	Mobile	Wills 3	1857-1870	254
Cleveland, James	Clarke	PCR M	1864-1866	239
Cleveland, James S.	Dallas	Wills B	1850-1871	267
Cleveland, Larkin	Coosa	W&OCR 2	1843-1883	46
Cleveland, Larkin D.	Mobile	Wills 3	1857-1870	577
Cleveland, March	Bibb	Loose	Dated 1858	
Cleveland, Robert W.	Coosa	W&OCR 2	1843-1883	13
Cleveland, Sarah	Coosa	W&OCR 2	1843-1883	91
Clew, David	Lauderdale	Wills 3	1821-1825	16
Clifton, Malinda	Dallas	Wills B	1850-1871	421
Clinton, Matthew	Sumter	Wills 1	1828-1851	213
Clinton, Patrick	Tuscaloosa	Wills 3	1858-1865	91

TESTATOR	COUNTY	WHERE FOUND		PAGE
Clitheral, Alex B.	Montgomery	Wills 5	1863-1887	12
Clopton, Sally	Macon	Records 4	1850-1852	167
Cloud, William	Madison	PR 16	1831-1861	258
Cloyd, Joseph	Madison	Wills 1	1853-1875	16
Coate, William	Clarke	PCR N	1866-1870	344
Cobb, Jacob	Barbour	OCR 12	1861-1863	862
Cobb, McCuin	Barbour	OCR 5	1852-1853	345
Cobbs, John B.	Sumter	Wills 1	1828-1851	5
Cobbs, Nicholas Hamner	Montgomery	Wills 4	1853-1869	333
Cobbs, Thomas	Sumter	Wills 1	1828-1851	134
Coburn, Headley	Lauderdale	Wills 4	1821-1825	45
Cochran, Andrew	Talladega	W&I A	1852-1857	488
Cochran, Hiram	Tuscaloosa	Wills 1	1821-1855	157
Cochrane, William	Tuscaloosa	Wills 1	1821-1855	299
Cockburn, Elizah?	Lauderdale	Wills 4	1821-1825	116
Cockburn, Garrish	Lauderdale	Wills 3	1821-1825	122
Cockburn, Headley	Lauderdale	Wills B	1859-1870	7
Cocke, James W.	Lauderdale	Wills A	1835-1858	49
Cocke, John	Madison	PR 11	1842-1849	8
Cocke, John R.	Greene	Wills A	1821-1827	61
Cocke, W. I.	Marengo	Wills A	1820-1864	323
Cockrell, James	Tuscaloosa	Wills 1	1821-1855	207
Cockrell, John R.	Greene	Wills D	1851-1888	36
Cocks, Sarah	Clarke	GE&W	1832-1839	48
Cody, Barnett	Henry	OCR K	1859-1860	448
Coffee, Elizabeth P.	Lauderdale	Wills B	1859-1870	12
Coffe, Joshua	Lauderdale	Wills B	1859-1870	168
Coffman, David	Limestone	Wills 4	1831-1837	475
Coil, Michael	Madison	Deeds A	1810-1816	231
Coker, Loving	Tuscaloosa	Wills 1	1821-1855	285
Coker, Mary	Lowndes	Wills B	1830-1859	261
Coker, Noah B.	Bibb	Deeds K	1869-1871	219
Coker, Sarah	Bibb	Loose	Dated 1846	
Coker, Thomas	Tallapoosa	Wills 1	1838-1866	39
Coker, William	Macon	Records 2	1838-1842	269
Colbert, Mary	Henry	OCR J	1857-1858	684
Colclough, Richard A.	Montgomery	Wills 4	1853-1859	512
Cole, Baylas	Jefferson	Wills A	1856-1880	78
Cole, James C.	Greene	Wills D	1851-1888	141
Cole, Jesse G.	Perry	Wills B	1858-1873	270
Cole, John	Mobile	Wills 2	1837-1857	139
Cole, Martin	Madison	Wills 1	1853-1875	512
Cole, William	Dallas	Wills A	1821-1849	105
Coleburn, John	Perry	Wills A	1821-1866	85
Coleman, Mrs. Caroline V.	Washington	Wills 1 ∅	1827-1888	246
Coleman, Mrs. Caroline V.	Washington	Wills B	1827-	144
Coleman, Charlas	Greene	Wills A	1821-1827	26
Coleman, Charles P.	Greene	Wills C	1840-1864	248
Coleman, Clarisa	Monroe	W&D E	1856-1861	405
Coleman, Daniel	Limestone	Wills 11	1865-1866	178
Coleman, Elizabeth	Montgomery	Wills 3	1840-1854	282

TESTATOR	COUNTY	WHERE FOUND		PAGE
Coleman, James B.	Dallas	Wills A	1821-1849	103
Coleman, Jesse	Marengo	Wills A	1820-1864	226
Coleman, Isaiah	Dallas	Wills A	1821-1849	333
Coleman, Martha	Lowndes	Wills B	1830-1859	185
Coleman, Mary C.	Butler	Wills 1	1853-1864	214
Coleman, Pleasant P.	Perry	Wills B	1858-1873	83
Coleman, Pleasant P.	Perry	Wills B	1858-1873	87
Coleman, Hadford	Greene	Wills C	1840-1864	110
Coleman, Ruffin	Limestone	Wills 9	1847-1850	1
Coleman, Samuel W.	Montgomery	Wills 2	1820-1845	213
Coleman, Spilsberry	Sumter	Wills 1	1828-1851	293
Coleman, Thomas K.	Perry	Wills B	1858-1873	230
Coleman, William	Dallas	Wills A	1821-1849	299
Coleman, William	Madison	Deeds D	1816-1818	79
Coleman, William A.	St. Clair	RE A	1858-1874	343
Coles, James Patton	Madison	Wills 1	1853-1875	212
Coley, Sanford	Mobile	Wills 3	1857-1870	13
Colgin, Sarah A. F.	Sumter	Wills 2	1851-1872	62
Colhin, William R.	Sumter	Wills 1	1828-1851	48
Colin, Faustin	Mobile	Wills 2	1837-1857	450
Colin, Polexene	Mobile	Wills 1	1813-1837	132
Collett ?, Louis	Mobile	Wills 2	1837-1857	52
Colley, John	Barbour	OCR 9	1858-1859	148
Colley, Rev. Thomas	Talladega	W&I B	1858-1864	504
Collier, B.	Lamar	Wills 1	1844-1910	9
Collier, Edward	Madison	PR 15	1850-1853	127
Collier, Henry W.	Tuscaloosa	Wills 3	1858-1865	1
Collier, John	Limestone	Wills 7	1844-1847	394
Collier, John	Marengo	Wills A	1820-1864	236
Collier, M. M.	Limestone	Wills 5	1836-1841	498
Collier, Mrs. Mary A.	Tuscaloosa	Wills 3	1858-1865	231
Collier, Sarah W.	Lamar	Wills 1	1844-1910	10
Collier, Thomas W.	Limestone	Wills 11	1865-1866	89
Collier, William E.	Limestone	Wills 4	1831-1837	291
Collier, Wyatt	Lauderdale	Wills A	1835-1858	269
Collins, Arthur	Dallas	Wills A	1821-1849	91
Collins, Honore	Mobile	Wills 1	1813-1837	76
Collins, James	Greene	Wills B	1817-1841	181
Collins, Jeremiah	St. Clair	RE A	1858-1874	336
Collins, John	Hale	Wills A	1867-1923	9
Collins, John	St. Clair	RE A	1858-1874	351
Collins, John	Tuscaloosa	Wills 1	1821-1855	324
Collins, Joseph (Negro)	Mobile	Wills 1	1813-1837	240
Collins, Joshua	Mobile	Wills 1	1813-1837	189
Collins, Martha	Lowndes	Wills B	1830-1859	162
Collins, Mary S.	St. Clair	RE A	1858-1874	349
Collins, N. F.	Lee	Wills A	1867-1898	39
Colquit, Walter T.	Russell	Wills 2	1850-1873	117
Coltart, Samuel	Madison	Wills 1	1853-1875	508
Colter, John	Lee	Wills A	1867-1898	53
Colvard, William	Macon	WAC&A 11	1862-1870	442

TESTATOR	COUNTY	WHERE FOUND		PAGE
Colvin, Alexander	Montgomery	Wills 2	1820-1845	136
Colvin, Daniel	Perry	Wills A	1821-1855	292
Colvin, James	Lowndes	Wills B	1830-1859	404
Colvin, Margaret	Lowndes	Wills B	1830-1859	271
Colvin, Savilla	Greene	Deeds V		482
Combash, Jane	Dallas	Wills B	1850-1871	301
Combs, William A.	Madison	PR 12	1845-1849	559
Comer, James	Russell	Wills 2	1850-1873	353
Commyns, Thomas	Baldwin	Wills A	1811-1881	180
Compton, Ann P.	Tuscaloosa	Wills 3	1858-1865	20
Compton, Mary E.	Marengo	Wills A	1820-1864	448
Comstock, Edwin P.	Tuscaloosa	Deeds U		164
Conally, Robert L.	Lowndes	Wills C	1861-1899	104
Conant, Jeremiah	Tallapoosa	Wills 1	1838-1866	93
Cone, Adam	Perry	Wills A	1821-1855	135
Cone, Dr. William N.	Montgomery	Wills 3	1840-1854	156
Coney, John C.	Lowndes	Wills C	1861-1899	48
Connally, Charles	Madison	Wills 1	1853-1875	196
Connally, John W.	Madison	OR 15	1850-1853	581
Connell, Simon	Mobile	Wills 2	1837-1857	462
Connelly, James Zechariah	Barbour	OCR 15	1865-1866	144
Conniff, Patrick	Montgomery	Wills 5	1863-1887	64
Connolly, Robert	Lowndes	Wills B	1830-1859	188
Connoway, William	Coosa	W&OCR 2	1843-1883	182
Conoway, John P.	Sumter	Wills 1	1828-1851	187
Constantine, George	Mobile	Wills 3	1857-1870	348
Constantine, Mary	Mobile	Wills 3	1857-1870	279
Conville, Allen	Bibb	Adr.R J	1865-1876	544
Conway, Charles	Baldwin	Wills A	1811-1881	37
Conway, Charles	Baldwin	Wills A	1811-1881	42
Conway, Charles	Mobile	Wills 1	1813-1837	1
Conway, Edward	Dallas	Wills A	1821-1849	59
Conway, Ruth	Baldwin	Wills A	1811-1881	93
Conyers, Martha E.	Montgomery	Wills 4	1853-1869	508
Coofer, Wiley	Lauderdale	Wills 4	1821-1825	112
Cook, Absolem Mastin	Wilcox	Wills 5	1855-1870	371
Cook, Anna	Lowndes	Wills C	1861-1899	49
Cook, Benjamin F.	Chambers	Wills 3	1856-1899	173
Cook, Christopher	Lauderdale	Wills B	1859-1870	110
Cook, Daniel	Wilcox	Wills 6	1862-1870	102
Cook, George M.	Lowndes	Wills C	1861-1899	11
Cook, James C.	Russell	Wills 1	1838-1849	125
Cook, James D.	Chambers	Wills 3	1856-1899	89
Cook, James Madison	Barbour	OCR 10	1859-1860	122
Cook, James Watkins	Lowndes	Wills C	1861-1899	95
Cook, John	Baldwin	Wills A	1811-1881	231
Cook, John Herbert	Wilcox	Wills 3	1826-1858	107
Cook, John P.	Lowndes	Wills C	1861-1899	41
Cook, John P.	Lowndes	Wills C	1861-1869	62
Cook, Joseph W.	Chambers	Wills 3	1856-1899	109
Cook, Mary	Dallas	Wills A	1821-1849	11

TESTATOR	COUNTY	WHERE FOUND		PAGE
Cook, Nancy	Lauderdale	Wills B	1859-1870	166
Cook, Nicholas	Baldwin	Wills A	1811-1881	60
Cook, Robert P.	Tuscaloosa	Wills 3	1858-1865	128
Cook, William D.	Montgomery	Wills 3	1840-1854	34
Cooke, Jesse J.	Wilcox	Wills 4	1847-1862	1
Cooper, Anthony	St. Clair	RE F	1862-1867	888
Cooper, Charles	Lawrence	I&W D	1835-1840	22
Cooper, Clara C.	Wilcox	Wills 5	1855-1870	442
Cooper, Cyntha	Macon	Records 7	1857-1859	147
Cooper, Dewitt	Tuscaloosa	Wills 3	1858-1865	96
Cooper, Isaac	Dallas	Wills A	1821-1849	272
Cooper, James	Madison	PR 7	1834-1837	51
Cooper, John E.	Butler	Wills 1	1853-1864	113
Cooper, Oliver A.	St. Clair	RE F	1862-1869	175
Cooper, Wade	Lawrence	I&W A	1850-1857	432
Cooper, Wiley	Lauderdale	Wills B	1859-1870	8
Copeland, David	Blount	PM B		442 ?
Copeland, James	Madison	Deeds A	1810-1816	25
Corbitt, William J.	Henry	OCR O	1864-1865	120
Cordier, Charles	Mobile	Wills 2	1837-1857	195
Corley, Adkin	Coosa	W&OCR 2	1843-1883	176
Cornelius, David	Lawrence	I&W D	1835-1840	179
Cornelius, Ellenor	Madison	Wills 1	1853-1875	297
Cornelius, Moses	Blount	PM B-1	1844-1851	149
Cornelius, Rowland	Madison	PR 2	1818-1823	364
Cornelius, Rowland	Madison	PR 11	1842-1849	233
Cornelius, William, Sr.	Blount	Records A	1837-1841	141
Corral, Andres	Mobile	Wills 2	1837-1857	145
Corri, Richard	Mobile	Wills 2	1837-1857	155
Cosby, William	Madison	PR 6	1832-1834	665
Cosley, John W.	Barbour	OCR 12	1861-1863	514
Cossman, Samuel H.	Sumter	Wills 1	1828-1851	61
Cost, John	Bibb	Loose	Dated 1847	
Costa, Peter	Mobile	Wills 2	1837-1857	325
Cottle, James	Chambers	Wills 3	1856-1899	129
Cotton, Cyrus	Russell	Wills 2	1850-1873	64
Cotton, George W.	Barbour	OCR 5	1852-1853	125
Cotton, George W.	Chambers	Wills 1-2	1833-1856	88
Cotton, Mary	Henry	OCR M	1861-1862	453
Cotton, Micajah	Talladega	Wills A	1833-1839	27
Cotton, Peggy	Talladega	Wills C	1845-1853	119
Cottrell, James L.	Autauga	Reports B	1829-1833	295
Coursen, Susan M.	Mobile	Wills 2	1837-1857	342
Coursey, Daniel	Madison	PR 10	1842-1842	16
Courts, James M.	Dallas	Wills B	1850-1871	415
Courtney, James	Mobile	Wills 3	1857-1870	59
Courtney, John	Montgomery	Wills 3	1840-1854	159
Cowan, Thomas	Washington	Wills 1 Ø	1827-1888	167
Cowan, Thomas	Washington	Wills B	1827-	105
Cowan, William L.	Barbour	OCR 9	1858-1859	900
Cowan, William R.	Barbour	OCR 12	1861-1863	778

TESTATOR	COUNTY	WHERE FOUND		PAGE
Cowart, James	Pike	Wills A	1845-1862	9
Cowart, William	Barbour	OCR 7	1854-1857	214
Cowden, Elijah	Blount	OCR		476
Cowen, James	Marshall	OCR 1	1836-1837	174
Cowen, Robert H.	Dallas	Wills B	1850-1871	87
Cowles, Thomas M.	Montgomery	Wills 4	1853-1869	126
Cowling, Slaughter	Lowndes	Wills B	1830-1859	63
Cowls, William	Dallas	Wills A	1821-1849	53
Cox, Benjamin	Tuscaloosa	Wills 1	1821-1855	6
Cox, Benjamin F.	Chambers	Wills 3	1856-1899	123
Cox, Daniel	Bibb	PM E	1852-1855	488
Cox, Eliza	Jackson	Wills L	1865-1866	2
Cox, Isham	Limestone	Wills 4	1831-1837	130
Cox, James	Clarke	PR L	1861-1864	112
Cox, James	Jackson	Records	1861-1881	614
Cox, John	Clarke	PR E	1840-1845	129
Cox, John W.	Marengo	Wills A	1820-1864	210
Cox, Margaret M.	Chambers	Wills 3	1856-1899	112
Cox, Mathew	Clarke	PR K	1858-1861	619
Cox, Matthew	Bibb	PM E	1852-1855	521
Cox, Nixon	Dallas	Wills B	1850-1871	372
Cox, Pleasant	Lowndes	Wills C	1861-1899	14
Cox, Robert L.	Marengo	Wills A	1820-1864	249
Cox, Runyon H.	Macon	Records 5	1853-1855	71
Cox, Samuel A.	Chambers	Wills 3	1856-1899	124
Cox, Sarah	Clarke	GE&W	1832-1839	48
Cox, Thomas	Clarke	PR G	1850-1854	71
Cox, William	Jackson	Wills	1865-1866	2
Cox, William H.	Clarke	PR L	1861-1864	138
Coyle, Eveline Belmont	Madison	Wills I	1853-1875	122
Cozby, James, Sr.	Jefferson	Wills I	1818-1840	151
Craddock, Pleasant	Tuscaloosa	Wills 3	1858-1865	24
Cragy, Sarah	Lowndes	Wills B	1830-1859	153
Craig, James	Butler	Wills 1	1853-1864	158
Craig, John	Dallas	Wills A	1821-1849	331
Craig, John	DeKalb	W&D	1837-1863	5
Craig, John	Lauderdale	Wills A	1835-1858	24
Craig, Nat H.	Dallas	Wills B	1850-1871	314
Craig, Robert	Dallas	Wills B	1850-1871	280 ?
Craig, Robert	Sumter	Wills 2	1851-1872	201
Craig, Sarah	Dallas	Wills B	1850-1871	227
Craig, Thomas	Dallas	Wills B	1850-1871	168
Craig, William	Perry	Wills A	1821-1855	261
Crail, Alex W.	Dallas	Wills B	1850-1871	362
Crain, Mary	Chambers	Wills 3	1856-1899	1
Cranford, John M.	Macon	WAC&A 11	1862-1870	318
Crapp, John C.	Barbour	OCR 2	1842-1847	201
Cravy, Hugh	Sumter	Wills 1	1828-1851	33
Crawford, Alexander	Barbour	OCR 4	1850-1852	682
Crawford, Alfred	Lowndes	Wills C	1861-1899	6
Crawford, Andrew J.	Chambers	Wills 3	1856-1899	116

TESTATOR	COUNTY	WHERE FOUND		PAGE
Crawford, Anna M.	Wilcox	Wills 3	1826-1858	384
Crawford, Enos	Wilcox	Wills 2	1832-1850	205
Crawford, James	Wilcox	Wills 5	1855-1870	140
Crawford, Mason	Mobile	Wills 2	1837-1857	213
Crawford, Richard	Lauderdale	Wills B	1859-1870	279
Crawford, Robert L.	Mobile	Wills 2	1837-1857	296
Crawford, Rosannah	Sumter	Wills 1	1828-1851	355
Crawford, William G.	Macon	WAC&A 11	1862-1870	457
Crawford, William H.	Wilcox	Wills 5	1855-1870	153
Crawley, Daniel	Jackson	Records	1861-1881	616
Crawley, John H.	Macon	Records 10	1863-1865	451
Crayton, Margaret	Lawrence	I&W D	1835-1850	415
Crayton, Mary	Chambers	Wills 1-2	1833-1856	379
Crayton, Nancy	Monroe	W&D E	1833-1870	130
Creamer, Mathew	Cleburne	Wills 1	1866-1884	14
Creigh, John G.	Wilcox	Wills 1	1821-1844	396
Creighton, John	Clarke	OCR	1825-1832	212
Crenshaw, Abner	Autauga	Wills 1	1862-1925	32
Crenshaw, Joseph	Perry	Wills A	1821-1855	113
Crews, John D.	Barbour	OCR 9	1858-1859	830
Crews, Thomas R.	Sumter	Wills 2	1851-1872	337
Cribbs, Jacob J.	Tuscaloosa	Wills 1	1821-1855	70
Criss, James	Madison	Deeds D	1816-1818	78
Criswell, Elijah	Sumter	Wills 1	1828-1855	370
Crittenden, Elizabeth G.	Lauderdale	Wills B	1859-1870	20
Crittenden, W. W.	Lauderdale	Wills B	1859-1870	299
Crittenden, William	Lauderdale	Wills 4	1821-1825	146
Critz, George F.	Limestone	Wills 11	1865-1866	91
Crocheron, John J.	Dallas	Wills B	1850-1871	307
Crocheron, Nicholas	Dallas	Wills A	1821-1849	61
Croft, W. F.	Greene	Wills C	1840-1864	212
Crommelin, Charles	Montgomery	Wills 4	1853-1869	146
Cronin, Joanna	Mobile	Wills 3	1857-1870	440
Croom, Evelina	Montgomery	Wills 5	1863-1887	54
Croom, I. H.	Greene	Wills C	1840-1864	152
Croom, Nichols P.	Sumter	Wills 2	1851-1872	339
Croom, Wiley	Greene	Wills C	1840-1864	194
Crosby, James J.	Lowndes	Wills B	1830-1859	107
Crosby, John J.	Lowndes	Wills C	1861-1899	28
Crosby, Wilbern	Monroe	W&D E	1833-1870	205
Crosby, William	Mobile	Wills 2	1837-1857	97
Crosby, William	Monroe	W&D C	1833-1870	7
Cross, Maclin	Jackson	PM	1856-1859	211
Cross, Richard	Lauderdale	Wills 3	1821-1825	162
Cross, William	Shelby	Wills D	1841-1846	517
Croswell, Robert	Greene	Wills C	1840-1864	229
Croswell, William	Pike	Wills B	1862-1879	142
Crothers, William	Mobile	Wills 2	1837-1857	405
Crotwell, George	Jefferson	PM	1831-1832	334
Crow, Jacob	Russell	Wills 2	1850-1873	133
Crow, Johnson	Morgan	Records 1	1821-1834	115

TESTATOR	COUNTY	WHERE FOUND		PAGE
Crowder, Thomas	Russell	Wills 1	1838-1849	107
Crowell, Cautey	Russell	Wills 2	1850-1873	209
Crowell, Henry	Russell	Wills 1	1838-1849	42
Crowell, John, Sr.	Russell	Wills 1	1838-1849	134
Crowson, Aaron	Sumter	Wills 1	1828-1851	19
Crozier, Arthur	Calhoun	Loose	Probated 1848	
Crozier, Elizabeth	Calhoun	Loose	Probated 1855	
Crozier, Lucinda S.	Calhoun	Loose	Probated 1851	
Crum, George Bowman	Wilcox	Wills 4	1847-1862	233
Crum, Mrs. Jerusha R.	Lowndes	Wills C	1861-1899	83
Crump, Sally	Tuscaloosa	Wills 3	1858-1865	10
Crumpton, W. P.	Dallas	Wills B	1850-1871	324
Crumpton, William Z.	Wilcox	Wills 5	1855-1870	249
Crunley, George	Lauderdale	Wills B	1859-1870	434
Cruse, Samuel	Madison	Wills 1	1853-1875	346
Crutcher, William	Madison	Wills 1	1853-1875	393
Cubley, John K.	Sumter	Wills 1	1828-1851	78
Culbert, Mathew	Marshall	PR 2	1857-1858	697
Culbert, Mathew	Marshall	FR 9	1867-1869	210
Culbreath, Newton T.	Chambers	Wills 3	1856-1899	165
Culbreth, Eunice	Russell	Wills 2	1850-1873	6
Cullen, Bridget	Mobile	Wills 2	1837-1857	250
Cullen, Maxmillain	Mobile	Wills 3	1857-1870	724
Cully, Edward	Marengo	Wills A	1820-1864	275
Culp, W. A.	Henry	OCR U	1869-1870	715
Culpeper, Martha	Henry	OCR L	1860-1861	223
Culpeper, Martha	Henry	OCR T	1868-1870	146
Culpepper, Mariner	Talladega	W&I D	1867-1880	251
Culver, Isaac	Henry	OCR K	1859-1860	444
Cummings, John, Jr.	Clarke	OCR	1825-1832	265
Cummings, Thomas	Tuscaloosa	Wills 3	1858-1865	149
Cunning, John	Pike	Wills A	1845-1862	215
Cunningham, Mrs. Agnes	Talladega	W&I B	1858-1864	621
Cunningham, Hugh M.	Talladega	Wills C	1845-1853	140
Cunningham, James	Madison	PR 4	1826-1829	406
Cunningham, John	Jackson	Wills	1866-1867	29
Cunningham, John	Perry	Wills A	1821-1855	287
Cunningham, John D.	Talladega	Wills B	1839-1845	86
Cunningham, John H.	Talladega	W&I A	1852-1857	373
Cunningham, Joseph	Shelby	Wills L	1838-1858	537
Cunningham, Joseph T.	Talladega	Wills C	1845-1853	270
Cunningham, Louisa	Montgomery	Wills 4	1853-1869	64
Cunningham, Robert C.	Mobile	Wills 3	1857-1870	292
Cunningham, Robert M.	Tuscaloosa	Wills 1	1821-1855	123
Cunningham, Samuel	Talladega	Wills C	1845-1853	345
Cunningham, William	Conecuh	OB A	1865-1870	137
Cunningham, William A.	Perry	Wills B	1858-1873	168
Curb, Thomas	Perry	Wills B	1858-1873	268
Cureton, William	Henry	Deeds A-B	1822-1840	61
Curless, Meredith	Coosa	W&OCR 2	1843-1883	165
Currence, John M.	Russell	Wills 1	1838-1849	102

TESTATOR	COUNTY	WHERE FOUND		PAGE
Curry, Angus	Barbour	OCR 2	1842-1847	79
Curry, Edwin	Perry	Wills A	1821-1855	145
Curry, John S.	Greene	Wills B	1817-1841	81
Curry, Louisa A.	Talladega	W&I B	1858-1864	234
Curry, William	Barbour	OCR 9	1858-1859	437
Curry, William	Talladega	W&I A	1852-1857	62
Curtin, Patrick	Mobile	Wills 3	1857-1870	521
Curtis, Daniel	Marengo	Wills A	1820-1864	530
Curtis, Elizabeth	Marengo	Wills A	1820-1864	310
Curtis, Hardey	Baldwin	Wills A	1811-1881	83
Curtis, Nathaniel	Marengo	Wills A	1820-1864	281
Curtis, Samuel	Marengo	Wills A	1820-1864	272
Curtis, William L.	Marengo	Wills A	1820-1864	256
Cusac, Corrine D.	Sumter	Wills 2	1851-1872	422
Cusack, Thomas	Sumter	Wills 2	1851-1872	407
Cutts, Sharade	Bibb	Loose	1859	
Dabney, Thomas	Clarke	PR K	1858-1861	142
Dacy, John	Clarke	PR N	1866-1870	267
Dade, A. P.	Mobile	Wills 1	1813-1837	113
Dade, Harriet	Mobile	Wills 2	1837-1857	433
Dade, Robert T.	Mobile	Wills 3	1857-1870	287
Dade, Sarah H.	Mobile	Wills 2	1837-1857	149
Dade, Susan T.	Mobile	Wills 2	1837-1857	5
Dade, Susan T.	Mobile	Wills 1	1813-1837	280
Daffin, John	Clarke	PR K	1858-1861	633
Dailey, Owen D.	Monroe	W&D B	1841-1845	58
Daily, Abbigail	Wilcox	Wills 4	1847-1862	121
Daily, David	Wilcox	Wills 4	1847-1862	64
Daily, Jacob	Monroe	W&D E	1856-1861	326
Daily, William	Monroe	W&D E	1856-1861	10
Dalrymple, Thomas	Lauderdale	Wills A	1835-1858	298
Dancy, James	Lauderdale	Wills 3	1821-1825	9
Dandridge, Robert H.	Lawrence	I&W D	1835-1840	420
Danelly, Sarah	Macon	Records 10	1863-1865	560
Daniel, Ellen	Lowndes	Wills B	1830-1859	112
Daniel, Ephraim	Sumter	Wills 2	1851-1872	16
Daniel, James	Greene	Wills A	1821-1827	10
Daniel, John	Chambers	Wills 3	1856-1899	207
Daniel, John T.	Wilcox	Wills 3	1826-1858	263
Daniel, John William	Barbour	OCR 2	1842-1847	151
Daniel, Robert L.	Macon	Records 2	1838-1842	341
Daniel, Thomas J.	Chambers	Wills 3	1856-1899	111
Daniel, William	Lowndes	Wills B	1830-1859	58
Daniel, Willie	Madison	Deeds A	1810-1816	156
Danner, Thomas G.	Sumter	Wills 2	1851-1872	264
Dansby, Elenor	Sumter	Wills 1	1828-1851	197
Dansby, John C.	Marengo	Wills A	1820-1864	537
Danzy, John	Henry	OCR H	1855-1857	338

TESTATOR	COUNTY	WHERE FOUND		PAGE
Danzy, Mahala Jane	Clarke	PR N	1866-1870	274
Darby, James	Pike	Wills A	1845-1862	55
Darden, Abner	Talladega	W&I D	1867-1880	536
Darden, George	Tuscaloosa	Wills 1	1821-1855	198
Darden, James	Greene	Wills B	1817-1841	289
Darden, John	Tallapoosa	Wills 1	1838-1866	58
Darling, Susan	Mobile	Wills 3	1857-1870	434
Darmond, Richard	Morgan	OCR 7	1837-1843	25
Darrington, Robert	Clarke	GE&W	1832-1839	200
Darrow, Mary	Etowah	Wills A	1866-1870	6
Darwin, George	Madison	Wills 1	1853-1875	316
Darwin, William	Morgan	OCR 7	1837-1843	101
Daudell, James, Sr.	Chambers	Wills 1-2	1833-1856	471
D'Avadie, Martha	Mobile	Wills 2	1837-1857	281
Davenport, Gorham	Mobile	Wills 3	1857-1870	524
Davenport, James M.	Marengo	Wills A	1820-1864	234
Davenport, Nelson	Tuscaloosa	Wills 4	1868-1897	215
Daves, Andrew C.	Marshall	FR 9	1867-1869	183
Davidson, Elihu L.	Lowndes	Wills C	1861-1899	8
Davidson, John H.	Marengo	Wills A	1820-1864	535
Davidson, Samuel C.	Jackson	Wills 1	1865-1866	6
Davidson, Sarah	Marengo	Wills A	1820-1864	269
Davidson, William	Mobile	Wills 2	1837-1857	256
Davie, Robert	Madison	PR 12	1845-1849	595
Davis, Benjamin	Lauderdale	Wills 3	1821-1825	38
Davis, Benjamin	Lauderdale	Wills 4	1821-1825	134
Davis, Christopher H.	Chambers	Wills 3	1856-1899	24
Davis, D. R.	Calhoun	Loose	Probated 1858	
Davis, Daniel	Jefferson	Wills A	1856-1880	253
Davis, Eli W.	Lowndes	Wills C	1861-1899	158
Davis, Frederick	Perry	Wills A	1821-1855	69A
Davis, George	Mobile	Wills 2	1837-1857	293
Davis, George Franklin	Coosa	Wills & OCR 2	1843-1883	101
Davis, Gilcrease	Lauderdale	Wills 4	1821-1825	149
Davis, Helen T.	Mobile	Wills 2	1837-1857	441
Davis, Henry	Jackson	Records	1861-1881	585
Davis, Henry G.	Clarke	PR E	1840-1845	409
Davis, Hugh	Perry	Wills B	1858-1873	306
Davis, Ishmael	Montgomery	Wills 3	1840-1854	107
Davis, Israel	Wilcox	Wills 1	1821-1844	374
Davis, Jessee C.	Autauga	Reports C	1834-1838	388
Davis, John	Dallas	Wills A	1821-1849	180
Davis, John	Madison	PR 9	1839-1841	244
Davis, John	Tallapoosa	Wills 1	1838-1866	45
Davis, John L.	Tuscaloosa	Wills 3	1858-1865	33
Davis, John T.	Chambers	Wills 1-2	1833-1856	226
Davis, Josiah	Pike	Wills B	1862-1879	146
Davis, Leonardus	Dallas	Wills A	1821-1849	48
Davis, Leonidas S.	Clarke	PR M	1864-1866	238
Davis, Lewis C.	Autauga	Reports C	1834-1838	91
Davis, Madison C.	Macon	Records 3	1845-1850	311

TESTATOR	COUNTY	WHERE FOUND		PAGE
Davis, Nancy P.	Morgan	FR 23	1866-1867	306
Davis, Nephlet	Clarke	GE&W	1832-1839	472
Davis, Person	Talladega	W&I A	1852-1857	216
Davis, Polly	Lauderdale	Wills B	1859-1870	125
Davis, Presley	Pike	Wills B	1862-1879	25
Davis, Robert W.	Madison	PR 8	1831-1839	193
Davis, Samuel	Madison	PR 10	1842-1842	24
Davis, Samuel	Sumter	Wills 2	1851-1872	35
Davis, Sarah	Autauga	Reports C	1834-1838	272
Davis, Sugar R.	Clarke	PR J	1856-1858	258
Davis, William	Baldwin	Wills A	1811-1881	57
Davis, William	Dallas	Wills A	1821-1849	1
Davis, William	Greene	Wills D	1851-1888	10
Davis, William	Lowndes	Wills C	1861-1899	108
Davis, Wilson A.	Calhoun	Loose	Dated 1844	
Davison, John L.	Monroe	W&D F	1861-1867	160
Davitt, William	Greene	Wills B	1817-1841	255
Dawes, James	Mobile	Wills 2	1837-1857	99
Dawkins, Reuben	Russell	Wills 2	1850-1873	347
Dawson, Edward	Mobile	Wills 2	1837-1857	132
Dawson, Georgia A.	Russell	Wills 2	1850-1873	239
Dawson, Hugh B.	Barbour	OCR 12	1861-1863	533
Dawson, Lemuel G.	Chambers	Wills 1-2	1833-1856	299
Day, Ameriah	Barbour	OCR 12	1861-1863	724
Day, David	Montgomery	Wills 4	1853-1869	524
Day, Edward	Dallas	Wills A	1821-1849	198
Day, Elias H.	Chambers	Wills 1-2	1833-1856	302
Day, John	St. Clair	Deeds B	1831-1849	234
Day, Joseph	Chambers	Wills 3	1856-1899	127
Day, Martin H.	Pike	Wills A	1845-1862	208
Day, Mary Ann	Chambers	Wills 3	1856-1899	197
Day, William, Sr.	Dallas	Wills A	1821-1849	125
Dean, Alexander	Sumter	Wills 2	1851-1872	298
Dean, Charles P.	Talladega	Wills C	1845-1853	416
Dean, Elizabeth	Montgomery	Wllls 3	1840-1854	241
Dean, James	Mobile	Wills 1	1813-1837	103
Dean, James M.	Montgomery	Wills 4	1853-1869	507
Dean, John	Lauderdale	Wills B	1850-1870	431
Dean, Josiah	Madison	Deeds B	1810-1816	119
Dean, Moses	St. Clair	RE C	1852-1859	321
Dean, Sarah	Chambers	Wills 3	1856-1899	162
Dean, Thomas M.	Butler	Wills 2	1864-1875	33
Dean, William	Lauderdale	Wills B	1850-1870	49
Deanart, Michael	Mobile	Wills 2	1837-1850	356
Dearing, A. T.	Tuscaloosa	Wills 4	1868-1897	10
Dearing, James H.	Tuscaloosa	Wills 3	1856-1865	106
Dearington, Robert	Clarke	GE&W	1832-1839	200
Dearman, Beersheba	Washington	Wills 1 ∅	1827-1888	227
Dearman, Beersheba	Washington	Wills B	1827-	135
Dearman, Gillum	St. Clair	Deeds B	1831-1849	810
Deas, James S.	Mobile	Wills 3	1857-1870	420

TESTATOR	COUNTY	WHERE FOUND		PAGE
Deavenport, Martin S.	Chambers	Wills 1-2	1833-1856	409
Deavor, Sheba	Blount	PM B	1852-1856	3
DeBardelaben, F. F.	Lowndes	Wills C	1861-1899	102
DeBardelaben, Henry	Autauga	Reports G	1850-1853	503
DeBardelaben, William A.	Russell	Wills 1	1838-1849	26
DeBow, Solomon T.	Madison	Wills 1	1853-1875	289
DeCastro, Alex	Marengo	Wills A	1820-1864	243
DeCourcey, Elizabeth	Mobile	Wills 2	1837-1857	290
Dedman, Henry H.	Madison	PR 3	1823-1826	301
Dedman, Philip	Madison	Wills 1	1853-1875	12
Deerman, Richard	St. Clair	Deeds C	1846-1855	192
Deerman, Solomon	St. Clair	Deeds A½	1822-1857	30
Dees, A.	Monroe	W&D 8	1870-1871	66
Dees, James	Monroe	W&D 8	1870-1871	370
Degrushe, William S.	Mobile	Wills 3	1857-1870	284
DeJarnette, Eliza W.	Jefferson	Wills A	1856-1880	233
DeJarnett, John P.	Autauga	Reports G	1850-1853	600
DeJarnett, Joseph P.	Autauga	Reports H	1853-1857	324
Dejernatte, Elias	Jefferson	OCR	1824-1831	7
Dejornatte, Elias	Jefferson	Wills I	1818-1840	28
Delage, Charles L.	Mobile	Wills 2	1837-1857	192
DeLaunay, Francis L.	Barbour	OCR 12	1861-1863	355
Delbecco, John B.	Mobile	Wills 2	1837-1857	323
Delbridge, James	Macon	WAC&A 11	1862-1870	183
Dellehay, Thomas	Macon	Records 5	1853-1855	1
Dellette, James	Monroe	W&D C	1845-1850	449
Deloach, Augustus W.	Coosa	W&OCR 2	1843-1883	143
Deloach, John	Jefferson	Deeds 1	1818-1828	27
Dement, Charles	Madison	PR 2	1818-1823	143
Dement, John	Madison	PR 14	1846-1850	181
Demony, Augustine	Mobile	Wills 3	1857-1870	527
Dennard, John E.	Barbour	OCR 16	1866-1868	76
Dennis, Charles	Pike	Wills B	1862-1879	20
Dennis, Coleman C.	Talladega	Wills B	1839-1845	3
Dennis, Daniel	Pike	Wills A	1845-1862	245
Dennis, Samuel	Dallas	Wills B	1850-1871	134
Denson, Mrs. Elizabeth	Talladega	W&I C	1862-1866	175
Denson, Jethro	Barbour	OCR 4	1850-1852	115
Denson, Nancy	Dallas	Wills B	1850-1871	19
Denton, R. Watson	Russell	Wills 2	1850-1873	239
Denton, Thomas	Montgomery	Wills 2	1820-1845	2
Deplous, Pierce	Conecuh	OB A	1865-1870	141
Depriest, Martin	Coosa	W&OCR 2	1843-1883	145
DeRamus, George	Autauga	Reports K	1859-1861	709
Deramus, Jacob A.	Autauga	Wills 1	1862-1925	59
Derrick, Henry	Jackson	Records	1861-1881	77
Derrick, John	Madison	Wills 1	1853-1875	308
Derrick, William W.	Marshall	FR 5	1855-1859	114
Desha, Robert, Sr.	Mobile	Wills 2	1837-1857	181
Deshler, David	Colbert	Wills A	1861-1903	40
Desloges, Auguste	Mobile	Wills 1	1813-1837	128

TESTATOR	COUNTY	WHERE FOUND		PAGE
Desloges, Lucy P.	Mobile	Wills 3	1857-1870	247
DeVan, Margaret Moore	Wilcox	Wills 5	1855-1870	413
DeVaubercy, Lewis F.A.E.L.	Mobile	Wills 1	1813-1837	262
DeVaux, Marie Louise	Mobile	Wills 3	1857-1870	251
DeVendel, Emilius	Mobile	Wills 3	1857-1870	1
Develin, Joseph	Mobile	Wills 3	1857-1870	415
Devenport, Elizabeth	Pike	Wills A	1845-1862	206
Devenport, William M.	Autauga	Reports C	1834-1838	340
Devine, James	Mobile	Wills 3	1857-1870	220
Devlin, Patrick	Montgomery	Wills 4	1853-1869	542
Devore, Elias	Macon	Records 5	1853-1855	352
Devotie, N. L.	Dallas	Wills B	1850-1871	229
Dewan?, Edmund	Mobile	Wills 3	1857-1870	55
Dewberry, Jesse	Lauderdale	Wills B	1859-1870	2
Dewberry, Jesse	Lauderdale	Wills B	1859-1870	47
Dewey, Joseph M.	Dallas	Wills B	1850-1871	126
Dewitt, John	Barbour	OCR 2	1842-1847	214
Dexter, Andrew A.	Montgomery	Wills 3	1840-1854	296
Dexter, William J.	Wilcox	Wills 4	1847-1862	151
Deyampert, Lucius Q. C.	Perry	Wills B	1858-1873	296
Dial, James	Sumter	Wills 2	1851-1872	401
Diamond, William J.	Montgomery	Wills 5	1863-1887	11
Dickens, Hancil	Butler	Wills 2	1864-1875	87
Dickens, Robert	Mobile	Wills 3	1857-1870	358
Dickerson, Archeleus	Butler	Wills 2	1864-1875	146
Dickerson, John Barney	Wilcox	Wills 1	1821-1844	341
Dickerson, L. H.	Montgomery	Wills 4	1853-1869	428
Dickey, George	Madison	W&I	1810-1820	139
Dickinson, John	Marshall	PR 2	1857-1888	691
Dickinson, John	Marshall	FR 6	1859-1867	513
Dickinson, Shadrach	Talladega	W&I C	1862-1866	360
Dickson, Eveline	Madison	Wills 1	1853-1875	431
Dickson, Ezekiel	Lauderdale	Wills B	1859-1870	350
Dickson, John S.	Madison	Wills 1	1853-1875	351
Dickson, Joseph	Barbour	OCR 4	1850-1852	691
Dickson, Joseph	Russell	Wills 1	1838-1849	146
Dickson, Robert	Clarke	GE&W	1832-1839	16
Dickson, Samuel B.	Marengo	Wills A	1820-1864	246
Dickson, William	Clarke	GE&W	1832-1839	227
Dickson, William	Madison	PR 14	1846-1850	459
Dill, John F.	St. Clair	RE B	1834-1857	6
Dillahunty, Sally N.	Lauderdale	Wills A	1835-1858	106
Dillard, Frances W.	Macon	Records 10	1863-1865	731
Dillard, Francis	Lowndes	Wills B	1830-1859	396
Dillard, John J?	Sumter	Will 1	1828-1851	372
Dillard, Joshua	Madison	Wills 1	1853-1875	215
Dilworth, George	Madison	Wills 1	1853-1875	204
Dines, John	Madison	PR 9	1839-1841	244
Dinkins, Edward	Pike	Wills B	1862-1879	152
Dinnard, Abner	Monroe	W&D A	1833-1841	213
Dismucks, J. Finney	Butler	Wills 1	1853-1864	222

TESTATOR	COUNTY	WHERE FOUND		PAGE
Dixon, Elizabeth	Dallas	Wills A	1821-1849	10
Dixon, Jerusha A.	Marengo	Wills A	1820-1864	458
Dixon, John	Clarke	OCR B	1818-1824	209
Dixon, John	Conecuh	OB A	1865-1870	260
Dixon, Joseph (Joel)	Marengo	Wills A	1820-1864	539
Dixon, Samuel R.	Tuscaloosa	Wills 3	1858-1865	177
Dixon, Thomas	Chambers	Wills 1-2	1833-1856	110
Dixon, Thomas	Mobile	Wills 2	1837-1857	206
Doanart, Michael	Mobile	Wills 2	1837-1857	356
Dobbin, Alexander	Greene	Wills B	1817-1841	282
Dobbs, Jesse, Sr.	Tallapoosa	Wills 1	1838-1866	46
Dobbs, Kiziah	Tallapoosa	Wills 1	1838-1866	136
Dobbuis, Oza R.	Perry	Wills B	1858-1873	237
Doddridge, Eli	Clarke	PR E	1840-1846	268
Doddridge, Noah, Sr.	Clarke	GE&W	1832-1839	401
Dodson, Joel	Talladega	Wills C	1845-1853	85
Dodson, Mary	Madison	PR 12	1845-1849	1
Dodson, Reuben	Tuscaloosa	Wills 3	1858-1865	86
Dolive, Genevieve	Mobile	Wills 1	1813-1837	139
Dorrance, Mary A.	Mobile	Wills 3	1857-1870	477
Donaghey, William	Dallas	Wills B	1850-1871	155
Donald, Thomas	Sumter	Wills 1	1828-1851	175
Donald, Thomas J.	Sumter	Wills 2	1851-1872	358
Donald, William S.	Sumter	Wills 2	1851-1872	81
Donaldson, Crawford H.	Tuscaloosa	Wills 1	1821-1855	219
Donaldson, Peter	Tuscaloosa	Wills 1	1821-1855	185
Donaldson, William	Washington	Wills 1 ∅	1827-1888	225
Donaldson, William	Washington	Wills B	1827-	134
Donaldson, William H.	Talladega	Wills A	1833-1839	127
Donaldson, William M.	Limestone	Wills 6	1841-1846	224
Donalson, Thomas	Morgan	OCR 27	1868-1869	188
Donelson, Edward B.	Lauderdale	Wills A	1835-1858	222
Donelson, Eliza Eleanor	Lauderdale	Wills A	1835-1858	190
Donelson, Mary J.	Lauderdale	Wills A	1835-1858	118
Donoho, Cornelius K.	Tuscaloosa	Wills 3	1858-1865	95
Donohoo, Henry	Lauderdale	Wills A	1835-1858	237
Donohoo, John	Lauderdale	Wills A	1835-1858	148
Donovan, James	Perry	Wills B	1858-1873	51
Dorman, Azoline	Mobile	Wills 2	1837-1857	193
Dorn, Abner	Pike	Wills A	1845-1862	112
Dorsett, John	Chambers	Wills 1-2	1833-1856	264
Dorsey, Thomas	Montgomery	Wills 4	1853-1869	234
Dortch, Isaac F.	Wilcox	Wills 5	1855-1870	315
Dortch, Isaac F.	Wilcox	Wills 5	1855-1870	366
Dortch, Mary Ann	Madison	Wills 1	1853-1875	83
Dortch, Robert	Madison	PR 7	1834-1837	195
Doss, George W.	Marengo	Wills A	1820-1864	519
Doss, Jeremiah	Coosa	W&PM A	1834-1842	247
Doss, Richard W.	Marshall	FR 8	1856-1867	41
Doss, Samuel T.	Autauga	Reports G	1850-1853	474
Doss, Stephen H.	Marengo	Wills A	1820-1864	277

TESTATOR	COUNTY	WHERE FOUND		PAGE
Doss, T. A. K.	Dallas	Wills B	1850-1871	286
Doss, William W.	Marengo	Wills A	1820-1864	302
Dossey, Alonzo R. C.	Mobile	Wills 2	1837-1857	339
Doswell, Thomas	Henry	OCR M	1861-1862	357
Doughan, Sharp	Blount	PM B	1852-1856	190
Douglas, Leonora D.	Madison	Wills 1	1853-1875	106
Douglas, Mary Jane	Madison	Wills 1	1853-1875	281
Douglas, Roxy L.	Russell	Wills 2	1850-1873	381
Douglass, Edward	Madison	PR 14	1846-1850	377
Doughty, Joseph	Tuscaloosa	Wills 1	1821-1855	242
Doughty, M. F.	Tuscaloosa	Wills 4	1868-1897	38
Douthit, James	Colbert	Wills A	1861-1903	10
Dox, Matilda W.	Madison	Wills 1	1853-1875	499
Doxey, Jeremiah	Jefferson	Wills 1	1818-1840	58
Doxey, Jeremiah, Jr.	Jefferson	Deeds 1	1818-1828	92
Dozier, James	Perry	Wills A	1821-1855	121
Dozier, Richard	Henry	OCR L	1860-1861	190
Dozier, Richard	Perry	Wills A	1821-1855	156
Drake, Benjamin F.	Jefferson	OCR	1824	10
Drake, James	Madison	PR 10	1842-1842	267
Drake, John	Madison	PR 9	1839-1841	1
Drake, William	Sumter	Wills 2	1851-1872	214
Drakeford, Mary	Macon	Records 8	1859-1860	509
Draper, David	Madison	PR 4	1826-1829	132
Draper, David	Madison	PR 4	1826-1829	182
Draper, Joshua	Calhoun	Loose	Probated 1857	
Draughan, Miller C.	Monroe	W&D C	1845-1850	71
Drennon, Amelia	Talladega	Wills C	1845-1853	79
Drew, Timothy	Mobile	Wills 2	1837-1857	383
Drewry, James A.	Barbour	OCR 14	1863-1865	410
Drinkard, John M.	Clarke	PR L	1861-1864	122
Drinkard, Smith	Chambers	Wills 3	1856-1899	164
Drinkard, William R.	Marengo	Wills A	1820-1864	397
Drish, John R.	Tuscaloosa	Wills 3	1858-1865	204
Driskill, Ambrose F.	Madison	Wills 1	1853-1875	550
Driskill, John	Madison	Wills 1	1853-1875	32
Driver, Eli M.	Calhoun	Loose	Probated 1851	
Driver, John C.	Perry	Wills B	1858-1873	195
Driver, Julia S.	Madison	Wills 1	1853-1875	3
Duane, Edmund	Mobile	Wills 3	1857-1870	55
Dubose, David	Shelby	Wills B	1818-1840	162
Dubose, Isaac	Dallas	Wills A	1821-1849	64
Dubose, Jeremiah	Pike	Wills A	1845-1862	75
Dubose, Pete	Dallas	Wills A	1821-1849	191
Dubose, William J.	Monroe	W&D C	1845-1850	106
Dubroca, Benjamin	Mobile	Wills 1	1813-1837	42
Dubroca, Hiliare	Mobile	Wills 1	1813-1837	115
Dubroca, Jane	Mobile	Wills 2	1837-1857	60
Dubroca, Maximillian	Mobile	Wills 1	1813-1837	131
Dubroca, Sebastian	Mobile	Wills 1	1813-1837	151
Du Brutz, Deborah	Marengo	Wills A	1820-1864	230

TESTATOR	COUNTY	WHERE FOUND		PAGE
Duckell, John	Lauderdale	Wills A	1835-1858	280
Duckette, Mary	Lauderdale	Wills A	1835-1858	213
Duckworth, Randel	Dallas	Wills B	1850-1871	28
Ducoutumane, Clement	Mobile	Wills 1	1813-1837	275
Ducouturnani, Clement	Mobile	Wills 2	1837-1857	1
Dudley, Edward, Jr.	Mobile	Wills 1	1813-1837	243
Dudley, John	Russell	Wills 2	1850-1873	348
Dudley, Joseph	Russell	Wills 2	1850-1873	408
Dudley, H. L.	Monroe	W&D F	1861-1867	113
Dudley, Mary R.	Lowndes	Wills C	1861-1899	37
Dudley, Thomas H.	Dallas	Wills B	1850-1871	333
Dudley, W. A.	Monroe	W&D F	1861-1867	316
Duerson, James	Perry	Wills B	1858-1873	245
Duffee, William	Tallapoosa	Wills 2	1864-1907	49
Duffey, John	Tuscaloosa	Deeds 4	Dated 1855	44
Dugger, Sampson	Macon	Records 7	1857-1859	765
Dugger, Eldred	Greene	Wills B	1817-1841	232
Duke, R. John	Greene	Wills A	1821-1827	38
Dulaney, Clement B.	Wilcox	Wills 4	1847-1862	236
Dulany, Benjamin	Wilcox	Wills 3	1826-1858	110
Dulany, Elisha	Calhoun	Loose	Probated 1857	
Dumas, Amos	Monroe	W&D B	1833-1870	426
Dumas, Azariah	Wilcox	Wills 3	1826-1858	305
Dumas, James	Wilcox	Wills 3	1826-1858	357
Dumas, Mary A.	Wilcox	Wills 2	1832-1850	248
Dumas, Obadiah	Wilcox	Wills 1	1821-1844	253
Dumee, Adrien S.	Mobile	Wills 3	1857-1870	214
Dunaway, Amos	Dallas	Wills B	1850-1871	84
Dunaway, David	Tallapoosa	Wills 2	1864-1907	63
Dunbar, Young	Washington	Wills 1 Ø	1827-1888	120
Dunbar, Young	Washington	Wills B	1827-	77
Duncan, Annie	Lauderdale	Wills B	1859-1870	146
Duncan, Benjamin	Clarke	PR N	1866-1870	258
Duncan, James	Russell	Wills 2	1850-1873	38
Duncan, John	Lauderdale	Wills A	1835-1858	288
Duncan, John J.	Lauderdale	Wills B	1859-1870	10
Duncan, Susanna	Chambers	Wills 3	1856-1899	206
Dunham, W. P.	Dallas	Wills A	1821-1849	337
Dunington, Elizabeth	Shelby	Wills E	1845-1850	293
Dunkin, David	Madison	PR 16	1831-1861	176
Dunkin, David	Perry	Wills B	1858-1873	172
Dunklin, Ann H.	Lowndes	Wills C	1861-1899	148
Dunklin, William	Dallas	Wills A	1821-1849	41
Dunklin, William A.	Dallas	Wills B	1850-1871	279
Dunlap, David	Chambers	Wills 1-2	1833-1856	474
Dunlap, James	Greene	Wills B	1817-1841	269
Dunlap, Jane	Tuscaloosa	Wills 1	1821-1855	258
Dunlap, Mary	Montgomery	Wills 3	1840-1854	68
Dunlap, Robert	Tuscaloosa	Wills 3	1858-1865	126
Dunlap, William, Jr.	Russell	Wills 2	1850-1873	73
Dunlap, William	Tuscaloosa	Wills 1	1821-1855	167

TESTATOR	COUNTY	WHERE FOUND		PAGE
Dunn, Cornelius	Baldwin	Wills A	1811-1881	1
Dunn, David A.	Pike	Wills A	1845-1862	62
Dunn, Elizabeth	Jefferson	Wills A	1856-1880	82
Dunn, Ellis	Barbour	OCR 9	1858-1859	427
Dunn, George	Wilcox	Wills 3	1826-1858	416
Dunn, John	Lauderdale	Wills A	1835-1858	68
Dunn, Nancy C.	Tuscaloosa	Will 1	1821-1855	76
Dunn, Thomas W.	Lee	Wills A	1867-1898	8
Dunn, William B.	Madison	Wills 1	1853-1875	114
Dunnahaw, John	Lawrence	I&W D	1835-1840	474
Dunnam, Green L.	Wilcox	Wills 4	1847-1862	217
Dunnan, Robert	Baldwin	Wills A	1811-1881	11
Dunsmore, Adam	Madison	Deeds A	1810-1816	163
Dunson, George W.	Chambers	Wills 3	1856-1899	191
Dunwoody, James	Mobile	Wills 1	1813-1837	115
Dupree, Mildred Arthur	Madison	PR 15	1850-1853	539
Dupree, Sarah	Monroe	W&D B	1841-1845	375
Dupree, William E.	Lauderdale	Wills A	1835-1858	2
Durand, Alexis D.	Mobile	Wills 2	1837-1857	84
Durand, Martin	Mobile	Wills 2	1837-1857	108
Durden, (Mrs.) Gilly	Autauga	Reports K	1859-1861	375
Duret, Genvieve	Mobile	Wills 1	1813-1837	225
Durham, Harris J.	Lowndes	Wills B	1830-1859	294
Duseh, Isadore	Mobile	Wills 3	1857-1870	604
Dutton, William	Mobile	Wills 2	1837-1857	269
Duval, Elisha	Clarke	PR H	1854-1856	470
Dyche, Minerva I?	Marengo	Wills A	1820-1864	296
Dye, James	Talladega	W&I D	1867-1880	153
Dyer, Eliza Ann	Madison	Wills 1	1853-1875	474
Dyer, Jane Ann	Montgomery	Wills 3	1840-1854	245
Dykes, Noah	Dallas	Wills A	1821-1849	87
Dyson, Charles	Lauderdale	Wills B	1850-1870	295
Eades, John	Wilcox	Wills 1	1821-1844	286
Eady, Benjamin	Russell	Wills 2	1850-1873	248
Earl, James W.	Washington	Wills 1 ∅	1827-1888	126
Earl, James W.	Washington	Wills B	1827-	80
Earle, Elizabeth	Baldwin	Wills A	1811-1881	89
Earle, James	Baldwin	Wills A	1811-1881	62
Earle, James Wood	Mobile	Wills 2	1837-1857	142
Earle, Richard G.	Calhoun	PR A-2	1856-1866	93
Earle, Samuel S.	Jefferson	Wills A	1856-1880	335
Earle, Thomas W.	Jefferson	Wills A	1856-1880	210
Earley, William	Jefferson	PM	1831-1832	316
Early, Reuben	St. Clair	RE F	1862-1868	325
Early, William	Jefferson	OCR	1831-1832	316
Earp, William	Sumter	Wills 1	1828-1851	222
Easley, Daniel W.	Greene	Wills B	1817-1841	62
Easley, Edward	Perry	Wills A	1821-1855	165

TESTATOR	COUNTY	WHERE FOUND		PAGE
Easley, Hugh	Madison	Wills 1	1853-1875	515
Easley, John W.	Calhoun	PR A-2	1856-1866	344
Easley, John W.	Calhoun	Loose	Probated 1865	
Easley, Roderick	Marengo	Wills A	1820-1864	188
Easley, Warham	Sumter	Wills 1	1828-1851	54
Easley, William	Talladega	W&I A	1852-1857	25
Eason, Edmond W.	Madison	Wills 1	1810-1820	545
Eason, Ichiel	Sumter	Wills 2	1851-1872	47
Eason, John T.	Sumter	Wills 2	1851-1872	299
Eason, Obed	Tallapoosa	Wills 1	1838-1866	224
Eason, William	Madison	PR 7	1834-1837	530
East, William	Madison	PR 13	1838-1848	358
Easterling, Bennett	Butler	Wills 2	1864-1875	42
Eastland, William	Madison	Wills 1	1853-1875	347
Eberhart, Francis P.	Barbour	OCR 14	1863-1865	41
Eberhart, James	Chambers	Wills 1-2	1833-1856	312
Echols, John	Madison	PR 3	1823-1826	355
Echols, Josephine	Russell	Wills 2	1850-1873	383
Echols, Margaret	Dallas	Wills B	1850-1871	131
Echols, Obadiah	Macon	OCM 2	1835-1842	180
Echols, Rowena M.	Russell	Wills 2	1850-1873	423
Eckelberger, Samuel	Limestone	Wills 11	1865-1866	5
Eddins, Benjamin	Madison	Wills 1	1853-1875	106
Eddins, John S.	Pike	Wills B	1862-1879	113
Eddins, Simeon J.	Tuscaloosa	Wills 3	1858-1865	70
Edens, James	Morgan	OCR 6	1831-1837	531
Edmondson, Levi	Limestone	Wills 4	1831-1837	124
Edmondson, Martha A.	Dallas	Wills B	1850-1871	336
Edmondson, William	Jefferson	Wills 1	1818-1840	67
Edmondson, William	Jefferson	Wills 1	1818-1840	68
Edmondson, William	Jefferson	Deeds 1	1818-1828	71
Edmonson, Thomas	Sumter	Wills 1	1828-1851	199
Edmunds, Henry	Lauderdale	Wills B	1850-1870	342
Edmunds, Samuel	Baldwin	Wills A	1811-1881	108
Edwards, Achilles	Greene	Wills B	1817-1841	216
Edwards, Anna	Sumter	Wills 1	1828-1851	392
Edwards, B. W.	Lowndes	Wills C	1861-1899	102
Edwards, Charles G.	Dallas	Wills B	1850-1871	174
Edwards, Eliza M.	Greene	Wills B	1817-1841	286
Edwards, Francis R.	Lowndes	Wills C	1861-1899	87
Edwards, George T.	Lowndes	Wills C	1861-1899	159
Edwards, Isaac P.	Lowndes	Wills B	1830-1859	275
Edwards, J. W.	Russell	Wills 2	1850-1873	336
Edwards, James W.	Autauga	Reports F	1845-1850	588
Edwards, Jane	Marshall	OCR 1	1836-1837	243
Edwards, Jesse R.	Autauga	Reports I	1856-1858	18
Edwards, John	Chambers	Wills 1-2	1833-1856	473
Edwards, John	Jefferson	Wills A	1856-1880	351
Edwards, John	Perry	Wills A	1821-1855	59
Edwards, John	Pike	Wills B	1862-1879	102
Edwards, John	St. Clair	Deeds B	1831-1849	872

TESTATOR	COUNTY	WHERE FOUND		PAGE
Edwards, John S.	Talladega	Wills B	1839-1845	66
Edwards, Matilda	Dallas	Wills B	1850-1871	310
Edwards, Michael	Russell	Wills 2	1850-1873	47
Edwards, Mildred M.	St. Clair	Deeds B	1831-1849	842
Edwards, Nancey	Russell	Wills 2	1850-1873	122
Edwards, Reps	Greene	Wills B	1817-1841	273
Edwards, W. B.	Russell	Wills 2	1850-1873	335
Edwards, William B.	Madison	Wills 1	1853-1875	523
Eggleston, Elbridge F.	Lawrence	I&W A	1850-1857	166
Eggleston, Matthew I?	Lawrence	I&W D	1835-1840	619
Eiland, Asa	Perry	Wills A	1821-1855	4
Eiland, Jincy	Perry	Wills B	1858-1873	88
Eiland, Stephen	Russell	Wills 2	1850-1873	61
Elam, Hiram	Bibb	Admr.R J	1865-1876	477
Elder, Samuel	Madison	Deeds A	1810-1816	41
Eldridge, John R. B.	Madison	Wills 1	1853-1875	383
Eldridge, Martha B.	Dallas	Wills B	1850-1871	36
Eldridge, Millicent T.	Madison	Wills 1	1853-1875	380
Eldridge, Thomas	Madison	PR 2	1818-1823	366
Eley, Eli	Tallapoosa	Wills 1	1838-1866	10
Eley, Mills	Madison	PR 3	1823-1826	419
Eliott, Anna	Sumter	Wills 1	1828-1851	378
Elison, James	Montgomery	Wills 3	1840-1854	237
Elkins, Eli	Chambers	Wills 1-2	1833-1856	202
Ellenbee, John	Dallas	Wills B	1850-1871	113
Ellett, Edmond	Colbert	Wills A	1861-1903	14
Ellett, James	Henry	OCR N	1862-1864	313
Ellington, Dewie	Talladega	W&I A	1852-1857	458
Ellington, Erasmus	Tuscaloosa	Wills 1	1821-1855	223
Elliott, Amos	Shelby	Wills D	1841-1846	134
Elliott, Elizabeth	Tuscaloosa	Wills 1	1821-1855	313
Elliott, Rebecca	Lawrence	I&W D	1835-1840	256
Elliott, Samuel	Lawrence	I&W C	1866-1880	282
Ellis, Catherine	Wilcox	Wills 2	1832-1850	337
Ellis, Charlotte	Greene	Wills D	1851-1888	156
Ellis, Edward	Montgomery	Wills 2	1820-1845	119
Ellis, Eli	Tuscaloosa	Wills 1	1821-1855	83
Ellis, Ezekiel	Clarke	PR L	1861-1864	99
Ellis, Henry A.	Mobile	Wills 1	1813-1837	209
Ellis, James	Mobile	Wills 3	1857-1870	389
Ellis, Jesse	Elmore	Wills A	1866-1906	1
Ellis, John	Wilcox	Wills 1	1821-1844	102
Ellis, Moody R.	Dallas	Wills B	1850-1871	128
Ellis, Nathan	Coosa	W&OCR 2	1843-1883	231
Ellis, Radford	Butler	Wills 1	1853-1864	256
Ellisoe, Adam	Montgomery	Wills 3	1840-1854	55
Ellison, Jacob	Montgomery	Wills 4	1853-1869	23
Ellison, Thomas	Mobile	Wills 2	1837-1857	36
Ellison, W. L.	Blount	PM B-1	1844-1851	302
Ellitt, Davis	Pike	Wills A	1845-1862	104
Ellzey, Elizabeth	Madison	PR 15	1850-1853	481

TESTATOR	COUNTY	WHERE FOUND		PAGE
Elmore, Ann	Autauga	Reports H	1855-1857	494
Elston, David A.	Talladega	W&I B	1858-1864	259
Elston, John	Calhoun	Loose	Probated 1853	
Elston, Oliver H.	Talladega	W&I A	1852-1857	553
Elston, William L.	Talladega	W&I B	1858-1864	102
Ely, Michael	Macon	Records 2	1838-1842	71
Emather-Nee-Othak	Chambers	Wills 1-2	1833-1856	7
Embry, Briton	Tuscaloosa	Wills 1	1821-1855	44
Embry, Elizabeth	Coosa	W&OCR 2	1843-1883	144
Embry, Enoch	Tallapoosa	Wills 1	1838-1866	105
Embry, Nancy	Talladega	Wills C	1845-1853	118
Embry, T. J.	Calhoun	PR A-2	1856-1866	337
Emerson, Margaret S.	Montgomery	Wills 4	1853-1869	564
Emfinger, Elizabeth	Dallas	Wills B	1850-1871	197
Emmons, John	Monroe	W&D D	1850-1856	247
Emmons, William	Monroe	W&D 9	1871-1872	93
Enfinger, Henry	Russell	Wills 2	1850-1873	324
English, Alexander	Talladega	Wills C	1845-1853	369
English, Charles A.	Monroe	W&D A	1833-1841	324
English, Johnathan	Monroe	W&D A	1833-1841	213
English, Joshua	Clarke	PR E	1840-1845	41
English, M.	Lauderdale	Wills B	1859-1870	429
English, Robert	Dallas	Wills B	1850-1871	153
English, Sarah	Baldwin	Wills A	1811-1881	51
English, Thomas	Monroe	W&D A	1833-1841	270
English, William	Montgomery	Wills 2	1820-1845	306
Engram, Oliver	Barbour	OCR 8	1856-1858	196
Engster?, John	Mobile	Wills 3	1857-1870	385
Enlow, Daniel	Dallas	Wills A	1821-1849	334
Enlow, Nancy	Dallas	Wills B	1850-1871	107
Ent?, John	Mobile	Wills 1	1813-1837	91
Epes, Richard J.	Sumter	Wills 2	1851-1872	330
Erskine, Alexander	Madison	Wills 1	1810-1820	135
Ervin, Lucy	Wilcox	Wills 3	1826-1858	106
Erwin, Alexander R.	Madison	Wills 1	1853-1875	222
Erwin, Isaac H.	Clarke	PR E	1840-1845	301
Erwin, Isom H.	Mobile	Wills 2	1837-1857	85
Erwin, William	Perry	Wills A	1821-1855	78
Erylist, Matthew	Lauderdale	Wills 4	1821-1825	69
Espy, Elizabeth G.	Barbour	OCR 9	1858-1859	921
Estes, Caldwell	Sumter	Wills 1	1828-1851	214
Estes, Carter	Sumter	Wills 1	1828-1851	205
Estes, Mathew	Madison	PR 4	1826-1829	51
Estes, Randal	Lauderdale	Wills A	1835-1858	290
Etheridge, A. W.	Monroe	W&D F	1861-1867	168
Etheridge, James	Mobile	Wills 2	1837-1857	26
Etheridge, M. E.	Monroe	W&D F	1861-1867	80
Ethridge, Isaac	Lowndes	Wills B	1830-1859	56
Eugster?, John	Mobile	Wills 3	1857-1870	385
Eustis, Ozel	Mobile	Wills 3	1857-1870	120
Eut, John	Mobile	Wills 1	1813-1837	91

TESTATOR	COUNTY	WHERE FOUND		PAGE
Evans, Amy	Lauderdale	Wills A	1835-1858	237
Evans, A. N.	Monroe	W&D D	1850-1856	306
Evans, Cyrus (Negro)	Mobile	Wills 2	1837-1857	148
Evans, Duncan	Talladega	W&I C	1862-1866	160
Evans, Ellington	Sumter	Wills 2	1851-1872	363
Evans, Eliza Ann	Dallas	Wills B	1850-1871	179
Evans, Freeman C.	Mobile	Wills 3	1857-1870	466
Evans, Jesse	Lauderdale	Wills B	1859-1870	11
Evans, Jesse	Lauderdale	Wills 3	1821-1825	64
Evans, John	Lawrence	I&W D	1835-1840	55
Evans, Peter	Lowndes	Wills B	1830-1859	358
Evans, Samuel	Jackson	Records	1861-1881	407
Evans, Stokely	Chambers	Wills 1-2	1833-1856	381
Evans, William P.	Pike	Wills B	1862-1879	111
Everell, Ray	Clarke	PR K	1858-1861	297
Everett, Enoch	Washington	Wills 1 ∅	1827-1888	60
Everett, Enoch	Washington	Wills B	1827-	39
Everett, John	Washington	Wills 1 ∅	1827-1888	122
Everett, John	Washington	Wills B	1827-	78
Everitt, Ann B.	Mobile	Wills 2	1837-1857	107
Ewing, Alexander	Madison	Wills 1	1853-1875	155
Ewing, James L.	Mobile	Wills 3	1857-1870	484
Ezell, Jane	Macon	Records 10	1863-1865	501
Ezell, Lewis	Lauderdale	Wills A	1835-1858	107
Fabriques, Benito	Mobile	Wills 1	1813-1837	261
Fackler, Elizabeth M.	Madison	Wills 1	1853-1875	467
Faek, Margaret	Lauderdale	Wills B	1859-1870	125
Fair, Dr. Drewry	Dallas	Wills B	1850-1871	133
Faircloth, Cordial	Lawrence	I&W A	1850-1857	271
Faircloth, Mandiah C.	Lawrence	I&W A	1850-1857	438
Fairly, John P.	Wilcox	Wills 3	1826-1858	96
Faison, Thomas J.	Barbour	OCR 1	1833-1843	304
Faith, Jackson W.	Washington	Wills 1 ∅	1827-1888	238
Faith, Jackson W.	Washington	Wills B	1827-	140
Falconer, Caroline	Montgomery	Wills 4	1853-1869	85
Falconer, John	Montgomery	Wills 4	1853-1869	16
Falconer, William	Montgomery	Wills 2	1820-1845	224
Fambro, W. W.	Dallas	Wills B	1850-1871	251
Fancher, Richard	Bibb	Loose	1849	
Fannin, A. P.	Macon	WAC&A 11	1862-1870	595
Fannin, Jacob	Montgomery	Wills 3	1840-1854	113
Fannin, Mary	Dallas	Wills A	1821-1849	215
Farish, Eliza	Sumter	Wills 1	1828-1851	62
Fariss, William B.	Montgomery	Wills 4	1853-1869	527
Farley, Henry Benner	Montgomery	Wills 4	1853-1869	368
Farley, James	Chambers	Wills 1-2	1833-1856	158
Farley, Michael F.	Madison	Wills 1	1853-1875	121
Farmer, Millicent	Sumter	Wills 1	1828-1851	337

TESTATOR	COUNTY	WHERE FOUND		PAGE
Farnell, John	Monroe	W&D B	1841-1845	311
Farr, John B.	Baldwin	Wills A	1811-1881	23
Farrar, Abel	Monroe	W&D A	1833-1841	12
Farrar, Rich	Perry	Wills B	1858-1871	264
Farrar, Samuel M.	Tuscaloosa	Wills 1	1821-1855	164
Farraw, Henry, Sr.	Perry	Wills A	1821-1855	250
Farrell, William	Shelby	Wills B	1818-1840	104
Farrell, William	Shelby	Wills C	1818-1827	194
Farrer, Sarah F.	Limestone	Wills 7	1844-1847	74
Farrer, William J.	Limestone	Wills 9	1847-1850	278
Farris, Cornelius	Lauderdale	Wills A	1835-1858	67
Fasin, Domingo	Mobile	Wills 2	1837-1857	262
Faucett, Richard	Tuscaloosa	Wills 1	1821-1855	269
Faulk, John	Monroe	W&D B	1841-1845	67
Faulk, Henry Lawson	Barbour	OCR 18	1870-	82
Faulkner, Vincent	Perry	Wills A	1821-1855	87
Favor, John	Limestone	Wills 9	1847-1850	43
Favor, William	St. Clair	Deeds B	1831-1849	733
Favre, Clara	Mobile	Wills 2	1837-1857	87
Fawn, William W.	Monroe	W&D F	1861-1867	120
Fay, James	Dallas	Wills A	1821-1849	192
Feagen, Samuel	Barbour	OCR 3	1847-1851	205
Fearn, Eliza Maria	Madison	Wills 1	1853-1875	313
Fearn, (Dr.) Richard Lee	Mobile	Wills 3	1857-1870	593
Fearn, Robert	Madison	Wills 1	1853-1875	96
Fearn, Thomas	Madison	Wills 1	1853-1875	304
Fears, Mary E.	Tuscaloosa	Wills 3	1858-1865	78
Fears, Mary E. A.	Tuscaloosa	Wills 3	1858-1865	45
Felder, Adam	Montgomery	Wills 4	1853-1869	325
Felder, Richard	Montgomery	Wills 4	1853-1869	167
Fellow?, John	Chambers	Wills 3	1856-1899	187
Felter, Moses Y?	Mobile	Wills 1	1813-1837	262
Felton?, John	Chambers	Wills 3	1856-1899	187
Fennel, Francis M.	Jackson	Wills	1870-1872	241
Fennel, Sallie	Morgan	OCR 6	1831-1837	372
Fennell, Isham	Madison	Deeds B	1810-1816	239
Fennell, James	Morgan	OCR 11	1850-1852	50
Fenner, Jim (Negro)	Mobile	Wills 3	1857-1870	192
Fenner, Jim	Tuscaloosa	Wills 3	1858-1865	75
Ferguson, Catherine	Chambers	Wills 1-2	1833-1856	443
Ferguson, Clement	Lawrence	I&W A	1850-1857	523
Ferguson, D. A. McD.	Russell	Wills 2	1850-1873	407
Ferguson, Frederick	Macon	Records 10	1863-1866	223
Ferguson, Jacob	Butler	Wills 1	1853-1864	29
Ferguson, James	Russell	Wills 2	1850-1873	380
Ferguson, T. P.	Shelby	Wills H	1847-1866	367
Fernandez, Clare	Mobile	Wills 2	1837-1857	110
Ferrell, James	Sumter	Wills 2	1851-1872	231
Ferrell, William	Macon	Records 5	1853-1855	709
Ferrent, Peter	Mobile	Wills 3	1857-1870	696
Ferror, Cammillus	Barbour	OCR 14	1863-1865	551

TESTATOR	COUNTY	WHERE FOUND		PAGE
Feticks, Eliza J.	Wilcox	Wills 4	1847-1862	206
Fickling, Isabella	Butler	Wills 2	1864-1876	86
Field, Edmund	Baldwin	Wills A	1811-1881	16
Field, Richard	Mobile	Wills 2	1837-1857	9
Fielder, L? B.	Pike	Wills B	1862-1879	9
Fielder, T. L.	Pike	Wills B	1862-1879	12
Fields, J. M.	Tuscaloosa	Wills 3	1856-1865	88
Fields, Samuel	Jefferson	Wills A	1856-1880	131
Figures, William B.	Madison	Wills 1	1853-1875	488
Fike, William	Perry	Wills A	1821-1855	62
Finch, Daniel W. E.	Marengo	Wills A	1820-1864	298
Finch, Ed. G.	Marengo	Wills A	1820-1864	198
Finch, Elizabeth	Marengo	Wills A	1820-1864	359
Finch, Harvey	Calhoun	PR A-2	1856-1865	335
Finch, Jared M.	Mobile	Wills 2	1837-1857	215
Fincher, John	Mobile	Wills 2	1837-1857	189
Finis?, Joseph	Lowndes	Wills B	1830-1859	16
Finnigan, Henry	Lowndes	Wills B	1830-1859	412
Finklea, John C.	Monroe	W&D C	1845-1850	533
Finklea, Thomas	Monroe	W&D C	1845-1850	272
Finley, Ann	Sumter	Wills 1	1828-1851	272
Finley, Samuel	Marshall	FR 5	1855-1859	419
Finn, Dennis N.	Talladega	W&I B	1858-1864	132
Figuet, C. J.	Tuscaloosa	Wills 4	1868-1897	4
Fishburne, E. B.	Russell	Wills 2	1850-1873	304
Fisher, Jacob	Macon	Records 3	1845-1850	371
Fisher, James R.	Wilcox	Wills 5	1855-1870	119
Fisher, William	Wilcox	Wills 1	1821-1844	332
Fitten, James	Limestone	Wills 4	1831-1837	288
Fitts, James H.	Marengo	Wills A	1820-1864	200
Fitts, Walker	Bibb	PM E	1852-1855	289
Fitzgerald, Elizabeth	Coosa	W&OCR 2	1843-1883	173
Fitzgerald, William, Sr.	Lawrence	I&W A	1850-1857	142
Fitzpatrick, Benjamin	Elmore	Wills A	1866-1906	21
Fitzpatrick, Catherine	Mobile	Wills 3	1857-1870	553
Fitzpatrick, Fannie	Montgomery	Wills 4	1853-1869	153
Fitzpatrick, Joseph	Montgomery	Wills 2	1820-1845	242
Fitzpatrick, W. J.?	Montgomery	Wills 4	1853-1869	462
Flake, Seaborn J.	Montgomery	Wills 4	1853-1869	437
Flanagan, Mary J.	Wilcox	Wills 5	1855-1870	68
Flanagin, William C.	Dallas	Wills A	1821-1849	124
Flannery, Edmund	Mobile	Wills 3	1857-1870	234
Flash, Alexander	Mobile	Wills 3	1857-1870	432
Fleming, George	Calhoun	Loose	Probated 1849	
Fleming, James	Autauga	Reports I	1856-1858	96
Fleming, John W.	Greene	Wills B	1817-1841	189
Fleming, Margaret	Clarke	OCR F	1846-1850	320
Fleming, Robert	Sumter	Wills 1	1828-1851	362
Fleming, Sarah M.	Madison	Wills 1	1850-1875	447
Fleming, William	Madison	Wills 1	1853-1875	379
Flemming, John	Coosa	W&OCR 2	1843-1883	40

TESTATOR	COUNTY	WHERE FOUND		PAGE
Flennoy, John	Madison	Wills 1	1853-1875	521
Fletcher, James N.	Limestone	Wills 12	1866-1872	585
Fletcher, Mathew M.	Washington	Wills B	1827-	96
Fletcher, Mathew M.	Washington	Wills 1 ∅	1827-1888	152
Fletcher, Nathan	Morgan	PCTR C(15)	1854-1858	453
Fletcher, Richard	Madison	PR 7	1834-1837	45
Fletcher, William	Madison	Deeds A	1810-1818	240
Fletcher, Ziba	Chambers	Wills 1-2	1833-1856	208
Flewellen, Eaton	Russell	Wills 1	1838-1849	17
Flewellen, Elvin	Russell	Wills 2	1850-1873	195
Flinn, R. J.	Barbour	OCR 14	1863-1865	476
Flippin, Francis	Madison	PR 15	1850-1853	509
Florence, David	Talladega	W&I B	1858-1864	201
Florence, John	Barbour	OCR 15	1865-1866	603
Florence, Obadiah	Barbour	OCR 14	1863-1865	557
Florence T.	Russell	Wills 2	1850-1873	302
Flournoy, J. C.	Pike	Wills B	1862-1879	149
Flournoy, James Gibson	Madison	PR 2	1818-1823	249
Flournoy, Josiah	Barbour	OCR 2	1842-1847	98
Flournoy, Marcus A.	Chambers	Wills 1-2	1833-1856	292
Flowers, Bennett	Sumter	Wills 1	1828-1851	381
Flowers, Eleanor M. A.	Montgomery	Wills 3	1840-1854	57
Flowers, John	Pike	Wills A	1845-1862	101
Flowers, John	Sumter	Wills 2	1851-1872	243
Flowers, John L.	Montgomery	Wills 3	1840-1854	42
Flowers, Sarah M.	Sumter	Wills 2	1851-1872	404
Floyd, James C.	Chambers	Wills 3	1856-1899	161
Floyd, John L.	Chambers	Wills 3	1856-1899	93
Floyd, Larkin	Chambers	Wills 3	1856-1899	226
Floyd, Prudence	Autauga	Reports J	1858-1859	654
Floyd, Robert	Chambers	Wills 1-2	1833-1856	162
Floyd, Shadrick	Chambers	Wills 1-2	1833-1856	269
Floyd, William	Chambers	Wills 1-2	1833-1856	25
Floyd, William J.	Macon	Records 6	1856-1858	626
Fluker, George	Wilcox	Wills 1	1821-1844	289
Fluker, Hardy	Clarke	PR K	1858-1861	103
Fluker, William	Sumter	Wills 2	1851-1872	66
Flynt, Perry	Madison	PR 16	1831-1861	517
Foard, Francis	Sumter	Wills 1	1828-1851	358
Foard, Wyatt	Montgomery	Wills 2	1820-1845	122
Follin, M. N.	Mobile	Wills 2	1837-1857	232
Fonde, Camilla V.	Mobile	Wills 3	1857-1870	152
Forbes, John	Mobile	Wills 1	1813-1837	153
Forbes, Roger	Montgomery	Wills 5	1863-1887	80
Forbes, Thomas	Mobile	Wills 2	1837-1857	64
Ford, Elizabeth	Dallas	Wills B	1850-1871	30
Ford, James M.	Perry	Wills B	1858-1873	225
Ford, Kendrick	Clarke	PR H	1854-1856	294
Ford, Marianne	Madison	Wills 1	1853-1875	481
Ford, Matilda	Chambers	Wills 3	1856-1899	223
Ford, Merrick H.	Russell	Wills 2	1850-1873	150

TESTATOR	COUNTY	WHERE FOUND		PAGE
Ford, William M.	Perry	Wills B	1858-1873	117
Fore, William	Monroe	W&D C	1845-1850	325
Foreman, Isaac	Autauga	Reports B	1829-1833	407
Forest, Lire Le	Mobile	Wills 2	1837-1857	277
Forman, Benjamin	St. Clair	Wills	1821-1827	2
Forndrew, Penelope	Bibb	Loose	Dated 1848	
Forsyth, Frank D.	Mobile	Wills 3	1857-1870	264
Forsyth, J. H.	Russell	Wills 2	1850-1873	413
Fort, Burwell J?	Dallas	Wills A	1821-1849	129
Fort, Henry	Lawrence	I&W D	1835-1840	414
Fort, Henry	Sumter	Wills 1	1828-1851	303
Fort, Isaac	Barbour	Loose Box 90	Probated 1840	
Forte, Drury	Monroe	W&D A	1833-1841	344
Forthand, Palmer?	Monroe	W&D D	1850-1856	382
Foscue, Amos	Macon	Records 8	1859-1860	230
Foscue, Augustus	Marengo	Wills A	1820-1854	555
Foscue, Elizabeth	Macon	Records 2	1838-1842	293
Foshee, William	Bibb	Loose	Dated 1856	
Foster, Andrew	Limestone	Wills 3	1826-1831	97
Foster, Arthur	Monroe	W&D A	1833-1841	200
Foster, Elizabeth	Monroe	W&D A	1833-1841	111
Foster, Elizabeth	Tuscaloosa	Wills 1	1821-1855	51
Foster, Elizabeth W.	Tuscaloosa	Wills 4	1868-1897	164
Foster, Frederick	Greene	Wills B	1817-1841	211
Foster, G. W.	Monroe	W&D F	1861-1867	101
Foster, Hillary	Mobile	Wills 2	1837-1857	379
Foster, Isaiah	Greene	Wills A	1821-1827	1
Foster, J.R.W.	Tuscaloosa	Wills 1	1821-1855	330
Foster, James	Tuscaloosa	Wills 1	1821-1855	176
Foster, James H.	Greene	Wills B	1817-1841	271
Foster, James J.	Sumter	Wills 1	1828-1851	339
Foster, John W.	Sumter	Wills 1	1828-1851	227
Foster, John W.	Tuscaloosa	Wills 1	1821-1855	144
Foster, Joseph	Montgomery	Wills 4	1853-1869	573
Foster, Mary	Greene	Wills B	1817-1841	151
Foster, Robert S.	Tuscaloosa	Wills 1	1821-1855	189
Foster, William H.	Clarke	OCR	1825-1832	197
Fowler, Harriet	Mobile	Wills 3	1857-1870	708
Fowler, Hickman	Monroe	W&D D	1850-1856	480
Fowler, John	Blount	PM B-1	1844-1851	301
Fowler, John	Morgan	OCR 11	1850-1852	96
Fowler, Newton	Sumter	Wills 1	1828-1851	131
Fowler, Oxury	Montgomery	Wills 2	1820-1845	302
Fowler, Thomas	Henry	OCR J	1857-1858	427
Fowler, William	Limestone	Wills 3	1826-1831	101
Fowlkes, Ransom C.	Madison	Wills 1	1853-1875	354
Fox, Benjamin	Limestone	Wills 3	1826-1831	95
Fox, John	Limestone	Wills 4	1831-1837	111
Fox, John B.	Morgan	OCR 6	1831-1837	583
Foxhall, Robert H.	Montgomery	Wills 4	1853-1869	137
Foxworth, John C.	Wilcox	Wills 3	1826-1858	17

TESTATOR	COUNTY	WHERE FOUND		PAGE
Foy, Catherine	Mobile	Wills	3	532	1857-1870	532
Foy, Edward	Sumter	Wills	1	1828-1851	261
Foy, Margaret	Mobile	Wills	3	1857-1870	144
Foy, Margaret	Perry	Wills	A	1821-1855	126
Foy, Philip	Mobile	Wills	2	1837-1857	70
Fralick, Henry	Autauga	Reports	E-B	1841-1845	59
Fralick, John D.	Autauga	Reports	K	1859-1861	100
Franklin, Abner	Dallas	Wills	A	1821-1849	40
Franklin, Abraham	Madison	PR	3	1823-1826	366
Franklin, John	Madison	PR	3	1823-1826	304
Franklin, Mary	Coosa	W&OCR	2	1843-1883	220
Franklin, Thomas	Jefferson	OCR		1824-1831	154
Fraser, Allen	Montgomery	Wills	4	1853-1869	546
Frazar, Elizabeth	Madison	PR	6	1832-1834	692
Frazar, James	Madison	PR	2&5	1818-1826	204
Frazer, Henry A.	Macon	Records	10	1863-1865	605
Frazer, J. H.	Russell	Wills	2	1850-1873	294
Frazer, John A.	Chambers	Wills	3	1856-1899	76
Frazer, Kerenhappuch	Autauga	Reports	C	1834-1838	220
Frazer, Lewis	Jefferson	OCR		1841-1844	594
Frazer, William A.	Pike	Wills	A	1845-1862	2
Frazer, William D.	Montgomery	Wills	4	1853-1869	340
Frazier, John L.	Macon	Records	10	1863-1865	757
Frazier, Richerson	Jefferson	Wills	A	1856-1880	7
Frederick, Diana Maria	Chambers	Wills	3	1856-1899	134
Frederick, William	Chambers	Wills	1-2	1833-1856	206
Freeman, Claiborne A.	Madison	PR	10	1821-1855	12
Freeman, James	Tuscaloosa	Wills	1	182,-1855	357
Freeman, John	Lowndes	Wills	B	1830-1859	240
Freeman, Joseph L.	Chambers	Wills	3	1856-1899	183
Freeman, Josiah	Sumter	Wills	1	1828-1851	266
Freeman, Mrs. Nancy	Talladega	W&I	D	1867-1880	441
Freeman, Sarah	Montgomery	Wills	4	1853-1869	93
Freeman, Taylor	Chambers	Wills	1-2	1833-1856	413
Freeman, Thomas (Negro)	Madison	PR	2	1818-1823	262
Freeman, Young E.	Madison	PR	8	1831-1839	100
French, Amos	Limestone	Wills	12	1866-1872	500
French, Benjamin	Lauderdale	Wills	A	1835-1858	168
French, Lardner C.	Dallas	Wills	A	1821-1849	111
French, Robert	Clarke	GE&W		1832-1839	35
Frencher, Annell?	Dallas	Wills	B	1850-1871	200
Fricke, Anton	Mobile	Wills	3	1857-1870	610
Friend, Hugh B.	Madison	PR	11	1842-1849	569
Friend, John	Madison	PR	2&5	215	215
Friend, John N.	Madison	PR	8	1818-1826	252
Friend, Judith C.	Madison	PR	11	1842-1849	548
Frierson, John	Lowndes	Wills	B	1830-1859	74
Frierson, Robert	Tuscaloosa	Wills	1	1821-1855	244
Frith, Elizabeth A.	Autauga	Wills	1	1862-1925	6
Frith, Dr. Thomas P.	Autauga	Wills	1	1862-1925	62
Frye, George	Monroe	W&D	A	1833-1841	254

TESTATOR	COUNTY	WHERE FOUND		PAGE
Frye, Lucy	Monroe	W&D D	1850-1861	223
Fryer, Richard H.	Barbour	OCR 15	1865-1866	412
Fulford, Stephen	Sumter	Wills 1	1828-1851	305
Fulghum, Lavinia	Greene	Wills D	1851-1888	47
Fulks, J. P.	Dallas	Wills B	1850-1871	448
Fuller, Erastus B.	Barbour	OCR 3	1847-1851	182
Fuller, J. B.	Greene	Wills D	1851-1888	199
Fuller, James M.	Chambers	Wills 3	1856-1899	362
Fuller, James M.	Chambers	Wills 3	1856-1899	108
Fuller, Mordeca	St. Clair	Deeds A	1824-1832	589
Fuller, Stephen	Coosa	W&OCR 2	1843-1883	96
Fuller, Tryon	Calhoun	Loose	Probated 1860	
Fuller, Tryon	Talladega	W&I B	1858-1864	372
Fulton, Robert	Talladega	Wills A	1833-1839	168
Funderburgh, Sarah	Autauga	Reports E-A	1838-1841	158
Fuqua, Giles	Lauderdale	Wills B	1859-1870	418
Fuqua, Peyton	Lauderdale	Wills B	1859-1870	433
Fuqua, Seth	Madison	PR 2	1818-1823	266
Fuqua, William	Lauderdale	Wills A	1835-1858	315
Furgeson, Clairborn	Tallapoosa	Wills 1	1838-1866	183
Furlow, Cynthia	Macon	Records 2	1838-1842	357
Furlow, Margaret	Perry	Wills A	1821-1855	161
Furman, Samuel	Barbour	OCR 2	1842-1847	82
Furr, Charles	Dallas	Wills A	1821-1849	322
Fyler?, Harriett	Coosa	W&OCR 2	1843-1883	54
Gachet, Nicholas	Macon	Records 10	1863-1865	8
Gaffed, J. Milton	Butler	Wills 2	1864-1875	160
Gage, Charles P.	Mobile	Wills 3	1857-1870	600
Gage, James M.	Mobile	Wills 2	1837-1857	373
Gage, Margaret E.	Mobile	Wills 3	1857-1870	238
Gaillard, Thomas	Mobile	Wills 3	1857-1870	406
Gaines, Benjamin	Sumter	Wills 1	1828-1851	60
Gaines, Williams F.	Cleburne	Wills 1	1866-1884	104
Gallagher, John	Mobile	Wills 3	1857-1870	355
Galliher, William P.	Dallas	Wills A	1821-1849	78
Gallup, Benjamin C.	Mobile	Wills 3	1857-1870	645
Gamble, Ann	Wilcox	Wills 1	1821-1844	372
Gamage, Lucretia	Dallas	Wills A	1821-1849	107
Gamage, Thomas	Dallas	Wills A	1821-1849	34
Gamble, James	Wilcox	Wills 1	1821-1844	414
Gamble, James C.	Mobile	Wills 1	1813-1837	118
Gamble, Samuel J.	Wilcox	Wills 1	1821-1844	330
Gamble, William	Tallapoosa	Wills 1	1838-1866	86
Gamboni, Joseph	Mobile	Wills 3	1857-1870	297
Gambrell, John	Chambers	Wills 1-2	1833-1856	157
Gammon, William	Henry	Deeds A-B	1822-1840	226
Gandy, John	Bibb	Loose	Dated 1851	
Gandy, John P.	Bibb	Adm.R G	1851-1854	68

TESTATOR	COUNTY	WHERE FOUND		PAGE
Gandy, T. K.	Dallas	Wills B	1850-1871	399
Gannard, Babett	Mobile	Wills 1	1813-1837	92
Gantt, C. M.	Dallas	Wills A	1821-1849	295
Gantt, Robert	Dallas	Wills A	1821-1849	66
Garden, Catherine	Monroe	W&D C	1845-1850	510
Gardiner, James	Madison	PR 8	1831-1839	261
Gardner, Bardall	Dallas	Wills B	1850-1871	108
Gardner, Charles	Mobile	Wills 3	1857-1870	536
Gardner, David	Madison	PR 14	1846-1860	241
Gardner, Emma B.	Madison	Wills 1	1853-1875	372
Gardner, Garland F.	Dallas	Wills B	1850-1871	142
Gardner, Jason	Dallas	Wills A	1821-1849	24
Gardner, Wade E.	Wilcox	Wills 5	1855-1870	135
Gardner, William	Dallas	Wills B	1850-1870	34
Garner, A. L.	Colbert	Wills A	1861-1903	3
Garner, Charles Horace	Mobile	Wills 3	1857-1870	670
Garner, Hesikioh F.	Morgan	OCR 28	1869-1872	209
Garner, John S.	Madison	Wills 1	1810-1820	225
Garner, Sturday	Madison	PR 13	1838-1848	271
Garner, William W.	Bibb	Adm.R I	1858-1865	462
Garrard, Lewis G.	Marengo	Wills A	1820-1864	305
Garrard, Thomas	Lauderdale	Wills A	1835-1858	31
Garrard, William	Lauderdale	Wills A	1835-1858	20
Garratt, Isham W.	Perry	Wills B	1858-1873	186
Garrett, B. L.	Russell	Wills 2	1850-1873	235
Garrett, Nathan B.	Chambers	Wills 1-2	1833-1856	471
Garrett, William	Coosa	W&OCR 2	1843-1883	275
Garrett, William, Sr.	Coosa	W&OCR 2	1843-1883	64
Garrison, William	Madison	PR 3	1823-1826	201
Garth, Jesse W.	Morgan	FR 23	1866-1867	453
Garton, Rebecca	Perry	Wills A	1821-1855	32
Gary, Alfred B.	Coosa	W&OCR 2	1843-1883	136
Gary, G. L.	Tuscaloosa	Wills 3	1858-1865	151
Gary, William	Perry	Wills A	1821-1855	88
Gary, William B.	Sumter	Wills 1	1828-1851	246
Gascoigne, Charles	Mobile	Wills 3	1857-1870	2
Gaskeys, Thomas	Sumter	Wills 1	1828-1851	113
Gaston, Hugh	Wilcox	Wills 1	1821-1844	328
Gaston, Jon	Wilcox	Wills 3	1826-1858	327
Gaston, Robert	Autauga	Reports A	1825-1830	296
Gaston, William	Wilcox	Wills 1	1821-1844	318
Gates, George	Tuscaloosa	Wills 1	1821-1855	153
Gatewood, Thomas	Sumter	Wills 2	1851-1872	276
Gathings, Sampson	Baldwin	Wills A	1811-1881	91
Gauntt, Jacob	Tallapoosa	Wills 1	1838-1866	121
Gause, Austin B.	Mobile	Wills 3	1857-1870	136
Gause, Eliza	Montgomery	Wills 2	1820-1845	234
Gause, James	Montgomery	Wills 2	1820-1845	19
Gause, William	Montgomery	Wills 2	1820-1845	232
Gay, Francis	Mobile	Wills 2	1837-1857	235
Gay, Gilbert S.	Coosa	W&OCR 2	1843-1883	98

TESTATOR	COUNTY	WHERE FOUND		PAGE
Gay, Mills	Tuscaloosa	Wills 1	1821-1855	132
Gayle, Billups	Clarke	OCR	1825-1832	237
Gayle, John	Mobile	Wills 3	1857-1870	149
Gayle, Miles	Perry	Wills A	1821-1855	286
Gayle, Scarborough	Dallas	Wills B	1850-1871	71
Gayle, William	Mobile	Wills 2	1837-1857	408
Gazzam, George G.	Mobile	Wills 3	1857-1870	400
Gee, Albert G.	Dallas	Wills B	1850-1871	99
Gee, Mark W.	Wilcox	Wills 1	1821-1844	387
Geiger, Alexander	Sumter	Wills 2	1851-1872	413
Geiger, Jacob	Lowndes	Wills B	1830-1859	22
Genewick, Amelia	Greene	Wills A	1821-1827	46
Gentry, Archibald W.	Russell	Wills 2	1850-1873	87
George, Alexander	Perry	Wills A	1821-1855	110
George, Benjamin C.	Calhoun	Loose	Probated 1856	
George, Charles D.	DeKalb	PR	1857-1861	2
George, James F.	Perry	Wills B	1858-1873	380
George, John	Wilcox	Wills 5	1855-1870	241
George, Richard	Perry	Wills A	1821-1855	26
George, Richard	Perry	W&I	1823-1833	124
George, Samuel	Madison	PR 8	1831-1839	160
George, William	Chambers	Wills 1-2	1833-1856	295
Gerald, Camilla D.	Montgomery	Wills 5	1863-1887	28
Gerald, Daniel N.	Russell	Wills 2	1850-1873	282
Germany, F. M.	Macon	WAC&A 11	1862-1870	322
Geron, Jehu W.	Madison	Wills 1	1853-1875	402
Geudreau, Mary Louise	Mobile	Wills 2	1837-1857	165
Gholson, Greenville	Sumter	Wills 1	1828-1851	87
Gibbes, William H.	Lowndes	Wills B	1830-1859	45
Gibbons, William D.	Mobile	Wills 2	1837-1857	8
Gibbs, Charles R.	Sumter	Wills 2	1851-1872	425
Gibbs, William S.	Perry	Wills A	1821-1855	48
Gibson, Anna Maria	Wilcox	Wills 3	1826-1858	264
Gibson, Jane	Montgomery	Wills 2	1820-1845	214
Gibson, John	Mobile	Wills 3	1857-1870	130
Gibson, John	Morgan	OCR 3	1827-1832	55
Gibson, John R.	Morgan	OCR 11	1850-1852	401
Gibson, Patience	Tallapoosa	Wills 1	1838-1866	11
Gibson, Samuel	Sumter	Wills 1	1828-1851	17
Gibson, Samuel Royal	Pike	Wills A	1845-1862	239
Gibson, Susannah	Coosa	W&OCR 2	1843-1883	269
Gier, Emily S.	Bullock	Wills A	1868-1902	1
Gilbert, Mary	Limestone	Wills 9	1847-1850	442
Gilbert, Nancy	Wilcox	Wills 1	1821-1844	251
Gilbert, William	Sumter	Wills 2	1851-1872	394
Gilbreath, Alexander	Marshall	FR 8	1858-1867	108
Gilchrist, A.	Lowndes	Wills B	1830-1859	311
Gilchrist, Daniel	Lawrence	I&WA	1850-1872	440
Gilchrist, Elizabeth	Lowndes	Wills B	1830-1859	233
Gilder, Lucy	Chambers	Wills 3	1856-1899	65
Gilder, Sinot (Sennot?)	Chambers	Wills 1-2	1833-1856	109

TESTATOR	COUNTY	WHERE FOUND		PAGE
Gilfert, James M.	Sumter	Wills	2	1851-1872	32
Giles, John	Clarke	OCR		1825-1832	2
Gill, Benjamin	Perry	Wills	A	1821-1855	23
Gill, Benjamin	Perry	W&I		1823-1833	98
Gill, Daniel P.	Morgan	FR	18	1859-1860	204
Gill, James	Greene	Wills	C	1840-1864	21
Gill, James	Montgomery	Wills	4	1853-1869	477
Gill, Jerome B.	Sumter	Wills	1	1828-1851	390
Gill, Thomas W.	Dallas	Wills	B	1850-1871	244
Gill, William	Perry	Wills	A	1821-1855	171
Gillahan, Nancy	Lauderdale	Wills	3	1821-1825	1
Gillam, Robert	Tallapoosa	Wills	2	1864-1907	46
Gilleland, Abel	St. Clair	Deeds	A	1824-1832	141
Gillespie, D. H.	Russell	Wills	2	1850-1873	294
Gillespie, Joseph	Sumter	Wills	2	1851-1872	48
Gillespie, Margaret	Tuscaloosa	Wills	1	1821-1855	184
Gillespie, Mary	Sumter	Wills	2	1851-1872	176
Gillespie, Seaborn	Tuscaloosa	Wills	1	1821-1855	71
Gilliam, John W.	Marengo	Wills	A	1820-1864	329
Gilliland, Sarah	St. Clair	RE	D	1859-1867	110
Gilliland, Nancy	Lauderdale	Wills	B	1859-1870	9
Gilmer, Caroline	Tallapoosa	Wills	1	1838-1866	141
Gilmer, Elizabeth L.	Montgomery	Wills	4	1853-1869	81
Gilmer, Francis L.	Montgomery	Wills	4	1853-1869	463
Gilmer, Micajah W.	Montgomery	Wills	2	1820-1845	220
Gilmer, Peachy R.	Montgomery	Wills	4	1853-1869	336
Gilmer, Rebecca	Dallas	Wills	B	1850-1871	35
Gilmer, William B. S.	Chambers	Wills	3	1856-1899	138
Gilmer, William B. S.	Chambers	Wills	3	1856-1899	346
Gilmore, Archibald	Clarke	OCR	B	1818-1824	76
Gilmore, H. F.	Clarke	PR	L	1861-1864	189
Gilmore, James W.	Chambers	Wills	3	1856-1899	145
Gilmore, John	Chambers	Wills	1-2	1833-1856	269
Gilmore, John	Marengo	Wills	A	1820-1864	229
Gilmore, John W.	Henry	Deeds	A-B	1822-1840	132
Gilmore, Nathaniel Green	Sumter	Wills	1	1828-1851	300
Ginn, Jesse	St. Clair	Deeds	C	1846-1855	51
Girard, Eugene	Mobile	Wills	1	1813-1837	256
Girard, Joseph	Baldwin	Wills	A	1811-1881	140
Girard, Margueritte LeFleau	Mobile	Wills	1	1813-1837	167
Ginion, Dominique	Mobile	Wills	3	1857-1870	690
Givhan, Jacob	Dallas	Wills	A	1821-1849	218
Givhan, Thomas J.	Dallas	Wills	B	1850-1871	24
Gladden, Joseph	Calhoun	Loose		Probated 1859	
Glanson, James	Pike	Wills	A	1845-1862	196
Glasgow, Thomas	Cleburne	Wills	1	1866-1884	21
Glass, B. W.	Dallas	Wills	B	1850-1871	305
Glass, Mary	Chambers	Wills	3	1856-1899	33
Glasscock, Thomas G.	Montgomery	Wills	5	1863-1887	108
Glaze, Milton J.	Tallapoosa	Wills	1	1838-1866	205
Gleen, Mary	Autauga	Wills	1	1862-1925	23

TESTATOR	COUNTY	WHERE FOUND		PAGE
Glen, Francis Marion	Jefferson	Wills A	1856-1880	170
Glenn, Nancy	Lauderdale	Wills B	1859-1870	56
Glenn, Robert	Sumter	Wills 1	1828-1851	110
Glenn, Robert	Sumter	Wills 1	1828-1851	116
Glenn, Robert B.	Autauga	Reports B	1829-1833	39
Glenn, Tyre	Montgomery	Wills 4	1853-1869	307
Glover, Allen	Marengo	Wills A	1820-1864	204
Glover, Benjamin	Marengo	Wills A	1820-1864	1
Glover, Henry	Clarke	PR J	1856-1858	398
Glover, John B.	Lee	Wills A	1867-1898	32
Glover, John P.	Barbour	OCR 12	1861-1863	500
Glover, John S.	Coosa	W&OCR 2	1843-1883	117
Glover, Mary A.	Marengo	Wills A	1820-1864	465
Glover, Polly	Marengo	Wills A	1820-1864	214
Glover, Richard	Madison	Wills 1	1853-1875	105
Glover, Thomas	Henry	OCR M	1861-1862	163
Godbold, Leonard D.	Wilcox	Wills 5	1855-1870	127
Godbold, Zachariah	Baldwin	Wills A	1811-1881	55
Godden, Henry F.	Perry	Wills B	1858-1873	17
Godfrey, William	Sumter	Wills 2	1851-1872	41
Godwin, Wyley	Pike	Wills A	1845-1862	33
Goff, Lazarus	Mobile	Wills 1	1813-1837	217
Goff, Lewis	Mobile	Wills 2	1837-1857	11
Goggans, James	Coosa	W&OCR 2	1843-1883	68
Golden, Elizabeth	Pike	Wills A	1845-1862	223
Golden, Martha Ann	Tallapoosa	Wills 2	1864-1907	33
Golden, Seaborn	Tallapoosa	Wills 1	1838-1866	137
Goldsby, M. Sarah W.	Dallas	Wills B	1850-1871	251
Goldsby, Thornton B.	Dallas	Wills B	1850-1871	177
Goldsmith, John T.	Chambers	Wills 1-2	1833-1856	256
Goldsmith, William H.	Butler	Wills 2	1864-1875	76
Goldthwaite, Robert H.	Montgomery	Wills 2	1820-1845	259
Golightly, David	Tuscaloosa	Wills 1	1821-1855	212
Golson, Ann	Butler	Wills 2	1864-1875	69
Golson, Emanuel	Autauga	Wills 1	1862-1925	49
Golson, John W.	Autauga	Reports J	1858-1859	630
Gomillion, Henry	Pike	Wills A	1845-1862	113
Gooch, Albert G.	Tuscaloosa	Wills 3	1858-1865	37
Goode, Frances F.	Montgomery	Wills 4	1853-1869	390
Goode, Robert	Jefferson	Deeds 1	1818-1828	65
Goode, Thomas, Sr.	Jefferson	Deeds 1	1818-1828	170
Goode, William	Clarke	GE&W	1832-1839	494
Goodehill, Jacob	Mobile	Wills 2	1837-1857	224
Gooding, Hardy	Dallas	Wills A	1821-1849	124
Gooding, John L.	Mobile	Wills 3	1857-1870	301
Goodman, Duke W.	Mobile	Wills 3	1857-1870	502
Goodman, John H.	Mobile	Wills 3	1857-1870	405
Goodman, Mildred	Mobile	Wills 2	1837-1857	317
Goodner, David	Madison	PR 14	1846-1850	241
Goodson, James	Autauga	DMR 17	1820-1864	52
Goodson, William	Macon	Records 10	1863-1865	271

TESTATOR	COUNTY	WHERE FOUND		PAGE
Goodwin, Neophlet	Clarke	PR L	1861-1864	105
Goodwin, Jordan M.	Russell	Wills 1	1838-1849	182
Goodwin, Julius	Bibb	OCR	1846-1851	328
Goodwin, Young	Bibb	Loose	Dated 1847	
Goodwyn, Jane	Greene	Wills B	1817-1841	192
Gordon, Archibald W.	Mobile	Wills 3	1857-1870	504
Gordon, Alexander	Wilcox	Wills 1	1821-1844	338
Gordon, Amanda H.	Autauga	Wills 1	1862-1925	15
Gordon, James	Clarke	GE&W	1832-1839	105
Gordon, James	Madison	Wills 1	1853-1875	304
Gordon, Nancy	Mobile	Wills 2	1837-1857	278
Gordon, Posey	Greene	Wills B	1817-1841	60
Gordon, Robert G.	Wilcox	Wills 1	1821-1844	389
Gordon, Verlinda	Lowndes	Wills B	1830-1859	129
Gordon, William	Lowndes	Wills B	1830-1859	339
Gordy, John	Washington	Wills B	1827-	33
Gordy, John	Washington	Wills 1 ∅	1827-1888	52
Goree, James L.	Perry	Wills A	1821-1855	115
Goree, John R.	Perry	Wills A	1821-1855	283
Gorham, Ann	Montgomery	Wills 4	1853-1869	248
Gorman, Starling	Perry	Wills A	1821-1855	103
Goslin, Simon	Russell	Wills 2	1850-1873	135
Goss, Eliza	Greene	Wills B	1817-1841	226
Gould, Daniel	Sumter	Wills 1	1828-1851	391
Gould, Malichi	Greene	Wills A	1821-1827	6
Goyne, James	Tuscaloosa	Wills 1	1821-1855	119
Goyne, John	Jefferson	Wills 1	1818-1840	227
Grace, James M.	Henry	OCR O	1864-1865	125
Gracier, E. H.	Dallas	Wills B	1850-1871	363
Gracy, Minor W.	Marengo	Wills A	1820-1864	317
Grady, Nathaniel	Chambers	Wills 1-2	1833-1856	266
Grady, Robert	Sumter	Wills 2	1851-1872	30
Graggs, William	Chambers	Wills 3	1856-1899	184
Graham, Archibald	Autauga	Deeds B		32
Graham, Archibald	Montgomery	Wills 4	1853-1869	413
Graham, Charles	Sumter	Wills 1	1828-1851	357
Graham, Charles W.	Sumter	Wills 2	1851-1872	83
Graham, Dugald B.	Autauga	Reports C	1834-1838	236
Graham, Elijah	Sumter	Wills 2	1851-1872	73
Graham, Dempsey A.	Sumter	Wills 2	1851-1872	60
Graham, Elizabeth	Madison	Wills 1	1853-1875	344
Graham, James	Coosa	W&OCR 2	1843-1883	4
Graham, James B.	Morgan	OCR 8	1844-1848	344
Graham, Job P.	Lowndes	Wills B	1830-1859	3
Graham, John P.	Perry	Wills B	1858-1873	420
Graham, Margaret	Talladega	Wills C	1845-1853	19
Graham, Peter	Tallapoosa	Wills 1	1838-1866	2
Graham, Thomas B.	Coosa	W&OCR 2	1843-1883	14
Graham, William	Autauga	Reports K	1859-1861	382
Graham, William	Mobile	Wills 2	1837-1857	283
Graham, William	Montgomery	Wills 4	1853-1869	11

TESTATOR	COUNTY	WHERE FOUND		PAGE
Graney, Martin	Lauderdale	Wills B	1859-1870	158
Granger, Hiram	Dallas	Wills B	1850-1871	347
Granger, John C.	Pike	Wills A	1845-1862	86
Grant, Catherine	Lowndes	Wills B	1830-1859	344
Grant, Giles	Barbour	OCR 17	1868-1870	332
Grant, John H.	Barbour	OCR 4	1850-1852	565
Grant, Martha H.	Tallapoosa	Wills 1	1838-1866	226
Grant, William	Madison	PR 4	1826-1829	24
Gras, Sylvanie	Mobile	Wills 3	1857-1870	367
Graves, Adaline	Lauderdale	Wills A	1835-1858	148
Graves, Archibald	Pike	Wills A	1845-1862	127
Graves, Catherine	Madison	PR 14	1846-1850	178
Graves, David	Pike	Wills A	1845-1862	183
Graves, James	Pike	Wills A	1845-1862	185
Graves, James M.	Madison	PR 10	1842-1842	149
Graves, John	Pike	Wills A	1845-1862	121
Graves, Jonathan	Lauderdale	Wills 3	1821-1825	26
Graves, Nancy	Madison	PR 4	1826-1829	117
Graves, Robert	Sumter	Wills 1	1828-1851	110
Graves, William, Sr.	Autauga	Reports C	1834-1838	347
Graves, William	Lowndes	Wills B	1830-1859	315
Graves, William	Montgomery	Wills 2	1820-1845	25
Gravitte, Vincent	Madison	Wills 1	1853-1875	293
Gray, George Senr.	Autauga	Reports B	1829-1833	29
Gray, James	Tuscaloosa	Wills 1	1821-1855	204
Gray, James W.	Tallapoosa	Wills 1	1838-1866	178
Gray, John	Greene	Wills A	1821-1827	68
Gray, John	Greene	Wills B	1817-1841	3
Gray, John G.	Lauderdale	Wills A	1835-1858	211
Gray, Jonathan	Lawrence	I&W C	1866-1880	230
Gray, Joseph	Washington	Wills 1 ∅	1827-1888	235
Gray, Joseph	Washington	Wills B	1827-	139
Gray, Joshua	Wilcox	Wills 4	1847-1862	127
Gray, Parker	Montgomery	Wills 2	1820-1845	126
Gray, Roderick	Mobile	Wills 1	1813-1837	49
Gray, Sallie C.	Madison	PR 15	1850-1853	105
Gray, W. C.	Wilcox	Wills 2	1832-1850	244
Gray, Walter	Limestone	Wills 5	1836-1841	330
Gray, William	Madison	PR 6	1832-1834	678
Grayson, Benjamin	Madison	PR 2	1818-1823	216
Grayson, Benjamin	Madison	PR 2	1818-1823	268
Grayson, John	Madison	PR 4	1826-1829	19
Grayson, W. J.	Marengo	Wills A	1820-1864	473
Grayson, Young W.	Marengo	Wills A	1820-1864	274
Grayson, Young W.	Sumter	Wills 2	1851-1872	229
Green, Boling	Sumter	Wills 1	1828-1851	296
Green, Daniel	Sumter	Wills 1	1828-1851	166
Green, George	Jefferson	OCR	1841-1844	143
Green, Jesse	Marengo	Wills A	1820-1864	268
Green, Moses T.	Montgomery	Wills 4	1853-1869	35
Green, Peter A.	St. Clair	RE F	1862-1868	131

TESTATOR	COUNTY	WHERE FOUND		PAGE
Green, Richard	Marengo	Wills A	1820-1864	366
Green, William	Marengo	Wills A	1820-1864	228
Green, W. Frederick	Dallas	Wills A	1821-1849	33
Green, Zacheus	Marengo	Wills A	1820-1864	249
Green, Elizabeth	Marengo	Wills A	1820-1864	542
Greene, James B.	Mobile	Wills 2	1837-1857	295
Greening, John	Dallas	Wills A	1821-1849	69
Greenwood, William H.	Shelby	Wills B	1818-1840	160
Greer, Alexander W.	St. Clair	RE C	1852-1859	234
Greer, Henry H.	Chambers	Wills 1-2	1833-1856	385
Greer, Joseph, Sr.	Tallapoosa	Wills 1	1838-1866	14
Greer, Marion N.	Marengo	Wills A	1820-1864	398
Greer, Priscilla	Chambers	Wills 1-2	1833-1856	382
Greer, Samuel	Tallapoosa	Wills 1	1838-1866	214
Greer, William	Marengo	Wills A	1820-1864	292
Greer, William D.	Chambers	Wills 1-2	1833-1856	205
Gregg, Elisha	Lowndes	Wills C	1861-1899	165
Gregg, Robert H.	Wilcox	Wills 4	1847-1862	240
Gregory, Byrd	Limestone	Wills 12	1866-1872	274
Gregory, D.	Sumter	Wills 2	1851-1872	305
Gregory, Edward	Blount	PM B	1852-1856	360
Gregory, George W.	Mobile	Wills 2	1837-1857	438
Gregory, Noah H.	Montgomery	Wills 4	1853-1869	384
Gregory, William	Montgomery	Wills 2	1820-1845	117
Grelot, Bartholomew	Mobile	Wills 2	1837-1857	256
Grenberry, Langley B.	Henry	OCR J	1857-1858	582
Gresham, Archibald	Talladega	Deeds D		34
Gressom, William B.	Lauderdale	Wills 3	1821-1825	84
Grider, Benjamin	Pike	Wills A	1845-1862	60
Grier, Mary	Dallas	Wills A	1821-1859	36
Grier, Moses Sen.	Autauga	Reports C	1834-1838	514
Grier, Robert	Dallas	Wills A	1821-1849	3
Griffain, S.	Mobile	Wills 1	1813-1837	149
Griffen, Claibon	Sumter	Wills 1	1828-1851	186
Griffin, Archibald	Coosa	W&PM	1834-1842	172
Griffin, Archibald M.	Mobile	Wills 3	1857-1870	580
Griffin, Drury	Montgomery	Wills 2	1820-1845	115
Griffin, H. W.	Macon	WAC&A 11	1862-1870	320
Griffin, Ira	Mobile	Wills 1	1813-1837	250
Griffin, James	Washington	Wills 1 ∅	1827-1888	63
Griffin, James P.	Washington	Wills B	1827-	41
Griffin, John	Marshall	OCR 1	1836-1837	3
Griffin, John	Montgomery	Wills 2	1820-1845	18
Griffin, Joseph	Chambers	Wills 1-2	1833-1856	32
Griffin, Joseph	Chambers	Wills 1-2	1833-1856	33
Griffin, Joseph	Madison	PR 15	1850-1853	510
Griffin, Joseph	Montgomery	Wills 2	1820-1845	24
Griffin, Naomi	Wilcox	Wills 4	1847-1862	198
Griffin, William	Tallapoosa	Wills 1	1838-1866	203
Griffis, John	Autauga	Reports E-A	1838-1841	31
Griffis, John	Clarke	PR E	1840-1846	360

TESTATOR	COUNTY	WHERE FOUND		PAGE
Griffith, Joel	Chambers	Wills	1-2	1833-1856	308
Griffith, John	Marengo	Wills	A	1820-1864	198
Griffith, Joshua J.	Chambers	Wills	1-2	1833-1856	351
Grigg, William	Russell	Wills	2	1850-1873	51
Griggs, James	Barbour	OCR	16	1866-1868	45
Griggs, Leonard B.	Perry	Wills	A	1821-1855	80
Griggs, W. John	Greene	Wills	A	1821-1827	54
Grigsby, Levi M.	Marengo	Wills	A	1820-1864	305
Grimes, Allen	Marengo	Wills	A	1820-1864	128
Grimes, Jesse	Talladega	W&I	A	1852-1857	361
Grimes, Wiley	Wilcox	Wills	5	1855-1870	367
Grinnell, Michael D.	Mobile	Wills	3	1857-1870	556
Grisby, Sarah	Sumter	Wills	1	1828-1851	4
Grisby, Uriah	Dallas	Wills	A	1821-1849	161
Grisham, Eaton	Lauderdale	Wills	A	1835-1858	56
Grissett, Mary Jane	Wilcox	Wills	3	1826-1858	414
Grizzell, Joel, Sr.	Greene	Wills	B	1817-1841	82
Grooms, Council	Coosa	W&OCR	2	1843-1883	90
Groves?, William Sen.	Autauga	Reports	C	1834-1838	347
Grubs, William	Barbour	OCR	3	1847-1851	325
Grumbles, C. G.	Dallas	Wills	B	1850-1871	367
Gue, Joseph	Montgomery	Wills	4	1853-1869	548
Gunion?, Dominique	Mobile	Wills	3	1857-1870	690
Gunn, George B.	Coosa	W&OCR	2	1843-1883	233
Gunn, James M.	Chambers	Wills	3	1856-1899	154
Gunn, Jesse, Sr.	Chambers	Wills	1-2	1833-1856	383
Gunn, Larkin R.	Chambers	Wills	1-2	1833-1856	437
Gunn, N. P.	Tallapoosa	Wills	1	1838-1866	123
Gunn, Peter R.	Marengo	Wills	A	1820-1864	212
Gunter, John	Blount	Records	A	1837-1845	102
Guphill, Willie J.	Montgomery	Wills	2	1820-1845	264
Gurley, Jeremiah	Madison	PR	11	1842-1849	45
Gutherie, William J.	Bullock	Wills	A	1868-1902	22
Guthrey, Bernard	Madison	PR	2	1818-1823	381
Guy, Joseph	Shelby	Wills	B	1818-1840	166
Gwin, Jeremiah	Tuscaloosa	Wills	1	1821-1855	154
Hadden, Elizabeth	Sumter	Wills	1	1828-1851	297
Hadden, Isaac	Sumter	Wills	1	1828-1851	320
Hadnot, William S.	Autauga	Reports	G	1850-1853	438
Hadnot, William S.	Autauga	PM	11		211
Hagerty, Abel	Montgomery	Wills	3	1840-1854	271
Hagerty, Jackson	Montgomery	Wills	4	1853-1869	21
Hagerty, William	Montgomery	Wills	2	1820-1845	83
Haggard, Noah	Shelby	Wills	H	1847-1866	926
Haggerty, Blasengame	Montgomery	Wills	2	1820-1845	300
Haggerty, Hugh	Lauderdale	Wills	4	1821-1825	49
Haggerty, Hugh	Lauderdale	Wills	B	1859-1870	145
Hagler, Henry	Barbour	OCR	4	1850-1852	524

TESTATOR	COUNTY	WHERE FOUND		PAGE
Hagler, Peter	Barbour	OCR 4	1850-1852	471
Hagood, Mary E.	Lowndes	Wills B	1830-1859	335
Haig, Eliza	Mobile	Wills 2	1837-1857	344
Haight, Jacob N.	Mobile	Wills 1	1813-1837	120
Haile, James C.	Jackson	Wills	1866-1867	306
Hailey, John C.	Barbour	OCR 14	1863-1865	527
Hainsworth, Aurelia	Sumter	Wills 2	1851-1872	364
Hainsworth, Levin	Washington	Wills 1 Ø	1827-1888	50
Hainsworth, Levin	Washington	Wills B	1827-	32
Hair, James	Sumter	Wills 2	1851-1872	272
Halaway, S. T.	Tuscaloosa	Wills 3	1858-1865	165
Halbert, Joshua	Tuscaloosa	Wills 1	1821-1855	210
Halbrook, Jacob	Greene	Wills C	1840-1864	757
Hale, Harriet C.	Sumter	Wills 2	1851-1872	179
Hale, John	Dallas	Wills A	1821-1849	132
Hale, Lydia	Madison	Deeds B	1810-1816	220
Hale, Mary A.	Sumter	Wills 2	1851-1872	204
Hale, Stephen F.	Greene	Wills C	1840-1864	687
Hale, William	Madison	Wills 1	1853-1875	263
Haley, James	Tuscaloosa	Wills 4	1868-1897	45
Halfman, Ethelbert	Montgomery	Wills 4	1853-1869	402
Halizan, James	Lauderdale	Wills 3	1821-1825	16
Hall, Adam	Madison	Wills 1	1853-1875	188
Hall, Amy G.	Dallas	Wills A	1821-1849	205
Hall, Ann	Baldwin	Wills A	1811-1881	217
Hall, Archibald	Sumter	Wills 2	1851-1872	126
Hall, Bolling	Autauga	Reports C	1834-1838	259
Hall, Dixon	Autauga	Reports E-A	1838-1841	80
Hall, Dixon	Montgomery	Wills 2	1820-1845	5
Hall, Henry	Limestone	Wills 5	1836-1841	27
Hall, Henry	Morgan	PCTRC (15)	1854-1858	490
Hall, James	Greene	Wills B	1817-1841	150
Hall, James	Talladega	Wills B	1839-1845	52
Hall, James M.	Barbour	OCR 12	1861-1863	386
Hall, Jane	Madison	Wills 1	1853-1875	124
Hall, John	Coosa	W&OCR 2	1843-1883	66
Hall, John	Dallas	Wills A	1821-1849	18
Hall, John	Greene	Wills D	1851-1888	196
Hall, John	Mobile	Wills 1	1813-1837	207
Hall, John P.	Madison	PR 10	1842-1842	142
Hall, Joseph	Montgomery	Wills 4	1853-1869	110
Hall, Margaret	Madison	PR 9	1839-1841	277
Hall, Margaret	Talladega	W&I B	1858-1864	245
Hall, Marshall H.	Lowndes	Wills C	1861-1899	29
Hall, Mary	Tallapoosa	Wills 1	1838-1866	4
Hall, Meridith	Calhoun	Loose	Probated 1856	
Hall, Samuel E.	Chambers	Wills 3	1856-1899	41
Hall, Samuel T.	Tuscaloosa	Wills 3	1858-1865	22
Hall, Stephen	Jefferson	OCR	1824-1831	17
Hall, Thomas	Madison	PR 3	1823-1826	12
Hall, Thomas	Talladega	W&I B	1858-1864	438

TESTATOR	COUNTY	WHERE FOUND		PAGE
Hall, William	Baldwin	Wills A	1811-1881	88
Hall, William	Mobile	Wills 3	1857-1870	289
Hall, William R.	Monroe	W&D F	1861-1867	152
Hall, William T.	Autauga	Wills 1	1862-1925	51
Hallonquist, Sophia	Montgomery	Wills 5	1863-1887	34
Hallum, Thomas	Calhoun	Loose	Probated 1834	
Halsell, S. P.	Sumter	Wills 1	1828-1851	382
Halsey, George Allen	Shelby	Wills L	1838-1858	534
Halsey, Stephen	Madison	PR 6	1832-1834	53
Hamblin, John	Madison	PR 13	1838-1848	199
Hamblin, Martha	Madison	Wills 1	1853-1875	48
Hambrick, John	Lowndes	Wills B	1830-1859	55
Hamer, Daniel	Tuscaloosa	Wills 1	1821-1855	202
Hamer, Elizabeth	Tuscaloosa	Wills 1	1821-1855	354
Hamill, Louisa H. A.	Greene	Wills C	1840-1864	305
Hamilton, Andrew	Chambers	Wills 1-2	1833-1856	277
Hamilton, Audley	Jefferson	Wills 1	1818-1840	194
Hamilton, James	Dallas	Wills B	1850-1871	156
Hamilton, Leonard Hawes	Coosa	W&OCR 2	1843-1883	25
Hamilton, Lucy B.	Mobile	Wills 2	1837-1857	459
Hamilton, Lucy B.	Mobile	Wills 3	1857-1870	374
Hamilton, Margaret S.	Lowndes	Wills C	1861-1899	151
Hamilton, N. A. V. E.	Russell	Wills 2	1850-1873	292
Hamilton, Philip	Lowndes	Wills B	1830-1859	230
Hamilton, Thomas	Lowndes	Wills B	1830-1859	145
Hamilton, William C.	Talladega	Wills C	1845-1853	101
Hamilton, William J.	Greene	Wills D	1851-1888	52
Hamlet, Robert	Madison	PR 12	1845-1849	580
Hamlett, Elizabeth	Greene	Wills B	1817-1841	8
Hamlett, William R.	Greene	Wills C	1840-1864	365
Hammond, Eli	Madison	PR 10	1842-1842	74
Hammond, Richmond	St. Clair	RE D	1859-1867	101
Hammond, Samuel E.	Talladega	Wills C	1845-1853	364
Hammond, W. P.	Mobile	Wills 4	1870-1878	65
Hamner, Samuel	Madison	PR 3	1823-1826	178
Hampton, Ephraim	Russell	Wills 1	1838-1849	165
Hampton, James	Calhoun	Loose	Probated 1857	
Hampton, John	Madison	W&I	1810-1820	111
Hampton, John M.	Tallapoosa	Wills 1	1838-1866	60
Hampton, Obediah W.	Sumter	Wills 1	1828-1851	20
Hancock, Clem	Limestone	Wills 9	1847-1850	171
Hancock, Joseph	Chambers	Wills 1-2	1833-1856	205
Hancock, Robert	Madison	PR 2&5	1818-1826	396
Hand, Joseph R.	Macon	WAC&A 11	1862-1870	514
Hand, Obatiah	Sumter	Wills 1	1828-1851	37
Handcock, Isaiah	St. Clair	Deeds B	1831-1849	898
Handley, Justina A.	Wilcox	Wills 5	1855-1870	183
Hanesworth, James L.	Sumter	Wills 2	1851-1872	147
Haney, Patrick	Mobile	Wills 2	1837-1857	190
Hanna, Benjamin? B.	Greene	Wills C	1840-1864	563
Hanna, Robert C.	Greene	Wills C	1840-1864	1

TESTATOR	COUNTY	WHERE FOUND		PAGE
Hanna, Samuel	Greene	Wills C	1840-1864	87
Hannah, Andrew M.	Greene	Wills B	1817-1841	249
Hannah, M. M.	Calhoun	PR A-2	1856-1866	402
Hannay, Mary E.	Lauderdale	Wills B	1859-1870	16
Hanson, Jacob	Mobile	Wills 3	1857-1870	365
Hanson, Johanna	Mobile	Wills 3	1857-1870	653
Hanson, John C., Sr.	Lee	Wills A	1867-1898	16
Hanson, William	Chambers	Wills 1-2	1833-1856	71
Hanu, Martin	Mobile	Wills 2	1837-1857	50
Haraway, Samuel	Lauderdale	Wills A	1835-1858	93
Hardin, Jesse	Talladega	W&I D	1867-1880	723
Hardin, Joshua	Lauderdale	Wills A	1835-1858	202
Hardin, Levi	Tallapoosa	Wills 1	1838-1866	94
Hardin, Polly	Lauderdale	Wills A	1835-1858	33
Harding, Edward	Baldwin	Wills A	1811-1881	236
Harding, James L.	Marengo	Wills A	1820-1864	254
Harding, William W.	Baldwin	Wills A	1811-1881	240
Hardwick, Charles A.	Russell	Wills 1	1838-1849	176
Hardwick, Garland	Tuscaloosa	Wills 1	1821-1855	112
Hardwick, Garland	Tuscaloosa	Wills 3	1858-1865	188
Hardwick, George	St. Clair	Deeds A	1824-1832	23
Hardwick, John L.	Lauderdale	Wills A	1835-1858	242
Hardwick, William	Montgomery	Wills 4	1853-1869	24
Hardy, Alfred	Macon	Records 3	1845-1850	745
Hardy, Aquilla	Greene	Wills D	1851-1888	28
Hardy, B. F.	Lowndes	Wills B	1830-1859	329
Hardy, Daniel M.	Dallas	Wills B	1850-1871	70
Hardy, Jefferson	Dallas	Wills B	1850-1871	335
Hardy, Jesse Willy	Dallas	Wills A	1821-1849	263
Hardy, John, Sr.	Dallas	Wills B	1850-1871	32
Hardy, John	Lowndes	Wills B	1830-1859	132
Hardy, John	Russell	Wills 2	1850-1873	99
Hardy, Jonathan	Madison	Deeds C	1816-1818	101
Hardy, Robert	Coosa	W&OCR 2	1843-1883	7
Hardy, William, Sr.	Lowndes	Wills B	1830-1859	104
Harewood, John	Wilcox	Wills 1	1821-1844	310
Hargranes, James T.	Lauderdale	Wills B	1859-1870	136
Hargraves, William	Jefferson	OCR	1841-1844	438
Hargroves, Abner	Limestone	Wills 3	1836-1841	388
Hargrove, John	Tuscaloosa	Wills 1	1821-1855	344
Hargrove, A. William	Greene	Wills A	1821-1827	31
Hargroves, James	Madison	Deeds D	1816-1818	10
Harkey, John Senr.	Tuscaloosa	Wills 1	1821-1855	59
Harkins, Andrew	Shelby	Wills E	1845-1850	441
Harkins, Robert	Tallapoosa	Wills 1	1838-1866	111
Hariston, Mary H.	Greene	Wills D	1851-1888	126
Harlan, James	Madison	PR 4	1826-1829	403
Harless, David	Madison	Deeds A	1810-1816	119
Harless, Henry	Madison	Deeds A	1810-1816	115
Harman, Stephen	Lauderdale	Wills 3	1821-1825	65
Harmon, Stephen	Lauderdale	Wills 4	1821-1825	10

TESTATOR	COUNTY	WHERE FOUND		PAGE
Harmon, Violetta	St. Clair	RE B	1834-1857	68
Harp, Dudley	St. Clair	RE F	1862-1868	214
Harper, Benjamin A.	Perry	Wills B	1858-1873	246
Harper, Edward	Perry	Wills B	1858-1873	100
Harper, James M.	Montgomery	Wills 3	1840-1854	1
Harper, John	Jefferson	Wills 1	1818-1840	202
Harper, John	Tallapoosa	Wills 1	1838-1866	17
Harper, John J., Jr.	Macon	Records 3	1845-1850	383
Harper, Joseph	Montgomery	Wills 3	1840-1854	45
Harper, R. W.	Marengo	Wills A	1820-1864	267
Harper, Sophia	Sumter	Wills 2	1851-1872	366
Harper, William	Dallas	Wills A	1821-1849	133
Harper, William	Tallapoosa	Wills 1	1838-1866	117
Harper, William H.	Montgomery	Wills 3	1840-1854	304
Harper, William T.	Perry	Wills B	1858-1873	120
Harper, Wyatt	Sumter	Wills 2	1851-1872	319
Harpin, John	Mobile	Wills 2	1837-1857	75
Harralson, Burgess B.	Chambers	Wills 3	1856-1899	133
Harralson, Jonathan A.	Chambers	Wills 1-2	1833-1856	416
Harrell, Alfred	Chambers	Wills 3	1856-1899	193
Harrell, Fanny	Dallas	Wills A	1821-1849	162
Harrell, George P.	Madison	PR 4	1826-1829	34
Harrell, Jesse T.	Talladega	W&I B	1858-1864	541
Harrell, Susanna	Chambers	Wills 3	1856-1899	63
Harrell, Thomas J.	Coosa	W&OCR 2	1843-1883	72
Harrington, Drury	Chambers	Wills 1-2	1833-1856	229
Harrington, G.	Greene	Wills D	1851-1888	214
Harrington, George D.	Elmore	Wills A	1866-1906	4
Harrington, John	Wilcox	Wills 2	1832-1850	254
Harris, Abraham	Calhoun	Loose	Probated 1860	
Harris, Archibald	Greene	Wills C	1840-1864	411
Harris, B. H.	Russell	Wills 2	1850-1873	399
Harris, Benjamin F.	Mobile	Wills 4	1870-1878	57
Harris, Benjamin W.	Lowndes	Wills C	1861-1899	43
Harris, Dewitt C.	Talladega	W&I B	1858-1864	743
Harris, Dinguid?	Wilcox	Wills 2	1832-1850	305
Harris, Edward	Madison	PR 6	1832-1834	106
Harris, Elijah	Greene	Wills C	1840-1861	305
Harris, Eliza G.	Madison	PR 16	1831-1861	299
Harris, Francis E.	Madison	PR 4	1826-1829	404
Harris, Frederick	Limestone	Wills 3	1826-1831	380
Harris, Henry P.	Russell	Wills 2	1850-1873	36
Harris, John H.	Limestone	Wills 6	1841-1846	417
Harris, Joshua	Chambers	Wills 1-2	1833-1856	246
Harris, Kinchen	Lowndes	Wills B	1830-1859	81
Harris, Lucy N.	Morgan	PCFR 20	1860-1865	199
Harris, Lud W.	Washington	Wills 1 Ø	1827-1888	71
Harris, L. W.	Washington	Wills B	1827-	46
Harris, Margaret	Montgomery	Wills 4	1853-1869	399
Harris, Marshall D.	Wilcox	Wills 4	1847-1862	160
Harris, Martha C.	Wilcox	Wills 4	1847-1862	56

TESTATOR	COUNTY	WHERE FOUND		PAGE
Harris, Mary	Greene	Wills C	1840-1864	472
Harris, Matthew	Madison	PR 4	1826-1829	361
Harris, Micajah	Chambers	Wills 1-2	1833-1856	267
Harris, Micajah	Clarke	PCR H	1854-1856	364
Harris, Moses	Macon	Records 10	1863-1865	353
Harris, Narcissa A.	Macon	Records 10	1863-1865	497
Harris, Nathan	Montgomery	Wills 4	1853-1869	71
Harris, Polly	Mobile	Wills 2	1837-1857	16
Harris, Rachel M.	Macon	Records 7	1857-1859	729
Harris, Randal	Clarke	GE&W	1832-1839	122
Harris, Rebecca B.	Sumter	Wills 2	1851-1872	279
Harris, Richard	Madison	PR 16	1831-1861	299
Harris, Richard	Sumter	Wills 2	1851-1872	1
Harris, Samson W.	Coosa	W&OCR 2	1843-1883	94
Harris, Sarah	Pike	Wills A	1845-1862	35
Harris, Simon	Limestone	Wills 12	1866-1872	501
Harris, Thomas W.	Henry	OCR P	1864-1866	101
Harris, William	Madison	PR 2&5	1818-1826	367
Harris, William	Montgomery	Wills 2	1820-1845	13
Harris, William K.	Macon	Records 10	1863-1865	10
Harrison, Benjamin	Jefferson	OCR	1824-	304
Harrison, Benjamin	Madison	PR 16	1850-1853	196
Harrison, Catherine	Greene	Wills C	1840-1864	571
Harrison, Edward	Limestone	OCM	1830-1834	26
Harrison, J. N.	Lowndes	Wills C	1861-1899	22
Harrison, Jethro	Greene	Wills C	1840-1864	60
Harrison, R. B.	Dallas	Wills A	1821-1849	203
Harrison, Samuel?	Wilcox	Wills 1	1821-1844	370
Harrison, Simmons	Sumter	Wills 2	1851-1872	248
Harrison, Stewart	Montgomery	Wills 2	1820-1845	111
Harrison, Thomas	Russell	Wills 2	1850-1873	317
Harrison, Thomas A.	Marengo	Wills A	1820-1864	443
Harrison, William	Greene	Wills D	1851-1888	81
Harrison, Willoughby B.	Montgomery	Wills 2	1820-1845	72
Harriss, Francis	Wilcox	Wills 3	1826-1858	25
Harriss, Joshua	Perry	Wills A	1821-1855	182
Harriss, William Henry	Wilcox	Wills 3	1826-1858	414
Harry, Charley W.	Tallapoosa	Wills 1	1838-1866	50
Harry, Thomas	Greene	Wills C	1840-1864	481
Harry, William H.	Sumter	Wills 2	1851-1872	420
Hart, Benjamin	Mobile	Wills 2	1837-1857	274
Hart, Benjamin	Montgomery	Wills 3	1840-1854	130
Hart, Henry	Conecuh	OB A	1865-1870	320
Hart, Henry William	Tuscaloosa	Wills 1	1821-1855	94
Hart, James K.	Tallapoosa	Wills 2	1864-1907	60
Hart, John T.	Wilcox	Wills 3	1826-1858	45
Hart, Susan	Colbert	Wills A	1861-1903	24
Hart, William	Greene	Wills B	1817-1841	284
Harten, Hardy	Tuscaloosa	Wills 1	1821-1855	129
Harten, Samuel	Tuscaloosa	Wills 1	1821-1855	109
Hartley, Daniel	Mobile	Wills 2	1837-1857	236

TESTATOR	COUNTY	WHERE FOUND		PAGE
Hartley, Thomas L.	Marengo	Wills	A	1820-1864	546
Harve, William	Lauderdale	Wills	3	1821-1825	115
Harvey, Benjamin	Henry	Deeds	A-B	1822-1840	6
Harvey, John	Henry	Deeds	A-B	1822-1840	13
Harvey, John	Lauderdale	Wills	A	1835-1858	6
Harvey, Margaret	Mobile	Wills	2	1837-1857	461
Harvill, Thomas	Perry	Wills	A	1821-1855	234
Harwell, Mrs. Burchet	Barbour	OCR	14	1863-1865	107
Harwell, J. W.	Pike	Wills	B	1862-1879	37
Harwell, James	Montgomery	Wills	2	1820-1845	239
Harwell, James B.	Lauderdale	Wills	A	1835-1858	118
Harwell, John B.	Greene	Wills	B	1817-1841	228
Harwell, Samuel	Montgomery	Wills	3	1840-1854	161
Harwell, William T.	Sumter	Wills	2	1851-1872	45
Harwood, Samuel M.	Sumter	Wills	1	1828-1851	173
Haslip, Henry	Shelby	Wills	H	1847-1866	123
Hassell, Benjamin D.	Montgomery	Wills	4	1853-1869	54
Hassell, Lavina	Tuscaloosa	Wills	3	1858-1865	61
Hassell, Mary S.	Greene	Wills	C	1840-1864	144
Hassell, Webster R.	Greene	Wills	C	1840-1864	142
Hasselvander, Anne	Dallas	Wills	B	1850-1871	444
Hasskew, S. E.	Dallas	Wills	A	1821-1849	278
Hastie, John H.	Baldwin	Wills	A	1811-1881	214
Hastings, Edmund M.	Montgomery	Wills	5	1863-1887	59
Hatch, Durant	Greene	Wills	B	1817-1841	168
Hatch, George N.	Sumter	Wills	1	1828-1851	248
Hatcher, Griffin	Clarke	PR	N	1866-1870	325
Hatcher, James	Dallas	Wills	A	1821-1849	142
Hatcher, John	Dallas	Wills	B	1850-1871	210
Hatter, John	Greene	Wills	B	1817-1841	6
Hatter, Richard	Greene	Wills	C	1840-1864	18
Hatter, William R. B.	Greene	Wills	D	1851-1888	184
Hatton, Frances	Madison	PR	9	1839-1841	581
Hatton, James	Madison	PR	13	1838-1848	198
Hatton, Polly	Greene	Wills	A	1821-1827	49
Hatton, Thomas L.	Autauga	Wills	1	1862-1925	1
Haupt, George	Mobile	Wills	1	1813-1837	178
Haupt, George	Mobile	Wills	1	1813-1837	196
Hawkins, Daniel	Clarke	OCR	F	1846-1850	145
Hawkins, Josias	Lauderdale	Wills	B	1859-1870	46
Hawkins, Robert Z.	Morgan	OCR	7	1837-1843	93
Hawkins, Thomas	Lowndes	Wills	B	1830-1859	228
Hawley, Susan	Montgomery	Wills	4	1853-1869	433
Hawthorn, Sarah Ann	Wilcox	Wills	4	1847-1862	159
Hawthorn, William J.	Wilcox	Wills	4	1847-1862	242
Hay, David	Perry	Wills	A	1821-1855	273
Hay, David	Perry	Wills	A	1821-1855	276
Hayden, James	Lowndes	Wills	C	1861-1899	55
Hayes, Jesse	Russell	Wills	2	1850-1873	237
Hayes, John M.	Limestone	Wills	11	1865-1866	67
Hayes, John	Mobile	Wills	3	1857-1870	563

TESTATOR	COUNTY	WHERE FOUND		PAGE
Hayes, Patrick W.	Talladega	Wills A	1833-1839	1
Hayes, Samuel B.	Cleburne	Wills 1	1866-1886	7
Haygood, James	Lowndes	Wills B	1830-1859	414
Haygood, James E.	Chambers	Wills 1-2	1833-1856	350
Haygood, Willis	Lauderdale	Wills A	1835-1858	106
Haynie, C. Richard	Montgomery	Wills 2	1820-1845	255
Haynie, Luke	Coosa	W&OCR 2	1843-1883	48
Haynie, William E.	Barbour	OCR 17	1868-1870	454
Hays, George	Greene	Wills B	1817-1841	204
Hays, John	Lowndes	Wills B	1830-1859	55
Hays, Martin J.	Sumter	Wills 2	1851-1872	31
Hays, Patrick	Dallas	Wills A	1821-1849	63
Hays, Thomas	Butler	Wills 1	1853-1864	240
Hazard, John B.	Mobile	Wills 2	1837-1857	13
Hazard, John B.	Washington	Wills 1 Ø	1827-1888	56
Hazard, John B.	Washington	Wills B	1827-	37
Hazarde, Charles C.	Mobile	Wills 3	1857-1879	8
Hazes, Martha B.	Dallas	Wills B	1850-1871	331
Head, James	Greene	Wills C	1840-1864	189
Head, William	Barbour	OCR 8	1856-1858	195
Healy, Daniel	Mobile	Wills 3	1857-1870	606
Heard, Elias J.?	Tallapoosa	Wills 1	1838-1866	16
Heard, Jesse	Perry	Wills A	1821-1856	133
Hearin, Nancy	Clarke	OCR F	1846-1850	412
Hearin, Robert	Clarke	GE&W	1832-1839	469
Hearn, A. J.	Macon	WAC&A 11	1862-1870	504
Hearn,? Barney	Montgomery	Wills 4	1853-1869	164
Hearn, James	Sumter	Wills 2	1851-1872	95
Hearn, Mary	Wilcox	Wills 4	1847-1862	3
Hearne, Abigail	Lowndes	Wills B	1830-1859	324
Hearne, William, Sr.	Lowndes	Wills B	1830-1859	23
Hearston, Major	Lauderdale	Wills 3	1821-1825	6
Hearts, Richard	Lauderdale	Wills A	1835-1858	160
Heartsfield, Wiley W.	Pike	Wills A	1845-1862	159
Heath, Alexander W.	Madison	PR 8	1831-1839	260
Heath, Alexander W.	Talladega	Wills B	1839-1845	264
Heath, George W.	Wilcox	Wills 5	1855-1870	311
Heathcock, John	Madison	Wills 1	1853-1875	376
Heisen, Chas. & Conradina	Talladega	W&I D	1867-1880	429
Heisen, Chas. & Conradina	Talladega	W&I D	1867-1880	520
Heisen, Conradina	Talladega	W&I D	1867-1880	528
Hellen, Mary Ann	Hale	Wills A	1867-1923	29
Hellums, William	Madison	Deeds A	1810-1816	76
Hemphill, Alexander	Greene	Wills B	1817-1841	213
Hemphill, F. F.	Tuscaloosa	Wills 4	1868-1897	388
Hemphill, William	Jefferson	OCR	1824-1831	335
Henderson, Alexander	Mobile	Wills 2	1837-1857	288
Henderson, D. R.	Marengo	Wills A	1820-1864	293
Henderson, David	Chambers	Wills 1-2	1833-1856	359
Henderson, Eli	Pike	Wills A	1845-1862	172
Henderson, James Viral	Coosa	W&OCR 2	1843-1883	330

TESTATOR	COUNTY	WHERE FOUND		PAGE
Henderson, John	Henry	Deeds A-B	1822-1840	371
Henderson, Richard	Limestone	Wills 4	1831-1837	281
Henderson, Simeon	Shelby	Wills D	1841-1846	176
Henderson, Solomon J.?	Macon	Records 3	1845-1850	255
Henderson, Thomas O.	Sumter	Wills 1	1828-1851	325
Henderson, W.	Monroe	W&D 8	1870-1871	382
Hendon, Harry T.	Greene	Wills C	1840-1864	401
Hendon, William T., Sr.	Hale	Wills A	1867-1923	59
Hendrick, Hance	Talladega	W&I D	1867-1880	167
Hendrick, Mathias	Lowndes	Wills B	1830-1859	250
Hendrick, Micajah	Barbour	OCR 1	1833-1843	185
Hendrick, Nimrod	Tuscaloosa	Wills 3	1858-1865	138
Hendrick, W. W.	Talladega	W&I B	1858-1864	658
Hendrick, William Y.	Talladega	W&I D	1867-1880	357
Hendricks, Mary M.	Barbour	OCR 6	1854-1856	481
Hendrix, James	Tuscaloosa	Wills 1	1821-1855	249
Hendrix, Jonathan D.	Sumter	Wills 2	1851-1872	177
Hendrix, Larkin	Lauderdale	Wills A	1835-1858	132
Hendrix, Larkin	Lauderdale	Wills B	1859-1870	150
Hennigan, Samuel	Lawrence	I&W A	1850-1857	269
Henry, Charles A.	Mobile	Wills 2	1837-1857	77
Henry, Dr. Charles F.	Mobile	Wills 3	1857-1870	304
Henry, Frederic	Tuscaloosa	Wills 1	1821-1855	45
Henry, Hugh	Marshall	FR 5	1855-1859	149
Henry, John	Lauderdale	Wills 4	1821-1825	20
Henry, John	Mobile	Wills 2	1837-1857	419
Henry, John	Mobile	Wills 3	1857-1870	455
Henshaw, Andrew	Clarke	PR H	1854-1856	147
Henshaw, Edmund	Baldwin	Wills A	1811-1881	208
Hereford, Robert H.	Madison	Wills 1	1853-1875	52
Herlong, John H.	Lowndes	Wills C	1861-1899	51
Herman, Jones	Lauderdale	Wills B	1859-1870	22
Herndon, Burrell	Pike	Wills B	1862-1879	125
Herndon, Elizabeth	Greene	Wills B	1817-1841	119
Herndon, George	Lauderdale	Wills B	1859-1870	54
Herndon, James	Pike	Wills A	1845-1862	67
Herndon, John P.	Pike	Wills B	1862-1879	69
Herndon, Susan	Greene	Wills B	1817-1841	132
Herndon, Thomas H.	Greene	Wills C	1840-1864	31
Herrin, William	Macon	Records 3	1845-1850	295
Herring, Amelia B.	Morgan	OCR 8	1844-1848	381
Herring, Lewis W.	St. Clair	RE A	1854-1874	330
Herring, John	Barbour	OCR 9	1858-1859	939
Herring, John A.	Madison	PR 3	1823-1826	230
Herrington, Sarah	Montgomery	Wills 2	1820-1845	287
Hester, John	St. Clair	Deeds B	1831-1849	115
Hester, Lucy	Shelby	Wills B	1818-1840	176
Hester, Lucy	Shelby	Wills D	1841-1846	31
Hester, Wiley G. W.	Tuscaloosa	Wills 1	1821-1855	262
Hester, William	Tuscaloosa	Wills 1	1821-1855	74
Hester, William G.	Autauga	Reports B	1829-1833	331

TESTATOR	COUNTY	WHERE FOUND		PAGE
Hewitt, George	Tuscaloosa	Wills 1	1821-1855	352
Hewitt, Goldsmith W.	Jefferson	Deeds 1	1818-1828	113
Hewitt, James H.	Jefferson	Wills A	1856-1880	55
Hewlett, John W.	Madison	PR 7	1834-1837	258
Hibbin, James	Dallas	Wills A	1821-1849	256
Hibbler, Martha B.	Sumter	Wills 2	1851-1872	362
Hibbler, William H.	Sumter	Wills 2	1851-1872	257
Hickenbottom, William	Lauderdale	Wills 3	1821-1825	756
Hickman, Ann	Marengo	Wills A	1820-1864	191
Hicks, Daniel	Chambers	Wills 1-2	1833-1856	228
Hicks, James K.	Autauga	Reports B	1829-1833	421
Hicks, Johnston	Tallapoosa	Wills 1	1838-1866	150
Hicks, Mary L.	Butler	Wills 2	1864-1875	124
Hicks, Mathew	Cleburne	Wills 1	1866-1884	106
Hickson, Richard S.	Montgomery	Wills 2	1820-1845	59
Hiern, Roger A.	Mobile	Wills 3	1857-1870	540
Higdon, R. B.	Conecuh	OB A	1865-1870	414
Higginbotham, Blakeley	Wilcox	Wills 2	1832-1850	171
Higginbotham, Charles	Madison	PR 3	1823-1826	53
Higginbotham, Graves B.	Wilcox	Wills 3	1826-1858	99
Higgins, Jack L.	Montgomery	Wills 2	1820-1845	203
Higgins, John (Negro)	Madison	Wills 1	1853-1875	466
Higgins, William H.	Chambers	Wills 3	1856-1899	217
Hightower, Joshua	Chambers	Wills 1-2	1833-1856	466
Hightower, Philemon	Autauga	Reports C	1834-1838	639
Hilbern, Richard	Dallas	Wills A	1821-1849	172
Hill, Able	Madison	PR 8	1831-1839	412
Hill, Abner	Henry	Deeds A-B	1822-1840	306
Hill, Adam	Coosa	W&OCR 2	1843-1883	200
Hill, Andrew Jackson	Jefferson	PM	1844-1854	457
Hill, Benjamin	Greene	Wills C	1840-1864	15
Hill, Elizabeth	Washington	Wills 1 Ø	1827-1888	66
Hill, Elizabeth	Washington	Wills B	1827-	43
Hill, Eugene D.	Hale	Wills A	1867-1923	70
Hill, Francis A.	Dallas	Wills B	1850-1871	407
Hill, Gabriel ? L.	Greene	Wills B	1817-1841	259
Hill, George	Talladega	W&I C	1862-1866	364
Hill, Gibson F.	Chambers	Wills 3	1856-1899	199
Hill, Harriet H.	Hale	Wills A	1867-1923	42
Hill, Henry	Dallas	Wills A	1821-1849	71
Hill, Henry L.	Montgomery	Wills 3	1840-1854	53
Hill, James R.	Greene	Wills C	1840-1864	252
Hill, John	Mobile	Wills 2	1837-1857	394
Hill, Lewis H.	Elmore	Wills A	1866-1906	15
Hill, Lucy G.	Madison	Wills 1	1853-1875	240
Hill, Mary	Tallapoosa	Wills 1	1838-1866	48
Hill, Mary A.	Greene	Wills C	1840-1864	549
Hill, Roswell W.	Lowndes	Wills C	1861-1899	112
Hill, Savilla	Greene	Wills C	1840-1864	77
Hill, Starky	Dallas	Wills A	1821-1849	44
Hill, Thomas	Autauga	Reports B	1829-1833	411

TESTATOR	COUNTY	WHERE FOUND		PAGE
Hill, Thomas	Tallapoosa	Wills 1	1838-1866	148
Hill, Thomas M.	Sumter	Wills 2	1851-1872	294
Hill, William	Calhoun	Loose	Probated 1841	
Hill, William	Clarke	PR G	1850-1854	127
Hill, William S.	Montgomery	Wills 4	1853-1869	544
Hill, William W.	Greene	Wills C	1840-1864	236
Hillhouse, Jane	Autauga	Reports J	1858-1859	628
Hillian, Wiley	Marshall	FR 9	1867-1869	543
Hilliard, Bartlett	Montgomery	Wills 4	1853-1869	14
Hilliard, Columbus	Madison	PR 16	1831-1861	364
Hilliard, William	Pike	Wills B	1862-1879	72
Hilliard, William A.	Madison	PR 16	1831-1861	365
Hillman, Nimrod	Sumter	Wills 2	1851-1872	34
Hilverson, John	Mobile	Wills 2	1837-1857	330
Hind, M. O.	Montgomery	Wills 4	1853-1869	454
Hinds, Moses	Montgomery	Wills 4	1853-1869	348
Hine, Calvin	Limestone	Wills 4	1831-1837	535
Hines, Angus	Monroe	W&D F	1833-1870	179
Hines, Bryant	Greene	Wills C	1840-1864	487
Hines, Frederick	Sumter	Wills 1	1828-1851	284
Hines, Joab	Lauderdale	Wills B	1859-1870	101
Hines, Joseph H.	Perry	Wills B	1858-1873	76
Hines, Lovet	Greene	Wills D	1851-1888	4
Hines, Michael	Mobile	Wills 3	1857-1870	393
Hines, Nancy	Monroe	W&D C	1845-1850	131
Hines, Sarah	Greene	Wills B	1817-1841	195
Hines, Willis	Montgomery	Wills 2	1820-1845	142
Hinson, John	Lowndes	Wills B	1830-1859	299
Hinson, John	Marengo	Wills A	1820-1864	250
Hinton, William	Greene	Wills C	1840-1864	150
Hiram, Elam?	Bibb	Loose	Dated 1870	
Hitchcock, Henry	Mobile	Wills 2	1837-1857	37
Hitt, Austin	Sumter	Wills 2	1851-1872	27
Hitt, Easter	Sumter	Wills 1	1828-1851	238
Hitt, Elizabeth	Dallas	Wills B	1850-1871	170
Hitt, Marshall M.	Dallas	Wills B	1850-1871	164
Hitts, Jackie S.	Lauderdale	Wills A	1835-1858	205
Hix, Richard	Madison	PR 4	1826-1829	165
Hixson, Samuel	Pike	Wills A	1845-1862	230
Hixson, W. L.	Pike	Wills B	1862-1879	40
Hobart, Peter H.	Mobile	Wills 1	1813-1837	162
Hobart, Euphrosine	Mobile	Wills 2	1837-1857	197
Hobbie, Mary Ann	Montgomery	Wills 3	1840-1854	157
Hobbs, John	Madison	PR 6	1832-1834	329
Hobbs, Mary W.	Limestone	Wills 5	1836-1841	178
Hobbs, William	Wilcox	Wills 1	1821-1844	107
Hobby, J. W.	Lowndes	Wills B	1830-1859	278
Hobdy, Edmund	Wilcox	Wills 4	1847-1862	221
Hodge, Benjamin M.	Montgomery	Wills 2	1820-1845	275
Hodge, Dennis	Butler	Wills 1	1853-1864	60
Hodge, George E.	Lee	Wills A	1867-1898	42

TESTATOR	COUNTY	WHERE FOUND		PAGE
Hodge, James	St. Clair	RE C	1852-1859	314
Hodge, John	Chambers	Wills 3	1856-1899	146
Hodges, Henry	Henry	OCR O	1864-1864	254
Hodges, Jesse	Madison	Deeds A	1810-1816	117
Hodges, John	Henry	Deeds A-B	1822-1840	4
Hodges, John	Madison	W&I	1810-1820	116
Hodges, Joseph	Jefferson	OCR	1841-1844	585
Hodges, Robert	Sumter	Wills 1	1828-1851	240
Hodges, Stephen	Jefferson	Wills A	1856-1880	344
Hodges, Thomas	Morgan	OCR 3	1827-1832	61
Hodges, William	Lawrence	I&W D	1835-1840	24
Hoefer, August	Mobile	Wills 3	1857-1870	512
Hoffman, Jacob	Macon	Records 5	1853-1855	439
Hoffman, Luke	Autauga	Reports G	1850-1853	177
Hogan, Elizabeth	Marengo	Wills A	1820-1864	413
Hogan, James	Tuscaloosa	Wills 1	1821-1855	283
Hogan, John A.	Marengo	Wills A	1820-1864	246
Hogan, John B.	Marengo	Wills A	1820-1864	271
Hogan, Maria S.	Marengo	Wills A	1820-1864	385
Hogan, Sarah	Talladega	W&I A	1852-1857	23
Hogan, William	Madison	PR 4	1826-1829	83
Hogg, Elizabeth	Autauga	Reports H	1853-1857	134
Hoggue, Matthew	Greene	Wills B	1817-1841	267
Hogins, John R.	Montgomery	Wills 2	1820-1845	120
Hoke, Daniel	Calhoun	Loose	Probated 1858	
Holcomb, A. H.	Sumter	Wills 2	1851-1872	29
Holcomb, Hosea H.	Shelby	Wills H	1847-1866	726
Holcomb, William H.	Mobile	Wills 2	1837-1857	201
Holcomb, Hosea	Jefferson	OCR	1841-1844	159
Holcroft, Braxton	Marengo	Wills A	1820-1864	307
Holdcroft, E. F. J.	Greene	Wills C	1840-1864	576
Holder, Charley	Sumter	Wills 2	1851-1872	304
Holditch, Wiliam	Sumter	Wills 1	1828-1851	68
Holland, Ann	Marengo	Wills A	1820-1864	162
Holland, J. C.	Dallas	Wills B	1850-1871	295
Holland, James M.	Jackson	Records	1861-1881	457
Holland, John	Sumter	Wills 1	1828-1851	171
Holland, John S.	Mobile	Wills 2	1837-1857	188
Holley, Elizabeth	Tallapoosa	Wills 1	1838-1866	71
Holley, Jesse J.	Sumter	Wills 2	1851-1872	285
Holley, Mary M.	Tallapoosa	Wills 1	1838-1866	70
Holley, Noel	Perry	Wills A	1821-1855	329
Hollifield, Jeremiah	Perry	Wills B	1858-1873	165
Hollifield, Jesse	Perry	Wills B	1858-1873	377
Hollinger, Alexander	Mobile	Wills 3	1857-1870	566
Hollingsworth, Benjamin	Calhoun	Loose Ø	Probated 1844	
Hollis, Worling	Lamar	Wills 1	1844-1910	12
Hollman, Capers W.	Butler	Wills 1	1853-1864	247
Holliday, Thomas	Greene	Wills C	1840-1864	5
Holloway, Anderson	Tuscaloosa	Wills 1	1821-1855	75
Holloway, Jesse H.	Limestone	Wills 3	1826-1831	109

TESTATOR	COUNTY	WHERE FOUND		PAGE
Holloway, John	Tuscaloosa	Wills 1	1821-1855	102
Holloway, Samuel	Madison	Wills 1	1853-1875	120
Holloway, William	St. Clair	Deeds B	1831-1849	148
Holloway, William, Sr.	St. Clair	Deeds B	1831-1849	648
Holloways, Judith	Autauga	Reports B	1829-1833	210
Hollowell, Mary	Madison	Wills 1	1853-1875	489
Holly, George	Greene	Wills C	1840-1864	396
Holly, Jackson D.	Montgomery	Wills 4	1853-1869	446
Holly, James	Lowndes	Wills B	1830-1859	273
Holly, Levi	Perry	Wills A	1821-1855	200
Holly, Mary A.	Mobile	Wills 2	1837-1857	221
Holman, B. O.	Wilcox	Wills 5	1855-1870	142
Holman, L. B.	Marengo	Wills A	1820-1864	222
Holman, Robert	Coosa	W&PM A	1834-1842	446
Holmes, Anderson	Perry	Wills B	1858-1873	333
Holmes, Benjamin	Perry	Wills B	1858-1873	277
Holmes, Hannah	Perry	Wills B	1858-1873	325
Holmes, Henry	Montgomery	Wills 4	1853-1869	534
Holmes, Jesse	Dallas	Wills B	1850-1871	185
Holmes, Mrs. Mildred	Perry	Wills A	1821-1855	267
Holmes, Richard	Madison	W&I	1810-1820	126
Holmes, Thomas	Lauderdale	Wills B	1859-1870	148
Holmes, Thomas G.	Baldwin	Wills A	1811-1881	123
Holms, Samuel	Perry	Wills B	1858-1873	193
Holstein, William	Chambers	Wills 1-2	1833-1856	231
Holstien, William	Chambers	Wills 1-2	1833-1856	336
Holt, Cadar	Marengo	Wills A	1820-1864	261
Holt, Charles W.	Chambers	Wills 3	1856-1899	126
Holt, Elbert A.	Montgomery	Wills 4	1853-1869	520
Holt, Hines, Sr.	Russell	Wills 1	1838-1849	81
Holt, John, Sr.	Chambers	Wills 1-2	1833-1856	381
Holt, Lewis	Clarke	PR N	1866-1870	360
Holt, Mary P.	Macon	Records 3	1845-1850	483
Holt, Meredith E.	Lauderdale	Wills B	1859-1870	186
Holt, Rebecca	Montgomery	Wills 5	1863-1887	90
Holt, William	Barbour	OCR 3	1847-1851	327
Holtam, E. S.	Clarke	PR N	1866-1870	379
Holton, William H.	Henry	OCR N	1862-1864	236
Holzworth, John	Madison	Wills 1	1853-1875	318
Hood, Bold Robin	Barbour	OCR 6	1854-1856	284
Hood, James	Lauderdale	Wills A	1835-1858	66
Hood, John M.	Lauderdale	Wills B	1859-1870	132
Hood, Mary A.	Lauderdale	Wills B	1859-1870	79
Hood, Robert	Dallas	Wills B	1850-1871	253
Hood, Samuel	Lauderdale	Wills B	1859-1870	276
Hood, Stephen W.	Chambers	Wills 3	1856-1899	213
Hood, Thomas	Dallas	Wills B	1850-1871	149
Hood, Thomas	Limestone	Wills 3	1826-1831	110
Hooe, Nathaniel Harris	Tuscaloosa	Deeds U		390
Hooks, George	Pike	Wills A	1845-1862	204
Hooks, Robert	Lawrence	I&W D	1835-1840	144

TESTATOR	COUNTY	WHERE FOUND		PAGE
Hooks, Susan	Sumter	Wills	2	1851-1872	110
Hooks, Tabitha	Macon	Records	6	1855-1858	176
Hooks, Thomas	Monroe	W&D	A	1833-1841	194
Hooper, Amelia V.	Lowndes	Wills	B	1830-1859	260
Hooper, Hugh	Greene	Wills	A	1821-1826	43
Hooper, John	Dallas	Wills	A	1821-1849	336
Hooper, Thomas B.	Greene	Wills	C	1840-1864	170
Hoot, H. C.	Dallas	Wills	B	1850-1871	302
Hooten, Henry	Pike	Wills	A	1845-1862	65
Hope, James A.	Clarke	PR	H	1854-1856	465
Hope, John	Clarke	PR	M	1864-1866	428
Hopkins, Arthur F.	Mobile	Wills	3	1857-1870	467
Hopkins, Hardy	Greene	Wills	B	1817-1841	54
Hopkins, Joseph	Greene	Wills	C	1840-1864	70
Hopkins, L. G.	Russell	Wills	2	1850-1873	278
Hopkins, Moses	Dallas	Wills	A	1821-1849	271
Hopper, George	Perry	Wills	B	1858-1873	259
Hopper, Mrs. Malinda J.	Perry	Wills	A	1821-1855	335
Horn, John	Marengo	Wills	A	1820-1864	427
Horn, John	Sumter	Wills	1	1828-1851	127
Horn, John I.?	Mobile	Wills	2	1837-1857	47
Horn, John W.	Sumter	Wills	1	1828-1851	189
Horne, Delitha	Mobile	Wills	2	1837-1857	440
Horne, Harris	Sumter	Wills	1	1828-1851	242
Horne, John	Montgomery	Wills	4	1853-1869	96
Horsefelt, John H.	Mobile	Wills	2	1837-1857	280
Horton, Archibald	Etowah	Wills	A	1866-1870	10
Horton, Edmund	Chambers	Wills	1-2	1833-1856	126
Horton, Jesse	DeKalb	Wills	A	1837-1863	3
Horton, George	Madison	Wills	1	1853-1875	206
Horton, James M.	Coosa	W&OCR	2	1843-1883	83
Horton, Lucy A. M.	Madison	Wills	1	1853-1875	286
Hottinguer, Jean Henri	Mobile	Wills	3	1857-1870	509
Houpt, Sebastian	Sumter	Wills	1	1828-1851	26
House, Isaac	Marengo	Wills	A	1820-1864	321
House, James	Madison	PR	4	1826-1829	245
House, John	Lauderdale	Wills	A	1835-1858	178
House, William	Coosa	W&OCR	2	1843-1883	21
House, (Mrs.) Winniford C.	Madison	Wills	1	1853-1875	38
Houseman, E.	Dallas	Wills	B	1850-1871	411
Houser, Churchill H.	Autauga	Wills	1	1862-1925	13
Houser, Ellen G.	Autauga	Wills	1	1862-1925	14
Houser, Lewis	Autauga	Reports	H	1853-1857	650
Houstan, David	Lauderdale	Wills	A	1835-1858	26
Houston, Mrs. Ann	Perry	Wills	A	1821-1855	143
Houston, Erastus L.	Sumter	Wills	2	1851-1872	263
Houston, Fanny T.	Madison	Wills	1	1853-1875	381
Houston, George V.	Jackson	Records		1861-1881	320
Houston, John	Sumter	Wills	1	1828-1851	340
Houston, Lewis T.	Autauga	DM&R	17	1820-1864	90
Houston, William	Perry	Wills	A	1821-1855	298

TESTATOR	COUNTY	WHERE FOUND		PAGE
Howard, Allen	Tuscaloosa	Wills 1	1821-1855	339
Howard, Annie	Macon	WAC&A 11	1862-1870	694
Howard, E. D.	Sumter	Wills 2	1851-1872	414
Howard, Elizabeth	Madison	PR 8	1831-1839	124
Howard, Horton	Madison	PR 7	1834-1837	177
Howard, James M.	Dallas	Wills B	1850-1871	56
Howard, John	Macon	Records 2	1838-1842	19
Howard, John H.	Barbour	OCR 13	1861-1864	16
Howard, Joseph	Macon	Records 3	1845-1850	127
Howard, Luke	Talladega	Wills A	1833-1839	155
Howard, Mariana	Madison	PR 9	1839-1841	497
Howard, Mark	Autauga	Reports G	1850-1853	397
Howard, Penelope	Madison	PR 10	1842-1842	117
Howard, Ralph O.	Russell	Wills 2	1850-1873	401
Howard, Robert H.	Macon	WAC&A 11	1862-1870	582
Howard, Samuel	Perry	Wills A	1821-1855	141
Howard, Stephen	Lauderdale	Wills B	1859-1870	435
Howard, Thomas S.	Madison	Deeds A	1810-1816	165
Howard, William	Madison	PR 12	1845-1849	195
Howe, Charles	Baldwin	Wills A	1811-1881	211
Howel, Ira E.	Marengo	Wills A	1820-1864	292
Howell, Caleb	Baldwin	Wills A	1811-1881	34
Howell, Eliza D.	Lowndes	Wills B	1830-1859	207
Howell, Joseph	Chambers	Wills 1-2	1833-1856	386
Howell, Levi	Lauderdale	Wills A	1835-1858	127
Howell, Lewis	Perry	Wills A	1821-1855	98
Howell, Mihill	Lawrence	I&W A	1850-1857	311
Howell, Patton	Lauderdale	Wills B	1859-1870	77
Howell, Thomas J.	Dallas	Wills B	1850-1871	229
Howell, William H.	Mobile	Wills 1	1813-1837	126
Howes, Daniel M.	Mobile	Wills 1	1813-1837	192
Howes, Malchus R.	Mobile	Wills 1	1813-1837	202
Howes, Sarah	Mobile	Wills 3	1857-1870	461
Howie, Samuel	Dallas	Wills A	1821-1849	63
Howland, Wing	Mobile	Wills 1	1813-1837	222
Howle, William A.	Cleburne	Wills 1	1866-1884	116
Howlett, Eliza G.	Perry	Wills A	1821-1855	272
Howson, John	Madison	Deeds C	1816-1818	103
Howson, Richard	Madison	Deeds C	1810-1816	81
Howson, Sarah	Madison	Ma	1816-1818	104
Howze, James	Chambers	Wills 1-2	1833-1856	230
Howze, James A.	Clarke	PR L	1861-1864	191
Hoxey, Asa	Montgomery	Wills 2	1820-1845	75
Hrabowski, H. R.	Lowndes	Wills B	1830-1859	224
Hrabowski, Thomas S.	Lowndes	Wills B	1830-1859	91
Hubbard, Abner	Perry	Wills B	1858-1873	170
Hubbard, James H.	Coosa	W&OCR 2	1843-1883	332
Hubbard, Thomas	Morgan	OCR 7	1837-1843	315
Huber, John Henry	Mobile	Wills 3	1857-1870	319
Huckabee, William T.	Marengo	Wills A	1820-1864	280
Huddleston, James	Autauga	Reports A	1825-1830	236

TESTATOR	COUNTY	WHERE FOUND		PAGE
Huddleston, Joseph	Dallas	Wills A	1821-1849	30
Huder, L. H.	Mobile	Wills 2	1837-1857	41
Hudgens, L. T.	Tuscaloosa	Wills 3	1858-1865	187
Hudgins, John W.	Barbour	OCR 14	1863-1865	180
Hudson, Abner	Perry	Wills B	1858-1873	354
Hudson, Charles O.	Limestone	Wills 11	1865-1866	32
Hudson, Isaac, Sr.	Lowndes	Wills B	1830-1859	7
Hudson, James G.	Perry	Wills B	1858-1873	214
Hudson, John H.	Calhoun	Loose	Probated 1846	
Hudson, Joseph	Greene	Wills A	1821-1827	24
Hudson, Lamech	Wilcox	Wills 1	1821-1844	433
Hudson, Robert	Calhoun	Loose	Probated 1849	
Hudson, W. Y.	Calhoun	Loose	Probated 1854	
Hudson, William Sen.	Marengo	Wills A	1820-1864	497
Huff, James	Russell	Wills 1	1838-1849	110
Hufman, S. H.	Montgomery	Wills 4	1853-1869	408
Hugeley,? Rowland	Lowndes	Wills B	1830-1859	121
Huggins, Burrel	Clarke	OCR	1825-1832	313
Hughes, Abner	Tallapoosa	Wills 1	1838-1866	181
Hughes, Agrippa A.	Madison	PR 12	1845-1849	306
Hughes, Ann Eliza.	Dallas	Wills B	1850-1871	354
Hughes, Charles J.	Macon	Records 2	1838-1842	38
Hughes, Daniel	Tuscaloosa	Wills 3	1858-1865	76
Hughes, Elizabeth	Montgomery	Wills 2	1820-1845	158
Hughes, George C. P.	Calhoun	Loose	Probated 1855	
Hughes, John	Montgomery	Wills 2	1820-1845	84
Hughes, Stephen T.	Coosa	W&OCR 2	1843-1883	245
Hughs, A. B.	Etowah	Wills A	1866-1870	2
Hughston, William F.	Talladega	W&I A	1852-1857	154
Hugon, Constance	Mobile	Wills 2	1837-1857	129
Huguenin, Sarah C.	Russell	Wills 2	1850-1873	233
Hull, Adam	Greene	Wills C	1840-1864	760
Hull, Thomas J.	Coosa	W&OCR 2	1843-1883	326
Humber, John	Tuscaloosa	Wills 1	1821-1855	328
Humphrey, Pheraba C.	Lowndes	Wills B	1830-1859	205
Humphries, L. B.	Sumter	Wills 2	1851-1872	398
Hunley, Ransom G.	Lowndes	Wills B	1830-1859	136
Hunly, Lucy	Lowndes	Wills B	1830-1859	366
Hunt, George	Coosa	W&OCR 2	1843-1883	86
Hunt, George W.	Chambers	Wills 1-2	1833-1856	279
Hunt, Isaiah	Jefferson	OCR	1824-1831	97
Hunt, Jonathan	Mobile	Wills 2	1837-1857	159
Hunt, Ralph S.	Greene	Wills D	1851-1888	85
Hunt, William	Coosa	W&OCR 2	1843-1883	141
Hunt, William R.	Madison	Wills 1	1853-1875	65
Hunter, Benjamin P.	Greene	Wills D	1851-1888	206
Hunter, C. D.	Clarke	PR L	1861-1864	141
Hunter, Charles D.	Clarke	PR M	1864-1866	213
Hunter, Clinton	Lowndes	Wills C	1861-1899	59
Hunter, Eleazor E.	Chambers	Wills 3	1856-1899	229
Hunter, Elizabeth S.	Dallas	Wills B	1850-1871	84

TESTATOR	COUNTY	WHERE FOUND		PAGE
Hunter, Elizabeth S.	Dallas	Wills B	1850-1871	298
Hunter, Elizabeth S.	Wilcox	Wills 3	1826-1858	155
Hunter, Mary H.	Dallas	Wills B	1850-1871	236
Hunter, William	Dallas	Wills B	1850-1871	102
Hurley, Thomas	Lawrence	I&W D	1835-1840	553
Hurley, William	Greene	Wills C	1840-1864	160
Hurst, Henry	Russell	Wills 2	1850-1873	22
Hurst, John A.	Chambers	Wills 3	1856-1899	83
Hurt, Joel, Sr.	Russell	Wills 1	1838-1849	81
Hurt, Martha	Russell	Wills 2	1850-1873	295
Hurt, William	Russell	Wills 1	1838-1849	149
Hurtel, Eliza	Mobile	Wills 3	1857-1870	571
Hurtel, Peter?	Greene	Wills A	1821-1827	36
Hurtt, John	Pike	Wills A	1845-1862	12
Huskabee?, James Johnston	Greene	Wills C	1840-1864	380
Hussey, Elijah	Madison	PR 2&5	1818-1826	541
Hussey, Stephen	Madison	PR 6	1832-1834	536
Hutchens, Thomas H.	Sumter	Wills 1	1828-1851	183
Hutcheson, Washington	Sumter	Wills 2	1851-1872	148
Hutching, Andrew J.	Lauderdale	Wills A	1835-1858	99
Hutchings, John	Madison	W&I	1810-1820	1
Hutchins, James L.	Sumter	Wills 2	1851-1872	418
Hutchinson, John	Tallapoosa	Wills 1	1838-1866	81
Hutchison, William	Tuscaloosa	Wills 1	1821-1855	33
Hutchison, Andrew	Clarke	PR L	1861-1864	519
Hutchison, Joseph	Montgomery	Wills 2	1820-1845	296
Hutchisson, James F.	Mobile	Wills 2	1837-1857	428
Hutson, Robert	Calhoun	Loose	Probated 1844	
Hutton, Aquilla D.	Greene	Wills C	1840-1864	311
Hyatt, Susan E. A.	Mobile	Wills 3	1857-1870	591
Ice, Nancy	Madison	PR 9	1839-1841	573
Ice, Thomas	Marshall	FR 6	1859-1867	599
Inge, John J.	Tuscaloosa	Wills 1	1821-1855	5
Inge, Richard, Sr.	Tuscaloosa	Wills 1	1821-1855	67
Ingram, Elizabeth	Chambers	Wills 1-2	1833-1856	338
Ingram, George	Russell	Wills 2	1850-1873	229
Ingram, Hezekiah Bussey	Calhoun	Loose	Probated 1838	
Ingram, John C.	Coosa	W&OCR 2	1843-1883	203
Ingram, Lemuel	Russell	Wills 2	1850-1873	14
Ingram, Martha C.	Dallas	Wills B	1850-1871	289
Ingram, Moses	Lauderdale	Wills B	1859-1870	69
Ingram, Samuel	Montgomery	Wills 2	1820-1845	221
Inman, John R.	Madison	PR 8	1831-1839	100
Inman, Isaac	Madison	PR 9	1839-1841	276
Inman, Isaac	Madison	PR 9	1839-1841	294
Ingersol, William J.	Mobile	Wills 2	1837-1857	43
Innerasity,? James	Mobile	Wills 2	1837-1857	233
Intone, John	Mobile	Wills 1	1813-1837	255

TESTATOR	COUNTY	WHERE FOUND		PAGE
Irby, Ann	Madison	PR 3	1823-1826	42
Irby, Ann	Wilcox	Wills 1	1821-1844	308
Irby, Edmond	Madison	Wills 1	1853-1875	193
Irby, John K.	Marengo	Wills A	1820-1864	10
Irby, Josiah E.	Wilcox	Wills 5	1855-1870	452
Irby, Mary G.	Madison	Wills 1	1853-1875	398
Irby, Moses	Sumter	Wills 1	1828-1851	346
Irby, Rebecca Ann	Wilcox	Wills 1	1821-1844	335
Irby, Susan E.	Madison	Wills 1	1810-1820	78
Irvin, Thomas	Mobile	Wills 2	1837-1857	66
Irvin, Mary	Henry	OCR M	1861-1862	140
Irvin, William	Henry	OCR F	1848-1853	251
Irvin, William	Henry	OCR F	1848-1853	123
Irving, Margaret	Mobile	Wills 3	1857-1870	39
Irwin, Alfred F.	Mobile	Wills 3	1857-1870	582
Irwin, Eliza A.	Mobile	Wills 4	1870-1878	100
Irwin, Joseph	Mobile	Wills 2	1837-1857	271
Irwin, S. B.	Morgan	FR 18	1859-1860	227
Irwin, Samuel P.	Talladega	W&I D	1867-1880	690
Isaacs, John W.	Jefferson	Wills A	1856-1880	181
Isbell, James	Clarke	PR G	1867-1880	410
Isbell, James	Talladega	W&I D	1867-1800	328
Isbell, Mrs. Rutelia	Talladega	W&I D	1867-1880	482
Ives, John	Madison	PR 6	1832-1834	81
Ives, John	Mobile	Wills 2	1837-1857	402
Ivey, Adams	Montgomery	Wills 2	1820-1845	148
Ivey, Bama	Macon	Records 6	1855-1858	385
Ivey, Benjamin	Sumter	Wills 2	1851-1872	153
Ivey, Elijah	Lowndes	Wills B	1830-1859	78
Ivey, John J.	Montgomery	Wills 4	1853-1869	309
Ivey, Robert	Barbour	OCR 13	1861-1867	37
Ivey, William	Lowndes	Wills B	1830-1859	289
Ivey, William E.	Dallas	Wills B	1850-1871	158
Ivy, Charles	Sumter	Wills 1	1828-1841	248
Ivie, Elisha	Perry	Wills B	1858-1873	411
Ivy, Henry	Perry	Wills B	1858-1873	407
Ivy, Turner	Dallas	Wills A	1821-1849	141
Jack, Jane Bowie	Talladega	Wills C	1845-1853	390
Jack, John	Mobile	Wills 4	1870-1878	53
Jack, Samuel A.	Talladega	W&I B	1858-1864	502
Jacks, (Mrs.) Ann Leslie	Talladega	W&I C	1862-1866	218
Jacks, James K.	Jefferson	Wills A	1856-1880	342
Jacks, John	Coosa	W&OCR 2	1843-1883	236
Jackson, A. D.	Macon	WAC&A 11	1862-1870	743
Jackson, Absolom	Chambers	Wills 1-2	1833-1856	117
Jackson, Absalom	Elmore	Wills A	1866-1906	35
Jackson, Alexander	Lauderdale	Wills B	1859-1870	182
Jackson, Alexander	Pike	Wills A	1845-1862	115

TESTATOR	COUNTY	WHERE FOUND		PAGE
Jackson, Benjamin	Lauderdale	Wills A	1835-1858	121
Jackson, Blake	Perry	Wills A	1821-1855	51
Jackson, Coleby	Madison	PR 4	1826-1829	22
Jackson, David A.	Calhoun	Loose	Probated 1847	
Jackson, Edwin	Perry	Wills A	1821-1855	354
Jackson, Green	Perry	Wills A	1821-1855	247
Jackson, Isaac	Madison	PR 2&5	1818-1826	409
Jackson, James	Autauga	Reports B	1829-1833	286
Jackson, James	Lauderdale	Wills A	1835-1858	73
Jackson, James	Marengo	Wills A	1820-1864	259
Jackson, James	Perry	W&I	1823-1833	47
Jackson, James	Perry	Wills A	1821-1855	13
Jackson, Jasen	Sumter	Wills 2	1851-1872	392
Jackson, Jefferson F.	Montgomery	Wills 4	1853-1869	357
Jackson, Jeremiah	Macon	Records 10	1863-1865	3
Jackson, Jesse	Tallapoosa	Wills 1	1838-1866	59
Jackson, Jesse M.	Chambers	Wills 1-2	1833-1856	466
Jackson, John	Marengo	Wills A	1820-1864	446
Jackson, John A.	Wilcox	Wills 5	1855-1870	137
Jackson, John F.	Greene	Wills C	1840-1864	508
Jackson, John Y.	Perry	Wills B	1858-1873	73
Jackson, Joseph	Perry	Wills B	1858-1870	244
Jackson, Lewis	Wilcox	Wills 3	1826-1858	118
Jackson, Mark	Russell	Wills 2	1850-1873	113
Jackson, Martha E.	Marengo	Wills A	1820-1864	548
Jackson, Mary	Clarke	PR E	1840-1845	17
Jackson, Nathan	Dallas	Wills A	1821-1849	26
Jackson, Robert	Chambers	Wills 1-2	1833-1856	303
Jackson, Temperance	Autauga	Wills 1	1862-1925	25
Jackson, Wilkins	Perry	Wills A	1821-1855	356
Jackson, William	Perry	Wills A	1821-1855	76A
Jackson, William F.	Macon	Records 6	1855-1858	297
Jackson, Wyche	Chambers	Wills 1-2	1833-1856	415
Jackson, Zanetta Mary	Macon	Records 7	1857-1859	100
Jacob, George	Lowndes	Wills B	1830-1859	22
Jacob, Mordecai	Chambers	Wills 1-2	1833-1856	309
Jacobs, Henry H.	Mobile	Wills 1	1813-1837	270
Jacobs, Capt. John	DeKalb	Wills A	1837-1863	15
Jacobs, Josiah	Coosa	W&OCR 2	1843-1883	134
Jacobs, Mordeca	Chambers	Wills 3	1856-1899	358
Jaggers, Daniel P.	Limestone	Wills 3	1826-1831	395
Jamar, Richard	Madison	Wills 1	1853-1875	483
James, Frederick	Bibb	Adm.R I	1858-1865	460
James, Frederick	Bibb	Loose	Dated1863	
James, John	Madison	PR 2	1818-1823	38
James, M. M.	Greene	Wills C	1840-1864	740
James, Mary	Clarke	OCR F	1846-1850	350
James, Mary	Pike	Wills A	1845-1862	178
James, Robert B.	Montgomery	Wills 3	1840-1854	80
James, Robert D.	Clarke	PR K	1858-1861	526
James, Thomas E.	Sumter	Wills 2	1851-1872	234

TESTATOR	COUNTY	WHERE FOUND		PAGE
James, Westwood W.	Lawrence	I&W	C	1866-1880	16
James, William	Sumter	Wills	1	1828-1851	6
Janatt, Thomas K.	Montgomery	Wills	3	1840-1854	133
Jarmon, Amos	Lawrence	I&W	C	1866-1880	392
Jarman, Thomas	Sumter	Wills	2	1851-1872	395
Jarrell, John S.	Chambers	Wills	3	1856-1899	6
Jarvis, Patrick F.	Chambers	Wills	1-2	1833-1856	363
Jay, Alvah	Greene	Wills	B	1817-1841	263
Jay, David	Conecuh	OB	A	1865-1870	95
Jay, John	Monroe	W&D	B	1833-1870	470
Jayrol, James	Montgomery	Wills	4	1853-1869	116
Jeandreau, John	Mobile	Wills	1	1813-1837	75
Jefcoat, Elijah	Pike	Wills	A	1845-1862	163
Jeffreys, James B.	Autauga	Reports	F	1845-1850	586
Jeffries, Alexander	Madison	PR	8	1831-1839	394
Jeffries, John	Elmore	Wills	A	1866-1906	18
Jeffries, Rolin	Tuscaloosa	Wills	3	1858-1865	98
Jelks, Robert	Russell	Wills	1	1838-1849	97
Jelton, Robert	Tuscaloosa	Deeds	U		161
Jemison, Humphrey	Perry	Wills	B	1858-1873	9
Jemison, John S.	Sumter	Wills	1	1828-1851	220
Jemison, Mims	Tuscaloosa	Wills	1	1821-1855	93
Jemison, Nancy	Perry	Wills	B	1858-1873	140
Jemison, Samuel	Perry	Wills	A	1821-1855	304
Jemison, Samuel	Talladega	W&I	B	1858-1864	584
Jenkins, Alexander	Henry	Deeds	A-B	1822-1840	155
Jenkins, Elizabeth	Lauderdale	Wills	A	1835-1858	314
Jenkins, James	Tuscaloosa	Wills	1	1821-1855	79
Jenkins, John	Wilcox	Wills	3	1826-1858	244
Jenkins, Joseph	Wilcox	Wills	1	1821-1844	114
Jenkins, Martha	Wilcox	Wills	5	1855-1870	115
Jenkins, Milton	Etowah	Wills	A	1866-1870	13
Jenkins, Richard	Sumter	Wills	2	1851-1872	173
Jenkins, Tempe	Barbour	OCR	3	1847-1851	350
Jenkins, Thomas	Lauderdale	Wills	B	1859-1870	419
Jenkins, Thomas	Lauderdale	Wills	4	1821-1825	73
Jenkins, William, Sr.	Talladega	W&I	A	1852-1857	31
Jenkins, William	Talladega	W&I	C	1862-1866	254
Jenkins, William S.	Talladega	W&I	A	1852-1857	122
Jenness, Nathaniel E.	Mobile	Wills	2	1837-1857	426
Jennings, Henry H.	Montgomery	Wills	4	1853-1869	360
Jennings, James	Tuscaloosa	Wills	3	1858-1865	13
Jennings, Stephen	Lauderdale	Wills	A	1835-1858	61
Jennings, William H.	Coosa	W&OCR	2	1843-1883	17
Jeter, James W.	Coosa	W&OCR	2	1843-1883	154
Jeter, Sarah	Chambers	Wills	3	1856-1899	50
Jeter, Sarah W.	Sumter	Wills	2	1851-1872	8
Jewett, Orgon S.	Clarke	PR	L	1861-1864	120
Jinkens, Elizabeth	Marengo	Wills	A	1820-1864	239
Johns, Robert	Chambers	Wills	3	1856-1899	79
John, Samuel W.	Perry	Wills	B	1858-1873	14

TESTATOR	COUNTY	WHERE FOUND		PAGE
Johns, Thomas	Cleburne	Wills 1	1866-1884	84
Johns, William	Chambers	Wills 3	1856-1899	171
Johnson, Agnes	Madison	PR 3	1823-1826	7
Johnson, Andrew N.	Barbour	OCR 2	1842-1847	380
Johnson, Ann	Tuscaloosa	Wills 1	1821-1855	49
Johnson, B.	Dallas	Wills A	1821-1849	210
Johnson, Burrell H.	Lowndes	Wills C	1861-1899	22
Johnson, Bushrod	Madison	PR 2	1818-1823	519
Johnson, Claiborne	Perry	Wills A	1821-1855	76
Johnson, David	Morgan	OCR 7	1837-1843	457
Johnson, Duncan	Jefferson	Wills 1	1818-1840	80
Johnson, Elizabeth	Bibb	Admr.R 1	1858-1865	459
Johnson, Elizabeth	Bibb	Loose	Dated 1864	
Johnson, Elizabeth	Sumter	Wills 1	1828-1851	327
Johnson, Enoch	Russell	Wills 2	1850-1873	252
Johnson, Ephraim O.	Mobile	Wills 3	1857-1870	31
Johnson, Francis C.	Dallas	Wills B	1850-1871	8
Johnson, George C.	Dallas	Wills B	1850-1871	410
Johnson, Henrietta	Jackson	Records	1861-1881	409
Johnson, Henry	Morgan	OCR 6	1831-1837	367
Johnson, James F.	Limestone	Wills 12	1866-1872	322
Johnson, Jessie	Macon	Records 3	1845-1850	490
Johnson, Jimmie	Dallas	Wills B	1850-1871	425
Johnson, John	Lauderdale	Wills 3	1821-1825	130
Johnson, John	Tuscaloosa	Wills 1	1821-1855	71
Johnson, John A.	Pike	Wills A	1845-1862	135
Johnson, John P.	Madison	Wills 1	1853-1875	61
Johnson, John R.	Montgomery	Wills 3	1840-1854	90
Johnson, Joseph	Washington	Wills B	1827-	49
Johnson, Joseph	Washington	Wills 1 ∅	1827-1888	74
Johnson, Joshua	Marshall	FR 1 (old)	1840-1844	246
Johnson, Lewis	Monroe	W&D D	1833-1870	280
Johnson, Mathew	Jefferson	PM	1848-1853	222
Johnson, Rachael	St. Clair	Deeds C	1846-1855	204
Johnson, Richard	Greene	Wills B	1817-1841	265
Johnson, Robert S.	Henry	OCR L	1860-1861	361
Johnson, Rosannah	Madison	Wills 1	1853-1875	50
Johnson, Samuel, Sr.	Limestone	Wills 4	1831-1837	139
Johnson, Sankey T.	Tallapoosa	Wills 1	1838-1866	26
Johnson, Sarah	Greene	Wills C	1840-1864	86
Johnson, Thomas H.	Sumter	Wills 2	1851-1872	274
Johnson, William	Butler	Wills 1	1853-1864	259
Johnson, William	Shelby	Wills K	1849	1
Johnson, William A.	Chambers	Wills 3	1856-1899	200
Johnson, William E.	Madison	PR 8	1831-1839	253
Johnson, Woodford A.	Montgomery	Wills 4	1853-1869	160
Johnston, Catherine	Bibb	Loose	Dated 1837	
Johnston, Clara	Washington	Wills 1 ∅	1827-1888	99
Johnston, Clara	Washington	Wills B	1827-	63
Johnston, Colyer	Calhoun	Loose	Probated 1844	
Johnston, Daniel	Calhoun	Loose	Probated 1851	

TESTATOR	COUNTY	WHERE FOUND		PAGE
Johnston, David	Macon	WAC&A 11	1862-1870	338
Johnston, David	Tuscaloosa	Wills 1	1821-1855	275
Johnston, George	Greene	Wills B	1817-1841	100
Johnston, George W.	Washington	Wills 1 Ø	1827-1888	139
Johnston, George W.	Washington	Wills B	1827-	89
Johnston, Isham	Barbour	OCR 2	1842-1847	295
Johnston, Jabez	Macon	Records 3	1845-1850	748
Johnston, James	Washington	Wills 1 Ø	1827-1888	142
Johnston, James	Washington	Wills B	1827-	90
Johnston, John	Greene	Wills C	1840-1864	59
Johnston, John	Madison	PR 6	1832-1834	494
Johnston, John	Mobile	Wills 1	1813-1837	58
Johnston, John	Montgomery	Wills 2	1820-1845	256
Johnston, John	Montgomery	Wills 4	1853-1869	311
Johnston, Joseph	Washington	Wills 1 Ø	1827-1888	74
Johnston, Joseph	Washington	Wills B	1827-	49
Johnston, Juliette	Greene	Wills C	1840-1864	409
Johnston, Mary	Barbour	OCR 7	1854-1857	501
Johnston, Robert	Mobile	Wills 3	1857-1870	522
Johnston, Thomas J.	Madison	PR 6	1832-1834	414
Johnston, Thomas J.	Madison	PR 6	1832-1834	464
Johnston, Thomas M.	Hale	Wills A	1867-1923	53
Johnston, V. J.	Dallas	Wills B	1850-1871	422
Johnston, William	Madison	Wills 1	1853-1875	355
Johnston, William	Mobile	Wills 2	1837-1857	92
Johnston, William B.	Greene	Wills C	1840-1864	540
Johnston, Woodford A.	Montgomery	Wills 4	1853-1869	160
Joiner, Elizabeth	Lowndes	Wills B	1830-1859	67
Joiner, Sarah	Lowndes	Wills B	1830-1859	96
Jones, Abner B.	St. Clair	RE D	1859-1867	605
Jones, Abram J.	Conecuh	OB A	1865-1870	304
Jones, Alford	Montgomery	Wills 4	1853-1869	296
Jones, Alpheus G.	Montgomery	Wills 3	1840-1854	275
Jones, Arthur W.	Madison	PR 6	1832-1834	362
Jones, Asenath	Montgomery	Wills 5	1863-1887	14
Jones, Benjamin A.	Sumter	Wills 2	1851-1872	161
Jones, Britton	Pike	Wills A	1845-1862	167
Jones, Cadwallader	Greene	Wills D	1851-1888	160
Jones, Charles M.	Madison	PR 3	1823-1826	336-3
Jones, Daniel	Perry	Wills A	1821-1855	11
Jones, David	Lauderdale	Wills B	1859-1870	9
Jones, David	Perry	W&I	1823-1833	1
Jones, David C.	Perry	Wills A	1821-1855	239
Jones, Edmund	Greene	Wills C	1840-1864	431
Jones, Edward S.	Dallas	Wills B	1850-1871	180
Jones, Eliza Jane	Montgomery	Wills 4	1853-1869	180
Jones, Francis	Mobile	Wills 3	1857-1870	249
Jones, Franklin	Madison	PR 4	1826-1829	286
Jones, Frily	Sumter	Wills 2	1851-1872	233
Jones, Gabriel	Sumter	Wills 1	1828-1851	168
Jones, Garner	Baldwin	Wills A	1811-1881	256

TESTATOR	COUNTY	WHERE FOUND		PAGE
Jones, George T.	Madison	Wills 1	1853-1875	453
Jones, Hamilton	Clarke	PR E	1840-1845	292
Jones, Hardy	Chambers	Wills 1-2	1833-1856	334
Jones, Hardy	Limestone	Wills 7	1844-1847	243
Jones, Hardy	Tallapoosa	Wills 1	1838-1866	32
Jones, Harwood	Perry	Wills A	1821-1855	74
Jones, Henry, Sr.	Barbour	OCR 4	1850-1852	120
Jones, Henry G.	Greene	Wills D	1851-1888	190
Jones, Humphrey	Perry	Wills A	1821-1855	341
Jones, J. H. Y.	Limestone	Wills 5	1836-1841	425
Jones, J. S.	Pike	Wills B	1862-1879	77
Jones, James	Chambers	Wills 1-2	1833-1856	197
Jones, James	Greene	Wills D	1851-1888	474
Jones, James	Mobile	Wills 2	1837-1857	23
Jones, James	St. Clair	RE A	1858-1874	325
Jones, James E.	Sumter	Wills 1	1828-1851	93
Jones, James F.	Greene	Wills D	1851-1888	210
Jones, James H.	Wilcox	Wills 3	1826-1858	269
Jones, James T.	Butler	Wills 2	1864-1875	73
Jones, James W.	Sumter	Wills 2	1851-1872	213
Jones, Jeremiah	Wilcox	Wills 5	1855-1870	441
Jones, Joel W.	Madison	PR 4	1826-1829	35
Jones, John	Dallas	Wills A	1821-1849	109
Jones, John	Lauderdale	Wills A	1835-1858	109
Jones, John	Lauderdale	Wills B	1859-1870	15
Jones, John	Madison	PR 4	1826-1829	317
Jones, John	Perry	Wills A	1821-1855	8
Jones, John C.	Wilcox	Wills 5	1855-1870	123
Jones, John W.	Limestone	Wills 7	1844-1847	162
Jones, Jonathan	Bibb	Adm.R D	1830-1838	116
Jones, Jonathan	Bibb	Loose	Dated 1833	
Jones, Joseph	Butler	Wills 1	1853-1864	106
Jones, Joshua	Montgomery	Wills 4	1853-1869	538
Jones, Len H.	Tuscaloosa	Wills 1	1821-1855	358
Jones, Lewellen	Madison	PR 2	1818-1823	42
Jones, Lewellen	Madison	PR 2	1818-1823	106
Jones, Lewellen	Madison	PR 4	1826-1829	410
Jones, Lewis	Autauga	Wills 1	1862-1925	4
Jones, Martha	Morgan	OCR 8	1844-1848	300
Jones, Martha A.	Perry	Wills A	1821-1855	160
Jones, Martha Eliz.	Mobile	Wills 2	1837-1857	42
Jones, Mary	Dallas	Wills A	1821-1849	110
Jones, Mary	Wilcox	Wills 4	1847-1862	235
Jones, Nancy	Dallas	Wills A	1821-1849	32
Jones, Nancy	Madison	PR 8	1831-1839	154
Jones, Nathan	Madison	W&I	1810-1820	141
Jones, Nathaniel S.	Autauga	Reports H	1853-1857	666
Jones, Oscar M.	Perry	Wills A	1821-1855	81
Jones, Rachel M.	Perry	Wills B	1858-1873	345
Jones, Randall	Barbour	OCR 12	1861-1863	512
Jones, Reuben	Tuscaloosa	Wills 1	1821-1855	89

TESTATOR	COUNTY	WHERE FOUND		PAGE
Jones, Sallie	Dallas	Wills	B	1850-1871	293
Jones, Samuel	Barbour	OCR	5	1852-1853	45
Jones, Samuel	Barbour	OCR	14	1863-1865	363
Jones, Samuel L.	Wilcox	Wills	5	1855-1870	271
Jones, Seaborn	Lowndes	Wills	B	1830-1859	388
Jones, Stephen	Wilcox	Wills	2	1832-1850	282
Jones, Stephen J.	Wilcox	Wills	4	1847-1862	264
Jones, Susannah	Marengo	Wills	A	1820-1864	334
Jones, Syrena	Sumter	Wills	2	1851-1872	264
Jones, T. Booth	Colbert	Wills	A	1861-1903	9
Jones, Thomas, Sr.	Lowndes	Wills	B	1830-1859	41
Jones, Thomas	Madison	PR	2	1818-1823	215
Jones, Thomas E.	Limestone	Wills	3	1826-1831	107
Jones, Thomas J? B.	Dallas	Wills	B	1850-1871	303
Jones, Thomas T.	Perry	Wills	B	1858-1873	163
Jones, Thomas W.	Greene	Wills	B	1817-1841	177
Jones, Thomas W.	Wilcox	Wills	3	1826-1858	301
Jones, Vincent	Shelby	Wills	B	1818-1840	178
Jones, Walter	Mobile	Wills	3	1857-1870	310
Jones, Whitmore	Lauderdale	Wills	A	1835-1858	174
Jones, Wiley	Wilcox	Wills	1	1821-1844	302
Jones, William, Jr.	Baldwin	Wills	A	1811-1881	156
Jones, William	Dallas	Wills	A	1821-1849	21
Jones, William	Greene	Wills	C	1840-1864	141
Jones, William	Macon	Records	2	1838-1842	332
Jones, William	Madison	W&I		1810-1820	210
Jones, William	Madison	Deeds	A	181o-1816	27
Jones, William	Madison	PR	6	1832-1834	131
Jones, William	Madison	PR	8	1831-1839	405
Jones, William	Mobile	Wills	2	1837-1857	12
Jones, William	Perry	Wills	B	1858-1873	27
Jones, William A.	Perry	Wills	A	1821-1855	316
Jones, William D.	Sumter	Wills	2	1851-1872	109
Jones, William E.	Lauderdale	Wills	B	1859-1870	8
Jones, William E.	Perry	Wills	A	1821-1855	210
Jones, William H.	Madison	Wills	1	1853-1875	116
Jones, William H.	Montgomery	Wills	4	1853-1869	322
Jones, William H.	St. Clair	RE	F	1862-1868	168
Jones, William Ian? (Jur)	Greene	Wills	C	1840-1864	674
Jones, William Roland	Madison	Wills	1	1853-1875	546
Jones, Willis	Chambers	Wills	3	1856-1899	231
Jordan, Charles S.	Jefferson	Wills	A	1856-1880	195
Jordan, Fleming	Madison	PR	2&5	1818-1826	460
Jordan, Henry	Madison	PR	8	1831-1839	28
Jordan, Henry C.	Madison	Wills	1	1853-1875	272
Jordan, Iredell	Dallas	Wills	A	1821-1849	236
Jordan, James P.	Baldwin	Wills	A	1811-1881	78
Jordan, John	Marengo	Wills	A	1820-1864	241
Jordan, R. G.	Madison	PR	12	1845-1849	57
Jordan, Sam	Limestone	Wills	6	1841-1846	225
Jordan, Stephen	St. Clair	Deeds	A	1824-1832	112

TESTATOR	COUNTY	WHERE FOUND		PAGE
Jordan, Warren J.	Barbour	Loose Box 159	Probated 1861	
Jordan, Warren J.	Barbour	OCR 11	1860-1861	523
Jordan, William	Washington	Wills 1 Ø	1827-1888	107
Jordan, William	Washington	Wills B	1827-	68
Jordan, William Henry	Dallas	Wills A	1821-1849	259
Jorden, Isaac	Monroe	W&D B	1833-1870	424
Jorden, Vincent	St. Clair	RE G	1866-1870	91
Joseph, Augustine	Mobile	Wills 2	1837-1857	392
Joseph, Philip	Mobile	Wills 1	1813-1837	203
Joyce, John	Montgomery	Wills 4	1853-1869	432
Joyce, Mathew	Mobile	Wills 1	1813-1837	268
Joyner, Benajah	Tallapoosa	Wills 1	1838-1866	44
Joyner, John A.	Mobile	Wills 3	1857-1870	41
Judge, George	Madison	W&I	1810-1820	119
Judge, George	Madison	W&I	1810-1820	491
Judge, J. L.	Greene	Wills C	1840-1864	630
Judkins, George	Montgomery	Wills 2	1820-1845	43
Jumper, Samuel, Sr.	Coosa	W&PM A	1834-1842	264
Juzan, Daniel	Mobile	Wills 1	1813-1837	110
Kaeiser, Andrew	Lawrence	I&W C	1866-1880	24
Kaeiser, Margaret R.	Morgan	OB 29	1867-1871	418
Kane, Patrick	Mobile	Wills 3	1857-1870	154
Keahey, Samuel J.	Talladega	W&I B	1858-1864	237
Kealing, John H.	Macon	WAC&A 11	1862-1870	265
Keane, Andrew	Mobile	Wills 3	1857-1870	317
Keaton, John	Tuscaloosa	Wills 1	1821-1855	110
Keel, Needom	Clarke	GE&W	1832-1893	13
Keel, William	Chambers	Wills 3	1856-1899	121
Keener, James M.	Pike	Wills A	1845-1862	251
Keener, J. F.	DeKalb	Wills A	1837-1863	19
Keener, William	Autauga	Reports C	1834-1838	334
Keith, John	Talladega	W&I B	1858-1864	527
Keith, Peyton	Greene	Wills C	1840-1864	67
Kellam, Willis	Chambers	Wills 1-2	1833-1856	380
Kellett, John	Tallapoosa	Wills 1	1838-1866	112
Kelley, D.	Coosa	W&OCR 2	1843-1883	253
Kelley, David A.	Perry	Wills A	1821-1855	231
Kelley, Margaret	Macon	Records 6	1855-1858	123
Kelly, David E.	Madison	Wills 1	1853-1875	113
Kelly, Elias	Pike	Inv. A	1845-1862	168
Kelly, (Dr.) James	Jefferson	OCR	1841-1844	52
Kelly, John	Wilcox	Wills 5	1855-1870	275
Kelly, Joseph	Chambers	Wills 1-2	1833-1856	4
Kelly, Moses	Jefferson	Wills A	1856-1880	221
Kelly, Patrick	Mobile	Wills 3	1857-1870	308
Kelly, Patrick	Mobile	Wills 3	1857-1870	688
Kelly, Reuben	Russell	Wills 2	1850-1873	427
Kelly, Sims	Calhoun	Loose Ø	Probated 1860	

TESTATOR	COUNTY	WHERE FOUND		PAGE
Kelly, Thomas	Limestone	Wills	4	1831-1837	276
Kelly, William J.	Madison	Wills	1	1853-1875	307
Kelly, William T.	Henry	OCR	N	1862-1864	221
Kelsey, N. J.	Mobile	Wills	1	1813-1837	224
Kemp, Nathan B.	Montgomery	Wills	2	1820-1845	187
Kemp, S. B.	Monroe	W&D	A	1833-1841	507
Kenan, Eliza	Dallas	Wills	B	1850-1871	21
Kenan, M. J?	Dallas	Wills	A	1821-1849	135
Kenan, Mrs. Mary R.	Dallas	Wills	B	1850-1871	145
Kenan, Thomas	Dallas	Wills	A	1821-1849	232
Kendle?, John	Montgomery	Wills	4	1853-1869	393
Kendricks, Anderson H.	Coosa	W&OCR	2	1843-1883	321
Kenebrew, Madison D.	Tallapoosa	Wills	2	1874-1907	13
Kenedy, Joshua	Mobile	Wills	2	1837-1857	27
Kennard, J? B.	Sumter	Wills	1	1828-1851	324
Kennard, James J.	Madison	PR	3	1823-1826	176
Kennedy, Charles	Madison	PR	2	1818-1823	204
Kennedy, D. L.	Lauderdale	Wills	B	1859-1870	154
Kennedy?, George	Lauderdale	Wills	B	1859-1870	76
Kennedy, George W.	Talladega	Wills	C	1845-1853	315
Kennedy, Hugh	Dallas	Wills	A	1821-1849	227
Kennedy, Joseph N.	Madison	Wills	1	1853-1875	153
Kennedy, Joseph P.	Mobile	Wills	1	1813-1837	107
Kennedy, Mary	Clarke	PR	H	1854-1856	230
Kennedy, Mary M.	Madison	Wills	1	1853-1875	386
Kennedy, Samuel C.	Clarke	PR	H	1854-1856	405
Kennedy, Thomas	Greene	Wills	C	1840-1864	526
Kennedy, William E.	Mobile	Wills	1	1813-1837	111
Kenniard, James	Greene	Wills	C	1840-1864	192
Kennon, Charles	Montgomery	Wills	3	1840-1854	120
Kennon, Lucy	Montgomery	Wills	4	1853-1869	229
Kennon, Robert W.	Tuscaloosa	Wills	1	1821-1855	192
Kenson, Charles L.	Greene	Wills	C	1840-1864	45
Kent, Robert F.	Perry	Wills	A	1821-1855	107
Kent, Thomas, Sr.	Russell	Wills	2	1850-1873	279
Kernahan, Robert	Lauderdale	Wills	B	1859-1870	65
Kerr, Maria M. S.	Dallas	Wills	B	1850-1871	276
Kerr, Moses	Montgomery	Wills	3	1840-1854	109
Kerr, Robert H.	Talladega	W&I	D	1867-1880	720
Kessinger, Jacob	Clarke	OCR	F	1846-1850	500
Ketchum, Emily Joyce	Mobile	Wills	2	1837-1857	72
Ketchum, John R.	Mobile	Wills	3	1857-1870	416
Ketlar, Elijah	Butler	Wills	1	1853-1864	209
Key, Ann	Lauderdale	Wills	A	1835-1858	133
Key, Flora A.	Limestone	Wills	12	1866-1872	461
Key, James	Lauderdale	Wills	B	1859-1870	160
Key, Job	Madison	PR	4	1826-1829	189
Key, Lar C.	Limestone	Wills	9	1847-1850	260
Key, Tandy	Russell	Wills	1	1838-1849	8
Key, Tandy	Russell	Wills	1	1838-1849	19
Key, Thomas?	Shelby	Deeds	H	1837-1842	368

TESTATOR	COUNTY	WHERE FOUND		PAGE
Key, William T.	Limestone	OCM	1830-1834	218
Keyes, Washington	Limestone	Wills 5	1836-1841	180
Kidd, John W.	Shelby	Wills H	1847-1866	685
Kidd, William	Shelby	Wills B	1818-1840	172
Kidd, William	Shelby	Wills D	1841-1846	18
Kiely?, Dennis	Montgomery	Wills 4	1853-1869	181
Kilgore, Benajah	Russell	Wills 2	1850-1873	31
Killen, James	Lauderdale	Wills B	1859-1870	398
Killen, John M.	Montgomery	Wills 4	1853-1869	68
Killen, Nancy A.	Montgomery	Wills 4	1853-1869	404
Killough, James	Jefferson	OCR	1831-1832	78
Killough, James	Jefferson	PM	1831-1832	78
Killough, John	Montgomery	Wills 3	1840-1854	232
Kimball, R. R.	Dallas	Wills B	1850-1871	45
Kimbell, Edward	Morgan	OCR 12	1853-1855	533
Kimble, Perlinny G.	Morgan	PCTR C (15)	1854-1858	250
Kimbrough, Nathaniel	Wilcox	Wills 4	1847-1862	213
Kincaid, William	Madison	PR 15	1850-1853	155
Kindall, James M.	Talladega	Wills B	1839-1845	2
King, Abner H.	Barbour	OCR 10	1859-1860	597
King, Abner H.	Barbour	OCR 11	1860-1861	298
King, Alexander	Greene	Wills C	1840-1864	271
King, Benajah	Dallas	Wills B	1850-1871	161
King, Caroline E.	Barbour	OCR 3	1847-1851	323
King, Celia T.	Dallas	Wills B	1850-1871	351
King, Charles	Madison	PR 3	1823-1826	162
King, Edmund	Shelby	Wills H	1847-1866	872
King, Edwin D.	Perry	Wills B	1858-1873	151
King, Edwin W.	Perry	Wills B	1858-1873	106
King, Elias W.	Marengo	Wills A	1820-1864	300
King, Elisha F.	Perry	Wills A	1821-1855	277
King, Elisha Ford	Perry	Wills B	1858-1873	257
King, Gary	Barbour	OCR 2	1842-1847	79
King, George	Montgomery	Wills 2	1820-1845	143
King, Harmon	Madison	PR 2	1818-1823	286
King, Henry	Barbour	OCR 6	1854-1856	227
King, Henry	Barbour	OCR 6	1854-1856	652
King, Henry	Henry	Deeds A-B	1822-1840	385
King, Henry	Marengo	Wills A	1820-1864	434
King, Henry	Mobile	Wills 2	1837-1857	353
King, Henry	Montgomery	Wills 2	1820-1845	29
King, Henry J?	Dallas	Wills B	1850-1871	74
King, J. N. R.	Shelby	Wills H	1847-1866	700
King, James B.	Dallas	Wills B	1850-1871	19
King, John	Greene	Wills C	1840-1864	162
King, John D.	Dallas	Wills A	1821-1849	100
King, John F.	Pike	Wills B	1862-1879	87
King, Josiah	Tallapoosa	Wills 2	1864-1907	54
King, Leroy W.	Marengo	Wills A	1820-1864	257
King, Margaret	Perry	Wills B	1858-1873	208
King, Miles J?	Madison	Wills 1	1853-1875	455

TESTATOR	COUNTY	WHERE FOUND		PAGE
King, Penelope	Madison	PR 9	1839-1841	34
King, Samuel	DeKalb	Wills A	1837-1863	33
King, Thomas	St. Clair	RE D	1859-1867	94
King, W. I?	Sumter	Wills 2	1851-1872	220
King, William	Macon	Records 7	1857-1859	661
King, William	Talladega	Wills B	1839-1845	27
King, William A.	Calhoun	Loose	Probated 1870	
King, William R.	Dallas	Wills B	1850-1871	83
King, William T. C.	Dallas	Wills B	1850-1871	151
Kinkle, Cornelia A.	Madison	Wills 1	1853-1875	200
Kinkle, Robert M.	Madison	Wills 1	1853-1875	14
Kinnaird, James	Greene	Wills C	1840-1864	206
Kinnard, John	Marengo	Wills A	1820-1864	260
Kinnebrew, L. B.	Tallapoosa	Wills 1	1838-1866	83
Kirby, John	Tuscaloosa	Wills 1	1821-1855	317
Kirby, Martin	Mobile	Wills 2	1837-1857	57
Kirby, Richard	Marshall	PR 2	1857-1888	456
Kirby,? Richard	Marshall	FR 6	1859-1867	467
Kirby, William	Lawrence	I&W A	1850-1857	108
Kirby, William	Madison	PR 13	1838-1848	239
Kirky,? Richard	Marshall	FR 6	1859-1867	467
Kirkland,	Greene	Wills C	1840-1864	485
Kirkland, Daniel	Morgan	FR 22	1865-1866	48
Kirkland, Moses	Henry	OCR E	1845-1851	398
Kirkland, Moses	Henry	Deeds A-B	1822-1840	398
Kirkland, William	Autauga	Reports C	1834-1838	677
Kirkman, Thomas	Lauderdale	Wills 5	1859-1870	386
Kirkpatrick,	Greene	Wills C	1840-1864	206
Kirkpatrick, James	Greene	Wills C	1840-1864	111
Kirkpatrick, James P.	Butler	Wills 1	1853-1864	128
Kirksey, J? E. F.	Tuscaloosa	Wills 3	1858-1865	185
Kirksey, Jane	Greene	Wills C	1840-1864	485
Kirksey, Jared	Tuscaloosa	Wills 1	1821-1855	278
Kirksey, R. B. W.	Marengo	Wills A	1820-1864	402
Kirksey, (Mrs.) Sarah Y.	Talladega	W&I D	1867-1880	714
Kirvin, William	Dallas	Wills A	1821-1849	267
Kitchen, John	Lawrence	I&W C	1866-1880	276
Kittrell, Bryant	Greene	Wills B	1817-1841	197
Knight, Cullen C.	Monroe	W&D B	1833-1870	17
Knight, Cynthia	Sumter	Wills 2	1851-1872	28
Knight, John	Lee	Wills A	1867-1898	1
Knight, Josiah	St. Clair	RE C	1852-1859	331
Knight, Lewis J.	Butler	Wills 2	1864-1875	9
Knight, Nancy	St. Clair	Deeds B	1831-1849	145
Knight, Peter	Madison	PR 2	1818-1823	382
Knight, Polly	Montgomery	Wills 3	1840-1854	79
Knight, Thomas J? G.	Sumter	Wills 1	1828-1851	92
Knowles, John F.	Greene	Wills C	1840-1864	276
Knowles, Robert	Pike	Wills B	1862-1879	106
Knox, Dean	Mobile	Wills 3	1857-1870	90
Knox, James C.	Talladega	W&I D	1867-1880	534

TESTATOR	COUNTY	WHERE FOUND		PAGE
Knox, John	Wilcox	Wills 1	1821-1844	425
Koen, Frederick J?.	Washington	Wills 1 ∅	1827-1888	204
Koen, Frederick J?.	Washington	Wills B	1827-	124
Koen, John W.	Washington	Wills 1 ∅	1827-1888	177
Koen, John W.	Washington	Wills B	1827-	110
Koen, Joseph	Washington	Wills 1 ∅	1827-1888	159
Koen, Joseph	Washington	Wills B	1827-	101
Koger, William	Lauderdale	Wills A	1835-1858	303
Kohl, Frank	Mobile	Wills 3	1857-1870	651
Kolb, James L.	Morgan	PCTR C (15)	1854-1858	532
Kolb, Joseph C.	Morgan	FR 20	1860-1865	482
Kolb, Samuel A.	Montgomery	Wills 3	1840-1854	66
Kornega, Mrs. T.	Dallas	Wills B	1850-1871	438
Kornicker, Fanny	Mobile	Wills 4	1870-1878	47
Krebs, Joseph	Mobile	Wills 2	1837-1857	334
Krebs, Rene	Mobile	Wills 2	1837-1857	376
Krepe?, Louise le Fleau	Mobile	Wills 1	1813-1837	25
Kresse,? Louise le Fleau	Mobile	Wills 1	1813-1837	25
Kunzelman, John	Clarke	PR J	1856-1858	104
Kurtland, Charles J.	Baldwin	Wills A	1811-1881	219
Kyle, George	Monroe	W&D E	1833-1870	295
Kyle, William J.	Coosa	W&OCR 2	1843-1883	75

Labulby, Henry	Mobile	Misc. D	1837-1857	639
Lacey, William	Jefferson	OCR	1841-1844	488
Lack, Solomon	Tallapoosa	Wills 1	1838-1866	72
Lacosta, Euphraise	Mobile	Wills 2	1837-1857	19
Lacoste, Augustine	Baldwin	Wills A	1811-1881	72
Lacoste, Cyrus	Mobile	Wills 2	1837-1857	284
Lacoste, Donat	Baldwin	Wills A	1811-1881	74
Lacoste, Nicholas	Mobile	Wills 2	1837-1857	212
Lacy, Alexander H.	Madison	Wills 1	1853-1875	323
Lacy, Elisha	Sumter	Wills 2	1851-1872	245
Lacy, John	Morgan	OCR 3	1827-1832	34
Lacy, Jordan	Madison	PR 9	1839-1841	291
Lafoy, James	Washington	Wills 1 ∅	1827-1888	80
Lafoy, James	Washington	Wills B	1827-	52
Laird, William	Mobile	Wills 2	1837-1857	189
Lake, Sarah L.	Sumter	Wills 2	1851-1872	406
Lamar, Benjamin B.	Montgomery	Wills 2	1820-1845	146
Lamar, Catharine	Autauga	Reports A	1825-1830	147
Lamar, Harmony	Barbour	OCR 2	1842-1847	126
Lamar, John	Autauga	Reports I	1856-1858	395
Lamb, Green E.	Russell	Wills 2	1850-1873	373
Lamb, James	Lauderdale	Wills B	1859-1870	73
Lamb, John	Lauderdale	Wills B	1859-1870	132
Lamb, Laben	Russell	Wills 2	1850-1873	?
Lambert, A.	Monroe	W&D 9	1871-1872	160
Lambert, Andrew	Monroe	W&D C	1845-1850	321

TESTATOR	COUNTY	WHERE FOUND		PAGE
Lambert, Thomas	Mobile	Wills 2	1837-1857	157
Lamkin, Bennett	Wilcox	Wills 6	1862-1870	43
Lamkin, William M.	Macon	Records 10	1863-1865	221
Lampkins, Robert	Madison	Wills 1	1853-1875	459
Lampkins, Rosannah	Madison	PR 2&5	1818-1826	406
Lampley, Harrison D.	Barbour	OCR 14	1863-1865	497
Lampley, John M.	Barbour	OCR 16	1866-1868	503
Lamplin, John	Macon	Records 3	1845-1850	747
Lamply, Ira	Barbour	OCR 9	1858-1859	283
Lamply, Ira	Barbour	OCR 9	1858-1859	291
Lancaster, Edward, Sr.	Baldwin	Wills A	1811-1881	146
Lancaster, Theron	Chambers	Wills 1-2	1833-1856	410
Lancy, Titus	Russell	Wills 2	1850-1873	125
Land, Berry	Greene	Wills B	1817-1841	266
Landers, James B. M.	Talladega	W&I D	1867-1880	397
Landman, William	Lauderdale	Wills A	1835-1858	192
Landman, William	Madison	PR 4	1826-1829	407
Landrum, Rebecca	Mobile	Wills 3	1857-1870	166
Lane, Isaac	Colbert	Wills A	1861-1903	31
Lane, (Rev.) J. H. Capers	Talladega	W&I D	1858-1864	295
Lane, John	Madison	PR 4	1826-1829	31
Lane, Joseph J.	Dallas	Wills B	1850-1871	27
Lane, Levin B.	Perry	Wills B	1858-1873	315
Lane, Nancy	Marengo	Wills A	1820-1864	336
Lane, Perele H.	Morgan	OCR 7	1837-1843	215
Lane, Rachel	Dallas	Wills B	1850-1871	48
Lane, Richard D.	Macon	Records 2	1838-1842	287
Lanford, Robert	Madison	PR 10	1842-1842	52
Langford, Champ	St. Clair	Deeds B	1831-1849	134
Langford, John	Madison	Wills 1	1853-1875	251
Langham, Lewis L.	Mobile	Wills 3	1857-1870	278
Langhorne, James C.	Marengo	Wills A	1820-1864	214
Langley, Osey	Tuscaloosa	Wills 3	1858-1865	159
Lanier, Ann	Madison	PR 10	1842-1842	59
Lanier, Ann	Madison	PR 12	1845-1849	36
Lanier, George W.	Chambers	Wills 3	1856-1899	13
Lanier, Isaac	Madison	PR 4	1826-1829	204
Lanier, James A.	Lawrence	I&W D	1835-1840	487
Lanier, Samson C.	Lauderdale	Wills A	1835-1858	253
Lanier, Sidney C.	Montgomery	Wills 4	1853-1869	515
Lanier, Sterling	Montgomery	Wills 5	1863-1887	49
Lanier, William	Madison	PR 9	1839-1841	328
Lanier, William D.	Madison	PR 8	1831-1839	207
Lankford, James	Clarke	PR E	1840-1845	116
Lansford, Pryor D.	Lawrence	I&W A	1850-1857	179
Lansford, T. A.	Lauderdale	Wills A	1835-1858	231
Lapsley, Joseph M.	Dallas	Wills B	1850-1871	295
Lapsley, Mary A.	Dallas	Wills B	1850-1871	371
Laraes, Jack	Marshall	PM	1836-1839	3
Larkin, Edmond	Lauderdale	Wills A	1835-1848	225
Larkins, Elizabeth	Lowndes	Wills B	1830-1859	107

TESTATOR	COUNTY	WHERE FOUND		PAGE
Larkins, James N.	Sumter	Wills 1	1828-1851	301
Larkins, William	Montgomery	Wills 4	1853-1869	253
Laroe, Jacob	Marshall	FR Estates	1835-1840	1
Larronil, Pascal	Mobile	Wills 3	1857-1870	463
Lary, Jeremiah	Autauga	Reports E-B	1841-1845	56
Lasseter, Clarissa	Lowndes	Wills B	1830-1859	71
Latady, Eugene	Mobile	Wills 3	1857-1870	306
Latham, Angela S.	Mobile	Wills 3	1857-1870	303
Laurendine, Louise	Mobile	Wills 2	1837-1857	174
Lavalle, John	Sumter	Wills 2	1851-1872	14
Lavendar, Charles E.	Dallas	Wills B	1850-1871	44
Lavender, Hugh	Greene	Wills B	1817-1841	154
Lavender, James	Sumter	Wills 1	1828-1851	313
Lavender, Lifus S.	Lowndes	Wills B	1830-1859	328
Lavender, Simeon	Lowndes	Wills B	1830-1859	322
Law, George E.	Macon	Records 10	1863-1865	699
Law, James	Marengo	Wills A	1820-1864	424
Law, Mrs. Margaret C.	Talladega	W&I D	1867-1880	671
Law, Peyton, Sr.	Marshall	FR 1	1840-1844	109
Lawler, Benjamin	Madison	Wills 1	1853-1875	328
Lawler, James	Madison	PR 2&5	1818-1826	100
Lawler, Jehu, Sr.	Madison	PR 16	1831-1861	30
Lawler, Jesse	Madison	PR 9	1839-1841	85
Lawler, John	Montgomery	Wills 5	1863-1887	86
Lawley, John	Jefferson	PM	1831-1832	7
Lawley, John	Jefferson	OCR	1831-1832	14
Lawley, Joseph	Bibb	Admr.R D	1830-1838	77
Lawrence, Abraham	Tallapoosa	Wills 1	1838-1866	43
Lawrence, Charity	Tuscaloosa	Wills 1	1821-1855	237
Lawrence, Charles A.	Tuscaloosa	Wills 3	1858-1865	178
Lawrence, Joseph	Dallas	Wills A	1821-1849	147
Lawrence, Sarah	Pike	Wills B	1862-1879	30
Lawrence, Stephen	Lowndes	Wills B	1830-1859	269
Lawson, Ann	Autauga	Reports H	1853-1857	692
Lawson, Charles M.	Dallas	Wills A	1821-1849	57
Lawson, James	Lowndes	Wills B	1830-1859	389
Lawson, Mary Ann	Autauga	Reports G	1850-1853	399
Lawson, Munford	Sumter	Wills 1	1828-1851	140
Layman, Rebekah	Madison	PR 4	1826-1829	510
Laysetter, John	Tallapoosa	Wills 1	1838-1866	47
Lazies, John Paul	Mobile	Wills 3	1857-1870	497
Lea, Charity	Madison	Wills 1	1853-1875	502
Lea, Tempee	Perry	Wills A	1821-1855	57
Leach, C. S.	Tuscaloosa	Wills 4	1868-1897	215
Leach, Fielding	Mobile	Wills 2	1837-1857	69
Leake, John M.	Madison	PR 2&5	1818-1826	61
Leath, George D.	DeKalb	Wills A	1837-1863	55
Leavens, Joshua B.	Mobile	Wills 1	1813-1837	229
Leawley, Joseph	Bibb	Loose	Dated1832	
LeCat, Ann	Mobile	Wills 1	1813-1837	93
Lecky, Alexander	Colbert	Wills A	1861-1903	11

TESTATOR	COUNTY	WHERE FOUND		PAGE
Ledlow, Adam	Dallas	Wills A	1821-1849	346
Lee, Ambrose	Greene	Wills D	1851-1888	60
Lee, David	Perry	Wills B	1858-1873	174
Lee, David	Perry	Wills C	1862-1895	1
Lee, Eliazer	Marengo	Wills A	1820-1864	143
Lee, Eliza J.	Clarke	PR L	1861-1864	94
Lee, George L.	Conecuh	OB A	1865-1870	130
Lee, Houston H.	Madison	Wills 1	1853-1875	29
Lee, Isaac	Tuscaloosa	Wills 3	1858-1865	11
Lee, Isaiah	Coosa	W&OCR 2	1843-1883	299
Lee, James B.	Greene	Wills B	1817-1841	218
Lee, John	Wilcox	Wills 2	1832-1850	212
Lee, John A.	Wilcox	Wills 5	1855-1870	113
Lee, John G.	Monroe	W&D D	1850-1856	396
Lee, Landon?	Dallas	Wills A	1821-1849	145
Lee, Needham, Sr.	Barbour	OCR 5	1852-1853	85
Lee, Peter	Wilcox	Wills 1	1821-1844	316
Lee, Pleasant	Dallas	Wills A	1821-1849	223
Lee, Ransom	Tuscaloosa	Wills 3	1858-1865	230
Lee, Richard	Perry	W&I	1823-1833	12
Lee, Richard	Perry	Wills A	1821-1855	11
Lee, Robert	Clarke	PR K	1858-1861	482
Lee, Samuel W.	Lowndes	Wills C	1861-1899	127
Lee, Sarah	Limestone	Wills 3	1826-1831	100
Lee, Susan	Sumter	Wills 2	1851-1872	269
Lee, Thomas	Lauderdale	Wills B	1859-1870	395
Lee, Thomas H.	Dallas	Wills B	1850-1870	148
Lee, William	Chambers	Wills 1-2	1833-1856	204
Lee, William	Montgomery	Wills 2	1820-1845	152
Lee, William	Pike	Wills B	1862-1879	156
Lee, William H.	Greene	Wills D	1851-1888	192
Lee, Woodson P.	Pike	Wills A	1845-1862	125
Leech, Samuel C.	Macon	Records 2	1838-1842	384
Leech, William	Madison	PR 8	1831-1839	415
Leeman, Joseph	Madison	PR 9	1839-1841	374
Leester, Moses	St. Clair	Deeds A	1824-1832	590
Leetch, Naomi	Lawrence	I&W A	1850-1857	368
Leetch, William	Lawrence	I&W D	1835-1840	408
Leforest,? L.	Mobile	Wills 2	1837-1857	277
Leftwich, John Briscoe	Lauderdale	Wills A	1835-1858	179
Legg, William	Limestone	Wills 11	1865-1866	21
Lehmberg, Henry	Madison	Wills 1	1853-1875	108
Leigh, William	Lauderdale	Wills B	1859-1870	122
Lenier, Mary	Autauga	Reports L	1862-1863	4
Lenoir, James M.	Dallas	Wills B	1850-1871	318
Lenore, William	Bibb	Loose	Dated 1849	
Leonard, Edward S.	Montgomery	Wills 4	1853-1869	383
Leonard, Van	Russell	Wills 2	1850-1873	267
Lerch, Margaret	Montgomery	Wills 4	1853-1869	498
Lesley, Elizabeth	St. Clair	Deeds B	1831-1849	163
Leslie, Cornelia R.	Madison	Wills 1	1853-1875	24

TESTATOR	COUNTY	WHERE FOUND		PAGE
Leslie, G. W.	Monroe	W&D C	1845-1850	398
Leslie, Jane	Monroe	W&D F	1861-1867	86
Leslie, John	Perry	Wills A	1821-1855	10
Leslie, Naomi	Madison	Wills 1	1853-1875	80
Lester, Daniel	Russell	Wills 2	1850-1873	5
Lester, John E.	Russell	Wills 2	1850-1873	55
Lester, Moses	St. Clair	Deeds A	1824-1832	590
Lesueur, Samuel	Russell	Wills 1	1838-1849	55
Lesuier, N. B.	Marengo	Wills A	1820-1864	490
Leverett, Gideon	Chambers	Wills 3	1856-1899	166
Leverett, Margaret	Marengo	Wills A	1820-1864	316
Leverett, Mary G.	Chambers	Wills 1-2	1833-1856	316
LeVert, Francis J.	Madison	Wills 1	1853-1875	412
Levie, John	Autauga	Reports C	1834-1838	214
Lewin, Charles	Tuscaloosa	Wills 1	1821-1855	146
Lewis, Abraham	Madison	PR 2	1818-1823	42
Lewis, Addin	Mobile	Wills 2	1837-1857	116
Lewis, Ann D.	Montgomery	Wills 2	1820-1845	274
Lewis, Arthur M.	Marengo	Wills A	1820-1864	523
Lewis, Burwell B.	Tuscaloosa	Wills 4	1868-1897	231
Lewis, Charles	Madison	PR 3	1823-1826	369
Lewis, Eliza	Montgomery	Wills 4	1853-1869	183
Lewis, Elizabeth	Greene	Wills B	1817-1841	138
Lewis, Enoch	Madison	PR 10	1842-1842	265
Lewis, Enoch	Madison	PR 12	1845-1849	35
Lewis, Francis	Limestone	Wills 4	1831-1837	523
Lewis, Frederick	Perry	Wills B	1858-1873	23
Lewis, George	Butler	Wills 1	1853-1864	236
Lewis, Henry	Macon	Records 4	1850-1852	13
Lewis, James	Tuscaloosa	Wills 1	1821-1855	181
Lewis, Jane	Mobile	Wills 2	1837-1857	246
Lewis, John H.	Madison	Wills 1	1810-1820	195
Lewis, Joshua	Sumter	Wills 2	1851-1872	184
Lewis, Levi	Madison	Wills 1	1853-1875	94
Lewis, Margaret	Madison	Wills 1	1853-1875	321
Lewis, Meriwether A.	Madison	Wills 1	1853-1875	275
Lewis, Nicholas P.	Morgan	PCTR C (15)	1854-1858	87
Lewis, Noland R.	Lee	Wills A	1867-1898	46
Lewis, Patrocles	Limestone	Wills 6	1841-1846	602
Lewis, Paul H.	Mobile	Wills 2	1837-1857	196
Lewis, Pearce A.	Russell	Wills 2	1850-1873	33
Lewis, Peter C.	Madison	PR 2&5	1818-1826	325
Lewis, Pierce L.	Russell	Wills 2	1850-1873	43
Lewis, Samuel	Madison	PR 2&5	1818-1826	544
Lewis, Samuel Seymour	Mobile	Wills 2	1837-1857	172
Lewis, Sarah	Macon	Records 6	1855-1858	260
Lewis, Zachariah	Montgomery	Wills 2	1820-1845	10
Leysath, James M.	Butler	Wills 2	1864-1875	127
Liddell, Sarah U.	Henry	OCR U	1869-1870	496
Lide, Hugh	Lowndes	Wills B	1830-1859	215
Lide, James	Dallas	Wills B	1850-1871	132

TESTATOR	COUNTY	WHERE FOUND		PAGE
Lide, Jane	Dallas	Wills B	1850-1871	260
Lide, R. P.	Dallas	Wills B	1850-1871	315
Liddle, John N.	Jefferson	OCR	1824-	74
Light, William	Mobile	Wills 1	1813-1837	163
Lightfoot, Clackston	Madison	PR 12	1845-1849	579
Lightfoot, Clara B.	Madison	Wills 1	1853-1875	338
Lightfoot, Henry C.	Perry	Wills A	1821-1855	55
Lightfoot, John	Madison	PR 12	1845-1849	2
Lightfoot, John F.	Lawrence	I&W A	1850-1857	156
Lightfoot, Philip	Greene	Wills D	1851-1888	118
Lightfoot, Philip C.	Greene	Wills D	1851-1888	154
Lightner, Michael	Barbour	OCR 15	1865-1866	527
Likens, Sarah R.	Calhoun	Loose	Probated 1855	
Likins, John	Calhoun	Loose	Probated 1841	
Lile, Victoria L.	Morgan	FR 20	1860-1865	547
Lile, Virginia E.	Madison	Wills 1	1853-1875	89
Lile, Virginia E.	Morgan	OCR 12	1853-1855	541
Lilley, William	Madison	PR 9	1839-1841	262
Lindsay, William	Limestone	Wills 5	1836-1841	305
Lindsey, Amelia Long	Wilcox	Wills 3	1826-1858	265
Lindsey, David	Talladega	W&I A	1852-1857	214
Lindsey, Jacob	Lauderdale	Wills 4	1821-1825	11
Lindsey, John	Tallapoosa	Wills 1	1838-1866	118
Lindsey, L. W.	Monroe	W&D 8	1870-1871	586
Lindsey, (Mrs.) Martha S.	Talladega	W&I B	1858-1864	556
Lindsey, Phebe	Tallapoosa	Wills 2	1864-1907	19
Lindsey, Samuel H.	Coosa	W&OCR 2	1843-1883	242
Lipscomb, A. E.	Greene	Wills D	1851-1888	326?
Lipscomb, Joel	Greene	Wills B	1817-1841	165
Lipscomb, Martha	Madison	Wills 1	1853-1875	33
Lipscomb, William C.	Marengo	Wills A	1820-1864	410
Lister, William	Barbour	OCR 3	1847-1851	198
Litsey, John	Tallapoosa	Wills 2	1864-1907	23
Litsinger, James	Lauderdale	Wills A	1835-1858	167
Little, Amariah	Sumter	Wills 1	1828-1851	219
Little, Ben B.	Sumter	Wills 2	1851-1872	310
Little, Ben B., Jr.	Sumter	Wills 2	1851-1872	354
Little, Edwin L.	Sumter	Wills 2	1851-1872	288
Little, Elizabeth	Sumter	Wills 2	1851-1872	359
Little, Sitto	Sumter	Wills 2	1851-1872	325
Littleton, Charles	Lauderdale	Wills A	1835-1858	158
Littleton, Reuben S.	Lauderdale	Wills B	1859-1870	16
Litzy, J. A.	Limestone	Wills 5	1836-1841	173
Litzy, Jacob	Limestone	Wills 5	1836-1841	126
Livingston, Rachel Rebecca	Autauga	Reports G	1850-1853	299
Livingston, Robert T.	Autauga	Reports F	1845-1850	440
Livingston, Taliafferro	Mobile	Wills 1	1813-1837	79
Lloyd, Benjamin	Butler	Wills 1	1853-1864	189
Lloyd, John F.	Lowndes	Wills C	1861-1899	36
Locke, Eliza A.	Morgan	FR 18	1859-1860	536
Locke, Joseph	Monroe	W&D D	1850-1856	11

TESTATOR	COUNTY	WHERE FOUND		PAGE
Locke, Richard	Pike	Wills B	1862-1879	44
Locket, Osbern	Wilcox	Wills 1	1821-1844	441
Lockett, Benjamin	Marengo	Wills A	1820-1864	210
Lockett, H. P.	Russell	Wills 2	1850-1873	307
Lockett, Napoleon	Perry	Wills B	1858-1873	321
Lockhart, Charles	Morgan	OCR 8	1844-1848	26
Lockhart, Julius C.	Butler	Wills 2	1864-1875	101
Lockhart, Mathew	Madison	W&I	1810-1820	118
Locklin, William	Monroe	W&D A	1833-1841	256
Lockwood, Paul S. Lee	Mobile	Wills 3	1857-1870	316
Lodge, Henry	Mobile	Wills 2	1837-1857	263
Lodor, John A.	Dallas	Wills B	1850-1871	308
Loeb, George	Montgomery	Wills 4	1853-1869	236
Loewi, Israel P.	Perry	Wills A	1821-1855	297
Loftin, Andrew J.	Montgomery	Wills 4	1853-1869	370
Loftin, James A.	Montgomery	Wills 3	1850-1854	7
Loftin, Samuel	Marengo	Wills A	1820-1864	300
Loftin, Sarah	Clarke	PR J	1856-1858	138
Logan, Catherine	Dallas	Wills A	1821-1849	150
Logan, Elizabeth H.	Tuscaloosa	Wills 3	1858-1865	63
Logan, Freeman	Tuscaloosa	Wills 4	1868-1897	74
Logan, John	Madison	PR 8	1831-1839	400
Logan, Martha	Madison	PR 10	1842-1842	265
Logan, Matilda	Madison	PR 10	1842-1842	265
Logan, Thomas	Madison	Deeds A	1810-1816	26
Logan, William	Chambers	Wills 3	1856-1899	228
Logwood, Thomas	Madison	PR 2	1818-1823	136
Lokey, Benjamin	Russell	Wills 2	1850-1873	20
Lolley, Christopher	Shelby	Deeds E	1822-1835	144
Lolley, Jeremiah	Shelby	Wills E	1845-1850	295
Lomax, Tennent	Montgomery	Wills 4	1853-1869	367
Long, Daniel	Dallas	Wills B	1850-1871	245
Long, Danial	Madison	PR 8	1831-1839	357
Long, Gabriel	Limestone	Wills 4	1831-1837	619
Long, Hiram A.	Mobile	Wills 2	1837-1857	282
Long, Jacob	Butler	Wills 1	1853-1864	8
Long, James D.	Sumter	Wills 2	1851-1872	157
Long, John	Washington	Wills 1 ∅	1827-1888	36
Long, John	Washington	Wills B	1827-	25
Long, Lunceford	Autauga	Wills 1	1862-1925	44
Long, Reuben	Greene	Wills B	1817-1841	79
Long, Richard B.	Sumter	Wills 2	1851-1872	312
Long, Simon E.	Sumter	Wills 1	1828-1851	62
Longgon, James	Marengo	Wills A	1820-1864	372
Longmire, Edmond	Monroe	W&D A	1833-1841	271
Longmire, Garrett	Monroe	W&D C	1845-1850	236
Longmire, John	Greene	Wills A	1821-1827	66
Longmire, John	Greene	Wills B	1817-1841	2
Longstreth, Isaac T.	Mobile	Wills 2	1837-1857	200
Loomis, James	Mobile	Wills 1	1813-1837	190
Loomis, John Q.	Elmore	Wills A	1866-1906	32

TESTATOR	COUNTY	WHERE FOUND		PAGE
Looney, Catherine	Lauderdale	Wills B	1859-1870	272
Looney, Rebecca	St. Clair	Deeds B	1831-1849	770
Loper,? Annie	Montgomery	Wills 5	1863-1887	84
Loper, Daniel R.	Montgomery	Wills 4	1853-1869	77
Loper, Joseph	Washington	Wills 1 Ø	1827-1888	200
Loper, Joseph P.	Washington	Wills B	1827-	122
Loper, Peter	Washington	Wills 1 Ø	1827-1888	218
Loper, Peter	Washington	Wills B	1827-	131
Loper, William	Montgomery	Wills 2	1820-1845	55
Lopez, Bartholomew	Mobile	Wills 3	1857-1870	116
Lorance, John	Tuscaloosa	Wills 1	1821-1855	14
Lott, Arthur	Barbour	OCR 10	1859-1860	166
Loughry, Eneas	Mobile	Wills 3	1857-1870	167
Louis, John	Greene	Wills D	1851-1888	105
Love, Chauncey	Wilcox	Wills 5	1855-1870	322
Love, Erasmus	Autauga	Reports G	1850-1853	396
Love, Jessee	St. Clair	RE F	1862-1868	186
Love, John	Dallas	Wills A	1821-1849	189
Love, John	Madison	W&I	1810-1820	30
Love, Joseph	Limestone	Wills 3	1826-1831	377
Love, Robertus	Washington	Wills 1 Ø	1827-1888	109
Love, Robertus	Washington	Wills B	1827-18	70
Lovejoy, Samuel	Tallapoosa	Wills 1	1838-1866	189
Lovelace, William P.	Macon	Records 3	1845-1850	249
Lovelady, William	Shelby	Wills E	1845-1850	49
Loveless, Clarissce	Marshall	PR 2	1857-1888	129
Loveleys, John	Tallapoosa	Wills 1	1838-1866	15
Lovett, Joshua	Barbour	OCR 2	1842-1847	240
Loving, Abraham	Madison	PR 10	1842-1842	11
Lovorn, Thomas	St. Clair	Deeds A	1824-1832	390
Lowe, Robert J.	Madison	Wills 1	1853-1875	282
Lowery,? Robert W.	Jefferson	OCR	1824-1831	293
Lowery, John	Limestone	Wills 3	1826-1831	256
Lowery, Samuel	Marshall	FR 3	1843-1844	1
Lowery, Thomas W.	Lauderdale	Wills 3	1821-1825	149
Lowery, William	Lowndes	Wills B	1830-1859	102
Lowry, Agnes	Calhoun	Loose	Probated 1846	
Lowry, Agness	Calhoun	Loose	Probated 1845	
Lowry, Vernal	Sumter	Wills 2	1851-1872	13
Lowther, Elizabeth	Montgomery	Wills 5	1863-1887	102
Lucas, John H.	Limestone	Wills 4	1831-1837	498
Lucas, Henry	Montgomery	Wills 4	1853-1869	272
Lucas, Mary	Montgomery	Wills 2	1820-1845	133
Lucas, Mary	Montgomery	Wills 3	1850-1854	40
Luch, David	Lauderdale	Wills B	1859-1870	351
Lucie, Batt Smith	Dallas	Wills B	1850-1871	299
Luckey, James	Chambers	Wills 1-2	1833-1856	225
Lucy, William A.	Marengo	Wills A	1820-1864	123
Lude, David	Mobile	Wills 4	1870-1878	66
Lude, John Pierre	Mobile	Wills 3	1857-1870	312
Ludlam,? Jeremiah	Pike	Wills B	1862-1879	59

TESTATOR	COUNTY	WHERE FOUND		PAGE
Ludlow?, Jeremiah	Pike	Wills B	1862-1879	59
Ludlow?, Obedience	Dallas	Wills B	1850-1871	112
Luke, Enoch	Montgomery	Wills 4	1853-1869	232
Luke, Mrs. Mary	Talladega	W&I B	1858-1864	199
Lumpkin, Jane H.	Montgomery	Wills 2	1820-1845	216
Lumpkin, Robert	Madison	Wills 1	1853-1875	459
Lunney, John	Mobile	Wills 2	1837-1857	219
Lunonier, Joseph	Mobile	Wills 1	1813-1837	235
Lunsford, Jesse	Madison	PR 4	1826-1829	25
Lunsford, John R.	Marengo	Wills A	1820-1864	279
Lyle, William A.	Coosa	W&OCR 2	1843-1883	167
Lyles,	Greene	Wills D	1851-1888	203?
Lynch, Augustine	Tuscaloosa	Wills 4	1868-1897	27
Lynch, John	Mobile	Wills 3	1857-1870	710
Lynch, John	Mobile	Wills 4	1870-1878	73
Lynch, John W.	Autauga	Reports B	1829-1833	339
Lynch, Levi W.	DeKalb	Wills B	1869-1905	1
Lynch, Thomas	Coosa	W&OCR 2	1843-1883	210
Lynn, William	Lauderdale	Wills B	1859-1870	345
Lynn, William	Russell	Wills 2	1850-1873	217
Lyon, Castleton	Tuscaloosa	Wills 1	1821-1855	256
Lyon, George R.	Jackson	Records	1861-1881	98
Lyon, James G.	Mobile	Wills 2	1837-1857	202
Lyon, John	Shelby	Wills K	1851-1854	165
Lyons, Michael	Madison	Wills 1	1853-1875	417
McAdams, James	St. Clair	Deeds B	1831-1849	129
McAdin, James	Clarke	PR K	1858-1861	512
McAdory, Robert	Tuscaloosa	Wills 1	1821-1855	118
McAdory, Thomas	Jefferson	Deeds 1	1818-1828	29
McAdory, William	Jefferson	Wills A	1856-1880	202
McAlister, James	Mobile	Wills 3	1857-1870	712
McAlister, Narcissus	Lauderdale	Wills B	1859-1870	174
McAlister, Thomas	Lowndes	Wills B	1830-1859	13
McAllister, Hugh	Monroe	W&D C	1845-1850	393
McAlpin, Henry	Macon	Records 4	1850-1852	135
McAlpine, Robert D.	Greene	Wills D	1851-1888	167
McAlpine, W. H.	Clarke	PR L	1861-1864	117
McAlpine, William	Greene	Wills D	1851-1888	77
McArthur, John	Wilcox	Wills 6	1862-1870	24
McAuley, Daniel	Calhoun	Loose	Probated 1851	
McBeth, Walter	Pike	Wills A	1845-1862	39
McBeth, Waters	Pike	Wills A	1845-1862	72
McBrayer, James F.	St. Clair	RE D	1843-1883	606
McBrayer, William H.	Coosa	W&OCR 2	1843-1883	105
McBride, Alex	Sumter	Wills 2	1851-1872	265
McBride, James F.	Mobile	Wills 2	1837-1857	258
McBride, John	Barbour	OCR 4	1850-1852	652
McBride, Margaret	Mobile	Wills 3	1857-1870	492

TESTATOR	COUNTY	WHERE FOUND		PAGE
McBride, Thomas	Lauderdale	Wills B	1859-1870	13
McBryde, Daniel	Macon	Records 10	1863-1865	668
McBryde, Thomas C.	Wilcox	Wills 5	1855-1870	323
McBurney, Hugh	Pike	Wills B	1862-1879	2
McBurney, John R.	Mobile	Wills 3	1857-1870	368
McCaghran, Henry	Dallas	Wills A	1821-1849	120
McCain, Alexander	Talladega	W&I A	1852-1857	554
McCain, William	Talladega	W&I D	1867-1880	243
McCaleb, William	Madison	PR 15	1850-1853	532
McCall, Christian	Monroe	W&D D	1850-1855	139
McCall, Elizabeth Mary Ann	Russell	Wills 1	1838-1849	31
McCall, Hugh	Lowndes	Wills B	1830-1859	68
McCall, Jane	Lowndes	Wills B	1830-1859	272
McCall, Martin	Greene	Wills B	1817-1841	162
McCall, Nancy	Monroe	W&D D	1850-1855	296
McCall, Sarah	Pike	Wills A	1845-1862	74
McCall, Solomon P.	Lowndes	Wills C	1861-1899	98
McCalley, Caroline M.	Madison	Wills 1	1853-1875	542
McCalley, Martha Ann	Madison	Wills 1	1853-1875	541
McCallister, William M.	Marengo	Wills A	1820-1864	342
McCallum, Emily	Madison	Wills 1	1853-1875	384
McCandess, Joseph	Mobile	Wills 1	1813-1837	67
McCann, Robert	Greene	Wills B	1817-1841	236
McCants, John	Wilcox	Wills 2	1832-1850	202
McCants, John L.	Sumter	Wills 1	1828-1851	34
McCarley, David	Chambers	Wills 1-2	1833-1856	396
McCarley, David, Sr.	Chambers	Wills 3	1856-1899	75
McCarley, Elias B.	Chambers	Wills 3	1856-1899	122
McCarta, Alexander	Lauderdale	Wills B	1859-1870	50
McCarter, B. L.	Henry	OCR M	1861-1862	402
McCarter, J. M.	Russell	Wills 2	1850-1873	
McCarter, James	Greene	Wills C	1840-1864	76
McCarter, John	Perry	Wills A	1821-1855	35
McCartney, Alexander A.	Morgan	FR 20	1860-1865	16
McCartney, Barney	St. Clair	RE D	1859-1867	63
McCartney, Charles	Madison	W&I	1810-1820	132
McCartney, Council K.	Talladega	W&I B	1858-1864	316
McCartney, Fleming J.	Madison	Wills 1	1853-1875	10
McCartney, Jane	Morgan	OB 29	1867-1871	57
McCartney, Joseph	Sumter	Wills 2	1851-1872	26
McCartney, Malachiah	Sumter	Wills 2	1851-1872	18
McCartney, Mary F.	Marengo	Wills A	1820-1864	382
McCasker,? Terry	Mobile	Wills 1	1813-1837	69
McCaw, Hugh	Mobile	Wills 3	1857-1870	618
McCaw, Robert	Mobile	Wills 3	1857-1870	624
McClanahan, William	Lauderdale	Wills A	1835-1858	4
McClarahan, James	Mobile	Wills 3	1857-1870	442
McClary, John	Mobile	Wills 2	1837-1857	56
McClellan, Francis A.	Talladega	W&I D	1867-1880	425
McClellan, James J.	Madison	Wills 1	1853-1875	67
McClellen, Thomas	Talladega	Wills A	1833-1839	489

TESTATOR	COUNTY	WHERE FOUND		PAGE
McClelon, Robert	Russell	Wills 1	1838-1849	37
McClendon, Jephtha	Chambers	Wills 3	1856-1899	203
McClendon, Samuel	Chambers	Wills 1-2	1833-1856	366
McClerkin, Jane	Jefferson	Wills 1	1818-1840	29
McClung, James W.	Madison	PR 14	1846-1850	136
McClure, John N.	Mobile	Wills 4	1870-1878	49
McClure, John N.	Dallas	Wills B	1850-1871	323
McClure, W. D.	Butler	Wills 1	1853-1864	84
McCollough, Henry O.	Barbour	OCR 1	1833-1843	309
McCollum, William B.	Morgan	OB 29	1867-1871	68
McComb, Ann	Madison	PR 13	1838-1848	3
McCondichee, Elizabeth	Wilcox	Wills 1	1821-1844	417
McCondichee, Jay	Wilcox	Wills 1	1821-1844	405
McCondichee, John	Wilcox	Wills 1	1821-1844	352
McConnell, Benjamin	Baldwin	Wills A	1811-1881	177
McConnell, John A.	Sumter	Wills 2	1851-1872	71
McConnell, Mary F.	Tuscaloosa	Wills 3	1858-1865	148
McConnelly, Robert	Wilcox	Wills 4	1847-1862	125
McConnico, Mary E.	Wilcox	Wills 3	1826-1858	231
McConnico, William W.	Wilcox	Wills 1	1821-1844	278
McCord, Robert C.	Lawrence	I&W A	1850-1857	249
McCorkle, Violet	Sumter	Wills 2	1851-1872	106
McCorkles, Joseph	Sumter	Wills 1	1828-1851	332
McCormack, George	Limestone	Wills 7	1844-1847	66
McCormick, Daniel	Tallapoosa	Wills 1	1838-1866	175
McCormick, Edward	Mobile	Wills 2	1837-1857	391
McCormick, James	Calhoun	Loose	Probated 1855	
McCorquodale, Eliza	Clarke	PR L	1861-1864	114
McCorvey, Daniel	Monroe	W&D G	1868-1870	753
McCorvey, C. G.	Monroe	W&D G	1868-1870	294
McCorstin, William	Lauderdale	Wills B	1859-1870	102
McCown, John	Mobile	Wills 2	1837-1857	20
McCoy, Anthony	Monroe	W&D G	1868-1870	650
McCoy, David Fell	Barbour	OCR 2	1842-1847	294
McCoy, Franklin W.	Mobile	Wills 2	1837-1857	254
McCoy, Leroy	Chambers	Wills 1-2	1833-1856	439
McCoy, Nealy, Sr.	Chambers	Wills 1-2	1833-1856	336
McCoy, Neely	Russell	Wills 2	1850-1873	68
McCoy, Susan	Mobile	Wills 2	1837-1857	254
McCracken, James	Madison	PR 3	1823-1826	152
McCracken, John	Macon	Records 6	1855-1858	477
McCrady, Thomas	Montgomery	Wills 2	1820-1845	239
McCracken, Robert	Barbour	OCR 6	1854-1856	168
McCrany, Malcolm	St. Clair	Deeds A	1824-1832	560
McCrary, James	Montgomery	Wills 2	1820-1845	3
McCrary, Lee	Perry	Wills A	1821-1855	93
McCrary, Thomas	Lawrence	I&W D	1835-1840	57
McCraw, G. N.	Dallas	Wills B	1850-1871	431
McCraw, Sarah M.	Mobile	Wills 3	1857-1870	16
McCreless, Elizabeth	Calhoun	Loose	Probated 1839	
McCrory, Nancy	Butler	Wills 1	1853-1864	70

TESTATOR	COUNTY	WHERE FOUND		PAGE
McCroskey, Pleasant P.	Morgan	OCR 11	1850-1852	320
McCroskey, Rachael	Morgan	OB 29	1867-1871	416
McCullock, Martha S.	Montgomery	Wills 4	1853-1869	190
McCullock, Robert	Montgomery	Wills 2	1820-1845	260
McCullogh, Jonathan C.	Butler	Wills 1	1853-1864	19
McCullogh, Rachel	Butler	Wills 1	1853-1864	91
McCullough, Daniel	Lamar	Wills 1	1844-1910	12
McCullough, William	Montgomery	Wills 4	1853-1869	257
McCully, Ephraim	Lauderdale	Wills A	1835-1858	129
McCune, Adam	Limestone	Wills 11	1865-1866	108
McCurdy, A. P.	Dallas	Wills B	1850-1871	209
McCurdy, Edward S.	Chambers	Wills 3	1856-1899	188
McCurdy, Milus	Wilcox	Wills 3	1826-1858	253
McCurten, Cornelius	Mobile	Wills 1	1813-1837	20
McCutchen, John	Madison	Chancery Record R ##		545
McDade, James	Montgomery	Wills 3	1840-1854	141
McDanel, Patrick	Autauga	Reports J	1858-1859	626
McDaniel, John	Tallapoosa	Wills 1	1838-1866	117
McDaniel, Mathew	Montgomery	Wills 4	1853-1869	356
McDaniel, Sarah A.	Morgan	Records 1	1821-1834	79
McDavid, James	Madison	PR 10	1842-1842	32
McDavid, Joel A.	Baldwin	Wills A	1811-1881	131
McDermott, Edward	Mobile	Wills 3	1857-1870	542
McDevitt, James	Mobile	Wills 2	1837-1857	327
McDonald, Alexander	Barbour	OCR 2	1842-1847	323
McDonald, Arabella	Lowndes	Wills B	1830-1859	306
McDonald, Archibald	Monroe	W&D A	1833-1841	578
McDonald, Daniel A.	Sumter	Wills 2	1851-1872	152
McDonald, Hugh L.	Sumter	Wills 2	1851-1872	282
McDonald, John	Baldwin	Wills A	1811-1881	67
McDonald, John	Macon	Records 10	1863-1865	258
McDonald, Martha P.	Barbour	OCR 17	1868-1870	865
McDonald, Michael	Mobile	Wills 2	1837-1857	86
McDonald, Peter	Mobile	Wills 2	1837-1857	225
McDonald, Reuben	Baldwin	Wills A	1811-1881	204
McDonald, William	Morgan	PCTR C (15)	1854-1858	575
McDonnell, Archibald	Madison	PR 2&5	1818-1826	56
McDonnell, John	Wilcox	Wills 2	1832-1850	301
McDonold, Learner B.	Shelby	Wills L	1838-1858	667
McDougall, Chaney	Lauderdale	Wills A	1835-1858	224
McDow, Authur	Greene	Wills B	1817-1841	229
McDowell, Frances	Wilcox	Wills 5	1855-1870	131
McDowell, Margaret C.	Madison	Wills 1	1853-1875	537
McDowell, William	Wilcox	Wills 3	1826-1858	249
McDowell, William D.	Pike	Wills A	1845-1862	82
McDowell, William T.	Wilcox	Wills 2	1832-1850	278
McDuffie, Jane A.	Limestone	Wills 6	1841-1846	502
McElroy, Henry	Sumter	Wills 2	1851-1872	33
McElroy, Isaac	Sumter	Wills 1	1828-1851	377
McElroy, James	Dallas	Wills A	1821-1849	226
McElroy, John, Sr.	Dallas	Wills B	1850-1871	300

TESTATOR	COUNTY	WHERE FOUND		PAGE
McElroy, Phebe	Coosa	W&OCR 2	1843-1883	169
McElroy, Patrick	Mobile	Wills 2	1837-1857	252
McFaddin, Alexander	Lauderdale	Wills 4	1821-1825	152
McFaddin, Frances	Greene	Wills B	1817-1841	300
McFarland, James	Lowndes	Wills B	1830-1859	198
McFarland, James L.	Lowndes	Wills B	1830-1859	293
McFarland, Peter	Lowndes	Wills C	1861-1899	143
McFerrin, Robert	Lowndes	Wills C	1861-1899	114
McGaha, Burgess	Marshall	FR $3\frac{1}{2}$	1847-1850	15
McGahaa, Robert M.	Madison	Wills 1	1853-1875	35
McGarahan, James	Mobile	Wills 3	1857-1870	442
McGaughey, Robert	Montgomery	Wills 2	1820-1845	1
McGee, David	Tuscaloosa	Wills 3	1858-1865	32
McGee, Elizabeth Ann	Montgomery	Wills 3	1840-1854	139
McGee, Thomas	Marengo	Wills A	1820-1864	238
McGehee, Abner	Montgomery	Wills 4	1853-1869	44
McGehee, John M.	Talladega	Wills A	1833-1839	53
McGehee, Martha C.	Lowndes	Wills C	1861-1899	168
McGehee, William	Limestone	Wills 3	1826-1831	63
McGehee, William	Madison	Deeds S	1840-1842	62
McGhee, Lynn	Baldwin	Wills A	1811-1881	98
McGhee, Thomas	Sumter	Wills 1	1828-1851	176
McGill, James	Mobile	Wills 3	1857-1870	621
McGill, William	Mobile	Wills 3	1857-1870	418
McGilvary, Janet	Barbour	OCR 6	1854-1856	655
McGinney, Moses S.	Lowndes	Wills B	1830-1859	406
McGinney, (Mrs.) Sarah Hails	Lowndes	Wills C	1861-1899	47
McGough, Robert	Dallas	Wills A	1821-1849	38
McGowen, Catherine	Sumter	Wills 1	1828-1851	314
McGrath, Roger	Macon	Records 7	1857-1859	326
McGraw, A. G.	Dallas	Wills B	1850-1871	224
McGraw, Charles	Wilcox	Wills 1	1821-1844	364
McGraw, James V.	Shelby	Wills H	1847-1866	944
McGraw, Lewis	Wilcox	Wills 4	1847-1862	146
McGraw, Simeon	Autauga	DM&R 17	1820-1864	118
McGraw,? Stephen	Perry	Wills A	1821-1855	3
McGregor, M. J.	Russell	Wills 2	1850-1873	264
McGregor, William	Lawrence	I&W C	1866-1880	398
McGuire, Elijah	Tuscaloosa	Wills 1	1821-1855	201
McGuire, Henry H.	Wilcox	Wills 5	1855-1870	388
McGuire, John J.	Macon	Records 10	1863-1865	517
McGuire, Isaac	Dallas	Wills A	1821-1849	68
McGuire, W.	Barbour	OCR 8	1856-1858	235
McIlny, Mary	Marengo	Wills A	1820-1864	229
McIllwaine, Andrew, Sr.	Washington	Wills 1 ∅	1827-1888	19
McIllwain, Andrew	Washington	Wills B	1827-	12
McInnis, John B.	Barbour	OCR 14	1863-1865	566
McIntire, James	Clarke	PR J	1856-1858	176
McIntire, Malcolm	Lauderdale	Wills 4	1821-1825	16
McIntosh, Alexander	Wilcox	Wills 2	1832-1850	370
McIntosh, Angus	Wilcox	Wills 1	1821-1844	294

TESTATOR	COUNTY	WHERE FOUND		PAGE
McIntosh, Ann	Perry	Wills B	1858-1873	137
McIntosh, Elizabeth	Montgomery	Wills 2	1820-1845	134
McIntosh, Lauchlin	Perry	Wills A	1821-1855	49
McIntosh, Nivin	Elmore	Wills A	1866-1906	2
McIntosh, Peter	Lee	Wills A	1867-1898	9
McIntyre, Archibald	Chambers	Wills 1-2	1833-1856	434
McIver, Evander	Talladega	Wills A	1833-1839	493
MacIver, John	Montgomery	Wills 2	1820-1845	130
McKay, Adam	Macon	Records 2	1838-1842	39
McKay, Lucinda	Mobile	Wills 3	1857-1870	425
McKay, Lucinda	Montgomery	Wills 4	1853-1869	366
McKay, William S. D.	Sumter	Wills 1	1828-1851	281
McKee, John	Greene	Wills B	1817-1841	88
McKee, William F.	Clarke	PR L	1861-1864	212
McKeeman, Monroe Fost	Colbert	Wills A	1861-1903	20
McKelvy, Henry	Tallapoosa	Wills 2	1864-1907	25
McKemie, John	Madison	PR 2	1818-1823	177
McKemie, Robert	Tuscaloosa	Wills 3	1858-1865	101
McKenney, Eli	Chambers	Wills 3	1856-1899	9
Mackenness, G. William	Etowah	Wills A	1866-1870	3
McKenzie, Alex	Mobile	Wills 2	1837-1857	151
McKenzie, Alex Leander	Montgomery	Wills 4	1853-1869	122
McKenzie, Christian	Dallas	Wills B	1850-1871	241
McKenzie, Kenneth	Dallas	Wills A	1821-1849	353
McKenzie, William A.	Madison	PR 15	1850-1853	108
McKeynolt, T. B.	Greene	Wills A	1821-1827	40
McKibbon, Mary	Mobile	Wills 4	1870-1878	88
McKinley, Daniel	Sumter	Wills 2	1851-1872	61
McKinney, A. H.	Limestone	Wills 5	1836-1841	325
McKinney, Harris	Coosa	W&OCR 2	1843-1883	191
McKinney, James	Limestone	Wills 11	1865-1866	43
McKinney, John	Limestone	Wills 11	1865-1866	12
McKinney, John F.	Limestone	Wills 9	1847-1850	193
McKinney, Wilson	Limestone	Wills 3	1826-1831	248
McKinney, Zach	Macon	Records 10	1863-1865	714
McKinnon, John L.	Lee	Wills A	1867-1898	4
McKinzie, John George	Barbour	OCR 18	1870-	230
McKnight, James	Lauderdale	Wills A	1835-1858	7
McKnight, James	Lauderdale	Wills A	1835-1858	203
McKnight, Thomas P.	Lauderdale	Wills B	1859-1870	42
McLane, Charles	Pike	Wills B	1862-1879	35
McLaren, Thomas	Mobile	Wills 1	1813-1837	174
McLaughlin, Andrew	Jefferson	Wills A	1856-1880	47
McLaughlin, James	Greene	Wills A	1821-1827	12
McLaughlin, John	Perry	Wills B	1858-1873	33
McLean, Dougald	Greene	Wills B	1817-1841	256
McLean, Duncan	Pike	Wills A	1845-1862	19
McLean, John M.	Autauga	Reports C	1834-1838	6
McLean, Neil	Talladega	W&I A	1852-1857	457
McLean, Sarah	Macon	Records 4	1850-1852	207
McLellan, William	Talladega	Wills C	1845-1853	377

TESTATOR	COUNTY	WHERE FOUND		PAGE
McLemore, Ann	Coosa	W&OCR 2	1843-1883	57
McLemore, Edna A.	Chambers	Wills 3	1856-1899	35
McLemore, Elizabeth	Montgomery	Wills 3	1840-1854	291
McLemore, James	Montgomery	Wills 2	1820-1845	112
McLemore, James J.	Montgomery	Wills 3	1840-1854	118
McLemore, Jesse	Montgomery	Wills 2	1820-1845	109
McLemore, John H.	Montgomery	Wills 3	1840-1854	24
McLemore, W. T.	Greene	Wills D	1851-1888	31
McLemore, William	Macon	Records 5	1853-1855	323
McLemore, William	Montgomery	Wills 2	1820-1845	150
McLemore, Wilson	Chambers	Wills 1-2	1833-1856	284
McLenden, Sarah Ann	Washington	Wills 1 Ø	1827-1888	217
McLenden, Sarah Ann	Washington	Wills B	1827-	130
McLendon, Sarah	Pike	Wills B	1862-1879	30
McLendon, Thomas	Chambers	Wills 1-2	1833-1856	506
McLendon, William	Macon	Records 2	1838-1842	50
McLennan, Alexander	Madison	PR 8	1831-1839	101
McLennon, Alexander	Barbour	OCR 13	1863-1864	152
McLeod, Charles	Tuscaloosa	Wills 3	1858-1865	6
McLeod, John	Mobile	Wills 2	1837-1857	75
McLeod, Lindsey	Barbour	OCR 6	1854-1856	282
McLeod, Norman	Pike	Wills B	1862-1879	164
McLeroy, Andrew	Madison	PR 3	1823-1826	19
McLeroy, James Tate	Barbour	OCR 11	1860-1861	243
McLintock?, Leonard	Dallas	Wills A	1821-1849	185
McLoskey, Philip	Mobile	Wills 2	1837-1857	102
McMackin, William K.	Lauderdale	Wills A	1835-1858	312
McMahan, D.	Lauderdale	Wills B	1859-1870	288
McMath, Fannie	Tuscaloosa	Wills 4	1868-1897	8
McMicken, Andrew	Lauderdale	Wills 3	1821-1825	158
McMicken, Andrew	Lauderdale	Wills 4	1821-1825	2
McMilion, Amon	Tuscaloosa	Wills 1	1821-1855	17
McMillan, Abner	Dallas	Wills A	1821-1849	270
McMillan, Abner	Greene	Wills D	1851-1888	76
McMillan, C. M.	Sumter	Wills 2	1851-1872	199
McMillan, Columbus F.	Wilcox	Wills 6	1862-1870	61
McMillan, Dougal	Monroe	W&D A	1833-1841	169
McMillan, Drury	Sumter	Wills 2	1851-1872	205
McMillan, Gilbert	Lauderdale	Wills B	1859-1870	426
McMillan, James	Dallas	Wills A	1821-1849	116
McMillan, James A.	Wilcox	Wills 5	1855-1870	444
McMillan, John	Barbour	OCR 3	1847-1851	246
McMillan, Mary	Barbour	OCR 14	1863-1865	316
McMillan, Sarah	Wilcox	Wills 3	1826-1858	389
McMillan, William	Baldwin	Wills A	1811-1881	194
Macmillian, Edward	Pike	Wills B	1862-1879	84
McMillian, John C.	Coosa	W&OCR 2	1843-1883	88
McMillian, Nancy	Coosa	W&OCR 2	1843-1883	280
McMillian, Sarah	Morgan	OCR 7	1837-1843	392
McMillion, Alexander	Tuscaloosa	Wills 1	1821-1855	342
McMurry, James	Lauderdale	Wills A	1835-1858	285

TESTATOR	COUNTY	WHERE FOUND		PAGE
McNamara, George	Mobile	Wills 1	1813-1837	32
McNamara, Stephen	Mobile	Wills 3	1857-1870	53
McNamee, James	Chambers	Wills 3	1856-1899	39
McNeil, Daniel	Lowndes	Wills B	1830-1859	347
McNeil, Jane	Montgomery	Wills 4	1853-1869	361
McNeill, A. C.	Dallas	Wills B	1850-1871	228
McNeill, Eliza F.	Wilcox	Wills 5	1855-1870	148
McNeill, Hector	Wilcox	Wills 5	1855-1870	308
McNeill, John	Coosa	W&OCR 2	1843-1883	11
McNeill, Malcolm	Wilcox	Wills 1	1821-1844	385
McNoir, Letita Ann	Dallas	Wills B	1850-1871	90
McPhail, Michael	Barbour	OCR 7	1854-1857	305
McPhaill, John	Madison	PR 2	1818-1823	213
McPherson, Alexander B.	Lowndes	Wills C	1861-1899	39
McPherson, Cyrus	Sumter	Wills 2	1851-1872	251
McPherson, Nathan	Wilcox	Wills 5	1855-1870	107
McQueen, James, Sr.	Lowndes	Wills B	1830-1859	29
McQueen, John	Lowndes	Wills B	1830-1859	391
McQueen, Samuel	Lowndes	Wills C	1861-1899	74
McQuire, John	Mobile	Wills 3	1857-1870	68
McRa, Duncan	Dallas	Wills A	1821-1849	281
McRa, Mary	Dallas	Wills A	1821-1849	288
McRae, Christian	Autauga	Reports E-B	1841-1845	449
McRae, Mrs. Christian	Barbour	OCR 2	1842-1847	119
McRae, Christopher	Marengo	Wills A	1820-1864	237
McRae, Christopher J.	Wilcox	Wills 4	1847-1862	67
McRae, Farquhar A.	Barbour	OCR 9	1858-1859	531
McRae, Farquhar A.	Barbour	OCR 17	1868-1870	188
McRae, Hugh D.	Lowndes	Wills B	1830-1859	85
McRae, John	Marengo	Wills A	1820-1864	378
McRae, John A.	Lowndes	Wills C	1861-1899	44
McRae, Mary	Barbour	OCR 11	1860-1861	798
McRae, Mary	Wilcox	Wills 3	1826-1858	331
McRae, Josephine	Hale	Wills A	1867-1923	64
McRee, Martha Ann	Lowndes	Wills B	1830-1859	334
McReynolds, John	Wilcox	Wills 3	1826-1858	242
McReynolds, John D.	Calhoun	Loose	Probated 1837	
McReynolds, Joseph	Talladega	W&I C	1862-1866	153
McReynolds,? T. B.	Greene	Wills A	1821-1827	40
McReynolds, William	Wilcox	Wills 2	1832-1850	203
McRoy, Q.	Pike	Wills A	1845-1862	68
McAshan, William	Jefferson	Deeds 1	1818-1828	61
McTyeire, E. H.	Russell	Wills 2	1850-1873	241
McTyeire, John	Barbour	OCR 11	1860-1861	39
McTyeire, John	Russell	Wills 2	1850-1873	197
McVay, Hugh	Lauderdale	Wills A	1835-1858	193
McVay, Zadock	Lawrence	I&W A	1850-1857	283
McVoy,? Susan	Mobile	Wills 2	1837-1857	254
McWhorter, A. B.	Montgomery	Wills 4	1853-1869	238
McWhorter, Alvin A.	Montgomery	Wills 3	1840-1854	116
McWhorter, George Gray	Montgomery	Wills 2	1820-1845	79

TESTATOR	COUNTY	WHERE FOUND		PAGE
McWhorter, John	Pike	Wills A	1845-1862	16
McWhorter, John	Wilcox	Wills 5	1855-1870	422
McWilliams, Andrew	Jefferson	OCR	1824-1831	35
McWilliams, Elizabeth	Jefferson	OCR	1841-1844	31
Mabry, J. A.	Tuscaloosa	Wills 1	1821-1855	103
Mabson, William S.	Bullock	Wills A	1868-1902	25
Mackey, George B.	Tallapoosa	Wills 2	1864-1907	35
Mackey, James	Lauderdale	Wills B	1859-1870	306
Mackey, John	Lauderdale	Wills A	1835-1858	5
Mackey, Solomon	Tallapoosa	Wills 1	1838-1866	95
Maclin, Benjamin	Talladega	Wills B	1839-1845	90
Maclin, Thomas	Limestone	Wills 7	1844-1847	123
Macon, Warner	Macon	Records 8	1859-1860	554
Madden, Jane	Russell	Wills 2	1850-1873	53
Madden, Toliver	Tallapoosa	Wills 2	1864-1907	7
Madding, Elisha	Lawrence	I&W A	1850-1857	180
Maddox, Benjamin	Limestone	Wills 3	1826-1831	173
Maddox, Henley	Tuscaloosa	Wills 1	1821-1855	63
Maddox, Mark	Tuscaloosa	Wills 1	1821-1855	231
Maddox, Nathan	Wilcox	Wills 1	1821-1844	437
Maddox, William	Tuscaloosa	Wills 3	1858-1865	66
Maddox, William S.	Tallapoosa	Wills 1	1838-1866	202
Maddux, James	Chambers	Wills 1-2	1833-1856	361
Madlock, Anderson	Pike	Inv. A	1845-1862	213
Magbee, William L.	Chambers	Wills 3	1856-1899	201
Magee, William	Baldwin	Wills A	1811-1881	134
Magoffin, Beriah	Mobile	Wills 3	1857-1870	444
Magoffin, James	Washington	Wills 1 Ø	1827-1888	209
Magoffin, James	Washington	Wills B	1827-	126
Mahan, Jane	Mobile	Wills 3	1857-1870	382
Mahon, Mary	Perry	Wills A	1821-1855	7
Mahone, Stephen M.	Macon	Records 7	1857-1859	64
Mahoney, Patrick,	Baldwin	Wills A	1811-1881	54
Mainair, James	Montgomery	Wills 2	1820-1845	22
Majors, Aaron	Wilcox	Wills 5	1855-1870	439
Malcomson, Jane Bruce	Mobile	Wills 3	1857-1870	717
Maline, Jane	Limestone	Wills 12	1866-1872	13
Mallard, James H.	Macon	Records 5	1853-1855	725
Mallory, George M.	Mobile	Wills 2	1837-1857	253
Mallory, James	Talladega	W&I D	1867-1880	545
Malloy, Duncan	Bullock	Wills A	1868-1902	3
Malone, Allen	Tuscaloosa	Wills 3	1858-1865	154
Malone, Annie G.	Monroe	W&D G	1868-1870	335
Malone, Benjamin	Madison	PR 6	1832-1834	1
Malone, Drury R.	Mobile	Wills 2	1837-1857	156
Malone, David	DeKalb	Wills A	1837-1863	43
Malone, Harper	Madison	PR 9	1839-1841	371
Malone, Henry B.	Limestone	Wills 12	1866-1872	434

TESTATOR	COUNTY	WHERE FOUND		PAGE
Malone, Thomas	Mobile	Wills 2	1837-1857	217
Malone, Thomas, Jr.	Limestone	Wills 4	1831-1837	546
Malone,? Thomas C.	Limestone	Wills 6	1841-1846	221
Malone, William P.	Russell	Wills 2	1850-1873	29
Mandeville, Henry	Mobile	Wills 3	1857-1870	67
Mangham, Jane	Chambers	Wills 1-2	1833-1856	306
Mangham, William	Russell	Wills 2	1850-1873	11
Mangram, Jane	Chambers	Wills 1-2	1833-1856	306
Mangum, B. W.	Lowndes	Wills B	1830-1859	176
Maning, John	Montgomery	Wills 3	1840-1854	71
Manley, F. F.	Coosa	W&OCR 2	1843-1883	227
Manley, Richard	Tallapoosa	Wills 1	1838-1866	41
Manly, Basil, Sr.	Tuscaloosa	Wills 4	1868-1897	5
Mann, Benjamin H.	Greene	Wills B	1817-1841	112
Mann, Daniel	Bullock	Wills A	1868-1902	30
Mann, James N.	Dallas	Wills B	1850-1871	100
Mann, James W.	Monroe	W&D A	1833-1841	197
Mann, John H.	Coosa	W&OCR 2	1843-1883	189
Manney, James	Mobile	Wills 2	1837-1857	168
Manning, Elijah L.	Sumter	Wills 1	1828-1851	388
Manning, James	Madison	PR 9	1831-1841	446'
Manning, Mrs. Louisiana	Marengo	Wills A	1820-1864	501
Manning, Simeon D.	Monroe	W&D A	1833-1841	216
Manning, William	Lawrence	I&W A	1850-1857	62
Manry, Henry	Mobile	Wills 3	1857-1870	648
Maples, Sarah Jane	Madison	Wills 1	1853-1875	540
Marbury, Leonard	Coosa	W&OCR 2	1843-1883	222
Marcum, Amy	Tuscaloosa	Wills 3	1858-1865	176
Marcum, William	Lauderdale	Wills B	1859-1870	3
Marcus, Joshua	Autauga	Reports H	1853-1857	341
Marcus, Martha B.	Chambers	Wills 1-2	1833-1856	349
Mardis, John W.	Shelby	Wills L	1838-1858	110
Markham, Fanny T.	Mobile	Wills 2	1837-1857	286
Markham, James B.	Dallas	Wills B	1850-1871	196
Marks, Adeline E.	Russell	Wills 2	1850-1873	81
Marks, E. W.	Dallas	Wills B	1850-1871	360
Marks, James	Montgomery	Wills 2	1820-1845	257
Marks, James	Montgomery	Wills 4	1853-1869	571
Marks, John H.	Montgomery	Wills 2	1820-1845	61
Marks, Nickolas M.	Montgomery	Wills 3	1840-1854	59
Marks, Samuel B.	Montgomery	Wills 4	1853-1869	575
Marler, Aminadab	Montgomery	Wills 2	1820-1845	219
Marlins, James S.	Lauderdale	Wills B	1859-1870	28
Maroney, Isaac	Shelby	Wills C	1818-1827	4
Marr, John H.	Tuscaloosa	Wills 1	1821-1855	141
Marr, Nancy G.	Tuscaloosa	Wills 3	1858-1865	8
Marr, William Miller	Tuscaloosa	Wills 1	1821-1855	54
Marrast, William D.	Tuscaloosa	Wills 3	1858-1865	104
Marsey, Edward	Limestone	Wills 4	1831-1837	133
Marsh, Bryan	Wilcox	Wills 4	1847-1862	232
Marsh, James	Mobile	Wills 3	1857-1870	728

TESTATOR	COUNTY	WHERE FOUND		PAGE
Marshall, Elizabeth	Monroe	W&D B	1841-1845	75
Marshall, Frances	Tuscaloosa	Wills 3	1858-1865	39
Marshall, Hugh	Dallas	Wills B	1850-1871	268
Marshall, John L.	Monroe	W&D G	1868-1870	239
Marshall, Joseph B.	Monroe	W&D F	1861-1867	186
Marshall, T. A. J.	Dallas	Wills B	1850-1871	254
Martin, Aaron D.	Henry	Deeds A-B	1822-1840	167
Martin, Andrew	Madison	PR 1	1842-1849	616
Martin, Andy	Clarke	OCR F	1846-1850	63
Martin, Benjamin Y.	Barbour	OCR 11	1860-1861	529
Martin, Mrs. Caroline A. V.	Montgomery	Wills 3	1840-1854	258
Martin, Claiborne	Perry	Wills A	1821-1855	302
Martin, Dabney A.	Morgan	OCR 11	1850-1852	150
Martin, Elizabeth	Mobile	Wills 2	1837-1857	246
Martin, George M.	Perry	Wills B	1858-1873	348
Martin, James	Greene	Wills B	1817-1841	149
Martin, James	Mobile	Wills 2	1837-1857	114
Martin, James D.	Henry	Deeds A-B	1822-1840	135
Martin, John	Chambers	Wills 3	1856-1899	235
Martin, John	Coosa	W&OCR 2	1843-1883	35
Martin, John	Jefferson	PM	1848-1853	11
Martin, Joshua L.	Tuscaloosa	Wills 3	1858-1865	17
Martin, Louis	Marshall	FR 10	1869-1871	32
Martin, Loving	Calhoun	Loose	Probated 1856	
Martin, Martin D.	Barbour	OCR 10	1859-1860	677
Martin, Mary	Montgomery	Wills 5	1863-1887	1
Martin, Mary Ann	Lauderdale	Wills B	1859-1870	48
Martin, Nancy	Madison	PR 13	1838-1848	516
Martin, Phares	Hale	Wills A	1867-1923	45
Martin, Richard	Madison	Wills 1	1810-1820	370
Martin, Mrs. Sarah	Jefferson	Wills A	1856-1880	108
Martin, Shadrach	Perry	Wills A	1821-1855	251
Martin, Solomon	Talladega	W&I A	1852-1857	24
Martin, Thomas	Madison	Wills 1	1853-1875	207
Martin, William	Jefferson	Wills A	1856-1880	346
Martin, William	Mobile	Wills 2	1837-1857	46
Martin, William	Montgomery	Wills 2	1820-1845	273
Martin, Zachariah	Madison	PR 2&5	1818-1826	53
Marvin, Mary M.	Mobile	Wills 1	1813-1837	258
Marx, Henry	Mobile	Wills 4	1870-1878	63
Masendorff, Ferdinand	Mobile	Wills 3	1857-1870	328
Mason, Ann	Madison	PR 2&5	1818-1826	478
Mason, David H.	Limestone	Wills 4	1831-1837	349
Mason, James J.	Limestone	Wills 3	1826-1831	203
Mason, Job	Shelby	Wills B	1818-1840	119
Mason, Job	Shelby	Wills C	1818-1827	239
Mason, Joseph B.	Lowndes	Wills C	1861-1899	169
Mason, Joseph C.	Lowndes	Wills B	1830-1859	101
Mason, Judith Ann	Autauga	Reports G	1850-1853	302
Mason, L. W.	Wilcox	Wills 5	1855-1870	340
Mason, Michael	Madison	PR 8	1831-1839	414

TESTATOR	COUNTY	WHERE FOUND		PAGE
Mason, Priscilla A.	Morgan	OB 29	1867-1871	414
Mason, Rebecca	Limestone	Wills 5	1836-1841	88
Mason, Sarah	Wilcox	Wills 5	1855-1870	447
Mason, Sara Mariah	Elmore	Wills A	1866-1906	8
Mason, William	Limestone	Wills 4	1831-1837	556
Massengal, Elisha	Madison	PR 2	1818-1823	332
Massengale, Solomon	Madison	PR 2&5	1818-1826	289
Massey, B. B.	Perry	Wills B	1858-1873	20
Massey, Benjamin F.	Jefferson	Wills A	1856-1880	63
Massey, Cordy	Barbour	OCR 4	1850-1852	311
Massey, Francesco S.	Sumter	Wills 1	1828-1851	306
Massey, George P.	Perry	Wills B	1858-1873	384
Massey, James	Jefferson	Wills A	1856-1880	16
Massey, Joseph	Perry	Wills A	1821-1855	211
Massey, Joseph D.	Lowndes	Wills B	1830-1859	351
Massey, Kesiah	Perry	Wills B	1858-1873	1
Massey, Oliver	Perry	Wills A	1821-1855	131
Massey, Warren	Marengo	Wills A	1820-1864	455
Massie, John	Limestone	Wills 3	1826-1831	263
Massie, Judith	Limestone	Wills 7	1844-1847	34
Massie, Rob.	Mobile	Wills 1	1813-1837	117
Masterson, Hugh	Mobile	Wills 2	1837-1857	313
Masterson, James	Mobile	Wills 2	1837-1857	198
Masterson, John	Lauderdale	Wills B	1859-1870	19
Masterson, Luke	Mobile	Wills 2	1837-1857	237
Mastin, Francis T.	Madison	Wills 1	1853-1875	330
Mastin, Peter B.	Montgomery	Wills 4	1853-1869	467
Mastin, William J.	Madison	PR 12	1845-1849	347
Mather, Thomas	Mobile	Wills 1	1813-1837	248
Matheson, William	Clarke	GE&W	1832-1839	315
Mathews, C. L.	Dallas	Wills A	1821-1849	221
Mathews, George E.	Montgomery	Wills 3	1840-1854	50
Mathews, James B.	Autauga	Reports B	1829-1833	124
Mathews, S. B.	Wilcox	Wills 5	1855-1870	117
Mathews, William R.	Montgomery	Wills 4	1853-1869	7
Mathiew, Charles	Mobile	Wills 2	1837-1857	65
Mathus, Newman S.	Coosa	W&OCR 2	1843-1883	266
Matthew, Charles L.	Wilcox	Wills 1	1821-1844	298
Matthews, Archur	Wilcox	Wills 1	1821-1844	394
Matthews, James	Marengo	Wills A	1820-1864	209
Matthews, Luke	Madison	Wills 1	1853-1875	544
Matthews, Rebecca	Dallas	Wills A	1821-1849	168
Matthews, Walker	Jackson	Records	1861-1881	586
Matthews, William	Limestone	OCM	1824-1830	279
Matthews, Willis	Tallapoosa	Wills 2	1864-1907	1
Mattingly, Frances	Lauderdale	Wills B	1859-1870	13
Maturin, Simon	Coosa	W&PM A	1834-1842	163
Maul, George	Lowndes	Wills C	1861-1899	133
Maul, James	Lowndes	Wills B	1830-1859	168
Maury, Alexander C.	Sumter	Wills 1	1828-1851	88
Maxwell, Allen J.	Coosa	W&OCR 2	1843-1883	314

TESTATOR	COUNTY	WHERE FOUND		PAGE
Maxwell, Reuben	Tallapoosa	Wills 1	1838-1866	164
May, Abbey	Lauderdale	Wills B	1859-1870	261
May, Claiborn	Lauderdale	Wills 3	1821-1825	8
May, Henry	Lauderdale	Wills 3	1821-1825	143
May, Henry	Lauderdale	Wills 4	1821-1825	3
May, James	Pike	Wills A	1845-1862	201
May, James B.	Sumter	Wills 1	1828-1851	44
May, John	Clarke	PR L	1861-1864	123
May, Johnathan	Sumter	Wills 2	1851-1872	226
May, Martha W.	Sumter	Wills 2	1851-1872	291
May, Moody H.	Greene	Wills D	1851-1888	14
May, Nathan L.	Lowndes	Wills C	1861-1899	18
May, Patrick	Hale	Wills A	1867-1923	37
May, Richard	Tuscaloosa	Deeds T		7
May, Susannah	Lowndes	Wills C	1861-1899	85
May, Theodore	Autauga	Reports B	1829-1833	102
May, William	Lowndes	Wills B	1830-1859	25
May, William	Montgomery	Wills 2	1820-1845	22
May, William A.	Sumter	Wills 2	1851-1872	327
May, Woodson	Lawrence	I&W D	1835-1840	537
Mayberry, George	Bibb	OCM	1846-1851	280
Mayberry, George S.	Bibb	Admr.R 1	1858-1865	464
Mayes, Ann	Perry	Wills A	1821-1855	293
Mayes, Drury	Lawrence	I&W C	1866-1880	19
Mayes, Edward	Greene	Wills B	1817-1841	276
Mayfield, Archibald	Tuscaloosa	Wills 1	1821-1855	66
Mayfield, Sanie	Tuscaloosa	Wills 3	1858-1865	173
Mayhan, Jane	Mobile	Wills 3	1857-1870	382
Mayhew, Elvira	Madison	Wills 1	1853-1875	374
Mayhew, Lucy M.	Montgomery	Wills 2	1820-1845	101
Maynard, John L.	Mobile	Wills 2	1837-1857	81
Maynor, John D.	Russell	Wills 2	1850-1873	200
Maynor, William H.	Russell	Wills 2	1850-1873	222
Mayo, John	Chambers	Wills 3	1856-1899	51
Mays, Lewis	Madison	PR 4	1826-1829	410
Mays, Mary K.	Lauderdale	Wills B	1859-1870	129
Mays, R. L.	Macon	WAC&A 11	1862-1870	81
Meacham, Banks	Madison	Deeds C	1816-1818	12
Meacham, Mark	Madison	Deeds A	1810-1816	77
Mead, Lemuel	Madison	PR 7	1834-1837	533
Meador, James	Greene	Wills B	1817-1841	165
Meador, John	Dallas	Wills A	1821-1849	98
Meador, Loving ?	Sumter	Wills 2	1851-1872	19
Meadors, James I.	Chambers	Wills 3	1856-1899	160
Meadors, Warner W.	Chambers	Wills 3	1856-1899	96
Meadows, Enoch	Henry	OCR R	1866-1867	248
Meadows, Isham	Lowndes	Wills B	1830-1859	154
Meadows, James	Jefferson	Wills A	1856-1880	325
Meadows, Jesse	Tallapoosa	Wills 2	1864-1907	90
Meadows, Thomas W.	Tallapoosa	Wills 2	1864-1907	39
Meads, John P.	Montgomery	Wills 4	1853-1869	149

TESTATOR	COUNTY	WHERE FOUND		PAGE
Mealing, Jonathan	Lowndes	Wills C	1861-1899	167
Mealing, Lucretia	Lowndes	Wills C	1861-1899	79
Means, Margaret	Greene	Wills B	1817-1841	185
Medcalf, Benjamin	Baldwin	Wills A	1811-1881	84
Meggs, William	St. Clair	Deeds B	1831-1849	911
Meek, Ann A.	Tuscaloosa	Wills 1	1821-1855	333
Megginson, Andrew J.	Clarke	PR L	1861-1864	111
Meincke, J. C.	Wilcox	Wills 6	1862-1870	77
Mejat, Geanty	Mobile	Wills 1	1813-1837	133
Melson, Nancy	Dallas	Wills B	1850-1871	386
Melton, Evander	Lowndes	Wills C	1861-1899	91
Melton, John	St. Clair	RE C	1852-1859	327
Melton, Robert	Washington	Wills 1 ∅	1827-1888	134
Melton, Robert	Washington	Wills B	1827-	85
Melton, Thomas	Perry	Wills A	1821-1855	222
Melton, Thompson	Greene	Wills A	1821-1827	48
Melton, William Allen	Perry	Wills B	1858-1873	253
Melvin, Scarborough	Baldwin	Wills A	1811-1881	264
Mendenhall, Ann B.	Wilcox	Wills 5	1855-1870	273
Mendenhall, Eli	Wilcox	Wills 3	1826-1858	246
Menefee, Albert	Chambers	Wills 3	1856-1899	99
Menifee, Tatum	Chambers	Wills 1-2	1833-1856	228
Mentzar, Jonas	Lauderdale	Wills 3	1821-1825	107
Meriwether, Joseph	Greene	Wills B	1817-1841	175
Meriwether, Zachy	Greene	Wills B	1817-1841	167
Merrell, Laura A.	Autauga	Reports C	1834-1838	92
Merrett, James	Tuscaloosa	Wills 1	1821-1855	341
Merrill, Jonathan	Lauderdale	Wills 4	1821-1825	83
Merrill, Lemuel	Macon	Records 5	1853-1855	454
Merrissey, Michael	Mobile	Wills 3	1857-1870	260
Merritt, Gabriel	Montgomery	Wills 4	1853-1869	20
Merritt, Thomas	Talladega	W&I B	1858-1864	339
Mervino, Elen C.	Montgomery	Wills 4	1853-1869	332
Mervino, Elizabeth	Montgomery	Wills 3	1840-1854	63
Meslier, Augustine Eliz.	Mobile	Wills 2	1837-1857	247
Messer, John	Jackson	Records	1861-1881	325
Mestaye, Michael	Greene	Wills A	1821-1827	17
Metcalf, Andrew	Madison	Deeds B	1810-1816	86
Methvin, Levi	Madison	PR 13	1838-1848	359
Meux, Richard	Madison	PR 3	1823-1826	353
Micholson, Malcksie	Lauderdale	Wills B	1859-1870	118
Middlebrooks, Thomas J.	Lee	Wills A	1867-1898	13
Middleton, A. W.	Montgomery	Wills 5	1863-1887	20
Middleton, Greenberry	Jackson	Records	1861-1881	316
Middleton, John	Madison	PR 2	1818-1823	113
Middleton, William	Monroe	W&D F	1861-1867	164
Milam, Almon G.	Lawrence	I&W C	1866-1880	159
Milam, Benjamin	Tallapoosa	Wills 1	1838-1866	207
Milam, James W.	Talladega	Wills B	1839-1845	198
Milam, John	Madison	PR 8	1831-1839	397
Milam, Jordan	Tallapoosa	Wills 1	1838-1866	107

TESTATOR	COUNTY	WHERE FOUND		PAGE
Miles, David	Pike	Wills A	1845-1862	42
Miles, George	Dallas	Wills A	1821-1849	59
Miles, Jacob	Jefferson	Deeds 1	1818-1828	67
Miles, Jacob	Jefferson	Wills 1	1818-1840	81
Miles, Robert	Mobile	Wills 2	1837-1857	302
Miles, William P.	Lowndes	Wills B	1830-1859	138
Milford, Robert	Russell	Wills 2	1850-1873	115
Millard, Nathaniel	Dallas	Wills A	1821-1849	348
Millender, William	Autauga	Reports C	1834-1838	272½
Miller, Abijah	Wilcox	Wills 5	1855-1870	325
Miller, Benjamin	Lawrence	I&W A	1850-1857	136
Miller, Charles	Sumter	Wills 1	1828-1851	157
Miller, David M.	Tuscaloosa	Wills 3	1858-1865	220
Miller, David R.	Mobile	Wills 3	1857-1870	552
Miller, Elijah	Perry	Wills A	1821-1855	207
Miller, Eliza	Mobile	Wills 3	1857-1870	236
Miller, Henry	Henry	OCR N	1862-1864	168
Miller, Henry	Madison	PR 15	1850-1853	152
Miller, Henry	Mobile	Wills 2	1837-1857	263
Miller, Israel	Mobile	Wills 3	1857-1870	427
Miller, Jacob	Mobile	Wills 2	1837-1857	224
Miller, James	Dallas	Wills B	1850-1871	5
Miller, James	Mobile	Wills 2	1837-1857	371
Miller, John	Mobile	Wills 3	1857-1870	327
Miller, John H.	Montgomery	Wills 4	1853-1869	423
Miller, Margaret	Jefferson	Deeds 1	1818-1828	125
Miller, Martin	Madison	Wills 1	1853-1875	237
Miller, Mary	Madison	Wills 1	1853-1875	6
Miller, Mary	Madison	Wills 1	1853-1875	504
Miller, George Poe	Mobile	Wills 3	1857-1870	387
Miller, R. M.	Lauderdale	Wills B	1859-1870	96
Miller, S. H.	Madison	Wills 1	1853-1875	517
Miller, Susan M.	Mobile	Wills 3	1857-1870	650
Miller, Thomas	Pike	Wills B	1862-1879	160
Miller, William	Calhoun	Loose	Probated 1860	
Miller, William	Chambers	Wills 1-2	1833-1856	435
Miller, William	Perry	Wills A	1821-1855	134
Miller, William E.	Sumter	Wills 1	1828-1851	309
Milligan, Hugh	Mobile	Wills 3	1857-1870	156
Millo, Vincent	Mobile	Wills 1	1813-1837	87
Mills, Abner B.	Montgomery	Wills 2	1820-1845	281
Mills, Augustus L.	Henry	OCR P	1864-1866	518
Mills, Benjamin	Montgomery	Wills 2	1820-1845	186
Mills, Jacob	Jefferson	Wills 1	1818-1840	81
Mills, James	Tuscaloosa	Wills 3	1858-1865	73
Mills, James	Tuscaloosa	Wills 3	1858-1865	239
Mills, John	Russell	Wills 1	1838-1849	82
Mills, Peter	Tuscaloosa	Wills 1	1821-1855	280
Mills, William	Coosa	W&OCR 2	1843-1883	132
Milner, John	Tallapoosa	Wills 1	1838-1866	63
Milner, William	Tallapoosa	Wills 1	1838-1866	155

TESTATOR	COUNTY	WHERE FOUND		PAGE
Milton, E. M.	Dallas	Wills B	1850-1871	105
Mims, Alexander	Baldwin	Wills A	1811-1881	95
Mims, Alexander F.	Dallas	Wills B	1850-1871	63
Mims, Britten	Monroe	W&D B	1841-1845	546
Mims, David	Baldwin	Wills A	1811-1881	86
Mims, Drewry	Barbour	OCR 9	1858-1859	308
Miner, William F.	Morgan	OCR 3	1827-1832	23
Minor, Henry	Greene	Wills B	1817-1847	212
Minor, Henry, Jr.	Greene	Wills B	1817-1841	292
Minshaw, Jacob	Barbour	OCR 1	1833-1843	323
Minter, Anthony M.	Dallas	Wills B	1850-1871	192
Minter, Joanna	Dallas	Wills A	1821-1849	81
Minter, Josiah	Morgan	PCTR C (15)	1854-1858	29
Minter, Robert R.	Dallas	Wills B	1850-1871	365
Minter, William I.	Tuscaloosa	Wills 3	1858-1865	131
Mitchell, Armstrong	Montgomery	Wills 4	1853-1869	377
Mitchell, Benjamin	Montgomery	Wills 3	1840-1854	104
Mitchell, Christian	Clarke	OCR F	1846-1850	150
Mitchell, Cullen	Limestone	Wills 4	1831-1837	138
Mitchell, Doctor Louica	Perry	Wills A	1821-1855	92
Mitchell, Frank	Mobile	Wills 1	1813-1837	108
Mitchell, Henry H.	Clarke	OCR	1825-1832	290
Mitchell, Hinchy	Tuscaloosa	Wills 1	1821-1855	13
Mitchell, Isaiah	Lauderdale	Wills A	1835-1858	161
Mitchell, Jabez	Tuscaloosa	Wills 1	1821-1855	208
Mitchell, James	Lee	Wills A	1867-1898	11
Mitchell, James	Montgomery	Wills 2	1820-1845	28
Mitchell, James	Sumter	Wills 2	1851-1872	93
Mitchell, James S.	Chambers	Wills 3	1856-1899	31
Mitchell, Jesse B.	Limestone	Wills 5	1836-1841	565
Mitchell, John	Dallas	Wills B	1850-1871	402
Mitchell, John	Macon	Records 10	1863-1865	706
Mitchell, John E.	Autauga	Reports E-B	1841-1845	274
Mitchell, Joseph	Tuscaloosa	Wills 1	1821-1855	114
Mitchell, Joshua S.	Chambers	Wills 1-2	1833-1856	101
Mitchell, M. E. A.	Dallas	Wills B	1850-1871	47
Mitchell, Margaret	Mobile	Wills 3	1857-1870	715
Mitchell, Mary	Montgomery	Wills 4	1853-1869	171
Mitchell, Mary Jane	Shelby	Wills H	1847-1866	635
Mitchell, Napoleon B.	Dallas	Wills B	1850-1871	98
Mitchell, Randolph	Barbour	OCR 13	1863-1864	172
Mitchell, Reuben	Chambers	Wills 3	1856-1899	26
Mitchell, Robert	Macon	WAC&A 11	1862-1870	604
Mitchell, Ruben A.	Coosa	W&OCR 2	1843-1883	198
Mitchell, Stephen	Perry	Wills A	1821-1855	19
Mitchell, Stephen	Perry	W&I	1823-1833	90
Mitchell, Thomas	Montgomery	Wills 2	1820-1845	262
Mitchell, Uriah G.	Dallas	Wills A	1821-1849	216
Mitchell, William	Mobile	Wills 1	1813-1837	96
Mitchell, William H.	Lauderdale	Wills B	1859-1870	111
Mitchell, Willis C.	Chambers	Wills 3	1856-1899	29

TESTATOR	COUNTY	WHERE FOUND		PAGE
Mitchell, Yancy	Sumter	Wills 2	1851-1872	352
Mitchem, L.	Lowndes	Wills B	1830-1859	261
Mitcherson, Rachel	Marengo	Wills A	1820-1864	467
Mitherson, John	Marengo	Wills A	1820-1864	230
Mixon, James	Henry	OCR S	1867-1868	488
Mizelle, John	Russell	Wills 1	1838-1849	100
Mobley, A. C.	Dallas	Wills B	1850-1871	281
Mobley, F. J.	Butler	Wills 1	1853-1864	199
Mobley, Thomas B.	Clarke	PR L	1861-1864	93
Moffitt, Henry	Perry	Wills A	1821-1855	34
Mohr, Christian S. G.	Mobile	Wills 3	1857-1870	339
Molton, Thomas	Montgomery	Wills 3	1840-1854	12
Moncrief, Sampson B.	Sumter	Wills 2	1851-1872	118
Monette, Rachel	Greene	Wills B	1817-1841	262
Monger, Hiram	Washington	Wills 1 ∅	1827-1888	185
Monger, Hiram	Washington	Wills B	1827-	114
Monroe, George	Madison	PR 2&5	1818-1826	111
Montague, R. A.	Perry	Wills B	1858-1873	114
Montgomery, James	Limestone	Wills 6	1841-1846	252
Montgomery, James	Talladega	W&I D	1867-1880	630
Montgomery, John P.	Calhoun	Loose	Probated 1864	
Montgomery, Joseph	Wilcox	Wills 4	1847-1862	207
Montgomery, Robert	Dallas	Wills B	1850-1871	234
Montgomery, Susan J.	Wilcox	Wills 5	1855-1870	297
Montgomery, William	Autauga	Reports K	1859-1861	7
Moody, David	Blount	Record PM B	1852-1856	186
Moody, Fabian	Chambers	Wills 1-2	1833-1856	195
Moon, Alexander	Marengo	Wills A	1820-1864	102
Moon, Thomas	Sumter	Wills 2	1851-1872	24
Mooney, Joseph	Madison	PR 2&5	1818-1826	545
Moor, Joseph	St. Clair	RE A	1858-1874	356
Moor, Lewis	Lowndes	Wills B	1830-1859	309
Moor, Pleasant	Henry	Deeds A-B	1822-1840	178
Moor, William	Lowndes	Wills B	1830-1859	10
Moor, William J.	Lowndes	Wills B	1830-1859	243
Moore, Aaron	Autauga	Reports C	1834-1838	347
Moore, Allen	Wilcox	Wills 1	1821-1844	250
Moore, Archibald	Tuscaloosa	Wills 1	1821-1855	224
Moore, B. F.	Pike	Wills B	1862-1879	33
Moore, David	Madison	PR 12	1845-1849	13
Moore, Edward	Tuscaloosa	Wills 1	1821-1855	12
Moore, Eli, Sr.	Mobile	Wills 2	1837-1857	115
Moore, Eliza M.	Perry	Wills A	1821-1855	106
Moore, Elizabeth A.	Mobile	Wills 3	1857-1870	565
Moore, Ezekiel	Madison	PR 2&5	1818-1826	290
Moore, Gabriel E.	Madison	PR 13	1838-1848	361
Moore, George T.	Wilcox	Wills 3	1826-1858	173
Moore, Henry	Madison	PR 13	1838-1848	571
Moore, Isaac	Dallas	Wills B	1850-1871	96
Moore, Jacob	Montgomery	Wills 3	1840-1854	253
Moore, Jacob E.	Montgomery	Wills 3	1840-1854	243

TESTATOR	COUNTY	WHERE FOUND		PAGE
Moore, James	Autauga	Reports	G	1850-1853	276
Moore, James, Sr.	Madison	PR 7	1834-1837	25
Moore, James	Mobile	Wills 1	1813-1837	173
Moore, James	Tallapoosa	Wills 1	1838-1866	115
Moore, James	Tallapoosa	Wills 1	1838-1866	125
Moore, James B.	Jefferson	Deeds 1	1818-1828	108
Moore, Jane B.	Perry	Wills B	1858-1873	91
Moore, John	Greene	Wills A	1821-1827	14
Moore, John	Lauderdale	Wills B	1859-1870	143
Moore, John	Marshall	FR 5	1855-1859	145
Moore, John	Monroe	W&D A	1833-1841	206
Moore, John B.	Jefferson	Wills A	1856-1880	21
Moore, John B.	Jefferson	Deeds 1	1818-1828	108
Moore, John E.	Lauderdale	Wills B	1859-1870	40
Moore, John F.	Limestone	Wills 4	1831-1837	459
Moore, John W.	Pike	Wills B	1862-1879	100
Moore, Joseph	Jefferson	PM	1848-1853	149
Moore, Josiah	Sumter	Wills 2	1851-1872	168
Moore, L. D.	Pike	Wills A	1845-1862	257
Moore, Leonard	Monroe	W&D A	1833-1841	208
Moore, Levin	Chambers	Wills 1-2	1833-1856	469
Moore, Lodrick	Sumter	Wills 1	1828-1851	137
Moore, Mary	Chambers	Wills 1-2	1833-1856	9
Moore, Nathaniel	Clarke	PR M	1864-1866	236
Moore, Samuel	Wilcox	Wills 1	1821-1844	296
Moore, Sithe	Wilcox	Wills 1	1821-1844	325
Moore, Thomas	Lauderdale	Wills A	1835-1858	277
Moore, Thomas	Madison	PR 2	1818-1823	176
Moore, Thomas	Tallapoosa	Wills 1	1838-1866	101
Moore, William	Madison	PR 2&5	1818-1826	405
Moore, William	Monroe	W&D G	1868-1870	600
Moore, William	Tuscaloosa	Wills 3	1858-1865	202
Moore, William Barnes	Mobile	Wills 3	1857-1870	245
Moore, William C.	Dallas	Wills B	1850-1871	141
Moore, William T.	Lee	Wills A	1867-1898	20
Moorer, John H.	Lowndes	Wills B	1830-1859	237
Moorer, John J.	Lowndes	Wills B	1830-1859	254
Moorer, John J.	Lowndes	Wills C	1861-1899	110
Mordecai, Jacob G.	Mobile	Wills 4	1870-1878	85
Mordecai, Solomon	Mobile	Wills 3	1857-1870	673
Moreland, E. N.	Pike	Wills B	1862-1879	38
Moreland, John T.	Chambers	Wills 1-2	1833-1856	276
Moreland, Turner	Russell	Wills 2	1850-1873	157
Morgan, Ashley	Autauga	Wills 1	1862-1925	19
Morgan, Elizabeth	Tallapoosa	Wills 1	1838-1866	220
Morgan, Francis L.	St. Clair	Deeds C	1846-1855	194
Morgan, Franklin H.	Madison	Wills 1	1853-1875	242
Morgan, George F.	Wilcox	Wills 4	1847-1862	245
Morgan, Henry R.	Tuscaloosa	Wills 1	1821-1855	325
Morgan, Isaiah	Dallas	Wills B	1850-1871	375
Morgan, John	Sumter	Wills 2	1851-1872	409

TESTATOR	COUNTY	WHERE FOUND		PAGE
Morgan, John D.	Wilcox	Wills 4	1847-1862	162
Morgan, Joseph, Jr.	Wilcox	Wills 4	1847-1862	44
Morgan, Mack	Wilcox	Wills 3	1826-1858	449
Morgan, Martin	Wilcox	Wills 2	1832-1850	193
Morgan, Martin	Wilcox	Wills 3	1826-1858	40
Morgan, Samuel	Calhoun	Loose	Probated 1857	
Morgan, William	Dallas	Wills B	1850-1871	102
Morgan, William C.	Chambers	Wills 3	1856-1899	88
Morris, Celia	Russell	Wills 1	1838-1849	1
Morris, Elizabeth	Mobile	Wills 3	1857-1870	614
Morris, Isham	Butler	Wills 1	1853-1864	178
Morris, Jesse	Tuscaloosa	Wills 1	1821-1855	236
Morris, Lewis	Chambers	Wills 1-2	1833-1856	453
Morris, Maurice	Lawrence	W&I C	1866-1880	162
Morris, Thomas A.	Perry	Wills B	1858-1873	149
Morris, William H.	Chambers	Wills 3	1856-1899	94
Morris, William H.	Chambers	Wills 3	1856-1899	111
Morrisen, Joseph	Mobile	Wills 3	1857-1870	111
Morrison, Andrew W.	Barbour	OCR 12	1861-1863	169
Morrison, Flora	Barbour	OCR 11	1860-1861	247
Morrison, James Brown	Henry	OCR F	1848-1853	304
Morrison, Josiah A.	Dallas	Wills B	1850-1871	9
Morrison, Robert C.	Marengo	Wills A	1820-1864	374
Morrison, William	Dallas	Wills A	1821-1849	167
Morrison, William R.	Dallas	Wills A	1821-1849	184
Morriss, Simcon	Talladega	W&I D	1867-1880	394
Morrow, George	Marshall	PR 2	1857-1888	494
Morrow, Isaac	Marshall	FR 1	1840-1844	183
Morrow, Malinda	Talladega	W&I D	1867-1880	587
Morrow, Margaret	Greene	Wills D	1851-1888	187
Morrow, Peter G.	Pike	Wills A	1845-1862	199
Morton, Alexander	Autauga	Reports C	1834-1838	567
Morton, John R.	Perry	Wills B	1858-1873	70
Morton, Thomas	Autauga	Reports F	1845-1850	356
Mosby, Hezekiah	Sumter	Wills 1	1828-1851	162
Moseley, A. K.	Dallas	Wills B	1850-1871	458
Moseley, Adra	Montgomery	Wills 4	1853-1869	569
Moseley, Elizabeth	Madison	PR 10	1842-1842	177
Moseley, George	Montgomery	Wills 2	1820-1845	286
Moseley, John	Madison	Wills 1	1853-1875	18
Moseley, Lewis	Dallas	Wills A	1821-1849	29
Moseley, Lewis A.	Dallas	Wills B	1850-1871	148
Moseley, Robert G.	Talladega	Wills A	1833-1839	487
Moseley, Sarah C.	Madison	PR 2	1818-1823	476
Mosely, John T.	Washington	Wills 1 ∅	1837-1888	189
Mosely, John T.	Washington	Wills B	1827-	116
Mosely, Robert	Perry	Wills B	1858-1873	143
Mosely, Robert T.	Montgomery	Wills 2	1820-1845	81
Mosely, Drury V.	Morgan	OCR 27	1868-1869	246
Mosley, William	Morgan	OCR 3	1827-1832	293
Mosley, William	Pike	Wills B	1862-1879	103

TESTATOR	COUNTY	WHERE FOUND		PAGE
Moss, Henry	Dallas	Wills A	1821-1849	134
Moss, James	Henry	OCR H	1855-1857	678
Mosser, Belinda	Pike	Wills A	1845-1862	136
Mosser, Samuel	Pike	Wills B	1862-1879	138
Mostillan, J. Sanford M.	Shelby	Wills E	1845-1850	50
Motley, Benjamin	Autauga	Wills 1	1862-1925	27
Motley, Robert	Autauga	Reports F	1845-1850	119
Motley, Robert, Sr.	Autauga	Reports C	1834-1838	242
Motley, William	Autauga	Reports C	1834-1838	333
Mottus, Silvain	Mobile	Wills 1	1813-1837	35
Moulton, C. M.	Sumter	Wills 2	1851-1872	131
Mounger, Henry H.	Washington	Wills 1 ∅	1827-1888	154
Mounger, Henry H.	Washington	Wills B	1827-	98
Mounger, Walter S.	Washington	Wills 1 ∅	1827-1888	157
Mounger, Walter S.	Washington	Wills B	1827-	99
Mowery, John	Limestone	OCM	1824-1830	249
Mowery, Judith	Limestone	Wills 4	1831-1837	657
Mudd, James	Jefferson	PM	1844-1854	306
Mudge, Albert	Mobile	Wills 2	1837-1857	187
Muldon, James	Mobile	Wills 4	1870-1878	70
Muldrow, James	Wilcox	Wills 1	1821-1844	391
Mullen, John	Russell	Wills 2	1850-1873	96
Mullinix, James	Tuscaloosa	Wills 1	1821-1855	240
Mumford, James	Perry	Wills A	1821-1855	179
Mund, Rosina	Baldwin	Wills A	1811-1881	222
Munroe, Malcolm	Talladega	W&I B	1858-1864	220
Murchison, John	Coosa	W&OCR 2	1843-1883	20
Murchison, Rora	Coosa	W&OCR 2	1843-1883	268
Murdock, James	Dallas	Wills A	1821-1849	152
Murph, John R.	Autauga	Reports F	1845-1850	296
Murphree, Daniel	Blount	PM B	1852-1856	46
Murphree, Solomon	Calhoun	Loose	Probated 1854	
Murphrey, William	Greene	Wills A	1821-1827	1
Murphy, Elizabeth	Montgomery	Wills 2	1820-1845	268
Murphy, Francis	Montgomery	Wills 5	1863-1887	8
Murphy, Hiram	Chambers	Wills 3	1856-1899	81
Murphy, John F.	Lauderdale	Wills B	1859-1870	3
Murphy, John H.	Montgomery	Wills 4	1853-1859	242
Murphy, M. E.	Lowndes	Wills B	1830-1859	285
Murphy, Moses	Sumter	Wills 1	1828-1851	97
Murphy, Murdock	Clarke	GE&W	1832-1839	77
Murphy, Nathan K.	Morgan	PCFR 18	1859-1860	250
Murphy, Thomas	Sumter	Wills 1	1828-1851	115
Murphy, William	Tallapoosa	Wills 2	1864-1907	85
Murray, Arthur	Montgomery	Wills 4	1853-1869	489
Murray, James	Chambers	Wills 1-2	1833-1856	508
Murray, Michael	Madison	PR 14	1846-1850	208
Murrell, Thomas W.	Chambers	Wills 1-2	1833-1856	317
Murrell, William	Clarke	GE&W	1832-1839	17
Murrell, William	Marengo	Wills A	1820-1864	175
Mushat, George L.	Lowndes	Wills C	1861-1899	13

TESTATOR	COUNTY	WHERE FOUND		PAGE
Musick, Jonathan	Chambers	Wills 1-2	1833-1856	203
Myatt, Aldridge	Lawrence	I&W A	1850-1857	13
Myers, Asberry	Sumter	Wills 1	1828-1851	200
Myers, Claiborne	Autauga	Reports G	1850-1853	574
Myers, Clairborne	Montgomery	Wills 3	1840-1854	306
Myers, William	Greene	Wills B	1817-1841	105
Myles, Josephus	Baldwin	Wills A	1811-1881	70
Myrick, John	Clarke	PR K	1858-1861	492
Nabors, Benjamin G.	Jefferson	Wills A	1856-1880	30
Nabors, Lewis	Calhoun	Loose	Probated 1843	
Nabors, Sam S.	Jefferson	Wills A	1856-1880	142
Naftel, St. John	Montgomery	Wills 3	1840-1854	249
Nails, Thomas P.	Lauderdale	Wills B	1859-1870	72
Nall, James	Perry	Wills A	1821-1855	205
Nance, Alfred	Dallas	Wills B	1850-1871	125
Nance, Daniel G.	Lauderdale	Wills A	1835-1858	199
Nance, Giles	Madison	PR 16	1831-1861	225
Nance, James, Sr.	Madison	PR 8	1831-1839	627
Nance, Nancy	Macon	Records 3	1845-1850	755
Nangle, Michael	Mobile	Wills 3	1857-1870	218
Napier, Leroy	Bullock	Wills A	1868-1902	32
Napier, Robert	Marengo	Wills A	1820-1864	235
Nash, Acton	Barbour	OCR 6	1854-1856	408
Nash, John	Jefferson	Wills A	1856-1880	316
Nash, John	Tuscaloosa	Wills 1	1821-1855	15
Nathan, Eli	Greene	Wills A	1821-1827	60
Nation, Edward	Blount	Records A	1837-1845	324
Nation, Hiram	St. Clair	RE D	1859-1867	90
Naugher, William	Tuscaloosa	Wills 1	1821-1855	356
Neal, John	Madison	Wills 1	1853-1875	25
Neal, L. B.	Tuscaloosa	Wills 4	1868-1897	7
Neal, Lydia	Tuscaloosa	Wills 1	1821-1855	174
Neal, William C.	St. Clair	RE C	1852-1859	241
Neal, Zachariah	Shelby	Wills B	1818-1840	168
Neale, Augustine	Marengo	Wills A	1820-1864	324
Neblett, Abel	Russell	Wills 2	1850-1873	
Needham, Benjamin	Washington	Wills 1 ∅	1827-1888	90
Needham, Benjamin	Washington	Wills B	1827-	58
Needham, James	Mobile	Wills 2	1837-1857	96
Neel, William	Tuscaloosa	Wills 1	1821-1855	268
Neely, James	Madison	Wills 1	1853-1875	421
Neely, John	Limestone	Wills 9	1847-1850	373
Neely, John	Madison	PR 3	1823-1826	193
Neil, Joseph	Chambers	Wills 1-2	1833-1856	143
Neil, William M.	Jefferson	Wills A	1856-1880	112
Neiley, Polly	Greene	Wills B	1817-1841	279
Nelms, ?David	Morgan	OCR 7	1837-1843	10
Nelms, Elisha Y.	Perry	Wills B	1858-1873	395

TESTATOR	COUNTY	WHERE FOUND		PAGE
Nelms, Samuel H.	Perry	Wills A	1821-1855	82
Nelson, Daniel	Autauga	Reports F	1845-1850	428
Nelson, ?David	Morgan	OCR 7	1837-1843	10
Nelson, George	Perry	Wills A	1821-1855	41
Nelson, Gideon E.	Hale	Wills A	1867-1923	15
Nelson, Nancy	Madison	PR 14	1846-1850	67
Nelson, Thomas	Russell	Wills 2	1850-1873	290
Nennelee, Margaret	Dallas	Wills B	1850-1871	106
Nertz, Elizabeth	Perry	Wills B	1858-1873	332
Nesbit, Thomas	Limestone	Wills 4	1831-1837	137
Nesmith, Martha	Lowndes	Wills C	1861-1899	15
NeSmith, Samuel P.	Lowndes	Wills C	1861-1899	15
Nettles, Elizabeth	Wilcox	Wills 4	1847-1862	158
Nettles, James L.	Wilcox	Wills 1	1821-1844	381
Nettles, John	Wilcox	Wills 1	1821-1844	383
Nettles, N. J.	Monroe	W&D F	1861-1867	97
Nettles, S. H.	Monroe	W&D D	1850-1856	304
Nevill, H. H.	Wilcox	Wills 5	1855-1870	180
Nevill, Mary Ann	Morgan	OCR LL	1850-1852	322
Nevill, Rebecca	Morgan	OCR 7	1837-1843	196
Newberry, Elizabeth	Lauderdale	Wills B	1859-1870	179
Newberry, James	Wilcox	Wills 1	1821-1844	316
Newberry, Peter	Wilcox	Wills 3	1826-1858	250
Newberry, William	Wilcox	Wills 1	1821-1844	346
Newbola, Ware S.	Mobile	Wills 2	1837-1857	74
Newell, John E.	Clarke	GE&W	1832-1839	251
Newman, Elizabeth	Tallapoosa	Wills 1	1838-1866	33
Newman, G. A.	Monroe	W&D A	1833-1841	255
Newman, James	Tallapoosa	Wills 1	1838-1866	31
Newman, Lemuel	Tallapoosa	Wills 1	1838-1866	152
Newman, Nancy	Lauderdale	Wills A	1835-1858	177
Newman, Samuel	Macon	Records 3	1845-1850	248
Newsom, Littlebury J.?	Dallas	Wills A	1821-1849	5
Newsom, Permelia C.	Perry	Wills B	1858-1873	434
Newsome, John J.	Lee	Wills A	1867-1898	48
Newton, Elizabeth	Wilcox	Wills 2	1832-1850	183
Newton, Isaac	Autauga	Deeds B		77
Newton, James E.	Calhoun	Loose	Probated 1852	
Newton, Mary	Marengo	Wills A	1820-1864	527
Newton, Thomas	St. Clair	Deeds B	1831-1849	836
Nicholas, Francoise	Mobile	Wills 1	1813-1837	28
Nicholas, James	Marengo	Wills A	1820-1864	532
Nicholas, Maggie	Mobile	Wills 3	1857-1870	384
Nicholas, Thomas	Montgomery	Wills 2	1820-1845	27
Nicholl, Robert A.	Mobile	Wills 2	1837-1857	47
Nichols, Benjamin F.	Mobile	Wills 3	1857-1870	646
Nichols, Edwin	Mobile	Wills 1	1813-1837	242
Nichols, Jimie Gray	Lowndes	Wills C	1861-1899	30
Nichols, Joel	Coosa	W&OCR 2	1843-1883	195
Nichols, William	Montgomery	Wills 2	1820-1845	209
Nicholson, Alexander	Coosa	W&OCR 2	1843-1883	119

TESTATOR	COUNTY	WHERE FOUND		PAGE
Nicholson, Alexander B.	Coosa	W&OCR 2	1843-1883	161
Nicholson, Cinthia	Lawrence	I&W D	1835-1840	631
Nicholson, Elijah	Morgan	OCR 6	1831-1837	532
Nicholson, Evan	St. Clair	Deeds B	1831-1849	213
Nicholson, James	Macon	Records 4	1850-1852	159
Nicholson, Josiah	Clarke	GE&W	1832-1839	30
Nicholson, William R.	DeKalb	Wills B	1869-1905	1
Nickols, Samuel	Perry	Wills A	1821-1855	90
Nicoll, Ellen	Mobile	Wills 3	1857-1870	285
Nimmo, Frances	Tuscaloosa	Wills 1	1821-1855	62
Nimmo, James F.	Madison	Wills 1	1853-1875	74
Nix, Zacheus	Henry	OCR M	1861-1862	395
Nixon, William O.	Lowndes	Wills C	1861-1899	137
Noble, Joseph C.	Tuscaloosa	Wills 1	1821-1855	229
Noble, Mary C.	Dallas	Wills B	1850-1871	95
Nobles, Luke	Montgomery	Wills 4	1853-1869	352
Noe, Peter G. ?	Lamar	Wills 1	1844-1910	5
Noe, Petter? G.	Lamar	Wills 1	1844-1910	5
Noel, James	Lauderdale	Wills A	1835-1858	182
Nolan, Thomas F.	Russell	Wills 2	1850-1873	290
Nolen, Berry	Lauderdale	Wills A	1835-1858	195
Nolen, Elijah	Montgomery	Wills 2	1820-1845	245
Nolen, James	Chambers	Wills 3	1856-1899	149
Nolly, Frances H.	Dallas	Wills B	1850-1871	122
Nolly, Richard M.	Dallas	Wills B	1850-1871	125
Nordlinger, Isaac J.	Clarke	PR L	1861-1864	215
Nored, Martha R.	Wilcox	Wills 4	1847-1862	266
Norman, Armsted	Perry	Wills A	1821-1855	54
Norman, Henderson	Montgomery	Wills 4	1853-1869	487
Norman, Joseph	Marshall	FR 4	1850-1855	52
Norman, William L.	Washington	Wills 1 ∅	1827-1888	105
Norman, William L.	Washington	Wills B	1827-	67
Norment, Eugene N.	Tuscaloosa	Wills 3	1858-1865	29
Norred, Martha R.	Wilcox	Wills 4	1847-1862	266
Norred, Millikon	Monroe	W&D C	1845-1850	19
Norris, Susan Ellen	Montgomery	Wills 4	1853-1869	62
Norris, Thomas J.	Tuscaloosa	Wills 1	1821-1855	115
Norris, William	Monroe	W&D A	1833-1841	326
Northington, Levi	Lamar	Wills 1	1844-1910	6
Northup, James Madison	Mobile	Wills 3	1857-1870	357
Norton, Nathaniel B.	Lauderdale	Wills 4	1821-1825	14
Norton, William	Mobile	Wills 3	1857-1870	50
Norville, Spencer	Lauderdale	Wills 4	1821-1825	131
Norwood, Alonza L.	Clarke	PR L	1861-1864	116
Norwood, Anna	Perry	Wills B	1858-1873	48
Norwood, Daniel H.	Dallas	Wills A	1821-1849	234
Norwood, David S.	Sumter	Wills 1	1828-1851	146
Norwood, Elias W.	Sumter	Wills 1	1828-1851	40
Norwood, Nathaniel	Marengo	Wills A	1820-1864	59
Norwood, Samuel	Marengo	Wills A	1820-1864	278
Norwood, Theophilus	Morgan	FR 20	1860-1865	271

TESTATOR	COUNTY	WHERE FOUND		PAGE
Norwood, William	Madison	PR 8	1831-1839	467
Nowlin, David	Madison	PR 9	1839-1841	81
Nuchols, Nat	Russell	Wills 2	1850-1873	387
Nungasser, Jacob	Mobile	Wills 2	1837-1857	321
Nunn, Elia	Morgan	OCR 7	1837-1843	365
Nunn, George	Chambers	Wills 1-2	1833-1856	254
Nunn, James	Autauga	Reports C	1834-1838	321
Nunn, James	Autauga	Reports C	Original	572
Nunn, Loftin	Chambers	Wills 1-2	1833-1856	152
Nunnagesser, Henry	Mobile	Wills 3	1857-1870	518
Nunnelee, Osburn F.	Conecuh	OB A	1865-1870	423
Nunnallee, Maria	Dallas	Wills B	1850-1871	285
Nunnallee, Willis	Dallas	Wills B	1850-1871	278
Nunnally, John C.	Madison	PR 4	1826-1829	285
Nurts, William	Perry	Wills A	1821-1855	149
Obanion, Mildred	Limestone	Wills 9	1847-1850	593
O'Bannon, James	Sumter	Wills 2	1851-1872	399
O'Bickley, Walter	Mobile	Wills 1	1813-1837	129
O'Brien, John	Mobile	Wills 3	1857-1870	267
O'Brien, Thomas	Mobile	Wills 2	1837-1857	380
O'Brien, W. J.	Mobile	Wills 3	1857-1870	354
O'Connell, John E.	Montgomery	Wills 3	1840-1854	31
O'Conner, Elija	Greene	Wills D	1851-1888	176
O'Connor, Brien	Mobile	Wills 2	1837-1857	333
O'Connor, Michael	Mobile	Wills 2	1837-1857	347
O'Daniel, Alex	Lowndes	Wills B	1830-1859	345
Odell, William C.	Lauderdale	Wills 3	1821-1825	63
Odelle, William	Lauderdale	Wills 4	1821-1825	64
Odom, Zantha	Lawrence	I&W A	1850-1857	487
Offutt, William E.	Montgomery	Wills 4	1853-1869	313
Ogbourne, Nicholas	Montgomery	Wills 2	1820-1845	189
Ogburn, Benjamin	Tallapoosa	Wills 1	1838-1866	65
Ogburn, William H.	Tuscaloosa	Wills 1	1821-1855	282
Ogden, Ann	Mobile	Wills 1	1813-1837	38
Ogden, Henrietta C.	Mobile	Wills 3	1857-1870	231
Ogden, Uyral	Mobile	Wills 2	1837-1857	264
Ogilby, Richard W.	Limestone	Wills 11	1865-1866	95
Ogletree, James B.	Macon	WAC&A 11	1862-1870	253
O'Hara, Mary L.	Dallas	Wills B	1850-1871	424
Olds, Paysun	Lowndes	Wills B	1830-1859	49
Olds, William W.	Dallas	Wills B	1850-1871	85
Olive, Jesse	Tuscaloosa	Wills 1	1821-1855	56
Olive, Nicholas M.	Montgomery	Wills 2	1820-1845	258
Oliver, Ann B.	Coosa	W&OCR 2	1843-1883	55
Oliver, E. T.	Lauderdale	Wills A	1835-1858	230
Oliver, Elizabeth	Sumter	Wills 1	1825-1851	282
Oliver, Florence M.	Chambers	Wills 1-2	1833-1856	410
Oliver, George W.	Lowndes	Wills C	1861-1899	7

TESTATOR	COUNTY	WHERE FOUND		PAGE
Oliver, John	Lowndes	Wills C	1861-1899	164
Oliver, John A.	Montgomery	Wills 2	1820-1845	272
Oliver, Lucinda	Perry	Wills B	1858-1873	95
Oliver, Margret S.	Lowndes	Wills B	1830-1859	326
Oliver, Samuel C.	Montgomery	Wills 5	1853-1887	3
Oliver, Samuel G.	Montgomery	Wills 3	1840-1854	96
Oliver, Samuel W.	Dallas	Wills A	1821-1840	157
Oliver, Thomas M.	Perry	Wills A	1821-1855	24
Oliver, Thomas M.	Perry	W&I	1823-1833	99
Oneal, Alvin	Sumter	Wills 1	1828-1851	208
Oneal, Eli	Sumter	Wills 2	1851-1872	320
O'Neil, George	Mobile	Wills 3	1857-1870	578
O'Neill, Hugh	Montgomery	Wills 2	1820-1845	284
Oram, Henry	Coosa	W&OCR 2	1843-1883	39
Ormond, J. J.	Tuscaloosa	Wills 3	1858-1865	194
Ormond, Evelina R.	Butler	Wills 1	1853-1865	254
Ormond, Thomas	Sumter	Wills 2	1851-1872	378
Ormsby, Clara T.	Autauga	Wills 1	1862-1925	55
Orr, Jacob	Morgan	OCR 7	1837-1843	148
Orr, Jonathan	Morgan	PCTR C (15)	1854-1858	576
Orr, Watkins	Morgan	OCR 8	1844-1848	399
Osborn, Alexander	Tallapoosa	Wills 1	1838-1866	173
Osborne, F. W. H.	Mobile	Wills 1	1813-1837	175
Orsburn, Christipher	Dallas	Wills B	1850-1871	123
Oswald, William	Mobile	Wills 2	1837-1857	389
Otey, John W.	Madison	Wills 1	1853-1875	1
Ott, William	Barbour	OCR 8	1856-1858	263
Otter, Harmon R.	Lawrence	I&W C	1866-1880	32
Otterson, John	Greene	Wills B	1817-1841	289
Otterson, Samuel	Greene	Wills B	1817-1841	199
Otts, Elizabeth A.	Lowndes	Wills B	1830-1859	258
Outerbridge, Ellen	Madison	Wills 1	1853-1875	528
Overton, Henry	Perry	Wills A	1821-1855	306
Overton, Penelope	Perry	Wills B	1858-1873	146
Owens, George W.	Mobile	Wills 2	1837-1857	2
Owen, Hopson	Tuscaloosa	Wills 1	1821-1855	334
Owen, John H.	Talladega	W&I C	1862-1866	216
Owen, Louisa S.	Mobile	Wills 3	1857-1870	332
Owen, Nathaniel Green	Macon	Records 10	1863-1865	587
Owen, Phil	Butler	Wills 2	1864-1875	186
Owen, Robert	Chambers	Wills 1-2	1833-1856	321
Owen, Samuel	Limestone	Wills 4	1831-1837	571
Owen, Susan R.	Mobile	Wills 3	1857-1870	704
Owen, Thomas	Tuscaloosa	Wills 3	1858-1865	68
Owen, William R. B.	Madison	PR 3	1823-1826	47
Owen, William J.	Barbour	OCR 9	1858-1859	514
Owens, Berry C.	Montgomery	Wills 5	1863-1887	286
Owens, Jesse	St. Clair	Deeds B	1831-1849	677
Owens, John N.	Tallapoosa	Wills 1	1838-1866	167
Owens, William	Morgan	OCR 8	1844-1848	440
Owings, Mary Ann	Montgomery	Wills 4	1853-1869	151

TESTATOR	COUNTY	WHERE FOUND		PAGE
Pace, Augusta D.	Lowndes	Wills B	1830-1859	139
Pace, David	Dallas	Wills A	1821-1849	67
Pace, Hardy	Chambers	Wills 1-2	1833-1856	133
Pace, Isaac S.	Macon	WAC&A 11	1862-1870	123
Pack, Joseph	Marengo	Wills A	1820-1864	185
Pack, Joseph	Sumter	Wills 1	1828-1851	98
Packard, Nathaniel T.	Madison	PR 8	1831-1839	177
Packer, Robert	Monroe	W&D A	1833-1841	195
Packer, Robert	Monroe	W&D A	1833-1841	492
Padelford, Joseph H.	Dallas	Wills A	1821-1849	193
Page, Benjamin	Chambers	Wills 3	1856-1899	143
Page, Jane B.	Greene	Wills B	1817-1841	280
Page, John R.	Russell	Wills 2	1850-1873	385
Page, William	Shelby	Wills H	1847-1866	789
Page, William F.	Chambers	Wills 3	1856-1899	102
Pages, Josiah	Lauderdale	Wills A	1835-1858	207
Paine, Thomas	Limestone	Wills 5	1836-1841	230
Palmer, Dabney	Mobile	Wills 3	1857-1870	46
Palmer, Stephen	Wilcox	Wills 2	1832-1850	306
Palmore, Marshall	Butler	Wills 2	1864-1875	168
Pape, T. R.	Monroe	W&D 8	1870-1871	584
Pargade?, Francis	Washington	Wills 1 ∅	1827-1888	73
Pargade?, Francis	Washington	Wills B	1827-	48
Parham, James A.	Barbour	OCR 14	1863-1865	390
Parham, Susan	Limestone	Wills 6	1841-1846	563
Parham, W. K.	Limestone	Wills 5	1836-1841	430
Parish, Henry	Perry	Wills B	1858-1873	29
Parish, Joel	Perry	Wills A	1821-1855	193
Parish, Mary	Tuscaloosa	Wills 1	1821-1855	360
Parish, William G.	Tuscaloosa	Wills 1	1821-1855	305
Park, Ezekiel E.	Russell	Wills 1	1838-1849	60
Park, Ezekiel S.	Lee	Wills A	1867-1898	40
Parkam, Young	Lawrence	I&W A	1850-1857	297
Parker, Bethany	Coosa	W&OCR 2	1843-1883	51
Parker, Dr. Bryant	Chambers	Wills 3	1856-1899	211
Parker, Con?	Sumter	Wills 2	1851-1872	210
Parker, Daniel	Dallas	Wills A	1821-1849	62
Parker, Henry	Butler	Wills 2	1864-1875	114
Parker, Henry J.	Butler	Wills 1	1853-1865	233
Parker, Isaac	Bibb	PM F	1855-1858	606
Parker, Isaac	Bibb	Loose	Dated 1859	
Parker, Isaac	Bibb	Admr. I	1858-1865	15
Parker, James	Sumter	Wills 2	1851-1872	89
Parker, James Volney	Sumter	Wills 2	1851-1872	192
Parker, Jesse	Clarke	OCR B	1818-1824	259
Parker, Josey	Monroe	W&D A	1833-1841	325
Parker, King	Perry	Wills B	1858-1873	239
Parker, Martha T.	Sumter	Wills 2	1851-1872	240
Parker, Milo B.	Barbour	OCR 7	1854-1857	151
Parker, Noah, Jr.	Butler	Wills 2	1864-1875	121
Parker, Owen	Tuscaloosa	Wills 3	1858-1865	5

TESTATOR	COUNTY	WHERE FOUND		PAGE
Parker, Peter S.	Lauderdale	Wills B	1859-1870	33
Parker, Samuel	Wilcox	Wills 3	1826-1858	355
Parker, Seth B.	Baldwin	Wills A	1811-1881	113
Parker, Susan?	Marengo	Wills A	1820-1864	201
Parker, Thomas	Limestone	Wills 3	1826-1831	50
Parkham, John C.	Butler	Wills 1	1853-1865	186
Parkham, Elias	Dallas	Wills B	1850-1871	97
Parks, Charles B.	Mobile	Wills 2	1837-1857	301
Parmer, E.	Lowndes	Wills B	1830-1859	301
Parmer, Josiah	Montgomery	Wills 5	1863-1887	26
Parmer, William	Montgomery	Wills 4	1853-1869	471
Parnall, Eleanor	Dallas	Wills B	1850-1871	127
Parnall, Jesse	Dallas	Wills A	1821-1849	127
Parr, John	Greene	Wills C	1840-1864	134
Parrish, Van S.	Mobile	Wills 1	1813-1837	237
Parsons, Enoch	Montgomery	Wills 2	1820-1845	241
Parsons, John	Jefferson	Wills A	1856-1880	274
Parton, Bennet	Perry	Wills A	1821-1855	233
Paschael, Milton	Coosa	W&OCR 2	1843-1883	147
Passos, Charles	Baldwin	Wills A	1811-1881	125
Pate, Charles	Tuscaloosa	Wills 1	1821-1855	107
Pate, Henry	Montgomery	Wills 4	1853-1869	435
Pate, Jeremiah	Morgan	OCR 5	1829-1831	419
Pate, John	St. Clair	RE B	1834-1857	450
Pate, John	Tuscaloosa	Wills 1	1821-1855	289
Pate, S. R.	Sumter	Wills 2	1851-1872	53
Pate, Stephen	Madison	W&I	1810-1820	129
Pathkiller, Peggy	St. Clair	Deeds B	1831-1849	65
Patrick, Elias	Marshall	FR 6	1859-1867	524
Patrick, Eliza	Perry	Wills B	1858-1873	375
Patrick, John	Lowndes	Wills B	1830-1859	35
Patrick, John	Perry	Wills B	1858-1873	293
Patterson, Alexander	Morgan	OCR 12	1853-1855	194
Patterson, John	Baldwin	Wills A	1811-1881	50
Patterson, John G.	Tallapoosa	Wills 1	1838-1866	52
Patterson, L. Thomas	Greene	Wills A	1821-1827	13
Patterson, Malcolm	Morgan	FR 18	1859-1860	275
Patterson, Malcolm	Talladega	Wills A	1833-1839	571
Patterson, Redmond	Montgomery	Wills 3	1840-1854	246
Patterson, W. J.	Russell	Wills 2	1850-1873	325
Patterson, William	Montgomery	Wills 2	1820-1845	160
Pattison, Charles S.	Washington	Wills 1 ∅	1827-1888	132
Pattison, Charles S.	Washington	Wills B	1827-	85
Patton, Isaac	Lauderdale	Wills B	1859-1870	368
Patton, M. W.	Dallas	Wills B	1850-1871	416
Patton, William	Sumter	Wills 1	1828-1851	46
Paul, Archibald	Dallas	Wills A	1821-1849	169
Paulett, Lewis M.	DeKalb	Wills A	1837-1863	8
Paulk, Elizabeth	Macon	Records 10	1863-1865	409
Paulk, Jonathan	Lauderdale	Wills B	1859-1870	82
Paulk, Thomas H.	Pike	Wills A	1845-1862	225

TESTATOR	COUNTY	WHERE FOUND		PAGE
Paulk, W. A.	Pike	Wills B	1862-1879	97
Paulk, William	Tallapoosa	Wills 1	1838-1866	12
Paulling, Daniel G. W.	Autauga	Wills 1	1862-1925	39
Paulling, John	Dallas	Wills B	1850-1871	46
Payler, R. T.	Sumter	Wills 2	1851-1872	390
Payne, Elias L.	Tuscaloosa	Wills 1	1821-1855	35
Payne, Hiram	Perry	Wills A	1821-1855	166
Payne, Laminda? W.	St. Clair	RE F	1862-1868	203
Payne, Samuel	Butler	Wills 2	1864-1875	49
Payne, Susan N.	Sumter	Wills 2	1851-1872	75
Payne, W. W.	Sumter	Wills 2	1851-1872	117
Payne, Williams	Barbour	OCR 3	1847-1851	388
Payton, Thomas	Morgan	OCR 6	1831-1837	221
Peacock, John	Coosa	W&OCR 2	1843-1883	107
Peacock, William	Montgomery	Wills 2	1820-1845	125
Pearce, Celia	Lowndes	Wills B	1830-1859	46
Pearce, Hilliard J.	Lowndes	Wills B	1830-1859	186
Pearson, Charles M.	St. Clair	RE D	1859-1867	281
Pearson, (Rev.) Edward	Talladega	Wills C	1845-1853	244
Pearson, Joel A.	Coosa	W&OCR 2	1843-1883	116
Pearson, John M.	Tallapoosa	Wills 1	1838-1866	61
Pearson, John M.	Tallapoosa	Wills 2	1864-1907	16
Pearson, Leonard	Marengo	Wills A	1820-1864	95
Pearson, Michael	Marengo	Wills A	1820-1869	19
Pearson, Penelope	Chambers	Wills 1-2	1833-1856	297
Pearson, Thomas G.	Tallapoosa	Wills 1	1838-1866	109
Pearson, William A.	Tallapoosa	Wills 1	1838-1866	6
Peavy, Joshua	Wilcox	Wills 3	1826-1858	103
Peay, Eliza Y.	Lowndes	Wills C	1861-1899	160
Peck, E. W.	Tuscaloosa	Wills 4	1868-1897	271
Peck, George	Coosa	W&OCR 2	1843-1883	152
Peden, John	Mobile	Wills 3	1857-1870	487
Peeples, Joseph	Tallapoosa	Wills 1	1838-1866	35
Peeples, Nathan	Autauga	Wills 1	1862-1925	40
Peeples, Tempey	Tallapoosa	Wills 1	1838-1866	3
Peerson, Thomas	Lawrence	I&W A	1850-1857	232
Peete, Alexander	Butler	Wills 2	1864-1875	62
Peete, Benjamin	Limestone	Wills 4	1831-1837	325
Pegues, George H.	Clarke	PR E	1840-1846	598
Pegues, Samuel B.	Tuscaloosa	Wills 1	1821-1855	84
Pegues, Sarah G.	Macon	Records 2	1838-1842	84
Pellam, John W.	Henry	OCR P	1864-1866	98
Pellum, Richard	Calhoun	Loose	Probated 1858	
Pelt, Henry	Clarke	GE&W	1832-1839	355
Pemberton, Joshua	Chambers	Wills 1-2	1833-1856	178
Pence, Enoch Bell	Dallas	Wills B	1850-1871	240
Pendergrass, John James	Chambers	Wills 3	1856-1899	114
Penfield, Daniel	Mobile	Wills 2	1837-1857	239
Peniers, John A.	Marengo	Wills A	1820-1864	80
Penn, Abner J.	Chambers	Wills 3	1856-1899	101
Penn, Margaret	Tuscaloosa	Wills 1	1821-1855	60

TESTATOR	COUNTY	WHERE FOUND		PAGE
Penn, Moses	Chambers	Wills 1-2	1833-1856	365
Penn, Peter L.	Talladega	Wills A	1833-1839	91
Penn, Stephens C.	Morgan	OCR 8	1844-1848	182
Penninger, W.	Tallapoosa	Wills 1	1838-1866	86
Pennington, John L.	Montgomery	Wills 2	1820-1845	104
Pennington, Ruth	Marengo	Wills A	1820-1864	280
Pennington, Sarah F.	Marengo	Wills A	1820-1864	183
Penny, James	Lauderdale	Wills A	1835-1858	8
Penrod, Daniel	Morgan	OCR 11	1850-1852	170
Percy, Thomas G.	Madison	PR 10	1842-1842	147
Perdue, A. B.	Lowndes	Wills B	1830-1859	87
Perdue, James H.	Butler	Wills 1	1853-1864	52
Perdue, John A. R.	Lowndes	Wills C	1861-1899	53
Perdue, John B.	Lowndes	Wills C	1861-1899	33
Perdue, John J.	Butler	Wills 1	1853-1864	195
Perdue, Sovering T.	Lowndes	Wills C	1861-1899	70
Peres, John Baptiste	Mobile	Wills 3	1857-1870	56
Perkins, Eliza C.	Tuscaloosa	Wills 1	1821-1855	300
Perkins, Frederick	Limestone	Wills 3	1826-1831	259
Perkins, Nicholas	Madison	PR 3	1823-1826	366
Perkins, Solomon	Wilcox	Wills 2	1832-1850	184
Perkins, William O.	Lauderdale	Wills A	1823-1858	90
Perkins, Williams	Greene	Wills D	1851-1888	21
Perle?, Anne	Mobile	Wills 2	1837-1857	351
Perrine, James	Mobile	Wills 2	1837-1857	385
Perry, Aaron	Calhoun	Loose	Probated 1857	
Perry, Ann	Sumter	Wills 1	1828-1851	96
Perry, Archibald	Henry	OCR F	1848-1853	179
Perry, Benjamin	Montgomery	Wills 4	1853-1869	341
Perry, Britton	Perry	Wills A	1821-1855	44
Perry, Edwin N.	Macon	Records 7	1857-1859	730
Perry, James R.	Barbour	OCR 7	1854-1857	144
Perry, John	Perry	Wills A	1821-1855	33
Perry, John	Russell	Wills 2	1850-1873	201
Perry, John A.	Perry	Wills A	1821-1855	165
Perry, John C.	Sumter	Wills 1	1828-1851	230
Perry, Obed	Chambers	Wills 3	1856-1899	92
Perry, William	Russell	Wills 1	1838-1849	73
Perryman, Alexander	Madison	Deeds D	1816-1818	2
Perryman, Edmund D.	Macon	Records 10	1863-1865	275
Person, James N.	Limestone	Wills 12	1866-1872	726
Person, William H.	Colbert	Wills A	1861-1903	6
Persons, Sarah	Russell	Wills 2	1850-1873	244
Persons, William	Sumter	Wills 1	1828-1851	18
Perteet, Solomon	Tuscaloosa	Wills 3	1858-1865	161
Pesnell, John R.	Cleburne	Wills 1	1866-1884	73
Peteet, John	Greene	Wills B	1817-1841	258
Peteet, Young	Perry	Wills A	1821-1855	153
Peterman, Newton J.	Henry	OCR N	1862-1864	523
Peters, Harriet	Montgomery	Wills 4	1853-1869	36
Peters, Harriet	Pike	Wills A	1845-1862	138

TESTATOR	COUNTY	WHERE FOUND		PAGE
Petters, Mrs. Mary	Lowndes	Wills C	1861-1899	88
Peters, Temperance T.	Lauderdale	Wills A	1835-1858	197
Peterson, Battle	Macon	Records 4	1850-1852	268
Peterson, Dolly	Macon	OCM 2	1835-1842	34
Peterson, James	Jefferson	Wills A	1856-1880	101
Pettey, Amy	Lauderdale	Wills 4	1821-1825	155
Pettey, William	Madison	PR 7	1834-1837	61
Pettibone, James V.	Dallas	Wills B	1850-1871	4
Pettigrew, Ebenezer	Greene	Wills A	1821-1827	3
Pettigrew, James	Greene	Wills B	1817-1841	287
Pettus, H. O.	Dallas	Wills B	1850-1871	400
Pettway, Mark H.	Wilcox	Wills 4	1847-1862	194
Petty, Benjamin F., Jr.	Barbour	OCR 18	1870-	80
Pfister, Amand	Montgomery	Wills 4	1853-1869	125
Pfister, Amand	Mobile	Wills 1	1813-1837	238
Phares, Isaac	Greene	Wills A	1821-1827	52
Pharoah, Francis	Montgomery	Wills 3	1840-1854	106
Pharr, Ephraim	Wilcox	Wills 2	1832-1850	210
Pharr, Harriet S.	Lowndes	Wills C	1861-1899	10
Pharr, Samuel K.	Lowndes	Wills C	1861-1899	153
Pharris, John C.	Sumter	Wills 2	1851-1872	382
Phelan, Joseph H.	Coosa	W&OCR 2	1843-1883	123
Phelps, Amariah B.	Montgomery	Wills 4	1853-1869	18
Phelps, John	Madison	PR 12	1845-1849	185
Phelps, Pleasants	Russell	Wills 2	1850-1873	219
Phelps, Thomas	Russell	Wills 2	1850-1873	284
Phelps, Welbourn	Limestone	Wills 4	1831-1837	130
Philipps, John	St. Clair	Deeds D	1855-1859	75
Philips, James	Montgomery	Wills 2	1820-1845	33
Philips, Joseph	St. Clair	RE F	1862-1868	199
Philips, Joseph H.	Dallas	Wills B	1850-1871	385
Phillips, Anthony	Limestone	Wills 5	1836-1871	424
Phillips, Charles	Russell	Wills 1	1838-1849	114
Phillips, David	Lauderdale	Wills B	1859-1870	340
Phillips, George	Dallas	Wills A	1821-1849	112
Phillips, James	Russell	Wills 2	1850-1873	328
Phillips, James D.	Tallapoosa	Wills 2	1864-1907	13
Phillips, John	Lauderdale	Wills B	1859-1870	313
Phillips, John	Sumter	Wills 1	1828-1851	276
Phillips, Mark	Perry	Wills B	1858-1873	281
Phillips, Richard	Madison	PR 12	1845-1849	193
Phillips, Winniford	Macon	Records 2	1838-1842	86
Philpot, M. D.	Dallas	Wills B	1850-1871	436
Pickens, Andrew L.	Mobile	Wills 2	1837-1857	314
Pickens, Israel	Greene	Wills A	1821-1827	58
Pickens, Joseph	Clarke	PR E	1840-1845	397
Picket, Reuben	Marengo	Wills A	1820-1864	197
Pickett, James	Autauga	Deeds A		95
Pickett, H. F.	Pike	Wills A	1845-1862	246
Pickett, Joseph W.	Wilcox	Wills 5	1855-1870	155
Pickett, R. M.	Pike	Wills A	1845-1862	256

130

TESTATOR	COUNTY	WHERE FOUND		PAGE
Pickett, Robert	Pike	Wills A	1845-1862	57
Pickett, Sarah	Autauga	Reports C	1834-1838	43
Pickett, Sarah	Autauga	Reports C	1834-1838	44
Pickett, William D.	Montgomery	Wills 2	1820-1845	187
Pickett, William R.	Autauga	Reports G	1850-1853	99
Pierce, John	Baldwin	Wills A	1811-1881	45
Pierce, John	Lowndes	Wills B	1830-1859	114
Pierson, John	Baldwin	Wills A	1811-1881	224
Pierson, Leah N.	Dallas	Wills B	1850-1871	382
Pigeon?, Henry	Mobile	Wills 1	1813-1837	105
Pilkington, Dura	Wilcox	Wills 3	1826-1858	167
Pilkington, James M.	Wilcox	Wills 5	1855-1870	145
Pilkington, John D.	Wilcox	Wills 5	1855-1870	181
Pilman, Isaac	Monroe	W&D A	1833-1841	211
Pinckard, William	Macon	Records 2	1838-1842	148
Pinkston, James	Montgomery	Wills 2	1820-1845	90
Pinson, Joseph	Calhoun	Loose	Probated 1849	
Pittman, Pheraba	Mobile	Wills 1	1813-1837	263
Pittman, Philip	Montgomery	Wills 2	1820-1845	9
Pitts, Aaron	Chambers	Wills 1-2	1833-1856	384
Pitts, David W.	Perry	Wills B	1858-1873	123
Pitts, George W.	Dallas	Wills A	1821-1849	86
Pitts, Silas	Shelby	Wills H	1847-1866	251
Pizzala, Joseph	Montgomery	Wills 5	1863-1887	30
Plant, Mary Ann	Dallas	Wills B	1850-1871	331
Platt, Harman	Pike	Wills A	1845-1862	98
Pledger, William H.	Wilcox	Wills 3	1826-1858	454
Poe, Francix	Mobile	Wills 3	1857-1870	376
Pogue, James T.	Coosa	W&OCR 2	1843-1883	187
Pogue, Susannah	Chambers	Wills 1-2	1833-1856	258
Poland, Nelson	Montgomery	Wills 2	1820-1845	285
Pollard, E. Justina	Mobile	Wills 2	1837-1857	320
Pollard, Phebe	Mobile	Wills 2	1837-1857	185
Pollard, Ryland T.	Montgomery	Wills 4	1853-1869	338
Pomeroy, Porter B.	Mobile	Wills 3	1857-1870	103
Pond, Amanda P.	Montgomery	Wills 4	1853-1869	118
Pond, Lewis W.	Montgomery	Wills 3	1840-1854	165
Ponder, Anna F.	Montgomery	Wills 4	1853-1869	298
Ponder, Benjamin	Montgomery	Wills 3	1840-1854	29
Ponder, James	Tallapoosa	Wills 1	1838-1866	34
Pool, Ephraim	Dallas	Wills B	1850-1871	163
Pool, Issac	Jefferson	Wills A	1858-1880	309
Pool, J. K. C.	Perry	Wills B	1858-1873	154
Pool, James	Perry	Wills A	1821-1855	91
Pool, Perkins P.	Lauderdale	Wills A	1835-1858	22
Pool, Stephen F.	Marengo	Wills A	1820-1864	510
Poole, Calvin	Butler	Wills 2	1864-1875	94
Poor, Moses	Madison	PR 2	1818-1823	41
Poor, Sarah	Madison	PR 2	1818-1823	264
Poore, James	Madison	PR 10	1842-1842	20
Pope, Alexander	Mobile	Wills 2	1837-1857	133

TESTATOR	COUNTY	WHERE FOUND		PAGE
Pope, Archelaus	Perry	Wills A	1821-1855	72
Pope, Britton J.	Marengo	Wills A	1820-1864	384
Pope, Dorothy	Mobile	Wills 2	1837-1857	226
Pope, E. W.	Morgan	PCFR 22	1865-1866	96
Pope, Ethelred	Morgan	OCR 7	1837-1843	521
Pope, Hermion	Marengo	Wills A	1820-1864	357
Pope, Mrs. Lucy E.	Talladega	W&I D	1867-1880	628
Pope, Minerva M.	Madison	PR 16	1831-1861	257
Pope, Sarah	Pike	Wills A	1845-1862	253
Pope, Susan	Russell	Wills 2	1850-1873	230
Pope, Tabitha S.	Mobile	Wills 3	1857-1870	314
Pope, William B.	Mobile	Wills 2	1837-1857	222
Pope, William H.	Madison	PR 14	1846-1850	141
Pope, Willis	Greene	Wills B	1817-1841	215
Pope, Willis	Mobile	Wills 3	1857-1870	625
Pope, Zachary	Autauga	Reports G	1850-1853	96
Porter, Frederick	Sumter	Wills 2	1851-1872	134
Porter, John C.	Washington	Wills 1 ∅	1827-1888	148
Porter, John C.	Washington	Wills B	1827-	94
Porter, John G.	Lowndes	Wills B	1830-1859	51
Porter, Joseph J.	Tuscaloosa	Wills 1	1821-1855	225
Porter, Lucy A.	Montgomery	Wills 4	1853-1869	493
Porter, Mary	Dallas	Wills A	1821-1849	232
Porter, Robert E.	Lauderdale	Wills A	1835-1858	10
Portier, Louis	Mobile	Wills 2	1837-1857	413
Portier, Michael	Mobile	Wills 3	1857-1870	135
Portis, Ira	Clarke	OCR	1825-1832	41
Portz, Nicholas G.	Mobile	Wills 3	1857-1870	349
Posey, Hezekiah	Calhoun	Loose	Probated 1847	
Posey, Jesse H.	Sumter	Wills 1	1828-1851	79
Posey, Sarah	Sumter	Wills 1	1828-1851	82
Posey, William	Lowndes	Wills B	1830-1859	280
Posey, William C.	Montgomery	Wills 4	1853-1869	83
Post, Mrs. Louisa A.	Mobile	Wills 2	1837-1857	415
Postes, Arthur	Mobile	Wills 1	1813-1837	48
Potts, Henry	Sumter	Wills 1	1828-1851	57
Potts, Henry	Sumter	Wills 1	1828-1851	195
Potts, Jonathan	Tuscaloosa	Wills 1	1821-1855	10
Potts, Mary M.	Chambers	Wills 3	1856-1899	67
Potts, Rachel	Tuscaloosa	Wills 1	1821-1855	100
Potts, Stephens	Bibb	Loose	Dated 1823	
Potts, Thomas W.	Tuscaloosa	Wills 1	1821-1855	53
Pouncy, Samuel	Montgomery	Wills 2	1820-1845	92
Pounds, Zachariah B.	Chambers	Wills 3	1856-1899	110
Powell, B. F.	Tuscaloosa	Wills 4	1868-1897	197
Powell, Cader	Montgomery	Wills 2	1820-1845	60
Powell, Drury	Montgomery	Wills 2	1820-1845	16
Powell, Elijah	Limestone	Wills 4	1831-1837	614
Powell, Elizabeth	Lowndes	Wills B	1830-1859	94
Powell, Genevieve (Dolive)	Mobile	Wills 1	1813-1837	139
Powell, Hozey ?	Coosa	W&OCR 2	1843-1883	140

TESTATOR	COUNTY	WHERE FOUND		PAGE
Powell, John	Limestone	Wills 9	1847-1850	140
Powell, John	Monroe	W&D A	1833-1841	168
Powell, John	Pike	Wills A	1845-1862	110
Powell, Leven	Madison	Wills 1	1853-1875	321
Powell, Penelope	Sumter	Wills 2	1851-1872	198
Powell, Peyton	Madison	PR 12	1845-1849	37
Powell, Sarah	Coosa	W&OCR 2	1843-1883	138
Powell, Sarah	Monroe	W&D A	1833-1841	199
Powell, Thomas	Mobile	Wills 1	1813-1837	40
Powell, William	Lowndes	Wills B	1830-1859	1
Power, Daniel M.	Madison	PR 4	1826-1829	103
Power, James F.	Coosa	W&OCR 2	1843-1883	180
Power, James L.	Madison	Wills 1	1853-1875	291
Power, William	Madison	Wills 1	1853-1875	260
Powers, Walter	Mobile	Wills 3	1857-1870	419
Powers, William	Madison	Wills 1	1853-1875	439
Powers, William H.	Madison	Wills 1	1853-1875	539
Powers, William L.	Mobile	Wills 3	1857-1870	105
Powley, John	Mobile	Wills 3	1857-1870	258
Pratt, Isabel A.	Tuscaloosa	Wills 3	1858-1865	170
Pratt, John	Lauderdale	Wills 3	1821-1825	62
Pratt, John	Lauderdale	Wills 4	1821-1825	138
Prele, Anne	Mobile	Wills 2	1837-1857	351
Preslar, Sarah T.	Butler	Wills 1	1853-1864	66
Presnell, James, Sr.	Clarke	GE&W	1832-1839	257
Prestridge, Benton R.	Perry	Wills B	1858-1873	35
Prestridge, John E.	Dallas	Wills B	1850-1871	369
Price, Alf C.	Dallas	Wills B	1850-1871	254
Price, Eleanor	Madison	PR 13	1838-1848	371
Price, Elizabeth	Greene	Wills D	1851-1888	133
Price, James F.	Perry	Wills B	1858-1873	205
Price, James L.	Perry	Wills B	1858-1873	339
Price, Jane	Marengo	Wills A	1820-1864	314
Price, John A.	Jackson	Wills	1866-1867	385
Price, John J.	Marengo	Wills A	1820-1864	299
Price, Ready Gun	Mobile	Wills 3	1857-1870	338
Price, Silas M.	Perry	Wills B	1858-1873	219
Price, Thomas	Mobile	Wills 1	1813-1837	5
Price, Thomas	Morgan	OCR 11	1850-1852	456
Price, William	Greene	Wills D	1851-1888	137
Price,William B.	Butler	Wills 2	1864-1875	28
Price, William H.	Lauderdale	Wills A	1835-1858	138
Prichard, Benjamin H.	Greene	Wills B	1817-1841	191
Pride, Willsey	Madison	PR 14	1846-1850	348
Pridnore, John	Marshall	FR 10	1869-1871	519
Prieto, Michael	Mobile	Wills 3	1857-1870	227
Prince, David	Morgan	PCFR 22	1865-1866	109
Prince, Edward	Tuscaloosa	Wills 3	1858-1865	109
Prince, Hudson	Talladega	Wills C	1845-1853	200
Pringle, James	Russell	Wills 2	1850-1873	79
Prior, Asa	Mobile	Wills 1	1813-1837	239

TESTATOR	COUNTY	WHERE FOUND		PAGE
Prior, Peter	Lauderdale	Wills 3	1821-1825	39
Pritchard, William	Tallapoosa	Wills 2	1864-1907	51
Pritchett, Christopher	Clarke	PR E	1840-1845	599
Pritchett, Marion	Marengo	Wills A	1820-1864	178
Pritchett, Martha W.	Marengo	Wills A	1820-1864	460
Probyn, William	Mobile	Wills 2	1837-1857	436
Proctor, John C.	Mobile	Wills 1	1813-1837	234
Promis, Eulalie	Marengo	Wills A	1820-1864	308
Prothro, James	Chambers	Wills 1-2	1833-1856	168
Pruit, Maria M.	Madison	Wills 1	1853-1875	424
Pruitt, Francis M.	Pike	Wills B	1862-1879	56
Pruitt, John	Sumter	Wills 2	1851-1872	11
Pruitt, Martin	Marengo	Wills A	1820-1864	203
Pruitt, Thomas	Lauderdale	Wills A	1835-1858	193
Pruitt, Thomas	Lauderdale	Wills A	1835-1858	293
Pruitt, Valentine G.	Madison	PR 9	1839-1841	21
Pruitt, William	Madison	Deeds D	1816-1818	77
Pryer, George	Mobile	Wills 1	1813-1837	205
Pryor, Joseph	Tuscaloosa	Wills 1	1821-1855	286
Pryor, Martha E.	Lauderdale	Wills 3	1821-1825	156
Pryor, Martha E.	Lauderdale	Wills 4	1821-1825	113
Ptomey, George W.	Wilcox	Wills 2	1832-1850	340
Pugh, Burwell B.	Pike	Wills A	1845-1862	129
Pugh, Jesse	Pike	Wills A	1845-1862	105
Pugh, William	Monroe	W&D C	1845-1850	512
Pugh, William W.	Tallapoosa	Wills 2	1864-1907	58
Pullian, George	Tallapoosa	Wills 1	1838-1866	149
Pullin, William	Chambers	Wills 1-2	1833-1856	350
Pumphrey, Jesse	Tuscaloosa	Wills 1	1821-1855	138
Purdy, Henry	Coosa	W&OCR 2	1843-1883	121
Purnell, William	Greene	Wills B	1817-1841	243
Purple, S. B.	Russell	Wills 2	1850-1873	164
Purvis, Burridge	Mobile	Wills 1	1813-1837	277
Puryear, Alexander	Monroe	W&D B	1841-1845	217
Puryear, James R.	Monroe	W&D C	1845-1850	429
Puryear, Lucy	Chambers	Wills 1-2	1833-1856	508
Puryear, Martha	Monroe	W&D B	1841-1845	297
Puryear, Mary F.	Monroe	W&D D	1850-1856	220
Puryear, Peter	Lawrence	I&W C	1866-1880	147
Putty, Betsy	Monroe	W&D B	1841-1845	94
Pychon, George A.	Lauderdale	Wills 3	1821-1825	76
Quandrell, Charles	Mobile	Wills 2	1837-1857	91
Quarles, Catharine	Dallas	Wills B	1850-1871	43
Quarles, Moses	Tuscaloosa	Wills 1	1821-1855	254
Quigley, Daniel	Mobile	Wills 3	1857-1870	386
Quinn, Lucy	Mobile	Wills 2	1837-1857	331

TESTATOR	COUNTY	WHERE FOUND		PAGE
Rabb, Robert S.	Pike	Wills A	1845-1862	119
Rabeale, Louisa	Mobile	Wills 3	1857-1870	533
Raby, Joseph	Mobile	Wills 2	1837-1857	71
Raby, K.	Marengo	Wills A	1820-1864	250
Rachael, Hamlin	Barbour	OCR 12	1861-1863	41
Radford, Robert R.	Perry	Wills B	1858-1873	271
Ragland, Nathaniel	Madison	PR 7	1834-1837	127
Ragsdale, Catherine	Madison	Wills 1	1853-1875	90
Raiford?, Campbell	Lee	Wills A	1867-1898	18
Rainbolt, Elisha	Madison	PR 2	1818-1823	265
Raines, John M.	Barbour	OCR 9	1858-1859	485
Rainey, D. W.	Greene	Wills B	1817-1841	177
Rainey, Tilman	Greene	Wills B	1817-1841	243
Ralph, Thomas H.	Tuscaloosa	Wills 4	1868-1897	32
Rambo, Darius D.	Lowndes	Wills C	1861-1899	84
Rambo, J. A.	Lowndes	Wills B	1830-1859	399
Ramsay, Samuel N.	Montgomery	Wills 4	1853-1869	113
Ramsey, Elizabeth A.	Wilcox	Wills 3	1826-1858	257
Ramsey, James H.	Coosa	W&OCR 2	1843-1883	79
Ramsey, John	Dallas	Wills A	1821-1849	207
Ramsey, John	Perry	Wills A	1821-1855	70A
Ramsey, John A.	Pike	Wills B	1862-1879	62
Ramsey, John R.	Lowndes	Wills B	1830-1859	190
Ramssen, C. M.	Mobile	Wills 3	1857-1870	114
Randal, Peter	Monroe	W&D D	1850-1856	79
Randall, Isaiah	Baldwin	Wills A	1811-1881	109
Randall, Samuel	Talladega	Wills B	1839-1845	282
Randle, Willis	Dallas	Wills A	1821-1849	12
Randolph, Cesaria	Mobile	Wills 3	1857-1870	300
Randolph, Corinna A.	Montgomery	Wills 5	1863-1887	9
Randolph, James D.	Montgomery	Wills 5	1863-1887	32
Randolph, N. F.	Jefferson	Wills 1	1818-1840	159
Randolph, Richard	Greene	Wills D	1851-1888	48
Rankin, James	Henry	Deeds A-B	1822-1840	366
Raoul, Carolina	Montgomery	Wills 2	1820-1845	197
Raoul, Frederic S.	Montgomery	Wills 5	1863-1887	55
Rap?, Frederick	Calhoun	PR B	1856-1866	533
Rapier, Richard	Lauderdale	Wills B	1859-1870	117
Rapiers, John H.	Lauderdale	Wills B	1859-1870	78
Rasberry, Daniel	Greene	Wills B	1817-1841	157
Rasco, Jesse	Dallas	Wills B	1850-1871	426
Rasco, Taylor L.	Dallas	Wills A	1821-1849	247
Raser, Laban	Dallas	Wills B	1850-1871	219
Ratchford, Ezekiel	Chambers	Wills 1-2	1833-1856	275
Ratcliff, Mary	Wilcox	Wills 1	1821-1844	321
Rathborn, Rufus C.	Madison	PR 10	1842-1842	142
Rather, Daniel	Madison	PR 3	1823-1826	105
Rather, Daniel R.	Madison	PR 6	1832-1834	163
Ratliff, James	Morgan	OCR 12	1853-1855	71
Ratliff, Rachael	St. Clair	Wills	1821-1827	34
Ravesies, Frederick	Mobile	Wills 2	1837-1857	452

TESTATOR	COUNTY	WHERE FOUND		PAGE
Rawdon, (Mrs.) Susan	Talladega	W&I C	1862-1866	321
Rawlinson, William	Autauga	Reports C	1834-1838	354
Rawls, Benjamin F.	Marengo	Wills A	1820-1864	302
Rawls, James B.	Mobile	Wills 2	1837-1857	312
Rawls, Thomas H.	Mobile	Wills 3	1857-1870	460
Ray, Elijah	Madison	PR 2	1818-1823	303
Ray, Frances	Tallapoosa	Wills 1	1838-1866	125
Ray, Frederick, Sr.	Tuscaloosa	Wills 1	1821-1855	106
Ray, Isaac	Macon	OCM 2	1835-1842	41
Ray, J. H.	Marengo	Wills A	1820-1864	221
Ray, James	Calhoun	Loose	Probated 1836	
Ray, Sarah	Tallapoosa	Wills 2	1864-1907	21
Ray, Silas	Tallapoosa	Wills 1	1838-1866	159
Ray, William T.	Tallapoosa	Wills 1	1838-1866	53
Raymond, David	Madison	PR 2	1818-1823	217
Rayner, Miles	Madison	PR 2	1818-1823	374
Rea, Luke	Bibb	Admr.R D	1830-1838	193
Rea, Robert	Chambers	Wills 1-2	1833-1856	358
Rea?, Robert G.	DeKalb	Wills A	1837-1863	29
Rea, Robert R.	Sumter	Wills 2	1851-1872	293
Read, Elias	Wilcox	Wills 1	1821-1844	411
Read, John	Madison	Wills 1	1853-1875	257
Read, Nathan	Macon	Records 4	1850-1852	239
Reardon, Ann	Mobile	Wills 3	1857-1870	343
Reardon, Letitia	Madison	PR 9	1839-1841	303
Reaves, Archibald	Wilcox	Wills 3	1826-1858	330
Reaves, James H.	Morgan	OCR 7	1837-1843	237
Reaves, John	Sumter	Wills 1	1828-1851	126
Reaves, Stephen	Lauderdale	Wills B	1859-1870	115
Reaves, William	Baldwin	Wills A	1811-1881	1
Reck, Jane A.	Montgomery	Wills 4	1853-1869	90
Reddoch, Sarah	Butler	Wills 1	1853-1864	121
Redman, John	Jackson	Records	1861-1881	476
Redmon, John	Pike	Wills A	1845-1862	1
Redmond, J. M.	Dallas	Wills B	1850-1871	445
Redmond, Robert W.	Chambers	Wills 3	1856-1899	115
Red Mouth	Coosa	W&PM A	1834-1842	1
Reed, Alfred P.	Russell	Wills 2	1850-1873	49
Reed, Asa	Macon	Records 2	1838-1842	46
Reed, Daniel	Washington	Wills 1 ∅	1827-1888	108
Reed, Daniel	Washington	Wills B	1827-	69
Reed, Delilah	Russell	Wills 2	1850-1873	183
Reed, James	DeKalb	Wills A	1837-1863	50
Reed, Joel	DeKalb	Wills A	1837-1863	11
Reed?, Joseph	Mobile	Wills 2	1837-1857	166
Reed, Nathan	Perry	Wills A	1821-1855	183
Reed, Rose	Washington	Wills 1 ∅	1827-1888	229
Reed, Rose	Washington	Wills B	1827-	136
Reed, Thomas	Limestone	Wills 4	1831-1837	609
Reed, William	Jefferson	Wills A	1856-1880	3
Reed, William	Perry	Wills A	1821-1855	96

TESTATOR	COUNTY	WHERE FOUND		PAGE
Reeder, Daniel	Lauderdale	Wills A	1835-1858	15
Reeder, Daniel	Lauderdale	Wills B	1859-1870	145
Reeder, David	Lauderdale	Wills A	1835-1858	119
Reedy, Elizabeth	Madison	Wills 1	1853-1875	249
Reedy, Michael	Tuscaloosa	Wills 1	1821-1855	8
Reel, Nancy Ann	Mobile	Wills 3	1857-1870	230
Reese, Anna	Chambers	Wills 1-2	1833-1856	351
Reese, Dixon	Autauga	Reports F	1845-1850	135
Reese, Hugh	St. Clair	Deeds C	1846-1855	67
Reese, Littleton	Autauga	Reports E-B	1841-1845	100
Reese, Margaret	Chambers	Wills 1-2	1833-1856	140
Reese, Nat	Lowndes	Wills B	1830-1859	401
Reese, William	Lowndes	Wills B	1830-1859	86
Reese, William J. ?	Marengo	Wills A	1820-1864	295
Reese, William J?, Jr.	Marengo	Wills A	1820-1864	329
Reeve, John, Sr.	Clarke	GE&W	1832-1839	92
Reeves, Ezekiel	Washington	Wills 1 ∅	1827-1888	114
Reeves, Ezekiel	Washington	Wills B	1827-	73
Reeves, Ichabod	Morgan	OCR 5	1829-1831	408
Reeves, Jeremiah B.	Chambers	Wills 1-2	1833-1856	365
Reeves, Thomas	Greene	Wills B	1817-1841	207
Reeves, William	Chambers	Wills 3	1856-1899	195
Register, Noel	Henry	Deeds C	1840-1846	37
Register, Reddin	Henry	Deeds C	1840-1846	84
Reid, John H.	Perry	Wills A	1821-1855	264
Reid, John, Sr.	Chambers	Wills 1-2	1833-1856	129
Reid?, Joseph	Mobile	Wills 2	1837-1857	166
Reide, Wiley B.	St. Clair	RE F	1862-1868	497
Reilly, James	Sumter	Wills 1	1828-1851	104
Relfe, D. J.	Lowndes	Wills B	1830-1859	304
Rembert, Sarah	Marengo	Wills A	1820-1864	279
Rencher, Daniel G.	Sumter	Wills 2	1851-1872	369
Rencher, William	Perry	Wills B	1858-1873	53
Rene, John	Mobile	Wills 2	1837-1857	430
Reno, Ramard	Mobile	Wills 2	1837-1857	46
Renshaw, Francis	Jackson	Records	1861-1881	609
Rey, Henry	Macon	WAC&A 11	1862-1870	126
Reynolds, A. J.	Montgomery	Wills 3	1840-1854	302
Reynolds, Caswell	Perry	Wills B	1858-1873	232
Reynolds, Charles L.	Mobile	Wills 2	1837-1857	273
Reynolds, George W.	Montgomery	Wills 3	1840-1854	289
Reynolds, Gideon	Greene	Wills B	1817-1841	234
Reynolds, James	Montgomery	Wills 4	1853-1869	185
Reynolds, Overton H.	Butler	Wills 2	1864-1875	20
Reynolds, Priscilla	Montgomery	Wills 4	1853-1869	421
Reynolds, Sarah A.	Dallas	Wills A	1821-1849	230
Reynolds, Susannah	Marengo	Wills A	1820-1864	184
Reynolds, Walker	Talladega	W&I D	1867-1880	234
Rhen, Maria	Henry	OCR H	1855-1857	204
Rhoden, Bryan	Greene	Wills B	1817-1841	183
Rhodes, Benjamin	Butler	Wills 1	1853-1864	165

TESTATOR	COUNTY	WHERE FOUND		PAGE
Rhodes, Charlotte	Butler	Wills 1	1853-1864	88
Rhodes, Jacob	Marengo	Wills A	1820-1864	322
Rhodes, Jarred	Butler	Wills 1	1853-1864	4
Rhodes, John	Clarke	GE&W	1832-1839	179
Rhodes, John	Sumter	Wills 1	1828-1851	271
Rhodes, Jonathan	Lauderdale	Wills A	1835-1858	213
Rhodes, Nancy	Pike	Wills A	1845-1862	153
Rice, Elisha H.	Madison	PR 15	1850-1853	21
Rice, Hugh H.	Morgan	FR 20	1860-1865	113
Rice, Joel	Blount	Deeds A		266
Rice, Joel	Madison	PR 6	1832-1834	322
Rice, Joel J.	Madison	PR 15	1850-1853	20
Rice, John	Dallas	Wills B	1850-1871	173
Rice, John	Madison	PR 6	1832-1834	686
Rice, Josiah	Autauga	Reports F	1845-1850	367
Rice, Mrs. Nancy C.	Talladega	W&I C	1862-1866	143
Rice, Richard	Lauderdale	Wills A	1835-1858	215
Rice?, Robert G.	DeKalb	Wills A	1837-1863	29
Rice, Thornton	Autauga	Reports E-B	1841-1845	391
Richards, Thomas L.	Chambers	Wills 1-2	1833-1856	262
Richards, William	Chambers	Wills 1-2	1833-1856	334
Richards, William	Coosa	W&OCR 2	1843-1883	38
Richardson, Amy	Limestone	Wills 5	1836-1841	481
Richardson, Benjamin	Macon	Records 2	1838-1842	146
Richardson, Charles	Shelby	Wills D	1841-1846	122
Richardson, Jane	Limestone	Wills 6	1841-1846	89
Richardson, John	Marengo	Wills A	1820-1864	440
Richardson, John	Washington	Wills B	1827-	117
Richardson, John	Washington	Wills 1 ∅	1827-1888	191
Richardson, John A.	Greene	Wills D	1851-1888	178
Richardson, Jonadab	Perry	Wills A	1821-1855	258
Richardson, Jonathan	Lauderdale	Wills A	1835-1858	117
Richardson, Mary	Pike	Wills A	1845-1862	50
Richardson, W. W.	Coosa	W&OCR 2	1843-1883	225
Richey, Alexander	Tuscaloosa	Wills 1	1821-1855	85
Richey, William, Sr.	Perry	Wills A	1821-1855	27
Ricks, Jesse	Pike	Wills A	1845-1862	87
Riddle, Abia T.	Greene	Wills D	1851-1888	43
Riddle, Alvis	Greene	Wills B	1817-1841	293
Riddle, Elizabeth	Dallas	Wills A	1821-1849	76
Riddle, Terry	Calhoun	Loose	Probated 1844	
Riddle, Thomas	Greene	Wills B	1817-1841	251
Riddle, Walter D.	Talladega	Wills C	1845-1853	432
Ridgill, William J.	Barbour	OCR 14	1863-1865	279
Riesgraf, Simon	Lauderdale	Wills B	1859-1870	127
Rieson, James	Dallas	Wills A	1821-1849	126
Rigby, Thomas	Dallas	Wills A	1821-1849	64
Rigby, Thomas	Dallas	Wills A	1821-1849	97
Riggin, Richard	Washington	Wills B	1827-	125
Riggin, Richard	Washington	Wills 1 ∅	1827-1888	207
Riggs, Joel	Dallas	Wills B	1850-1871	345

TESTATOR	COUNTY	WHERE FOUND		PAGE
Rikard, John R.	Monroe	W&D B	1841-1845	59
Riley, Allen	Autauga	Reports A	1825-1830	217
Riley, Allen	Autauga	Reports A	1825-1830	259
Riley, Ann	Monroe	W&D E	1856-1861	579
Riley, Enoch	Monroe	W&D A	1833-1841	305
Riley, George	Monroe	W&D E	1856-1861	302
Riley, James	Mobile	Wills 3	1857-1870	666
Riley, John	Jefferson	OCR	1831-1832	80
Riley, Joseph, Sr.	Jefferson	OCR	1824-1831	134
Ringold, Mary	Etowah	Wills A	1866-1870	12
Ringstaff, Adam	Lowndes	Wills B	1830-1859	51
Ripley, Thomas B.	Mobile	Wills 1	1813-1837	34
Riser, George	Talladega	W&I D	1867-1880	438
Rison, Archibald	Madison	Wills 1	1853-1875	288
Ritchie, James	Wilcox	Wills	1821-1844	94
Rivas, Jose	Mobile	Wills 1	1813-1837	112
Rivers, Richard	Clarke	PR N	1866-1870	496
Rivers, Thomas	Barbour	OCR 14	1863-1865	466
Rivers, William	Barbour	OCR 12	1861-1863	780
Rives, Amy	Montgomery	Wills 4	1853-1869	27
Rives, George M.	Montgomery	Wills 2	1820-1845	287
Rives, Green	Lowndes	Wills B	1830-1859	296
Rives, Jemima	Shelby	Wills L	1838-1858	561
Rives, John M.	Montgomery	Wills 3	1840-1854	10
Rives, Mary R.	Lowndes	Wills B	1830-1859	118
Rives, (Mrs.) R. M.	Dallas	Wills B	1850-1871	442
Rives, William H.	Montgomery	Wills 4	1853-1869	443
Roach, George	Lauderdale	Wills A	1835-1858	301
Roach, John D.	Dallas	Wills A	1821-1849	128
Roach, John D.	Monroe	W&D C	1845-1850	270
Roan, Jesse	Morgan	OCR 8	1844-1848	145
Robard, Thomas	Marengo	Wills A	1820-1864	43
Robb, Ann M.	Mobile	Wills 3	1857-1870	346
Robbins, Daniel	Coosa	W&OCR 2	1843-1883	45
Robbins, Hardy H.	Montgomery	Wills 5	1863-1887	77
Robbins, Henrietta	Wilcox	Wills 6	1862-1870	20
Robbins, Jethro	Montgomery	Wills 4	1853-1869	474
Robbins, John	Dallas	Wills B	1850-1871	40
Robbins, William R.	Sumter	Wills 2	1851-1872	124
Roberson, Amy	Macon	Records 7	1857-1859	67
Roberson, John, Sr.	St. Clair	Deeds B	1831-1849	934
Roberson, Mary	St. Clair	Deeds B	1831-1849	860
Roberson, William	Henry	Deeds A-B	1822-1840	71
Robert, John	Mobile	Wills 3	1857-1870	185
Roberto, Lorenzo	Dallas	Wills B	1850-1871	250
Roberts, James M.	Chambers	Wills 3	1856-1899	55
Roberts, Isaac	Jefferson	Wills A	1856-1880	241
Roberts, David P.	Calhoun	Loose	Probated 1838	
Roberts, James	Limestone	Wills 6	1841-1846	400
Roberts, Joseph M.	Mobile	Wills 3	1857-1870	690
Roberts, (Mrs.) M. A.	Dallas	Wills B	1850-1871	394

TESTATOR	COUNTY	WHERE FOUND		PAGE
Roberts, Sarah	Mobile	Wills 2	1837-1857	137
Roberts, William H.	Mobile	Wills 2	1837-1857	395
Robertson, Daniel S.	Chambers	Wills 1-2	1833-1856	470
Robertson, Elizabeth	Montgomery	Wills 4	1853-1869	394
Robertson, H. B.	Shelby	Wills D	1841-1846	130
Robertson, John	Madison	Deeds B	1810-1816	221
Robertson, Joel	Mobile	Wills 1	1813-1837	44
Robertson, Thomas	Madison	PR 6	1832-1834	120
Robertson, W. G.	Pike	Wills A	1845-1862	31
Robertson, William	Tuscaloosa	Wills 3	1858-1865	124
Robey, James D.	Lowndes	Wills B	1830-1859	255
Robinsen, R. E.	Monroe	W&D E	1856-1861	400
Robinson, Alfred	Lawrence	I&W C	1866-1880	132
Robinson, Arthur A.	Wilcox	Wills 4	1857-1862	247
Robinson, Daniel	Mobile	Wills 3	1847-1870	681
Robinson, Emeline	Madison	Wills 1	1853-1875	513
Robinson, James	Calhoun	Loose	Probated 1841	
Robinson, James B.	Autauga	Reports E-B	1841-1845	507
Robinson, James B.	Madison	PR 8	1831-1839	128
Robinson, James O. L.	Madison	PR 8	1831-1839	155
Robinson, John	Lauderdale	Wills A	1835-1858	218
Robinson, John	Marengo	Wills A	1820-1864	282
Robinson, John	Montgomery	Wills 4	1853-1869	270
Robinson, John George	Lee	Wills A	1867-1898	44
Robinson, Lemuel B.	Chambers	Wills 1-2	1833-1856	303
Robinson, Madison B.	Madison	PR 8	1831-1839	385
Robinson, Russell	Clarke	PR H	1854-1856	109
Robinson, Sarah	Chambers	Wills 3	1856-1899	84
Robinson, Thomas	Madison	PR 6	1832-1834	120
Robinson, Thornton	Sumter	Wills 1	1828-1851	94
Robinson, Todd, Sr.	Autauga	Reports C	1834-1838	600
Robinson, William	Madison	PR 2	1818-1823	107
Robinson, William A.	Clarke	OCR	1825-1832	314
Robisen, Edmond E.	Monroe	W&D E	1856-1861	312
Robison, Allen	Wilcox	Wills 1	1821-1844	305
Robison, Allen	Wilcox	Wills 2	1832-1850	289
Roby, Marcus	Morgan	OCR 5	1829-1831	184
Rochell, Anderson	Perry	Wills A	1821-1855	128
Rochell, John	Madison	PR 15	1850-1853	18
Rochell, Mrs. Nancy	Perry	Wills A	1821-1855	185
Rochon, Augustine	Baldwin	Wills A	1811-1881	6
Rochon, Maria	Mobile	Wills 1	1813-1837	14
Roden, Isham	Greene	Wills A	1821-1827	65
Roden, Jeremiah	DeKalb	Wills A	1837-1863	46
Roden, John B.	DeKalb	Wills A	1837-1863	58
Roden, Joshua	Greene	Wills B	1817-1841	1
Roden, Levi	Greene	Wills D	1851-1888	416
Rodes, Robert E.	Tuscaloosa	Wills 3	1858-1865	180
Rodgers, Laura A.	Macon	WAC&A 11	1862-1870	321
Rodgers, Thomas	Shelby	Wills B	1818-1840	2
Roger, Ara	Sumter	Wills 2	1851-1872	236

TESTATOR	COUNTY	WHERE FOUND		PAGE
Rogers, A. D.	Lowndes	Wills	C	1861-1899	106
Rogers, Abby T.	Mobile	Wills	3	1857-1870	544
Rogers, Alexander A.	Sumter	Wills	2	1851-1872	132
Rogers, B.	Dallas	Wills	B	1850-1871	451
Rogers, Catherine	Marshall	FR	10	1869-1871	140
Rogers, Daniel	Lee	Wills	A	1867-1898	28
Rogers, George W. A.	Morgan	OCR	11	1850-1852	444
Rogers, James B.	Tuscaloosa	Wills	3	1858-1865	30
Rogers, Larkin M.	Montgomery	Wills	2	1820-1845	205
Rogers, Mary	Tuscaloosa	Wills	1	1821-1855	293
Rogers, Robert, Sr.	Jefferson	Deeds	1	1818-1828	141
Rogers, Robert	Pike	Wills	A	1845-1862	23
Rogers, Robert	Talladega	Wills	C	1845-1853	242
Rogers, William	Madison	Wills	1	1853-1875	144
Rolen, Zachariah	Dallas	Wills	B	1850-1871	136
Rolfe, Oscar A.	Morgan	FR	23	1866-1867	24
Roling, John	Pike	Wills	A	1845-1862	4
Rolinson, William	Autauga	Reports	C	1834-1838	354
Rolton, Gilbert R.	Mobile	Wills	2	1837-1857	46
Romer, Ellena B.	Mobile	Wills	3	1857-1870	626
Ronalds, Thomas A.	Madison	Wills	1	1853-1875	128
Rondel, Marrio T.	Mobile	Wills	2	1837-1857	59
Ronville, Sustain	Mobile	Wills	2	1837-1857	12
Root, Richard	Montgomery	Wills	3	1840-1854	27
Roper, J. W.	Shelby	Wills	E	1845-1850	1
Roper, Joseph	Shelby	Wills	H	1847-1866	887
Roper, Mary	Madison	PR	6	1832-1834	435
Roper, Nancy J.	Mobile	Wills	4	1870-1878	50
Roper, Sarah L.	Lowndes	Wills	C	1861-1899	64
Roper, William F.	Dallas	Wills	A	1821-1849	159
Roquemore, Thomas	Barbour	OCR	14	1863-1865	2
Roquemore, Zach	Barbour	OCR	16	1866-1868	961
Rose, Charles	Dallas	Wills	A	1821-1849	122
Rose, Howell	Coosa	W&OCR	2	1843-1883	217
Rose, James	Marshall	PR	2	1857-1888	597
Rose, Mary R.	Russell	Wills	2	1850-1873	410
Rosewan, Joseph T.	Tuscaloosa	Wills	3	1858-1865	65
Ross?, Frederick	Calhoun	PR	B	1856-1865	533
Ross, George	Mobile	Wills	3	1857-1870	639
Ross, James W.	Perry	Wills	A	1821-1855	214
Ross, Julianna P.	Montgomery	Wills	2	1820-1845	100
Ross, L.	Lauderdale	Wills	A	1835-1858	243
Ross, William W.	Montgomery	Wills	3	1840-1854	86
Rosser-see Roper					
Rotherberry, Presley	Bibb	OCR		1846-1851	421
Roundtree, C. B.	Lauderdale	Wills	3	1821-1825	4
Roundtree, William	Madison	PR	7	1834-1837	605
Rouse, W. H.?	Pike	Wills	A	1845-1862	254
Rouseau, James	Russell	Wills	2	1850-1873	101
Routt, William	Madison	PR	14	1846-1850	222
Roux, Emil	Mobile	Wills	2	1837-1857	25

TESTATOR	COUNTY	WHERE FOUND		PAGE
Rowan, Samuel	DeKalb	Wills A	1837-1863	1
Rowe, James Gillespie	Mobile	Wills 3	1857-1870	295
Rowin, Hugh	Tuscaloosa	Wills 1	1821-1855	250
Roy, Isaac A.	Jefferson	OCR	1824-	59
Roy, Marianne	Mobile	Wills 1	1813-1837	12
Royen?, William	Morgan	OCR 26	1867-1869	163
Royster, Clark	Wilcox	Wills 4	1847-1862	188
Royster, Clarke	Monroe	W&D E	1856-1861	210
Royston, Robert	Dallas	Wills A	1821-1849	47
Royston, Thomas B.	Chambers	Wills 3	1856-1899	209
Rucker, Frances	Lauderdale	Wills A	1835-1858	105
Ruddell, George	Montgomery	Wills 3	1840-1854	39
Rudolp(h), Zeb, Jr.	Lowndes	Wills B	1830-1859	302
Rudolph, (Mrs.) Abigail	Lowndes	Wills C	1861-1899	113
Rudolph, Zeb, Sr.	Lowndes	Wills B	1830-1859	318
Ruffin, A. G.	Washington	Wills 1 ∅	1827-1888	31
Ruffin, Albert G.	Washington	Wills B	1827-	20
Rugeley?, Rowland	Lowndes	Wills B	1830-1859	121
Rumph, Thomas	Dallas	Wills B	1850-1871	199
Rush, Charles G.	Macon	Records 6	1855-1858	772
Rush, Leonard	Tuscaloosa	Wills 1	1821-1855	196
Rush, Sarah	Macon	Records 8	1859-1860	295
Rushin, William	Macon	Records 8	1859-1860	440
Rushing, Bryant	Shelby	Wills E	1845-1850	384
Rushing, Margaret	Coosa	W&OCR 2	1843-1883	250
Rushing, Mary	Sumter	Wills 1	1828-1851	44
Rushing, Mary	Sumter	Wills 1	1828-1851	74
Rushing, Stephen	Sumter	Wills 1	1828-1851	224
Russel, Wiley	Morgan	OCR 7	1837-1843	426
Russell, Andrew, Sr.	Perry	Wills A	1821-1855	219
Russell, Armstead	Autauga	Deeds B		59
Russell, Calvin A.	Talladega	W&D A	1852-1857	334
Russell, Daniel M.	Sumter	Wills 2	1851-1872	285
Russell, Ignatius	Talladega	W&I B	1858-1864	586
Russell, James	Dallas	Wills A	1821-1849	48
Russell, Jesse	Tallapoosa	Wills 2	1864-1907	31
Russell, Martha H.	Morgan	FR 20	1860-1865	251
Russell, Sarah	Tallapoosa	Wills 2	1864-1907	27
Russell, William	Clarke	PCR L	1861-1864	100
Ruth, John	Perry	Wills A	1821-1855	64
Rutherford, Nancy	Dallas	Wills A	1821-1849	35
Rutherford, Thomas	Dallas	Wills A	1821-1849	19
Rutherford, Thomas J.	Jefferson	Wills 1	1818-1840	139
Ruthledge, David	Morgan	OCR 6	1831-1837	353
Rutland, Martha	Autauga	Reports E-A	1838-1841	302
Rutland, Watson	Coosa	W&OCR 2	1843-1883	318
Rutledge, George	Limestone	Wills 3	1826-1831	261
Rutledge, John S.	Perry	Wills A	1821-1855	63
Rutledge, Mary	Perry	Wills B	1858-1873	371
Rutledge, Richard	Perry	Wills A	1821-1855	50
Rutledge, Spencer B.	Mobile	Wills 3	1857-1870	569

TESTATOR	COUNTY	WHERE FOUND		PAGE
Rutledge, Spencer B.	Mobile	Wills 3	1857-1870	741
Rutledge, William O.	Russell	Wills 2	1850-1873	309
Ryan, Ann	Calhoun	Loose	Probated 1865	
Ryan, Ann	Calhoun	PR A-2	1856-1866	312
Ryan, Hampton	Barbour	OCR 17	1868-1870	531
Ryan, John	Greene	Wills B	1817-1841	159
Ryan, John C.	Mobile	Wills 2	1837-1857	444
Ryan, T. T.?	Dallas	Wills B	1850-1871	349
Ryan, William W.	Montgomery	Wills 4	1853-1869	511
Ryder, Richard G.	Mobile	Wills 1	1813-1837	186
Rye, William J.	Chambers	Wills 1-2	1833-1856	447
Ryland, Nelson	Morgan	OCR 27	1868-1869	177
Saddler, Nancy T.	Jefferson	OCR	1831-1832	23
Saddler, Nancy T.	Jefferson	OCR	1824-1831	473
Saffold, May	Dallas	Wills B	1850-1871	212
Saffold, Reuben	Dallas	Wills A	1821-1849	296
Saffoon, William	Talladega	Deeds C	1821	427
Sager, Edmund Mayo	Mobile	Wills 2	1837-1857	276
Sale, Arabella	Wilcox	Wills 5	1855-1870	116
Sale, Caroline J.	Wilcox	Wills 5	1855-1870	287
Sale, Charles C.	Madison	Wills 1	1853-1875	268
Sale, Joseph	Madison	PR 8	1831-1839	505
Sale, Nancy	Madison	PR 14	1846-1850	486
Salger, Gill	Wilcox	Wills 6	1862-1870	54
Salomon, Adolph M.	Mobile	Wills 3	1857-1870	294
Salter, Watkins	Wilcox	Wills 5	1855-1870	124
Saltmarsh, A.	Dallas	Wills B	1850-1871	230
Samani, John Michael	Mobile	Wills 2	1837-1857	374
Samford, James	Mobile	Wills 3	1857-1870	361
Sammons, Grove W.	Bibb	OCR	1846-1851	502
Sample, Alexander	Autauga	Reports E-A	1838-1841	52
Sample, Barbara	Greene	Wills C	1840-1864	161
Sample, Margaret	Autauga	Reports G	1850-1853	300
Sample, Robert	Madison	PR 3	1823-1826	48
Sample, William N.	Marengo	Wills A	1820-1864	243
Sampler, Jeremiah	Calhoun	Loose	Probated 1842	
Samuels, Sampson	Marengo	Wills A	1820-1864	208
Sanders, Ezekiel	Tuscaloosa	Wills 1	1821-1855	3
Sanders, Francis E.	Perry	Wills B	1858-1873	286
Sanders, Francis E.	Pike	Wills A	1845-1862	71
Sanders, Hamlin	Montgomery	Wills 4	1853-1869	114
Sanders, Isaac	Pike	Wills B	1862-1879	130
Sanders, Jordan	Chambers	Wills 3	1858-1899	136
Sanders, William B.	Sumter	Wills 2	1851-1872	254
Sanderson, John G.	Limestone	Wills 3	1826-1831	393
Sanderson, Morris	Limestone	Wills 6	1841-1846	633
Sanderson, William	Greene	Wills B	1817-1841	53
Sandifer, Adelia	Jefferson	Wills A	1856-1880	157

TESTATOR	COUNTY	WHERE FOUND		PAGE
Sandifer, Philip	Jefferson	PM	1844-1854	287
Sandifer, William	Limestone	Wills 7	1844-1847	144
Sands, Mary	Madison	PR 3	1823-1826	378
Sanford, Caswell	Coosa	W&OCR 2	1843-1883	206
Sanford, Caswell	Elmore	Wills A	1866-1906	6
Sanford, Charles H.	Bibb	Admr.R 1	1858-1865	794
Sanford, Elizabeth	Mobile	Wills 2	1837-1857	443
Sanford, James	Mobile	Wills 3	1857-1870	361
Sankey, John S.	Montgomery	Wills 2	1820-1845	162
Sankey, Richard T.	Russell	Wills 1	1838-1849	104
Santini, Simon	Mobile	Wills 2	1837-1857	355
Sara?, Adolphe	Mobile	Wills 3	1857-1870	676
Sario?, Veto	Mobile	Wills 3	1857-1870	422
Sartwell, O. R.	Greene	Wills C	1840-1864	179
Sasser, Richard	Russell	Wills 2	1850-1873	421
Saterwhite, John	Dallas	Wills A	1821-1840	204
Satterwhite, Charles	Wilcox	Wills 4	1847-1862	145
Satterwhite, John W.	Wilcox	Wills 5	1855-1870	392
Satterwhite, Obe	Tallapoosa	Wills 1	1839-1866	126
Satterwhite, Ruben	Wilcox	Wills 1	1821-1844	431
Saucier, Marius	Mobile	Wills 3	1857-1870	607
Saunders, Claiborn	Madison	PR 2	1818-1823	112
Saunders, Thomas A.	Perry	Wills A	1821-1855	139
Saunders, Thomas A.	Sumter	Wills 1	1828-1851	59
Saunders, Thomas F.	Dallas	Wills B	1850-1871	93
Saunders, William B.	Sumter	Wills 2	1851-1872	254
Savage, Ann R.	Lawrence	I&W D	1835-1840	629
Savage, Benjamin	Wilcox	Wills 1	1821-1844	354
Savage, Charles B.	Wilcox	Wills 4	1847-1862	34
Savage, George M.	Lauderdale	Wills A	1835-1858	106
Savage, James	Calhoun	Loose	Probated 1841	
Savage, Robert	Conecuh	OB A	1865-1870	86
Savage, Samuel	Lauderdale	Wills A	1835-1858	41
Savage, W. F.	Lauderdale	Wills A	1835-1858	105
Sawyer, Ansel	Autauga	Reports F	1845-1850	84
Sawyer, Seymour B.	Montgomery	Wills 2	1820-1845	303
Saxon, Ann	Autauga	Reports E-B	1841-1845	170
Saxon, Benajah	Tallapoosa	Wills 1	1838-1866	54
Saxon, Samuel	Madison	Deeds D	1816-1818	74
Sayre, Mary V.	Montgomery	Wills 4	1853-1869	387
Sayre, P. D.	Montgomery	Wills 3	1840-1854	149
Sayre, Theodore	Marengo	Wills A	1820-1864	331
Sayre, William	Mobile	Wills 3	1857-1870	265
Scales, Elizabeth R.	Tuscaloosa	Wills 4	1868-1897	79
Scales, Peter P.	Sumter	Wills 1	1828-1851	32
Scales, Thomas H. P.	Talladega	Wills C	1845-1853	398
Scallorn, John	Madison	PR 2&5	1818-1826	464
Scanlon, Patrick	Mobile	Wills 3	1857-1870	679
Scarbrough, John W.	Greene	Wills C	1840-1864	560
Scattergood, Benjamin F.	Mobile	Wills 3	1857-1870	548
Schaffer, Jacob	Mobile	Wills 3	1857-1870	140

TESTATOR	COUNTY	WHERE FOUND		PAGE
Schall, John	Lauderdale	Wills B	1859-1870	142
Scheiffelin, George	Mobile	Wills 4	1870-1878	82
Schickner, Christian	Mobile	Wills 2	1837-1857	304
Schokley, Thomas C.	Russell	Wills 1	1838-1849	40
Schrobel, J. ? H.	Mobile	Wills 2	1837-1857	89
Schroeder, Charles Henry	Mobile	Wills 3	1857-1870	61
Schully, Lawrence	Marengo	Wills A	1820-1864	243
Scogin, William	Montgomery	Wills 2	1820-1845	140
Scogins, John	Pike	Wills A	1845-1862	14
Scogins, William C.	Montgomery	Wills 4	1853-1869	451
Scoggins, William	Montgomery	Wills 4	1853-1869	97
Scott, A. H.	Chambers	Wills 1-2	1833-1856	352
Scott, B. C.	Macon	Records 2	1838-1842	302
Scott, James	Limestone	Wills 3	1826-1831	105
Scott, James, Sr.	Perry	Wills A	1821-1855	119
Scott, James J.	Wilcox	Wills 5	1855-1870	138
Scott, Jane	Dallas	Wills B	1850-1871	187
Scott, John, Sr.	Lowndes	Wills B	1830-1859	76
Scott, John	Mobile	Wills 3	1857-1870	438
Scott, Lenord	Wilcox	Wills 1	1821-1844	448
Scott, Mary	Chambers	Wills 1-2	1833-1856	438
Scott, Nancy A.	Mobile	Wills 3	1657-1870	44
Scott, Nathaniel J.	Macon	Records 10	1863-1865	77
Scott, Robert T.	Jackson	Wills L	1665-1866	13
Scott, Thomas J.	Montgomery	Wills 4	1853-1869	401
Scovel, George	Montgomery	Wills 5	1863-1887	67
Scovel, Lyman	Montgomery	Wills 4	1853-1869	407
Scruggs, Edith	Madison	Wills 1	1853-1875	232
Scruggs, Edmond L.	Madison	PR 8	1831-1839	389
Scruggs, Gross	Madison	Wills 1	1853-1875	97
Scruggs, Jesse	Madison	W&I	1810-1820	135
Scruggs, Mary	Madison	PR 15	1850-1853	63
Scull, Dorcas	Mobile	Wills 2	1837-1857	106
Scurlock, Napoleon P.?	Sumter	Wills 1	1828-1851	247
Seagler, Elizabeth	Lowndes	Wills C	1861-1899	100
Seale, Barnabas	Bibb	PM F	1855-1858	592
Seale, Jarvis	Greene	Wills B	1817-1841	203
Seale, Littleton	Pike	Wills A	1845-1862	37
Seale, Ransom	Butler	Wills 1	1853-1864	173
Seale, William	Shelby	Deeds I	1842-1846	168
Seale, William	Shelby	Wills K	1846-1849	7
Seals, Barnabas	Bibb	Admr.R I	1858-1865	66
Seals, Spencer	Talladega	Wills C	1845-1853	204
Searcy, James W.	Henry	OCR H	1855-1853	338
Sears, Barnabas B.	Autauga	Wills 1	1862-1925	36
Seaver, Thomas	Wilcox	Wills 3	1826-1858	98
Seawell, G.	Marengo	Wills A	1820-1864	197
Seawell, Matilda A.	Butler	Wills 2	1864-1875	40
Seay, John W.	Barbour	OCR 9	1858-1859	594
Seegar, John	Russell	Wills 2	1850-1873	211
Sego, John	Lauderdale	Wills A	1853-1858	223

145

TESTATOR	COUNTY	WHERE FOUND		PAGE
Segrest, Jacob	Macon	Records 4	1850-1852	242
Segrest, Reuben	Macon	Records 8	1859-1860	481
Segur, Ann	Chambers	Wills 1-2	1833-1856	357
Seibels, John Jacob	Montgomery	Wills 4	1853-1869	500
Selers, Calvin C.	Wilcox	Wills 3	1826-1858	114
Sellars, Katherine	Lowndes	Wills B	1830-1859	110
Sellers, Cornelia	Bullock	Wills A	1868-1902	35
Sellers, Samuel	Pike	Wills A	1845-1864	155
Sellers, William	Clarke	PR L	1861-1864	58
Sells, James	Mobile	Wills 3	1857-1870	146
Selman, Elizabeth	Marengo	Wills A	1820-1864	240
Selman, William	Marengo	Wills A	1820-1864	145
Seloff, John	Lauderdale	Wills B	1859-1870	271
Seltzer, Levi D.	Mobile	Wills 3	1857-1870	182
Semple, Caroline A.	Montgomery	Wills 4	1853-1869	135
Semple, James	Perry	Wills A	1821-1855	187
Sentell, Samuel	Shelby	Wills B	1818-1840	164
Sentenne, Manuela Sorancia	Mobile	Wills 2	1837-1857	131
Serra, Battiste	Mobile	Wills 1	1813-1837	202
Serra, Clestine	Mobile	Wills 2	1837-1857	424
Sessions, John	Lowndes	Wills B	1830-1859	48
Sewell, John	Tallapoosa	Wills 1	1838-1866	119
Sexton, James	Mobile	Wills 3	1857-1870	631
Shackelford, Alex	Sumter	Wills 2	1851-1872	360
Shackelford, G. W.	Montgomery	Wills 4	1853-1869	550
Shackelford, James T.	Sumter	Wills 2	1851-1872	21
Shackelford, Richard	Coosa	W&OCR 2	1843-1883	215
Shackelford, Richard	Madison	PR 3	1823-1826	70
Shackleford, George	Montgomery	Wills 3	1840-1854	224
Shaddock, Samuel	Perry	Wills A	1821-1855	94
Shaddock, Thomas	Bibb	PM E	1852-1855	4
Shafer, William	Morgan	OCR 7	1837-1843	149
Shahan, John	St. Clair	RE C	1852-1859	23
Shanklin, Samuel J.	Madison	Wills 1	1853-1875	434
Shannon, David	Madison	Wills 1	1853-1875	295
Shannon, John H.	Dallas	Wills B	1850-1871	309
Shannon, Thomas	Chambers	Wills 3	1856-1899	174
Sharman, Clement	Chambers	Wills 1-2	1833-1856	274
Sharman, William C.	Chambers	Wills 3	1856-1899	144
Sharmon, Robert	Russell	Wills 2	1850-1873	36
Sharmon, Robert, Sr.	Russell	Wills 2	1850-1873	243
Sharp, Cambell	Monroe	W&D B	1841-1845	129
Sharp, James	Montgomery	Wills 4	1853-1869	381
Sharp, James C.	Dallas	Wills B	1850-1871	2
Sharp, John	Lauderdale	Wills B	1859-1870	58
Sharpe, Robert C.	Montgomery	Wills 4	1853-1869	178
Shaver, George	Montgomery	Wills 4	1853-1869	88
Shaver, James	Montgomery	Wills 3	1840-1854	173
Shaver, William	Morgan	OCR 7	1837-1843	149
Shaw, Adamson T.	Lawrence	I&W D	1835-1840	121
Shaw, Matthew	Washington	Wills 1 ∅	1827-1888	67

TESTATOR	COUNTY	WHERE FOUND		PAGE
Shaw, Mathew	Washington	Wills B	1827-	44
Shaw, Robert	Lauderdale	Wills B	1859-1870	161
Shaw, Thomas	Wilcox	Wills 3	1826-1858	322
Shaw, William W.	Coosa	W&OCR 2	1843-1883	324
Shearer, Gilbert	Dallas	Wills A	1821-1849	274
Shears, William A.	Dallas	Wills B	1850-1871	139
Sheffey, Lawrence B.	Madison	Wills 1	1853-1875	360
Sheffield, Isaac B.	Wilcox	Wills 5	1855-1870	15
Sheffield, Isam	Wilcox	Wills 1	1821-1844	368
Shelburn, Samuel	Lauderdale	Wills A	1835-1858	58
Shell, John W.	Pike	Wills B	1862-1870	115
Shell, Letty	Greene	Wills D	1851-1854	55
Shell, Vines T.	Greene	Wills B	1817-1841	131
Shelly, N. W.	Dallas	Wills B	1850-1871	216
Shelton, Azariah	Calhoun	Loose	Probated 1840	
Shelton, Charles T.	Tallapoosa	Wills 1	1838-1866	166
Shelton, H. C.	Lowndes	Wills B	1830-1859	232
Shelton, James T.	Mobile	Wills 3	1857-1870	633
Shelton, John	Mobile	Wills 2	1837-1857	211
Shelton, Lewis N.	Montgomery	Wills 4	1853-1869	301
Shepard, John	Dallas	Wills B	1850-1871	162
Sheperd, Elizabeth	Marshall	PR 2	1857-1888	662
Shepherd, Asa	Montgomery	Wills 2	1820-1845	154
Shepherd, Elizabeth C.	Morgan	FR 16	1857-1861	140
Shepherd, Susan P.	Mobile	Wills 2	1837-1857	215
Sheppard, James	Butler	Wills 2	1864-1875	23
Sheppard, Richard W.	Montgomery	Wills 3	1840-1854	267
Sheppard, William B.	Mobile	Wills 2	1837-1857	359
Sheridan, Nancy	Mobile	Wills 2	1837-1857	366
Sherman, James	Lauderdale	Wills B	1859-1870	21
Shevey, Joshua	Dallas	Wills B	1850-1871	241
Shields, J.?J.?	Sumter	Wills 2	1851-1872	218
Shinn, Carson	Mobile	Wills 2	1837-1857	361
Shirbet, William	Bibb	Admr.R 1	1858-1865	744
Shirley, Mary A.	Tuscaloosa	Wills 4	1868-1897	59
Shirly, Lewis	Etowah	Wills A	1866-1870	2
Shiva, Unity	Dallas	Wills A	1821-1849	229
Sholar, Benjamin	Lauderdale	Wills B	1859-1870	116
Shorter, Reuben C., Sr.	Barbour	OCR 5	1852-1853	503
Shorter, Reuben C.	Montgomery	Wills 3	1840-1854	265
Shotwell, Reuben	Madison	PR 13	1838-1848	357
Shuler, Barbara	Butler	Wills 1	1853-1864	26
Shultz, Frederick	Pike	Wills A	1845-1862	213
Shutes, Francis A.	Sumter	Wills 1	1828-1851	26
Sibley, Origen	Baldwin	Wills A	1811-1881	186
Sibley, William C.	Baldwin	Wills A	1811-1881	253
Sigler, Daniel	Monroe	W&D B	1841-1845	321
Siler, Solomon	Pike	Wills A	1845-1862	93
Sills, Henry C.	Lee	Wills A	1867-1898	6
Sills, James	Mobile	Wills 3	1857-1870	146
Silver, Joseph	Baldwin	Wills A	1811-1881	189

TESTATOR	COUNTY	WHERE FOUND		PAGE
Silvers, Jacob Jacob?	Dallas	Wills A	1821-1849	121
Siminton, James	Marengo	Wills A	1820-1864	240
Simison, John Andrew	Mobile	Wills 2	1837-1857	350
Simkins, Ada	Monroe	W&D D	1850-1856	59
Simmons, Catherine	Montgomery	Wills 4	1853-1869	476
Simmons, Jacob	Greene	Wills C	1840-1864	182
Simmons, James	Macon	WAC&A 11	1862-1870	583
Simmons, John	Madison	PR 2	1818-1823	379
Simmons, John	Talladega	Wills C	1845-1863	55
Simmons, Nathan	Macon	Records 6	1855-1858	466
Simmons, Robert	Sumter	Wills 2	1851-1872	86
Simmons, Ruben	Madison	PR 4	1826-1829	402
Simmons, Samuel	Autauga	Reports E-B	1841-1845	451
Simmons, Thomas	Bibb	Deeds J	1866-1869	320
Simms, Christiana N.	Dallas	Wills A	1821-1849	206
Simms, Harvell	Montgomery	Wills 2	1820-1845	174
Simms, James	Chambers	Wills 3	1856-1899	221
Simms, Matilda	Wilcox	Wills 3	1826-1858	112
Simms, Redding	Lowndes	Wills B	1830-1859	386
Simon, Lucy	Mobile	Wills 1	1813-1837	70
Simonton, Wm. Davidson	Lowndes	Wills C	1861-1899	25
Simpson, B. F.	Washington	Wills 1 ∅	1827-1888	242
Simpson, B. F.	Washington	Wills B	1827-	142
Simpson, Elisha	Washington	Wills 1 ∅	1827-1888	58
Simpson, Elisha	Washington	Wills B	1827-	38
Simpson, James	Sumter	Wills 2	1851-1872	315
Simpson, John	Lauderdale	Wills B	1859-1870	35
Simpson, John P.	Washington	Wills 1 ∅	1827-1888	231
Simpson, John P.	Washington	Wills B	1827-	137
Simpson, Philip	Washington	Wills 1 ∅	1827-1888	136
Simpson, Philip	Washington	Wills B	1827-	86
Simpson, Sarah J.	Mobile	Wills 3	1857-1870	333
Simpson, Thomas	Lauderdale	Wills B	1859-1870	23
Simpson, Thomas	Lauderdale	Wills B	1859-1870	60
Simpson, Uriah E.	Washington	Wills 1 ∅	1827-1888	163
Simpson, Uriah E.	Washington	Wills B	1827-	103
Simpson, William	Tallapoosa	Wills 1	1838-1866	145
Sims, Benjamin	Madison	PR 2	1818-1823	207
Sims, Downs	Autauga	Reports E-B	1841-1845	114
Sims, Edward	Tuscaloosa	Wills 1	1821-1855	134
Sims, George	Greene	Wills C	1840-1864	256
Sims, James	Russell	Wills 1	1838-1849	3
Sims, Jenny	Wilcox	Wills 5	1855-1870	454
Sims, John	Greene	Wills B	1817-1841	270
Sims, Julius H.	Greene	Wills B	1817-1841	235
Sims, Martha	Montgomery	Wills 3	1840-1854	196
Sims, Wilkins J.	Sumter	Wills 2	1851-1872	423
Sims, William	Autauga	Reports E-A	1838-1841	193
Sims, William	Butler	Wills 1	1853-1864	74
Sims, William	Limestone	Deeds 1	1819-1825	38
Sinard, J. D.	DeKalb	Wills B	1869-1905	5

TESTATOR	COUNTY	WHERE FOUND		PAGE
Sinclair, Mary J.?	Dallas	Wills A	1821-1849	325
Singletary, William J.	Henry	OCR S	1867-1868	484
Singleton, Enoch	Montgomery	Wills 4	1853-1869	139
Singleton, Irby	Clarke	PR E	1840-1845	266
Singleton, Sarah E.	Clarke	PCR L	1861-1864	139
Sinquefield, Moses	Pike	Wills B	1862-1879	53
Sistrunk, Joe	Macon	Records 3	1845-1850	573
Sivily, Joseph	Madison	W&I	1810-1820	124
Sivley, Andrew	Madison	Wills 1	1853-1875	41
Sizemore, Mary	Baldwin	Wills A	1811-1881	172
Sizemore, William	Baldwin	Wills A	1811-1881	128
Skains, Thomas	Butler	Wills 1	1853-1864	117
Skelton, Asa	Calhoun	PR A-2	1856-1866	279
Skelton, James J.	Calhoun	Loose	Probated 1854	
Skidmore, William	Morgan	OCR 11	1850-1852	189
Skilair?, Caleb Browning	Jackson	Wills	1870-1872	553
Skinner, Isaac	Tuscaloosa	Wills 1	1821-1855	220
Skinner, Lemuel	Wilcox	Wills 2	1832-1850	372
Skinner, William G.	Perry	Wills A	1821-1855	195
Slade, William B.	Washington	Wills 1 ∅	1827-1888	53
Slade, William B.	Washington	Wills B	1827-	34
Slater, George	Mobile	Wills 1	1813-1837	225
Slaton, John B.	Lee	Wills A	1867-1898	34
Slaton, Willoughby	Clarke	OCR	1825-1832	268
Slatter, Henry F.	Montgomery	Wills 3	1840-1854	123
Slaughter, Daniel	Barbour	OCR 8	1856-1858	200
Slaughter, Ezekiel	Tuscaloosa	Wills 4	1868-1897	1
Slaughter, Ezekiel	Tuscaloosa	Wills 4	1868-1897	2
Slaughter, J. R.	Tallapoosa	Wills 1	1838-1866	228
Slaughter, James	Limestone	Wills 3	1826-1831	64
Slaughter, John	Chambers	Wills 3	1856-1899	40
Slaughter, John	Madison	Deeds A	1810-1816	45
Slaughter, Samuel	Monroe	W&D C	1845-1850	183
Slawyer, Sarah F.	Greene	Wills C	1840-1864	733
Slayton, Arthur	Calhoun	Loose	Probated 1853	
Sledge, Alexander	Marengo	Wills A	1820-1864	540
Sledge, Oliver D.	Madison	Wills 1	1853-1875	505
Sledge, Washington A.	Madison	PR 8	1831-1839	155
Sligh, Emanuel	Macon	Records 6	1855-1858	374
Sloan, Archibald	St. Clair	Deeds B	1831-1849	179
Sloan, John	Barbour	OCR 16	1866-1868	563
Sloan, Joseph R.	Mobile	Wills 3	1857-1870	391
Sloan, Susannah	Wilcox	Wills 2	1832-1850	377
Sloane, B. W.	Lowndes	Wills B	1830-1850	174
Sloss, James L.	Lauderdale	Wills A	1835-1858	103
Smaw, Will	Perry	Wills A	1821-1855	150
Smedley, Thomas	Chambers	Wills 1-2	1833-1856	364
Smedly, Thomas M.	Chambers	Wills 3	1856-1899	186
Smetlin, Ann M.	Macon	Records 8	1859-1860	293
Smith, Albert	Wilcox	Wills 5	1855-1870	152
Smith, Angelina W.	Lowndes	Wills B	1830-1859	231

TESTATOR	COUNTY	WHERE FOUND		PAGE
Smith, Ann	Washington	Wills 1 ∅	1827-1888	48
Smith, Ann	Washington	Wills B	1827-	31
Smith, Ann B.	Lowndes	Wills C	1861-1899	27
Smith, Anna	Greene	Wills D	1851-1888	324
Smith, Arthur B.	Marengo	Wills A	1820-1864	328
Smith, B. C.	Lowndes	Wills B	1830-1859	66
Smith, Bart	Dallas	Wills A	1821-1849	317
Smith, Bartholomew	Lowndes	Wills B	1830-1859	40
Smith, Baxter	Dallas	Wills A	1821-1849	13
Smith, Benjamin	Lauderdale	Wills A	1835-1858	140
Smith, Benjamin J.	Lowndes	Wills C	1861-1899	124
Smith, Bird	Chambers	Wills 3	1856-1899	100
Smith, Bolin	Lowndes	Wills B	1830-1859	26
Smith, Bookajah	Washington	Wills 1 ∅	1827-1888	54
Smith, Bookajah	Washington	Wills B	1827-	35
Smith, Charles	Chambers	Wills 1-2	1833-1856	335
Smith, Charles	Limestone	Wills 11	1865-1866	66
Smith, D. K.	Monroe	W&D F	1861-1867	622
Smith, Daniel K.	Coosa	W&PM A	1834-1842	365
Smith, Delila	Sumter	Wills 1	1828-1851	217
Smith, Dialtha O.	Marengo	Wills A	1820-1864	487
Smith, Dudley	Dallas	Wills A	1821-1849	9
Smith, Edwin P.	Lowndes	Wills B	1830-1859	39
Smith, Elam	Greene	Wills C	1840-1864	633
Smith, Elijah	Perry	Wills A	1821-1855	100
Smith, Elizabeth	Lauderdale	Wills B	1859-1870	108
Smith, Elizabeth	Madison	PR 13	1838-1848	470
Smith, Elizabeth	Marengo	Wills A	1820-1864	348
Smith, Elizabeth	Mobile	Wills 2	1837-1857	411
Smith, Elizabeth R.	Tuscaloosa	Wills 1	1821-1855	217
Smith, Francis D.	Tuscaloosa	Wills 1	1821-1855	20
Smith, Frank	Colbert	Wills A	1861-1903	20
Smith, Gabriel	Limestone	Wills 5	1836-1841	202
Smith, Henry	Lauderdale	Wills A	1835-1858	130
Smith, Henry	Marengo	Wills A	1820-1864	201
Smith, Henry	Sumter	Wills 1	1828-1851	17
Smith, Isaac	Hale	Wills A	1867-1923	1
Smith, Isaac	Tallapoosa	Wills 1	1838-1866	170
Smith, Isaiah	Barbour	Loose Box 290 Probated 1857		
Smith, James	Morgan	OCR 8	1844-1848	250
Smith, James	Tallapoosa	Wills 1	1838-1866	191
Smith, James Bonnell	Mobile	Wills 3	1857-1870	498
Smith, James H.	Greene	Wills B	1817-1841	58
Smith, James H.	Lowndes	Wills C	1861-1899	128
Smith, Jenny	Wilcox	Wills 5	1855-1870	454
Smith, Jeremiah	Autauga	Reports C	1834-1838	81
Smith, John	Greene	Wills C	1840-1864	205
Smith, John	Lauderdale	Wills B	1859-1870	121
Smith, John	Lauderdale	Wills 4	1821-1825	127
Smith, John	Madison	W&I	1810-1820	47
Smith, John A.	Greene	Wills B	1817-1841	246

TESTATOR	COUNTY	WHERE FOUND		PAGE
Smith, John K.	Mobile	Wills 1	1813-1837	29
?Smiths? John W.	Greene	Wills C	1840-1864	9
Smith, John W.	Sumter	Wills 2	1851-1872	120
Smith, Jordan	Pike	Wills A	1845-1862	190
Smith, Joseph L. D.	Lauderdale	Wills A	1835-1858	34
Smith, Joseph W.	Perry	Wills A	1821-1855	246
Smith, Joshua	Sumter	Wills 2	1851-1872	277
Smith, Joshua T.	Sumter	Wills 1	1828-1851	86
Smith, Josiah	Barbour	OCR 8	1856-1858	228
Smith, Josiah P.	Montgomery	Wills 2	1820-1845	239
Smith, Leonora	Chambers	Wills 3	1856-1899	95
Smith, Maria Louisa	Montgomery	Wills 3	1840-1854	76
Smith, Martha	Clarke	PR J	1856-1858	535
Smith, Martha P.	Lauderdale	Wills B	1859-1870	62
Smith, Mary Ann	Mobile	Wills 3	1857-1870	561
Smith, Mrs. Mary	Perry	Wills A	1821-1855	159
Smith, Morris	Madison	PR 16	1831-1861	356
Smith, Nancey	Lowndes	Wills B	1830-1859	27
Smith, Nancy	Butler	Wills 1	1853-1864	38
Smith, Nathan	Perry	Wills A	1821-1855	66
Smith, Neal C.	Macon	Records 7	1857-1859	33
Smith, Needham	Butler	Wills 1	1853-1864	136
Smith, O. S.	Jefferson	Wills A	1856-1880	246
Smith, Octavius	Jefferson	Wills A	1856-1880	247
Smith, Rebecca	Montgomery	Wills 4	1853-1869	495
Smith, Rebecca	Russell	Wills 2	1850-1873	360
Smith, Reuben	Pike	Wills A	1845-1862	345
Smith, Richard	Montgomery	Wills 3	1840-1854	3
Smith, Robert W.	Coosa	W&OCR 2	1843-1883	5
Smith, Samuel	Limestone	Wills 6	1841-1846	53
Smith, Samuel	Madison	W&I	1810-1820	105
Smith, Samuel Henry	Perry	Wills A	1821-1855	167
Smith, Samuel P.	Lowndes	Wills C	1861-1899	15
Smith, Sarah Chester	Tuscaloosa	Wills 1	1821-1855	213
Smith, Simon	Henry	Deeds A-B	1822-1840	215
Smith, Solomon	Perry	Wills B	1858-1873	109
Smith, Solomon	Sumter	Wills 1	1828-1851	254
Smith, Solomon F.	Perry	Wills B	1858-1873	284
Smith, Stephens	Morgan	OCR 3	1827-1832	126
Smith, Thomas	Washington	Wills B	1827-	106
Smith, Thomas G.	Washington	Wils 1 ∅	1827-1888	170
Smith, Thomas H.	Macon	Records 10	1863-1865	556
Smith, Vines	Coosa	W&OCR 2	1843-1883	112
Smith, Virginius S.	Perry	Wills B	1858-1873	228
Smith, Wilkins	Russell	Wills 1	1838-1849	185
Smith, William	Madison	PR 9	1839-1841	268
Smith, William	Mobile	Wills 2	1837-1857	4
Smith, William	Mobile	Wills 4	1870-1878	75
Smith, William C.	Wilcox	Wills 4	1847-1862	16
Smith, William J.	Tuscaloosa	Wills 1	1821-1855	347
Smith, William M.	Morgan	OCR 27	1868-1869	388

TESTATOR	COUNTY	WHERE FOUND		PAGE
Smitherman, Jessee	Bibb	Admr.R 1	1858-1865	751
Smithers, Samuel	Madison	Wills 1	1853-1875	342
Smithsen, Ansen	Jefferson	Wills A	1856-1880	263
Smyly, James Senr.	Dallas	Wills B	1850-1871	17
Smyly, John	Dallas	Wills A	1821-1855	354
Smyth, Samuel M.	Pike	Wills B	1862-1879	158
Smythe, William M.	Marengo	Wills A	1820-1864	558
Snares, Peter	Baldwin	Wills A	1811-1881	121
Snead, Daniel W.	Bibb	OCR	1846-1851	97
Snead, Hermon B.	Madison	PR 2	1818-1823	290
Sneed, Stephen	Washington	Wills 1 ∅	1827-1888	145
Sneed, Stephen	Washington	Wills B	1827-	92
Snelgrove, Henry	Baldwin	Wills A	1811-1881	80
Snell, John	Monroe	W&D 8	1870-1871	576
Snell, John	Wilcox	Wills 1	1821-1844	356
Snider, Crusen	Madison	Wills 1	1853-1875	405
Snidow, Christian	Colbert	Wills A	1861-1903	49
Snipes, Maria A.	Barbour	OCR 9	1858-1859	563
Snipes, Martha	Barbour	OCR 4	1850-1852	434
Snipes, W. H.	Barbour	OCR 2	1842-1847	123
Snoddy, John	Madison	PR 2&5	1818-1826	55
Snoddy, William	Lauderdale	Wills B	1859-1870	38
Snoddy, William	Lauderdale	Wills 4	1821-1825	151
Snow, Caroline	Tuscaloosa	Wills 3	1858-1865	196
Snow, Elizabeth	Tuscaloosa	Wills 1	1821-1855	287
Snow, Henry A.	Tuscaloosa	Wills 3	1858-1865	147
Snow, Henry B.	Tuscaloosa	Wills 3	1858-1865	97
Snow, Samuel N.	Lowndes	Wills B	1830-1859	51
Snow, Stephen W.	Mobile	Wills 3	1857-1870	495
Snow, William H.	Jefferson	PM	1848-1853	212
Soale, L. A.	Lowndes	Wills C	1861-1899	146
Sofferans, Mary	Lauderdale	Wills A	1835-1858	251
Soloman, John G.	Monroe	W&D F	1861-1867	145
Solomon, Peter	Tuscaloosa	Wills 3	1858-1865	161
Somers, George	Sumter	Wills 2	1851-1872	230
Soost, Andrew D.	Mobile	Wills 3	1857-1870	277
Sorrell, Green	Chambers	Wills 1-2	1833-1856	227
Sorrell, John	Dallas	Wills A	1821-1849	194
Sorrell, K.	Dallas	Wills B	1850-1871	439
Sorsby, John T.	Greene	Wills D	1851-1858	111
Sorsby, Nicholas C.	Autauga	DM&R 17	1820-1864	51
Sorsby, Thomas J.	Hale	Wills A	1867-1923	62
Southerland, Alfred D.	Marshall	FR $3\frac{1}{2}$	1847-1850	89
Southerland, Samuel M.	Sumter	Wills 1	1828-1851	105
Sowell, James	Monroe	W&D C	1845-1850	526
Sowell, John	Henry	Deeds C	1840-1846	110
Sowerhaver, Conrad	Wilcox	Wills 2	1832-1850	375
Spain, Augustus	Madison	PR 16	1831-1861	243
Spain, M. D.	Lauderdale	Wills 4	1821-1825	59
Span, James G.	Lowndes	Wills C	1861-1899	116
Span, M. D.	Lauderdale	Wills B	1859-1870	24

TESTATOR	COUNTY	WHERE FOUND		PAGE
Spann, Mary J.	Hale	Wills A	1867-1923	68
Spaulding, E. M.	Lauderdale	Wills B	1859-1870	27
Spaulding, M. R.	Lauderdale	Wills B	1859-1870	140
Speaks, Thomas	Madison	Deeds D	1816-1818	1
Spear, Jesse P.	Montgomery	Wills 4	1853-1869	100
Spears, Martha E.	Limestone	Wills 11	1865-1866	11
Spears, Mary M.	Perry	Wills A	1821-1855	151
Specker, Cecelia	Lauderdale	Wills B	1859-1870	183
Speed, George W.	Perry	Wills A	1821-1855	61
Speed, Virginia M.	Perry	Wills B	1858-1873	183
Speed, William	Greene	Wills A	1821-1827	30
Speight, Edwin G.	Sumter	Wills 2	1851-1872	275
Speir, John	Pike	Wills A	1845-1862	52
Spence, Charlotte	Talladega	Wills A	1833-1839	496
Spence, Judy	Madison	PR 13	1838-1848	153
Spence, William	Talladega	W&I D	1867-1880	518
Spencer, Charles B.	Greene	Wills D	1851-1888	69
Spencer, Eliza N.	Tallapoosa	Wills 1	1838-1866	28
Spencer, Elizabeth	Greene	Wills C	1840-1864	347
Spencer, Henry S.	Tallapoosa	Wills 1	1838-1866	29
Spencer, James C.	Tuscaloosa	Wills 3	1858-1865	115
Spencer, John	Tuscaloosa	Wills 1	1821-1855	31
Spencer, John	Tuscaloosa	Wills 1	1821-1855	133
Spencer, Octavius, Sr.	Jefferson	Wills A	1856-1880	138
Spencer, Peter	Pike	Wills B	1862-1879	169
Spencer, Thomas B.	Jefferson	Wills A	1856-1880	227
Spinks, Henry N.	Chambers	Wills 1-2	1833-1856	362
Spinks, John E.	Macon	Records 10	1863-1865	711
Spiva, David	Perry	Wills A	1821-1855	340
Spiva, G. S.	Wilcox	Wills 3	1826-1858	105
Spivey, George B.	Greene	Wills C	1840-1864	430
Spivey, William E.	Lowndes	Wills C	1861-1899	142
Spong, William H.	Montgomery	Wills 4	1853-1869	439
Spotswood, Elliott	Madison	PR 9	1839-1841	62
Spotswood, Sally D.	Madison	Wills 1	1853-1875	44
Spraggins, Rebecca B.	Madison	PR 7	1834-1837	93
Spraggins, Robert S.	Madison	Wills 1	1853-1875	535
Spratling, Johnson	Chambers	Wills 1-2	1833-1856	307
Springer, Job	Greene	Wills B	1817-1841	91
Spuller?, Stephen	Mobile	Wills 3	1857-1870	395
Stack, Adam	Autauga	Reports A	1825-1830	235
Stafford, Nancy Anne	Lauderdale	Wills B	1859-1870	104
Staggers, John H.	Butler	Wills 1	1853-1864	123
Stainback, Julia Eliza	Mobile	Wills 2	1837-1857	369
Stainton, John	Monroe	W&D D	1850-1856	147
Stallworth, James	Pike	Wills A	1845-1862	169
Stallworth, M. P.	Monroe	W&D F	1861-1867	189
Stamps, Britton	Butler	Wills 2	1864-1875	140
Stamps, James, Sr.	Chambers	Wills 1-2	1833-1856	252
Stamps, Joshua	Lauderdale	Wills A	1835-1858	209
Stamps, William W.	Madison	PR 4	1826-1829	218

TESTATOR	COUNTY	WHERE FOUND		PAGE
Stanard, J. M.	Baldwin	Wills A	1811-1881	126
Stanback, Dixon	Morgan	OCR 6	1831-1837	232
Stanback, William	Lauderdale	Wills B	1859-1870	122
Standefer, James H.	Madison	Wills 1	1853-1875	213
Standifer, Abraham H.	Sumter	Wills 1	1828-1851	190
Standifer, Israel	Madison	PR 3	1823-1826	377
Standifer, Phebe	Madison	PR 8	1831-1839	411
Standley, James	Henry	OCR D	1842-1846	513
Stanford, George	Lamar	Wills 1	1844-1910	1
Stanley, Isaac	Wilcox	Wills 2	1832-1850	280
Stanley, Lewis	Barbour	OCR 6	1854-1856	478
Stanley, Peter	Autauga	Reports J	1858-1859	146
Stanley, Sandes	Henry	Deeds A-B	1822-1840	19
Stanton, Elizabeth	Sumter	Wills 1	1828-1851	191
Stanton, Henry T.	Sumter	Wills 1	1828-1851	243
Stanwood, Jacob	Lowndes	Wills C	1861-1899	194
Stapler, John	Madison	Wills 1	1853-1875	109
Stapler, William	Lauderdale	Wills B	1859-1870	58
Staples, Elizabeth J.	Wilcox	Wills 5	1855-1870	362
Stapleton, John E.	Baldwin	Wills A	1811-1881	112
Stark, John W.	Russell	Wills 2	1850-1873	128
Stark, Mary A.	Macon	WAC&A 11	1862-1870	458
Stark, William T.	Russell	Wills 2	1850-1873	352
Starke, Charlotte R.	Mobile	Wills 1	1813-1837	113
Starke, Douglass	Clarke	OCR	1825-1832	61
Starke, Lewis	Baldwin	Wills A	1811-1881	200
Starke, Thomas L.	Clarke	PR E	1840-1845	272
Statuz, George	Mobile	Wills 1	1813-1837	225
Stayler,? William	Mobile	Wills 2	1837-1857	64
Steadham, Edward, Sr.	Baldwin	Wills A	1811-1881	261
Stedham, Benjamin	Baldwin	Wills A	1811-1881	46
Stedham, Jesse, Sr.	Baldwin	Wills A	1811-1881	142
Stedham, Mary A.	Baldwin	Wills A	1811-1881	144
Steed, Frederick	Calhoun	Loose	Probated 1845	
Steel, Mary	Tuscaloosa	Wills 3	1858-1865	122
Steel, Michael	Mobile	Wills 3	1857-1870	507
Steel, Sylvester	Jefferson	PM	1844-1854	430
Steele, Abner A.	Greene	Wills C	1840-1864	2
Steele, Charles, Sr.	Mobile	Wills 2	1837-1857	219
Steele, George	Madison	Wills 1	1853-1875	69
Steele, George G.	Madison	Wills 1	1853-1875	220
Steele, Joseph	Madison	PR 15	1850-1853	526
Steele, Joseph G.	Greene	Wills C	1840-1864	587
Steele, William	Greene	Wills C	1840-1864	558
Steelman, Charles	Montgomery	Wills 2	1820-1845	236
Steenson, James W.	Lawrence	I&W A	1850-1857	409
Steger, Benjamin H.	Madison	Wills 1	1853-1875	352
Steger, John P.	Madison	PR 2&5	1818-1826	237
Steger, Rebekah M.	Madison	Wills 1	1853-1875	146
Stephen, Ann	Lauderdale	Wills B	1859-1870	141
Stephens, Hanson B.	Barbour	OCR 15	1865-1866	581

TESTATOR	COUNTY	WHERE FOUND		PAGE
Stephens, James	Greene	Wills D	1851-1888	62
Stephens, John H.	Sumter	Wills 2	1851-1872	101
Stephens, Lewis	Autauga	Reports A	1825-1830	166
Stephens, Martha	Russell	Wills 1	1838-1849	141
Stephens, Mary	Russell	Wills 2	1850-1873	176
Stephenson, James	Wilcox	Wills 4	1847-1862	19
Stephenson, John	Mobile	Wills 3	1857-1870	18
Stephenson, William D.	Lawrence	I&W A	1850-1857	530
Sterrett, David W.	Wilcox	Wills 3	1826-1858	462
Sterrett, J. W.	Montgomery	Wills 2	1820-1845	156
Stevens, Fatha	Chambers	Wills 3	1856-1899	72
Stevens, Lewis	Greene	Wills C	1840-1864	74
Stevens, Nancy	Monroe	W&D F	1861-1867	129
Stevens, Theophilus	Chambers	Wills 3	1856-1899	15
Stevens, William	Greene	Wills B	1817-1841	155
Stevenson, Charles, Sr.	Perry	Wills A	1821-1855	40
Stewart, Alexander	Dallas	Wills A	1821-1849	158
Stewart, Allen	Tuscaloosa	Wills 1	1821-1855	125
Stewart, Andrew J.	Perry	Wills B	1858-1873	404
Stewart, Charles A.	Mobile	Wills 2	1837-1857	143
Stewart, Eliza	Mobile	Wills 3	1857-1870	160
Stewart, Isaac	Wilcox	Wills 4	1847-1862	74
Stewart, Jacob	Dallas	Wills A	1821-1849	243
Stewart, James J.	Lowndes	Wills B	1830-1859	511
Stewart, James R.	Autauga	Reports C	1834-1838	123
Stewart, Jane	Russell	Wills 2	1850-1873	94
Stewart, John	Barbour	OCR 4	1850-1852	571
Stewart, Martha	Madison	Wills 1	1853-1875	143
Stewart, Martha E.	Madison	Wills 1	1853-1875	217
Stewart, Matilda	Mobile	Wills 1	1813-1837	46
Stewart, Roger	Mobile	Wills 3	1857-1870	37
Stewart, Samuel D.	Calhoun	Loose	Probated 1870	
Stewart, Sarah	Mobile	Wills 2	1837-1857	214
Stewart, Thomas	Madison	PR 13	1838-1848	388
Stewart, William A.	Mobile	Wills 1	1813-1837	223
Stewart, William A.	Talladega	Wills C	1845-1853	429
Stickney, Henry	Mobile	Wills 3	1857-1870	290
Stickney, Joseph B.	Greene	Wills C	1840-1864	123
Stiggins, Joseph	Baldwin	Wills A	1811-1881	9
Stinnett, William	Limestone	Wills 5	1836-1841	139
Stinson, Alexander	Barbour	Loose Box 304	Probated 1839	
Stinson, Jordan B.	Pike	Wills B	1872-1879	50
Stith, Cincinnatus	Washington	Wills 1 ∅	1827-1888	181
Stith, Cincinatus	Washington	Wills B	1827-	111
Stith, Harriett	Washington	Wills 1 ∅	1827-1888	183
Stith, Harriett	Washington	Wills B	1827-	112
St. john, Richard	Mobile	Wills 2	1837-1857	216
St. John, Sophia J.	Mobile	Wills 3	1857-1870	27
St. Leger, Margaret	Barbour	OCR 16	1866-1868	455
Stoddard, Jesse	Madison	PR 4	1826-1829	331
Stoddard, William	Mobile	Wills 1	1813-1837	37

TESTATOR	COUNTY	WHERE FOUND		PAGE
Stokes, Charles	Clarke	GE&W	1832-1839	541
Stokes, Elizabeth	Tuscaloosa	Wills 3	1858-1865	114
Stokes, Henry E.	Henry	OCR J	1857-1858	109
Stokes, Jeremiah	Perry	Wills A	1821-1855	336
Stokes, Joel A.	Montgomery	Wills 3	1840-1854	58
Stokes, Young	Chambers	Wills 1-2	1833-1856	441
Stone, Abner	Dallas	Wills B	1850-1871	233
Stone, Bentley	Calhoun	Loose	Probated 1863	
Stone, Daniel	Autauga	Reports A	1825-1830	185
Stone, Elias	Lauderdale	Wills 3	1821-1825	157
Stone, Joshua	Wilcox	Wills 1	1821-1844	303
Stone, Marble	Montgomery	Wills 2	1820-1845	37
Stone, Thomas B.	Tuscaloosa	Wills 1	1821-1855	155
Stone, Warren	Lowndes	Wills B	1830-1859	219
Stone, William	Talladega	Wills B	1839-1845	374
Storey, Margaret	Talladega	W&I B	1858-1864	195
Storrs, James S.	Perry	Wills B	1858-1873	221
Storrs, John S.	Shelby	Wills H	1847-1866	555
Storrs, Seth P.	Autauga	Reports H	1853-1857	220
Story, Charles	Chambers	Wills 1-2	1833-1856	271
Story, James	Greene	Wills A	1821-1827	50
Story, Susanna	Chambers	Wills 1-2	1833-1856	270
Stoudemier, John G.	Autauga	Reports E-B	1841-1845	230
Stoudenmire, Hilliard G.	Coosa	W&OCR 2	1843-1883	239
Stovall, Benjamin	Morgan	OCR 7	1837-1843	102
Stowers, Avery	Montgomery	Wills 3	1840-1854	215
Strade, Virginia	Monroe	W&D 8	1870-1871	179
Strain, Thomas A.	Morgan	FR 20	1860-1865	283
Strange, Abner A.	Limestone	Wills 4	1831-1837	391
Straughn, Fielding	Conecuh	OB A	1865-1870	164
Streater, Reddick	Barbour	OCR 8	1856-1858	524
Streator, Shepherd M.	Barbour	OCR 11	1860-1861	807
Street, Montford L.	Greene	Wills C	1840-1864	168
Street, William B.	Greene	Wills B	1817-1841	248
Streeters, William	Lauderdale	Wills B	1859-1870	44
Strickland, Eliza A.	Autauga	Reports H	1853-1857	538
Strickland, H. D.	Montgomery	Wills 3	1840-1854	140
Strickner?, John	Mobile	Wills 2	1837-1857	322
Stringer, James	Montgomery	Wills 2	1820-1845	64
Stringer, Williamson	Coosa	W&OCR 2	1843-1883	129
Stringfellow, Elizabeth	Greene	Wills C	1840-1864	334
Stringfellow, Enoch	Greene	Wills B	1817-1841	223
Stringfellow, Henry	Perry	Wills A	1821-1855	46
Stringfellow, William B.	Greene	Wills D	1851-1888	678
Stripling, Aaron	Pike	Wills A	1845-1862	193
Strong, Charles W.	Madison	Wills 1	1853-1875	450
Strong, Joshua S.	Russell	Wills 2	1850-1873	106
Strong, Nathan	Madison	PR 3	1823-1826	10
Strong, Pleasant	Madison	Wills 1	1853-1875	5
Strong, Robert	Madison	Wills 1	1853-1875	92
Strong, Thomas J.	Mobile	Wills 1	1813-1837	52

TESTATOR	COUNTY	WHERE FOUND		PAGE
Strosier, William	Chambers	Wills 3	1856-1899	103
Strother, E. H.	Sumter	Wills 1	1828-1851	233
Stroud, A. B.	Macon	Records 10	1863-1865	618
Stroud, De Lafayette	Montgomery	Wills 4	1853-1869	217
Strozier, William	Chambers	Wills 3	1856-1899	103
Strudwick, Martha	Marengo	Wills A	1820-1864	251
Strudwick, William F.	Marengo	Wills A	1820-1864	299
Stuardi, John	Mobile	Wills 2	1837-1857	268
Stuart, Charles A.	Mobile	Wills 2	1837-1857	143
Stuart, David	Morgan	OCR 6	1831-1837	564
Stuart, John	Morgan	OCR 11	1850-1852	348
Stuart, Joshua	Perry	Wills A	1821-1855	123
Stuart, Mary F.	Mobile	Wills 2	1837-1857	367
Stuart, Thomas A.	Autauga	Reports G	1850-1853	136
Stubbs, John A.	Dallas	Wills B	1850-1871	208
Stubblefield, Theodorick	Bibb	Admr.R F	1836-1846	49
Stubblefield, Theodorick	Bibb	Loose Box T	Dated 1821	
Stubbs, Lewis	Pike	Wills A	1845-1862	85
Stubbs, Nancy	Macon	Records 5	1853-1855	125
Sturdivant, Randolph	Tuscaloosa	Wills 1	1821-1855	4
Sturgis, Eli	Russell	Wills 2	1850-1873	265
Stuyler?, William	Mobile	Wills 2	1837-1857	64
Sudduth, M. H.	Tuscaloosa	Wills 4	1868-1897	317
Suffield, William	Lawrence	I&W D	1835-1840	623
Sulivan, William	Perry	Wills B	1858-1873	43
Sullan, John	Monroe	W&D C	1845-1850	72
Sullins, Bradford S.	Pike	Wills B	1862-1879	47
Sullivan, Charles	Lauderdale	Wills B	1859-1870	157
Sullivan, Jerry	Mobile	Wills 2	1837-1857	416
Sullivan, Louisa P.	Madison	PR 15	1850-1853	401
Summerhill, Elizabeth	Lauderdale	Wills B	1859-1870	41
Summers, Carlos	Montgomery	Wills 3	1840-1854	92
Summers, Elizabeth	Chambers	Wills 3	1856-1899	90
Summers, Jesse	Clarke	GE&W	1832-1839	287
Suther, John M.	Montgomery	Wills 3	1840-1854	73
Sutter, Jacob	Montgomery	Wills 4	1853-1869	455
Sutton?, James	Perry	Wills A	1821-1855	38
Sutton, Jesse	Barbour	OCR 10	1859-1860	507
Sutton, John	Tuscaloosa	Wills 1	1821-1855	69
Sutton, William C.	Mobile	Wills 2	1837-1857	265
Swan?, Isaac	Sumter	Wills 2	1851-1872	145
Swann, Tincy	Sumter	Wills 1	1828-1851	385
Swanson, Catherine	Mobile	Wills 2	1837-1857	45
Swanson, Francis	Lowndes	Wills B	1830-1859	150
Swearingen, J. W.	Macon	WAC&A 11	1862-1870	695
Sweeney, John	Mobile	Wills 3	1857-1870	529
Sweeney, James	Mobile	Wills 2	1837-1857	167
Swift, John	Dallas	Wills A	1821-1849	218
Swindle, Daniel	Tuscaloosa	Wills 1	1821-1855	316
Swindle, Jessee	Tuscaloosa	Wills 4	1868-1897	97
Swoop, Jacob K.	Lauderdale	Wills B	1859-1870	97

TESTATOR	COUNTY	WHERE FOUND		PAGE
Sykes, Benjamin	Tuscaloosa	Wills 1	1821-1855	214
Sylvester, James H.	Washington	Wills 1 Ø	1827-1888	77
Sylvester, James H.	Washington	Wills B	1827-	50
Tabb, Elizabeth	Dallas	Wills A	1821-1849	101
Tabb, Lucy	Dallas	Wills B	1850-1871	405
Tabb, Sally L.	Dallas	Wills A	1821-1849	240
Tait, James A.	Wilcox	Wills 3	1826-1858	294
Taite, Charles	Monroe	W&D A	1833-1841	210
Talbert, Ansel	Dallas	Wills B	1850-1871	271
Talbert, E. J.	Perry	Wills B	1858-1873	50
Talbert, J. A.	Wilcox	Wills 5	1855-1870	279
Talbert, Richard	Monroe	W&D E	1856-1861	18
Talbot, Hezekiah	Pike	Wills A	1845-1862	231
Talbot, John	Madison	Wills 1	1835-1875	389
Talbot, William H.	Sumter	Wills 2	1851-1872	271
Taliaferro, Mary E.	Montgomery	Wills 4	1853-1869	141
Taliaferro, R. H.	Jackson	PM	1869-	19
Taliaferro, David M.	Montgomery	Wills 2	1820-1845	42
Talley, John	Montgomery	Wills 2	1820-1845	254
Tally, George H.	Macon	Records 10	1863-1865	559
Tally, Henry Kiah	Montgomery	Wills 5	1863-1887	88
Tankersley, Frederick A.	Mobile	Wills 3	1857-1870	431
Tankersley, George	Greene	Wills B	1817-1841	250
Tankesley, George G.	Sumter	Wills 2	1851-1872	259
Tanner, Henry	Jackson	Records	1861-1881	441
Tanny?, William W.	Perry	Wills B	1858-1873	427
Tany, Sarah H.	Perry	Wills A	1821-1855	346
Tarlton, Abner	Wilcox	Wills 4	1847-1862	148
Tarrant, Francis L.	Jefferson	OCR	1831-1832	87
Tarrant, Francis L.	Jefferson	PM	1831-1832	87
Tarrant, James, Sr.	Jefferson	OCR	1841-1844	28
Tarrant, (Rev.) Leonard	Talladega	W&I B	1858-1864	564
Tarrant, Rowland	Jefferson	OCR	1824-1831	160
Tarrant, William C.	Jefferson	OCR	1824-1831	300
Tart, John G.	Monroe	W&D D	1850-1856	127
Tartt, Elanthan	Sumter	Wills 1	1828-1851	38
Tarver, Benjamin, Sr.	Lowndes	Wills B	1830-1859	75
Tarver, Benjamin F.	Montgomery	Wills 4	1853-1869	349
Tarver, Benjamin P.	Russell	Wills 1	1838-1849	29
Tarver, Catherine	Clarke	PR J	1856-1858	134
Tarver, Jonathan S.	Mobile	Wills 3	1857-1870	377
Tarver, Richard	Dallas	Wills A	1821-1849	38
Tarver, Williamson	Wilcox	Wills 4	1847-1862	14
Tarvin, Elisha	Baldwin	Wills A	1811-1881	138
Tarvin, William	Mobile	Wills 1	1813-1837	4
Tarwater, Lewis	Madison	PR 7	1834-1837	51
Tasker, William	Greene	Wills B	1817-1841	227
Tate, D.	Baldwin	Wills A	1811-1881	48

TESTATOR	COUNTY	WHERE FOUND		PAGE
Tate, John	Greene	Wills D	1851-1888	307
Tate, Margaret	Baldwin	Wills A	1811-1881	116
Tate, Sarah	Montgomery	Wills 2	1820-1845	206
Tate, Zedekiah	Lauderdale	Wills A	1835-1858	1
Tatom, Peter	Autauga	Reports F	1845-1850	357
Tatum, Abner	Madison	W&I	1810-1820	204
Tatum, Berry	Autauga	DM&R 17	1820-1864	48
Tatum, Edward	Jefferson	PM	1831-1832	201
Tatum, Judson C.	Chambers	Wills 1-2	1833-1856	505
Tatum, William	Calhoun	Loose	Probated 1850	
Taunton, Henry	Tallapoosa	Wills 2	1864-1907	9
Tawn, William U.?	Monroe	W&D F	1861-1867	120
Tayloe, George	Perry	Wills A	1821-1855	35
Tayloe, William H.	Perry	Wills B	1858-1873	406
Taylor, Andy B.	Lowndes	Wills B	1830-1859	62
Taylor, B. F.	Lowndes	Wills B	1830-1859	380
Taylor, Baxter	Chambers	Wills 1-2	1833-1856	198
Taylor, Benjamin	Autauga	Reports C	1834-1838	342
Taylor, D. M.	Sumter	Wills 2	1851-1872	357
Taylor, David A.	Barbour	OCR 14	1863-1865	418
Taylor, Eden	Chambers	Wills 1-2	1833-1856	284
Taylor, Edward L.	Lowndes	Wills C	1861-1899	92
Taylor, Emily J.	Talladega	W&I A	1852-1857	395
Taylor, George W.	Madison	PR 10	1842-1842	14
Taylor, Grant	Madison	PR 2&5	1818-1826	111
Taylor, Green B.	St. Clair	RE F	1862-1868	107
Taylor, Harris	Calhoun	Loose	Probated 1852	
Taylor, James, Sr.	Chambers	Wills 1-2	1833-1856	175
Taylor, James	Chambers	Wills 3	1856-1899	58
Taylor, James	St. Clair	Deeds A	1824-1832	355
Taylor, Jesse	Macon	Records 10	1863-1865	103
Taylor, Jesse M.	Talladega	W&I C	1862-1866	102
Taylor, Jesse P.	Montgomery	Wills 3	1840-1854	202
Taylor, Jessie	Jefferson	Wills A	1856-1880	117
Taylor, John, Sr.	Coosa	W&PM A	1834-1842	141
Taylor, John	Dallas	Wills A	1821-1849	117
Taylor, John	Madison	PR 4	1826-1829	21
Taylor, Ludwell F.	Montgomery	Wills 2	1820-1845	249
Taylor, M. B.	Sumter	Wills 2	1851-1872	221
Taylor, Peter	Limestone	Wills 3	1826-1831	257
Taylor, Samuel	Greene	Wills B	1817-1841	129
Taylor, Samuel	Sumter	Wills 2	1851-1872	56
Taylor, Sarah	Montgomery	Wills 3	1840-1854	181
Taylor, Shadrack	Mobile	Wills 3	1857-1870	143
Taylor, Syntha	Greene	Wills B	1817-1841	202
Taylor, Thompson W.	Greene	Wills D	1851-1888	352
Taylor, Walter	Clarke	GE&W	1832-1839	11
Taylor, William	Macon	Records 7	1857-1859	728
Taylor, William F.	Madison	PR 2	1818-1832	505
Teach, Thomas	Limestone	Wills 6	1841-1846	357
Teague, Elijah	Calhoun	Loose	Probated 1857	

TESTATOR	COUNTY	WHERE FOUND		PAGE
Teague, Frances	Madison	PR 7	1834-1837	545
Teague, Magness	Madison	PR 3	1823-1826	364
Teague, Unity	Madison	Wills 1	1853-1875	462
Teck, Abigal	Greene	Wills A	1821-1827	55
Tedder, Simon	Montgomery	Wills 3	1840-1854	151
Temple, Henry A.	Coosa	W&OCR 2	1843-1883	261
Terrell, Sarah	Sumter	Wills 1	1828-1851	386
Terrell, Susan	Sumter	Wills 1	1828-1851	139
Terry, David	Morgan	OCR 7	1837-1843	349
Terry, Eli	Autauga	Reports C	1834-1838	344
Terry, George	Madison	Wills 1	1853-1875	315
Terry, James	Perry	Wills A	1835-1855	147
Terry, W. B.	Lauderdale	Wills A	1835-1858	246
Tew, Wallis	Barbour	OCR 11	1860-1861	749
Tharp, Levi	Tuscaloosa	Wills 1	1821-1855	96
Thom, Ebenezer A.	Russell	Wills 2	1850-1873	377
Thomas, Betsy	Lauderdale	Wills B	1859-1870	177
Thomas, Constant C.	Tuscaloosa	Wills 4	1868-1897	44
Thomas, Darius B.	Coosa	W&OCR 2	1843-1883	9
Thomas, David	Macon	Records 5	1853-1855	120
Thomas, Ellis	Lauderdale	Wills 3	1821-1825	54
Thomas, Frederick G.	Macon	Records 4	1850-1852	133
Thomas, George	Lowndes	Wills C	1861-1899	133
Thomas, George W.	Jefferson	PM	1831-1832	131
Thomas, J. James	Montgomery	Wills 4	1853-1869	250
Thomas, Jessee	Lauderdale	Wills B	1859-1870	150
Thomas, John	Montgomery	Wills 2	1820-1845	144
Thomas, John	Pike	Wills A	1845-1862	21
Thomas, John H.	Chambers	Wills 3	1856-1899	142
Thomas, John L.	Autauga	Reports H	1853-1857	62
Thomas, John S.	Lauderdale	Wills A	1835-1858	65
Thomas, Jonathan Taylor	Montgomery	Wills 4	1853-1869	417
Thomas, Joshua	Tuscaloosa	Wills 1	1821-1855	32
Thomas, Josiah	Bibb	Loose	Dated 1862	
Thomas, Micajah	Limestone	Wills 5	1836-1841	490
Thomas, Michael	Russell	Wills 1	1838-1849	139
Thomas, Permelia R.	Perry	Wills B	1858-1873	226
Thomas, W. M.	Tuscaloosa	Wills 4	1868-1897	246
Thomas, William	Greene	Wills B	1817-1841	41
Thomas, William	Jefferson	OCR	1841-1844	458
Thomason, Arnold	St. Clair	Deeds A	1824-1832	339
Thomason, George	Lawrence	I&W D	1835-1840	177
Thomason, James	St. Clair	RE C	1852-1859	255
Thomason, John F.	Sumter	Wills 2	1851-1872	318
Thomason, Matthew D.	Mobile	Wills 3	1857-1870	398
Thompson, A. N.	Tuscaloosa	Wills 3	1858-1865	141
Thompson, Alexander	Greene	Wills A	1821-1827	40
Thompson, Alfred	Washington	Wills 1 Ø	1827-1888	42
Thompson, Alfred	Washington	Wills B	1827-	27
Thompson, Allen B.	Talladega	Wills C	1845-1853	420
Thompson, Altemant	Lauderdale	Wills A	1835-1858	292

TESTATOR	COUNTY	WHERE FOUND		PAGE
Thompson, Asa	Madison	PR 4	1826-1829	216
Thompson, Benjamin D.	Wilcox	Wills 3	1826-1858	238
Thompson, Bradford Henry	Russell	Wills 1	1838-1849	78
Thompson, Charles	Tallapoosa	Wills 1	1838-1866	57
Thompson, Edward	Morgan	OCR 6	1831-1837	374
Thompson, Elizabeth Swain	Perry	Wills A	1821-1855	105
Thompson, Francis	Tuscaloosa	Wills 1	1821-1855	318
Thompson, George	Montgomery	Wills 2	1820-1845	4
Thompson, H. B.	Russell	Wills 2	1850-1873	397
Thompson, Hezekiah	Wilcox	Wills 2	1832-1850	214
Thompson, James	Sumter	Wills 1	1828-1851	351
Thompson, James	Talladega	Wills A	1833-1839	89
Thompson, James	Washington	Wills 1 Ø	1827-1888	26
Thompson, James	Washington	Wills B	1827-	17
Thompson, James	Wilcox	Wills 3	1826-1858	168
Thompson, James E.	Wilcox	Wills 4	1847-1862	150
Thompson, John	Baldwin	Wills A	1811-1881	81
Thompson, John	Baldwin	Wills A	1811-1881	97
Thompson, John A.	Lauderdale	Wills B	1859-1870	123
Thompson, John E.	Dallas	Wills B	1850-1871	273
Thompson, Joseph	Lauderdale	Wills A	1835-1858	162
Thompson, Joseph	Washington	Wills 1 Ø	1827-1888	5
Thompson, Joseph	Washington	Wills B	1827-	3
Thompson, Josiah (negro)	Madison	Wills 1	1853-1875	519
Thompson, Louise S.	Russell	Wills 2	1850-1873	408
Thompson, Maria A.	Madison	PR 11	1842-1849	338
Thompson, Mary E.	Lauderdale	Wills A	1835-1858	111
Thompson, Nicholas	Mobile	Wills 3	1857-1870	352
Thompson, Polly	Madison	PR 8	1831-1839	26
Thompson, Polly	Marengo	Wills A	1820-1864	193
Thompson, Priscilla	Marengo	Wills A	1820-1864	192
Thompson, Robert	Madison	PR 4	1826-1829	460
Thompson, Samuel	Jefferson	Wills 1	1818-1840	218
Thompson, Sarah	Dallas	Wills A	1821-1849	233
Thompson, Sarah A.	Marengo	Wills A	1820-1864	364
Thompson, Sarah R.	Macon	Records 10	1863-1865	553
Thompson, Solomon	Tuscaloosa	Wills 1	1821-1855	16
Thompson, Thomas	Washington	Wills 1 Ø	1827-1888	21
Thompson, Thomas	Washington	Wills B	1827-1888	13
Thompson, Washington	Greene	Wills A	1821-1827	33
Thompson, William	Baldwin	Wills A	1811-1881	106
Thompson, William C.	Marengo	Wills A	1820-1864	332
Thompson, William J.	Macon	Records 10	1863-1865	405
Thompson, William N.	Autauga	Reports G	1850-1853	245
Thompson, W. A.	Montgomery	Wills 4	1853-1869	460
Thorington, Robert D.	Montgomery	Wills 2	1820-1845	210
Thorn, James	Greene	Wills B	1817-1841	233
Thornberry, Joseph A.	Lauderdale	Wills B	1859-1870	126
Thornhill, William, Sr.	Autauga	Reports G	1850-1853	419
Thornton, Caroline M.	Russell	Wills 2	1850-1873	228
Thornton, Deborah	Tuscaloosa	Wills 1	1821-1855	166

TESTATOR	COUNTY	WHERE FOUND		PAGE
Thornton, Dozier	Macon	Records 10	1863-1865	87
Thornton, Eleanor Brown	Mobile	Wills 3	1857-1870	269
Thornton, Green H.	Barbour	OCR 15	1865-1866	124
Thornton, Henry R.	Sumter	Wills 2	1851-1872	255
Thornton, Hudson A.	Russell	Wills 2	1850-1873	187
Thornton, Isaac	Madison	PR 7	1834-1837	290
Thornton, Jacob	Butler	Wills 2	1864-1875	155
Thornton, James	Clarke	PR H	1854-1856	232
Thornton, Luke	Greene	Wills D	1851-1888	130
Thornton, Reuben	Barbour	OCR 8	1856-1858	280
Thornton, Rueben	Russell	Wills 2	1850-1873	337
Thornton, Sarah A.	Greene	Wills D	1851-1888	220
Thornton, T. A.	Macon	Records 10	1863-1865	759
Thornton, Walker R.	Russell	Wills 2	1850-1873	288
Thornton, William E.	Barbour	OCR 12	1861-1863	443
Thornton, William G.	Sumter	Wills 1	1828-1851	43
Thorp, Edward R.	Mobile	Wills 3	1857-1870	401
Thrash, Nathan	Dallas	Wills A	1821-1849	154
Thrasher, Baston	Tallapoosa	Wills 2	1864-1907	42
Threadgill, Harvey	Wilcox	Wills 5	1855-1870	121
Threadgill, William, Sr.	Russell	Wills 2	1850-1873	286
Thweatt, Daniel	Shelby	Wills L	1838-1868	847
Thweatt, Henry	Greene	Wills B	1817-1841	239
Tice, Thomas C.	Pike	Wills B	1862-1879	122
Tichnor, Marianna	Tallapoosa	Wills 1	1838-1866	134
Tidmore, Mark	Sumter	Wills 2	1851-1872	97
Tidwell, Joseph Berry	Shelby	Wills E	1845-1850	48
Tidwell, Lewis	Dallas	Wills A	1821-1849	316
Tiller, Ann	Madison	Wills 1	1853-1875	449
Tiller, Eliza A.	Montgomery	Wills 4	1853-1869	397
Tillman, Daniel W.	Greene	Wills B	1817-1841	56
Tillman, Frederick J.	Perry	Wills A	1821-1855	204
Tillman, Jacob	Lowndes	Wills B	1830-1859	32
Tillman, Reuben	Limestone	Wills 4	1831-1837	324
Tillman, Samuel	Madison	PR 4	1826-1829	165
Timmens, Moses	Montgomery	Wills 3	1840-1854	121
Timmons, J. W.	Montgomery	Wills 4	1853-1869	491
Timmons, John	Madison	PR 12	1845-1849	70
Timmons, Sarah E.	Jefferson	Wills A	1856-1880	281
Tindall, Asa	Limestone	Wills 6	1841-1846	165
Tinnon, Robert	Lauderdale	Wills A	1835-1858	143
Tinsley, John S.	Dallas	Wills A	1821-1849	237
Tipton, John	Dallas	Wills B	1850-1871	78
Tison, Henry C.	Henry	OCR M	1861-1862	421
Tison, Hiram P.	Russell	Wills 2	1850-1873	293
Titus, Ebenezer	Madison	PR 3	1823-1826	88
Todd, Harriet	Montgomery	Wills 4	1853-1869	450
Todd, Haywood	Clarke	OCR	1825-1832	114
Todd, James E.	Dallas	Wills B	1850-1871	183
Todd, Jenet C.	Clarke	PR L	1861-1864	459
Todd, Josiah	Lowndes	Wills B	1830-1859	291

TESTATOR	COUNTY	WHERE FOUND		PAGE
Todd, Presley N.	Lauderdale	Wills A	1835-1858	200
Tolbert, Cyrus	Greene	Wills A	1821-1827	32
Tolbert, Rhoda	Sumter	Wills 2	1851-1872	328
Tom, (free negro)	Greene	Wills B	1817-1841	46
Tom, Moses	Sumter	Wills 1	1828-1851	133
Tom, Ohoyo	Sumter	Wills 1	1828-1851	204
Tomlison, Moses	Lauderdale	Wills A	1835-1858	87
Tompkins, Christopher	Bullock	Wills A	1868-1902	19
Tompkins, W. P.	Bullock	Wills A	1868-1902	11
Toney, R. A. E.	Tallapoosa	Wills 2	1864-1907	95
Toney, William	Henry	OCR J	1866-1867	655
Tool, David	Dallas	Wills A	1821-1849	6
Tool, J. E.	Dallas	Wills B	1850-1871	326
Tooseing, Joseph	Tuscaloosa	Wills 1	1821-1855	65
Torry, Pholby	Sumter	Wills 2	1851-1872	217
Tosh, John	Mobile	Wills 2	1837-1857	44
Toulmin, Harry	Washington	Wills 1 ∅	1827-1888	7
Toulmin, Harry	Washington	Wills B	1827-	4
Toulmin, John Butler	Mobile	Wills 3	1857-1870	198
Towers, Lewis	Chambers	Wills 1-2	1833-1856	440
Towns, Drury	Calhoun	Loose	Probated 1818	
Towns, Elisha	Calhoun	PR A-2	1856-1866	459
Townsend, Edmond	Madison	Wills 1	1853-1875	9
Townsend, Henry	Madison	PR 8	1831-1839	413
Townsend, Parks	Madison	PR 14	1846-1850	611
Townsend, Samuel	Madison	Wills 1	1853-1875	167
Townsend, Samuel C.	Madison	Wills 1	1853-1875	258
Townsend, Stith	Madison	PR 4	1826-1829	310
Townsend, William	Limestone	Wills 5	1836-1841	223
Townsley, Gertrude (Eslava)	Mobile	Wills 1	1813-1837	124
Toxey, William	Tuscaloosa	Wills 1	1821-1855	199
Trammell, Appling D.	Chambers	Wills 3	1856-1899	225
Trammell, James J.	Barbour	OCR 2	1842-1847	100
Trammell, Joel D.	Tallapoosa	Wills 1	1838-1866	113
Trammell, John	Chambers	Wills 3	1856-1899	158
Trammell, John	Chambers	Wills 3	1856-1899	367
Trammell, Mary	Chambers	Wills 1-2	1833-1856	351
Trapier, Sarah A.	Montgomery	Wills 2	1820-1845	290
Travis, Enoch	Sumter	Wills 1	1828-1851	108
Travis, Seaborn	Mobile	Wills 2	1837-1857	163
Traweek, Hugh	Tuscaloosa	Wills 1	1821-1855	266
Trawick, Green W.	Clarke	PR N	1866-1870	595
Trawick, Henry W.	Russell	Wills 2	1850-1873	319
Trawick, Moses	Russell	Wills 1	1838-1849	187
Traylor, John G.	Dallas	Wills B	1850-1871	1
Traywick, Elizabeth H.	Russell	Wills 2	1850-1873	434
Traywick, Henry	Russell	Wills 2	1850-1873	89
Trenier, John (Jean)	Mobile	Wills 3	1857-1870	485
Trenier,? John Baptiste	Mobile	Wills 1	1813-1837	165
Trice, James A.	Lawrence	I&W A	1850-1857	83
Trice, Jesse	Jackson	Wills L	1870-1872	25

TESTATOR	COUNTY	WHERE FOUND		PAGE
Trice, William	Madison	PR 2&5	1818-1826	267
Trigg, Abram	Perry	Wills A	1821-1855	125
Trigg, Mrs. Martha	Perry	Wills A	1821-1855	190
Trimble, James	Autauga	Reports H	1853-1857	42
Trimble, Moses	Tallapoosa	Wills 1	1838-1866	100
Tripp, Eliphalet	Mobile	Wills 2	1837-1857	50
Trippe, Henry	Perry	Wills A	1821-1855	154
Trippe, Leland	Marengo	Wills A	1820-1864	297
Trobaugh, John	Lauderdale	Wills A	1835-1858	220
Trotter, Silas F.	Talladega	W&I A	1852-1857	210
Trotter, William	Russell	Wills 2	1850-1873	145
Trouillet, Alexis (negro?)	Mobile	Wills 1	1813-1837	74
Trouillet, Margaritte (negro)	Mobile	Wills 1	1813-1837	176
Troillett, Isabel Eloisa (negro)	Mobile	Wills 1	1813-1837	84
Trousdale, Catherine	Lauderdale	Wills A	1835-1858	201
Troy, Mary A.	Dallas	Wills B	1850-1871	272
Troye, Edward	Madison	Wills 1	1853-1875	529
True, Samuel H.	Madison	PR 12	1845-1849	58
Truitt, Alfred S.	Macon	Records 10	1863-1865	712
Truss, Arthur	Talladega	W&I D	1867-1880	241
Tubb, James B.	Perry	Wills A	1821-1855	174
Tubbs, John	Perry	Wills A	1821-1855	73
Tucker, Allen	Marengo	Wills A	1820-1864	225
Tucker, Andrew B.	Jefferson	Wills A	1856-1880	348
Tucker, Ben F.	Limestone	Wills 9	1847-1850	407
Tucker, Ethel, Sr. (man)	Chambers	Wills 1-2	1833-1856	411
Tucker, George	Mobile	Wills 1	1813-1837	39
Tucker, Harriett	Limestone	Wills 7	1844-1847	70
Tucker, Henrietta	Chambers	Wills 3	1856-1899	22
Tucker, Hiram	Pike	Wills A	1845-1862	164
Tucker, J. M.	Bibb	Admr.R J	1865-1876	77
Tucker, Lavinia	Limestone	Wills 12	1866-1872	122
Tucker, Truhart	Marengo	Wills A	1820-1864	380
Tucker, W. L.	Marengo	Wills A	1820-1864	520
Turnbaugh, Isaac	Perry	Wills A	1821-1855	30
Turner, A. T.	Lamar	Wills 1	1844-1910	8
Turner, Anderson L.	Barbour	OCR 14	1863-1865	309
Turner, Bartholomew	Tallapoosa	Wills 1	1838-1866	66
Turner, Charles H.	Montgomery	Wills 2	1820-1845	45
Turner, Daniel B.	Madison	Wills 1	1853-1875	364
Turner, Elisha	Shelby	Wills D	1841-1846	128
Turner, Elizabeth M.	Dallas	Wills B	1850-1871	159
Turner, George F.	Chambers	Wills 3	1856-1899	237
Turner, Green B.	Bullock	Wills A	1868-1902	13
Turner, Henry G.	Chambers	Wills 3	1856-1899	56
Turner, James C.	Madison	Wills 1	1853-1875	284
Turner, Jesse M.	Tallapoosa	Wills 2	1864-1907	56
Turner, John B.	Madison	Wills 1	1853-1875	115
Turner, John F.	Calhoun	Loose	Probated 1856	
Turner, Joseph	Talladega	W&I D	1867-1880	15
Turner, Larkin	Chambers	Wills 1-2	1833-1856	316

TESTATOR	COUNTY	WHERE FOUND		PAGE
Turner, Lewis	St. Clair	RE F	1862-1868	850
Turner, Meshack	Macon	Records 2	1838-1842	418
Turner, Moses	Tuscaloosa	Wills 1	1821-1855	82
Turner, Patience	Sumter	Wills 1	1828-1851	393
Turner, Robert	Mobile	Wills 3	1857-1870	611
Turner, Robert H.	Macon	Records 10	1863-1865	554
Turner, Mrs. Roseina E.	Talladega	W&I B	1858-1864	494
Turner, Thomas	Madison	PR 2&5	1818-1826	172
Turner, Thomas U.	Lowndes	Wills B	1830-1859	248
Turner, William	Perry	Wills A	1821-1855	108
Turner, William D.	Clarke	PCR M	1864-1866	421
Turner, William S.	St. Clair	RE G	1866-1870	96
Turnipseed, Isabella	Bullock	Wills A	1868-1902	7
Turrentine, Harriet	Montgomery	Wills 4	1853-1869	389
Tuten, Zachariah	Limestone	Wills 3	1826-1831	84
Tutton, James	Perry	Wills A	1821-1855	38
Twelves, Stephen	Mobile	Wills 3	1857-1870	262
Tyler, Harriett	Coosa	W&OCR 2	1843-1883	54
Tyler, William	Jefferson	Wills A	1856-1880	288
Tyner, Wallis	Russell	Wills 2	1850-1873	321
Tyrone, Jacob	Limestone	Wills 9	1847-1850	338
Tyson, Abram?	Wilcox	Wills 2	1832-1850	187
Tyson, Mason	Marengo	Wills A	1820-1864	191
Ulmer, John J?	Dallas	Wills A	1821-1849	323
Ulmer, Margaret C.	Dallas	Wills A	1821-1849	324
Underwood, Green	Dallas	Wills B	1850-1871	60
Underwood, James	Autauga	Reports H	1853-1857	27
Underwood, James	Perry	Wills A	1821-1855	141
Underwood, M. M.	Perry	Wills B	1858-1873	156
Upshaw, James R.	Barbour	OCR 4	1850-1852	558
Upshaw, LeRoy	Barbour	OCR 1	1833-1843	228
Urban, Casper	Lauderdale	Wills A	1835-1858	194
Urquhart, London (negro)	Madison	PR 8	1831-1839	153
Utley, Benjamin K.	Baldwin	Wills A	1811-1881	32
Valients, James	Lauderdale	Wills A	1835-1858	61
Vance, James M.	Madison	Wills 1	1853-1875	192
Vance, John	Russell	Wills 1	1838-1849	123
Vance, William	Macon	OCM 2	1835-1842	94
Vandergraff, W. J.	Sumter	Wills 1	1828-1851	149
Vande Graffe?, William J.	Sumter	Wills 2	1851-1872	322
Vandergrift, Christopher	St. Clair	Deeds B	1831-1849	841
Van Epps, Barney W.	Mobile	Wills 2	1837-1857	337
Vann, Abner H.	Russell	Wills 2	1850-1873	116
Vann, James	Russell	Wills 2	1850-1873	350
Vann, Joseph	Sumter	Wills 2	1851-1872	52

TESTATOR	COUNTY	WHERE FOUND		PAGE
Vann, Joseph M.	Russell	Wills 2	1850-1873	207
Vann, Martha G.	Madison	Wills 1	1853-1875	53
Vann, Thomas	Madison	Wills 1	1853-1875	165
Vann, Thomas, Sr.	Madison	PR 9	1839-1841	270
Vann, William J.	Talladega	Wills C	1845-1853	290
Vanter, Mary A.	Marengo	Wills A	1820-1864	211
Varner, Benton	Marengo	Wills A	1820-1864	183
Varner, David M.	Pike	Wills A	1845-1862	235
Varner, James	Marengo	Wills A	1820-1864	89
Varner, John	Coosa	W&OCR 2	1843-1883	229
Varner, Samuel	Marengo	Wills A	1820-1864	182
Varner, Samuel, Sr.	Marengo	Wills A	1820-1864	291
Varner, W. G.	Lowndes	Wills B	1830-1859	363
Varner, William	Macon	WAC&A 11	1862-1870	677
Vasser, Little Berry	Dallas	Wills B	1850-1871	327
Vasser, John E.	Lowndes	Wills B	1830-1859	97
Vasser, Joseph P.	Limestone	Wills 12	1866-1872	549
Vasser, Lemuel	Dallas	Wills A	1821-1849	55
Vasser, Martha S.	Dallas	Wills A	1821-1849	89
Vasser, Sarah C.	Lowndes	Wills B	1830-1859	141
Vastbinder, Sarah	Baldwin	Wills A	1811-1881	87
Vastbinder, William G.	Baldwin	Wills A	1811-1881	136
Vaughan, A. G.	Marengo	Wills A	1820-1864	444
Vaughan, A. S.	Marengo	Wills A	1820-1864	528
Vaughan, Asa	Lawrence	I&W A	1850-1857	411
Vaughan, David V.	Talladega	W&I D	1867-1880	684
Vaughan, Eaton P.	Limestone	Wills 3	1826-1831	44
Vaughan, Mrs. Eddie	Talladega	W&I D	1867-1880	711
Vaughan, Fielding	Dallas	Wills B	1850-1871	389
Vaughn, Isaac S.	Sumter	Wills 1	1828-1851	345
Vaughn, William C.	Baldwin	Wills A	1811-1881	94
Vawter, William R.	Marengo	Wills A	1820-1864	459
Vaux, Marie Louise De	Mobile	Wills 3	1857-1870	251
Veal, Nancy L.	Russell	Wills 2	1850-1873	27
Veasey, Sarah	Montgomery	Wills 2	1820-1845	8
Veazey, J. H.	Tallapoosa	Wills 1	1838-1866	129
Vedmer, George	Mobile	Wills 2	1837-1857	179
Vendel, Emilius de	Mobile	Wills 3	1857-1870	1
Vernon, Ephraim J.	Wilcox	Wills 2	1832-1850	255
Vernon, George M.	Chambers	Wills 3	1856-1899	151
Vicers, Michael G.	Mobile	Wills 3	1857-1870	732
Vicker, Thomas	Montgomery	Wills 2	1820-1845	162
Vickers, James	Montgomery	Wills 2	1820-1845	172
Vickers, Joel	Henry	Deeds A-B	1822-1840	162
Vickers, Michael G.	Mobile	Wills 3	1857-1870	732
Vickery, Rhoda	Butler	Wills 2	1864-1875	1
Vicks, Richard	Clarke	PR J	1856-1858	105
Vidmer, George	Mobile	Wills 2	1837-1857	179
Vincent, Ann	Madison	Wills 1	1853-1875	26
Vincent, Ann Church	Mobile	Wills 3	1857-1870	42
Vincent, Columbus P.	Pike	Wills B	1862-1879	81

TESTATOR	COUNTY	WHERE FOUND		PAGE
Vincent, Elizabeth	Dallas	Wills A	1821-1849	262
Vincent, John	Wilcox	Wills 1	1821-1844	366
Vincent, Mary E.	Madison	Wills 1	1853-1875	187
Vincent, Pennington	Pike	Wills A	1845-1862	30
Viner, Charles	Mobile	Wills 2	1837-1857	61
Vines, Jabez	Tallapoosa	Wills 2	1864-1907	29
Vining, Mary	Limestone	Wills 3	1826-1831	104
Vinson, Olive	Jefferson	OCR	1831-1832	253
Vinson, Olly	Jefferson	PM	1831-1832	253
Vinson, Thomas	Jefferson	OCR	1824-1831	482
Vinson, Thomas	Jefferson	OCR	1831-1832	26
Vinson, West	Pike	Wills A	1845-1862	47
Violette, Sarah	Mobile	Wills 3	1857-1870	178
Voltz, Charles	Wilcox	Wills 3	1826-1858	237
Vurge, Alexander	Mobile	Wills 4	1870-1878	61
Waddill, Edmund	Wilcox	Wills 2	1832-1850	219
Waddilt, William	Dallas	Wills B	1850-1871	396
Wade, David	Madison	Wills 1	1853-1875	277
Wade, Lutitia	Jefferson	OCR	1841-1844	291
Wade, Reuben	Jefferson	Wills 1	1818-1840	154
Wade, Susan	Dallas	Wills A	1821-1849	106
Wade, William	Macon	Records 3	1845-1850	137
Wagets, William	Lowndes	Wills B	1830-1859	14
Waits, Levi	Coosa	W&OCR 2	1843-1883	107
Waldrip, Edmond	Tallapoosa	Wills 1	1838-1866	222
Waldrip, James	Lauderdale	Wills A	1835-1858	153
Waldrom, Charles	Lowndes	Wills B	1830-1859	62
Waldrop, Elisha	Calhoun	Loose	Probated 1849	
Waldrop, Robert	Jefferson	PM	1845-1853	196
Walker, Abraham	Clarke	GE&W	1832-1839	396
Walker, Augusta A.	Chambers	Wills 1-2	1833-1856	226
Walker, B. W.	Lowndes	Wills B	1830-1859	313
Walker, C. M.	Calhoun	Loose	Probated 1857	
Walker, Charles W.	St. Clair	Deeds B	1831-1849	402
Walker, Daniel M.	Calhoun	Loose	Probated 1857	
Walker, David	Limestone	Wills 5	1836-1841	109
Walker, David	Talladega	Wills C	1845-1853	139
Walker, Edwin C.	Macon	Records 3	1845-1850	270
Walker, Elias B.	Perry	Wills A	1821-1855	289
Walker, Fannie A.	Greene	Wills D	1851-1888	437
Walker, Francis	Perry	Wills A	1821-1855	146
Walker, James	Clarke	PR&K	1858-1861	491
Walker, James	Madison	PR 3	1823-1826	95
Walker, James	Montgomery	Wills 3	1840-1854	179
Walker, James D.	Greene	Wills A	1821-1827	55
Walker, Jessie	Cleburne	Wills 1	1866-1884	34
Walker, John	Calhoun	Loose Ø	Dated 1840	
Walker, John	Clarke	OCR F	1846-1850	192

TESTATOR	COUNTY	WHERE FOUND		PAGE
Walker, John F.	Limestone	Wills 3	1826-1831	62
Walker, John M.	Wilcox	Wills 2	1832-1850	280
Walker, Joseph K.	Dallas	Wills B	1850-1871	171
Walker, Julia A.	Macon	Records 10	1863-1865	561
Walker, L. D.	Montgomery	Wills 4	1853-1869	481
Walker, Martha	Clarke	PR E	1840-1845	484
Walker, Mary K.	Dallas	Wills B	1850-1871	197
Walker, Nathaniel	Clarke	OCR	1825-1832	74
Walker, Richard S.	Limestone	Wills 9	1847-1850	42
Walker, Richard W.	Madison	Wills 1	1853-1875	527
Walker, Robert	Tuscaloosa	Wills 1	1821-1855	170
Walker, Samuel	Madison	Wills 1	1853-1875	85
Walker, Samuel	Madison	PR 9	1839-1841	316
Walker, Sanders	Greene	Wills D	1851-1888	57
Walker, Thomas	Dallas	Wills B	1850-1871	434
Walker, Thomas H.	Marengo	Wills A	1820-1864	480
Walker, Thomas J.	Shelby	Wills D	1841-1846	504
Walker, Thomas J.	Calhoun	Loose	Probated 1842	
Walter, Thomas T.	Calhoun	Loose	Probated 1848	
Walker, Wyatt P.	Madison	PR 4	1826-1829	23
Wall, Mary	Madison	Wills 1	1853-1875	452
Wall, William	Montgomery	Wills 2	1820-1845	25
Wallace, Miss Harriett	Tuscaloosa	Wills 1	1821-1855	349
Wallace, James	Lowndes	Wills B	1830-1859	83
Wallace, James	Sumter	Wills 2	1851-1872	102
Wallace, John	Lauderdale	Wills A	1835-1858	64
Wallace, Lydia	Tallapoosa	Wills 2	1864-1907	37
Wallace, R. B.	Shelby	Wills L	1838-1858	494
Wallace, Stanhope L.	Perry	Wills B	1858-1873	389
Wallace, William	Dallas	Wills A	1821-1849	22
Waller, C. D.	Dallas	Wills B	1850-1871	322
Waller, John D.	Madison	PR 6	1832-1834	665
Wallis, John B.	Lauderdale	Wills B	1859-1870	147
Wallis, John F.	Perry	Wills A	1821-1855	136
Wallis, William	Lawrence	I&W A	1850-1857	484
Walls, William	Madison	PR 9	1839-1841	500
Walser, David	Tuscaloosa	Wills 1	1821-1855	206
Walsh, Ann	Tuscaloosa	Wills 3	1858-1865	192
Walsh, Edmond	Talladega	W&I D	1867-1880	353
Walsh, James H.	Tuscaloosa	Wills 3	1858-1865	120
Walters, E. Vander	Montgomery	Wills 5	1863-1887	52
Walters, John C.	Tuscaloosa	Wills 3	1858-1865	53
Walters, Thomas	Madison	PR 4	1826-1829	20
Walthall, Henry, Sr.	Marengo	Wills A	1820-1864	245
Walthall, John	Perry	Wills A	1821-1855	68
Walthall, Richard B.	Perry	Wills A	1821-1855	240
Walthall, Robert K.	Perry	Wills A	1821-1855	269
Walton, James F.	Sumter	Wills 1	1828-1851	228
Walton, Mary	Lowndes	Wills B	1830-1859	115
Walton, Mauring	Chambers	Wills 3	1856-1899	155
Walton, R. J.	Sumter	Wills 2	1851-1872	268

TESTATOR	COUNTY	WHERE FOUND		PAGE
Walton, Robert	Madison	PR 7	1834-1837	266
Walton, Thomas P.	Lowndes	Wills B	1830-1859	9
Ward, E. J.	Henry	OCR M	1861-1862	441
Ward, James G.	DeKalb	Wills A	1837-1863	52
Ward, John	Madison	Wills 1	1853-1875	56
Ward, John	Madison	PR 3	1823-1826	76
Ward, Joseph	Madison	Wills 1	1853-1875	494
Ward, Mathias	Talladega	Wills A	1833-1839	149
Ward, Samuel	Madison	Wills 1	1853-1875	340
Ward, Shadrack	Henry	OCR E	1845-1851	323
Ward, William	Montgomery	Wills 4	1853-1869	553
Ward, William J.	Henry	OCR R	1866-1867	452
Wardlaw, James	Wilcox	Wills 2	1832-1850	194
Wardlaw, William C.	Greene	Wills B	1817-1841	245
Wardlaw, William M.	Greene	Wills B	1817-1841	182
Ware, George	Jefferson	OCR	1841-1844	161
Ware, H. T.	Marengo	Wills A	1820-1804	346
Ware, James	Madison	PR 12	1845-1849	158
Ware, John	Jefferson	Wills A	1856-1880	89
Ware, Judith	Montgomery	Wills 4	1853-1869	94
Ware, Margaret	Autauga	Wills 1	1862-1925	5
Ware, Robert, Sr.	Montgomery	Wills 2	1820-1845	50
Ware, Robert J.	Montgomery	Wills 4	1853-1869	556
Ware, Rufus C.	Perry	Wills B	1858-1873	275
Ware, Susan	Sumter	Wills 2	1851-1872	388
Waring, Ellen	Lauderdale	Wills B	1859-1870	157
Warley, James	Mobile	Wills 4	1870-1878	59
Warren, Burrass	Barbour	OCR 2	1842-1847	213
Warren, David Talbot	Mobile	Wills 3	1857-1870	179
Warren, Malachi	Lowndes	Wills C	1861-1899	65
Warren, Malachia	Lowndes	Wills C	1861-1899	125
Warren, Milly	Greene	Wills B	1817-1841	164
Warren, Samuel D., Sr.	DeKalb	Wills B	1869-1905	3
Warren, Thomas	Barbour	OCR 1	1833-1843	293
Warren, Thomas, Sr.	Barbour	OCR 3	1847-1851	301
Warren, William, Sr.	Calhoun	Loose	Probated 1845	
Warren, William	Mobile	Wills 4	1870-1878	95
Warren, William S.	Tallapoosa	Wills 1	1838-1866	199
Warwick, Keziah	Talladega	W&I D	1867-1880	355
Warwick, Thomas	Talladega	W&I D	1867-1880	337
Washington, Bushrod W.	Madison	PR 2&5	1818-1826	519
Washington, E. A.	Sumter	Wills 2	1851-1872	99
Washington, N.	Monroe	W&D D	1850-1856	271
Washington, R. D.	Sumter	Wills 2	1851-1872	9
Washington, Robert	Sumter	Wills 2	1851-1872	139
Washington, John	Tuscaloosa	Wills 1	1821-1855	137
Waters, John W.	Talladega	W&I D	1867-1880	730
Waters, Samuel	Perry	Wills A	1821-1855	217
Watkins, B. O.	Marengo	Wills A	1820-1864	233
Watkins, Evan, Sr.	St. Clair	Deeds B	1831-1849	668
Watkins, Francis	Madison	PR 2&5	1818-1826	6

TESTATOR	COUNTY	WHERE FOUND		PAGE
Watkins, George W.	Marengo	Wills A	1820-1864	452
Watkins, Isam	Madison	PR 2	1818-1823	121
Watkins, Joel W.	Madison	Wills 1	1853-1875	20
Watkins, John	Greene	Wills B	1817-1841	209
Watkins, Samuel	Lawrence	I&W D	1835-1840	112
Watkins, Thompson	Montgomery	Wills 2	1820-1845	264
Watrous, Lydia Ann	Shelby	Wills L	1838-1858	54
Watson, Albert G.	Sumter	Wills 1	1828-1851	278
Watson, Aron	Lauderdale	Wills A	1835-1858	19
Watson, David	Greene	Wills D	1851-1888	102
Watson, Emily	Sumter	Wills 2	1851-1872	141
Watson, Gamiel	Marengo	Wills A	1820-1864	139
Watson, J. L.	Greene	Wills D	1851-1888	115
Watson, Jane	Shelby	Wills D	1841-1846	13
Watson, John	Coosa	W&OCR 2	1843-1883	42
Watson, John	St. Clair	Deeds B	1831-1849	670
Watson, John	St. Clair	Deeds B	1831-1849	685
Watson, John	Sumter	Wills 1	1828-1851	117
Watson, Joshua	Dallas	Wills A	1821-1849	351
Watson, Lewis	Talladega	Wills C	1845-1853	91
Watson, M. B.	Marengo	Wills A	1820-1864	276
Watson, Mary A. E.	Lowndes	Wills C	1861-1899	59
Watson, Thomas	Monroe	W&D A	1833-1841	203
Watson, Wade H.	Perry	Wills A	1821-1855	183
Watt, E. S.	Coosa	W&OCR 2	1843-1883	128
Watt, Thomas	Madison	PR 3	1823-1826	378
Watts, Comer B.	Dallas	Wills B	1850-1871	114
Watts, John	Monroe	W&D 9	1871-1872	182
Watts, Monroe P.	Mobile	Wills 3	1857-1870	634
Watts, Richard	Henry	OCR F	1848-1853	280
Watts, Thomas	Dallas	Wills A	1821-1849	174
Waugh, John	Dallas	Wills A	1821-1849	70
Wayland, Ann B.	Madison	PR 12	1845-1849	193
Weakley, James H.	Lauderdale	Wills A	1835-1858	258
Weatherford, Samuel	Limestone	Wills 7	1844-1847	94
Weatherly, Joseph	Calhoun	Loose Ø	Probated 1852	
Weatherly, Martin	Talladega	W&I A	1852-1857	474
Weatherly, Peter	Madison	Wills 1	1853-1875	493
Weathers, Elizabeth	Mobile	Wills 3	1857-1870	341
Weathers, Sarah	Chambers	Wills 1-2	1833-1856	412
Weathers, William	Lawrence	I&W D	1835-1840	354
Weaver, David	Dallas	Wills B	1850-1871	383
Weaver, George I.	Madison	PR 9	1839-1841	261
Weaver, George S.	Dallas	Wills A	1821-1849	225
Weaver, Henry	Tuscaloosa	Wills 1	1821-1855	195
Weaver, Holly	Chambers	Wills 3	1856-1899	113
Weaver, Joseph	Lauderdale	Wills B	1859-1870	61
Weaver, Philip I?, Sr.	Dallas	Wills B	1850-1871	356
Webb, Charles H.	Coosa	W&OCR 2	1843-1883	282
Webb, Elisha	Lowndes	Wills B	1830-1859	134
Webb, George W.	Tallapoosa	Wills 1	1838-1866	88

TESTATOR	COUNTY	WHERE FOUND		PAGE
Webb, Healey B.	Sumter	Wills 2	1851-1872	314
Webb, James	Autauga	Reports G	1850-1853	435
Webb, James	Lauderdale	Wills A	1835-1858	311
Webb, John	Lauderdale	Wills A	1835-1858	142
Webb, John C.	Chambers	Wills 1-2	1833-1856	165
Webb, Matilda	Lowndes	Wills B	1830-1859	247
Webb, Susan J.	Macon	WAC&A 11	1862-1870	260
Webb, Thomas	Perry	Wills A	1821-1855	225
Webster, Thomas J.	Dallas	Wills B	1850-1871	263
Weed, James L.	Coosa	W&OCR 2	1843-1883	74
Weeden, William	Madison	PR 12	1845-1849	272
Weekes, Modeste	Mobile	Wills 3	1857-1870	326
Weeks, Nicholas	Baldwin	Wills A	1811-1881	100
Weeks, Philip	Calhoun	Loose	Probated 1846	
Weeks, William	Baldwin	Wills A	1811-1881	198
Weems, Moses	Henry	OCR F	1848-1853	324
Weems, Penelope R.	Marengo	Wills A	1820-1864	297
Welborn, Thomas	Tuscaloosa	Wills 1	1821-1855	39
Welch, James	Butler	Wills 2	1864-1875	3
Welch, James	Tallapoosa	Wills 1	1838-1866	198
Welch, John	Lauderdale	Wills 3	1821-1825	128
Welch, John	Lauderdale	Wills B	1859-1870	14
Welch, Martha	Lauderdale	Wills 4	1821-1825	126
Welch, Mary	Talladega	Wills B	1839-1845	223
Welch, (Rev.) Oliver	Talladega	W&I D	1867-1880	418
Welch, Mrs. Sarah	Perry	Wills A	1821-1855	291
Welch, Thomas	Perry	Wills B	1858-1873	262
Welch, W. R.	Monroe	W&D F	1861-1865	146
Welding, James	Bibb	Admr.R F	1836-1846	424
Weldon, James	Bibb	Admr.R F	1836-1846	424
Wellborn, Alfred	Russell	Wills 2	1850-1873	160
Wellborn, Benjamin O.	Madison	PR 9	1839-1841	497
Wellborn, Elias	Madison	Wills 1	1853-1875	184
Wellborn, Isaac	Madison	PR 8	1831-1839	504
Wellborn, John Carleton	Barbour	OCR 5	1852-1853	507
Wellborn, Pollenia	Madison	Wills 1	1853-1875	30
Wells, James M.	Montgomery	Wills 2	1820-1845	96
Wells, John	Chambers	Wills 1-2	1833-1856	229
Wells, Lorenzo D.	Wilcox	Wills 3	1826-1858	262
Welsh, Mrs. Jane	Perry	Wills A	1821-1855	176
Welsh, Thomas	Dallas	Wills A	1821-1849	82
Welsh, Thomas	Montgomery	Wills 4	1853-1869	414
Wennemore, Lewis D.	Dallas	Wills B	1850-1871	205
Wesson, Harrison H.	Lauderdale	Wills B	1859-1870	164
Wesson, James W.	DeKalb	Wills A	1837-1863	61
West, Archibald	Mobile	Wills 2	1837-1857	231
West, Elizabeth	Tuscaloosa	Wills 1	1821-1855	9
West, Joshua	Shelby	Wills H	1847-1866	271
West, Mary Jones	Lowndes	Wills B	1830-1859	199
West, William	Bibb	Loose	Recorded 1870	
West, William	Morgan	FR 20	1860-1865	27

TESTATOR	COUNTY	WHERE FOUND		PAGE
West, Willis W.	Perry	Wills B	1858-1873	400
Westbrook, Durant	Dallas	Wills B	1850-1871	71
Westbrook, Moses	Marengo	Wills A	1820-1864	493
Westcott, Samuel T.	Montgomery	Wills 4	1853-1869	119
Wester, Edward	St. Clair	RE C	1852-1859	200
Westmoreland, A. A.	Lauderdale	Wills A	1835-1858	203
Westmoreland, E. B.	Lauderdale	Wills A	1835-1858	265
Weston, Robert	Sumter	Wills 1	1828-1851	259
Whaley, Archibald	Pike	Wills B	1862-1879	120
Wharton, George R.	Madison	Wills 1	1853-1875	510
Wharton, William	St. Clair	Deeds C	1846-1855	195
Whatley, George C.	Calhoun	Loose	Probated 1850	
Whatley, L. J.	Monroe	W&D 9	1871-1872	246
Whatley, Reuben	Mobile	Wills 3	1857-1870	490
Whatley, William H.	Lowndes	Wills C	1861-1899	107
Whatley, William J.	Calhoun	Loose	Probated 1866	
Whatley, Willis, Sr.	Clarke	OCR	1825-1832	375
Whatley, Wyatt	Chambers	Wills 1-2	1833-1856	79
Whealan, Thomas	Dallas	Wills B	1850-1871	433
Whealand, Thomas	Dallas	Wills B	1850-1871	429
Wheat, Artemisia	Chambers	Wills 3	1856-1899	44
Wheat, John	Tuscaloosa	Wills 1	1821-1855	323
Wheat, Moses	Chambers	Wills 1-2	1833-1856	294
Wheelan, Benjamin L.	Hale	Wills A	1867-1923	61
Wheeler, Noah	Barbour	OCR 8	1856-1858	345
Wheeler, William F.	Wilcox	Wills 5	1855-1870	465
Wheelis, Lewis	Chambers	Wills 3	1856-1899	4
Whelan, Mrs. Olivia L.	Dallas	Wills B	1850-1871	393
Whetstone, Henry	Autauga	Reports C	1834-1838	40
Whetstone, Jacob	Autauga	Reports G	1850-1853	158
Whetstone, Jacob	Autauga	PM 11		158
Whisenhunt, Catherine	Monroe	W&D F	1861-1867	84
Whitaker, J. B.	Montgomery	Wills 3	1840-1854	242
Whitaker, Wiggins W.	Autauga	Reports I	1856-1858	730
Whitaker, Wiggins W.	Montgomery	Wills 4	1853-1869	227
White, A. B.	Tuscaloosa	Wills 3	1858-1865	113
White, Absolum	Limestone	Wills 4	1831-1837	110
White, Benjamin	Lowndes	Wills B	1830-1859	151
White, David	Montgomery	Wills 2	1820-1845	246
White, David R.	Greene	Wills D	1851-1888	66
White, Eleanor	Russell	Wills 2	1850-1873	213
White, Henry	Montgomery	Wills 4	1853-1869	86
White, Henry C.	Clarke	PR L	1861-1864	119
White, J. F.	Perry	W&I	1823-1833	88
White, James	Macon	Records 4	1850-1852	59
White, James	Wilcox	Wills 1	1821-1844	312
White, John	Pike	Wills A	1845-1862	148
White, John	Russell	Wills 2	1850-1873	184
White, John F.	Perry	Wills A	1821-1855	17
White, John T.	Pike	Wills A	1845-1862	233
White, Mary S.	Mobile	Wills 2	1837-1857	306

TESTATOR	COUNTY	WHERE FOUND		PAGE
White, Mastin D.	Butler	Wills 2	1864-1875	80
White, Peter D.	Wilcox	Wills 4	1847-1862	156
White, Pleasant	Sumter	Wills 2	1851-1872	342
White, Reuben	Dallas	Wills A	1821-1849	44
White, Stringer	Lauderdale	Wills B	1859-1870	84
White, Theophilus	Russell	Wills 2	1850-1873	342
White, William	Tallapoosa	Wills 1	1838-1866	187
Whitehead, Jacob	Henry	OCR O	1864-1865	96
Whitehurst, Levi	Barbour	OCR 5	1852-1853	384
Whitfield, Benjamin	Tuscaloosa	Wills 3	1858-1865	223
Whitfield, Boaz	Marengo	Wills A	1820-1864	244
Whitfield, George	Sumter	Wills 1	1828-1851	164
Whithurst, Bentley	Russell	Wills 2	1850-1873	124
Whiting, James	Mobile	Wills 3	1857-1870	727
Whitley, Sarah A.	Lowndes	Wills C	1861-1899	38
Whitlow, John	Chambers	Wills 1-2	1833-1856	415
Whitney, D. S.	Sumter	Wills 1	1828-1851	71
Whitsett, Adoree?	Lauderdale	Wills 4	1821-1825	124
Whitsett, Joseph T.	Perry	Wills B	1858-1873	290
Whitsitt, John G.	Sumter	Wills 2	1851-1872	196
Whittle, Joseph	Bibb	Admr.R D	1830-1838	217
Whitworth, Claiborn, Sr.	Marshall	FR 6	1859-1867	585
Whytes, Thomas	Lauderdale	Wills B	1859-1870	188
Wier, Elizabeth	Tuscaloosa	Wills 1	1821-1855	1
Wiggins, Charlotte	Greene	Wills D	1851-1888	33
Wiggins, Charlotte	Greene	Wills D	1851-1888	40
Wiggins, Sarah	Sumter	Wills 2	1851-1872	22
Wiggins, Stephens	Monroe	W&D F	1861-1867	187
Wiggins, William	Autauga	Wills 1	1862-1925	21
Wightman, William	Lauderdale	Wills 4	1821-1825	120
Wightman, William	Lauderdale	Wills B	1859-1870	1
Wilbourn, William G.	Jackson	Wills L	1865-1866	7
Wilbourne, Charles	Jackson	Wills L	1865-1866	10
Wilbur, Jacob	Coosa	W&OCR 2	1843-1883	255
Wilcox, James W.	Jefferson	Wills A	1856-1880	192
Wilcox, Thomas	Greene	Wills B	1817-1841	139
Wilder, James S.	Lawrence	I&W D	1835-1840	302
Wildy, Jeremiah	Montgomery	Wills 2	1820-1845	86
Wiley, E. S.	Lowndes	Wills B	1830-1859	284
Wiley, Frances	Madison	PR 15	1850-1853	609
Wiley, Robert P.	Sumter	Wills 2	1851-1872	367
Wiley, Ruthy	Perry	Wills B	1858-1873	64
Wiley, Thomas	Chambers	Wills 1-2	1833-1856	433
Wilhite, Ezekiel	Morgan	OCR 11	1850-1852	377
Wilhite, John	Morgan	OCR 7	1837-1843	363
Wilkerson, A. J.	Tallapoosa	Wills 1	1838-1866	108
Wilkerson, Bethena L.	Macon	Records 5	1853-1855	649
Wilkerson, Jephthah	Chambers	Wills 1-2	1833-1856	352
Wilkerson, John	Perry	Wills A	1821-1855	308
Wilkeson, John	Perry	Wills A	1821-1855	6
Wilkins, John	Henry	Deeds C	1840-1846	390

TESTATOR	COUNTY	WHERE FOUND		PAGE
Wilkins, John L.	Chambers	Wills 3	1856-1899	46
Wilkins, William	Baldwin	Wills A	1811-1881	227
Wilkinson, Clare Ann	Perry	Wills B	1858-1873	39
Wilkinson, James	Limestone	Wills 7	1844-1847	340
Wilkinson, James	Montgomery	Wills 3	1840-1854	56
Wilkinson, John M.	Madison	PR 12	1845-1849	186
Wilkinson, John M.	Madison	PR 13	1838-1848	408
Wilkinson, Sidney	Coosa	W&OCR 2	1843-1883	62
Wilkison, John	Lauderdale	Wills B	1859-1870	181
Wilks, David	Morgan	OCR 7	1837-1843	114
Wilks, James	Morgan	OCR 7	1837-1843	145
Willborn, Eplorow?	Lauderdale	Wills 3	1821-1825	133
Willbourn, James	Madison	PR 12	1845-1849	424
Willensten, John (Jean)	Mobile	Wills 3	1857-1870	702
Willett, Frances	Lauderdale	Wills B	1859-1870	6
Williams, Aaron	Macon	Records 3	1845-1850	634
Williams, Abner	Montgomery	Wills 3	1840-1854	178
Williams, Alfred B.	Henry	OCR O	1864-1865	319
Williams, Amos	Lauderdale	Wills B	1859-1870	279
Williams, Arthur	Montgomery	Wills 2	1820-1845	14
Williams, B. S.	Macon	WAC&A 11	1862-1870	319
Williams, Benjamin O.	Madison	PR 9	1839-1841	497
Williams, Burges D.	Pike	Wills A	1845-1862	64
Williams, C. H.	Tuscaloosa	Wills 3	1858-1865	169
Williams, Daniel	Lauderdale	Wills B	1859-1870	18
Williams, David	Butler	Wills 2	1864-1875	71
Williams, E. J.	Sumter	Wills 1	1828-1851	334
Williams, Edward	Sumter	Wills 1	1828-1851	234
Williams, Emily	Dallas	Wills B	1850-1871	270
Williams, Henry	Lauderdale	Wills A	1835-1858	123
Williams, Horace H.	Clarke	PR L	1861-1864	102
Williams, Irene	Montgomery	Wills 4	1853-1869	362
Williams, Isaac B.	Lauderdale	Wills A	1835-1858	228
Williams, J. C.	Sumter	Wills 1	1828-1851	319
Williams, Jacob	Lauderdale	Wills A	1835-1858	135
Williams, James	Pike	Inv A	1845-1862	115
Williams, James A.	Monroe	W&D G	1868-1870	184
Williams, James W.	Perry	Wills B	1858-1873	288
Williams, Jared	Barbour	OCR 1	1833-1843	223
Williams, John G.	Barbour	OCR 8	1856-1858	205
Williams, John G.	Marengo	Wills A	1820-1864	505
Williams, John W.	Macon	Records 6	1855-1858	320
Williams, (Rev.) Jordan	Talladega	W&I D	1867-1880	427
Williams, Joseph	Clarke	GE&W	1832-1839	258
Williams, Josiah	Autauga	Deeds B		75
Williams, Judith	Tallapoosa	Wills 1	1838-1866	9
Williams, LeRoy	Barbour	OCR 1	1833-1843	228
Williams, Lewis M.	Chambers	Wills 1-2	1833-1856	136
Williams, Marmaduke	Tuscaloosa	Wills 1	1821-1855	271
Williams, Mary	St. Clair	RE A	1858-1874	327
Williams, Mary Ann	Mobile	Wills 1	1813-1837	260

TESTATOR	COUNTY	WHERE FOUND		PAGE
Williams, Mathew	Montgomery	Wills 2	1820-1845	20
Williams, Morris	Mobile	Wills 1	1813-1837	18
Williams, Robert W.	Barbour	OCR 9	1858-1859	589
Williams, Sherod	Madison	PR 2&5	1818-1826	508
Williams, Simeon	Madison	Wills 1	1853-1875	362
Williams, Simeon	Pike	Wills B	1862-1879	162
Williams, Stephen	Marengo	Wills A	1820-1864	6
Williams, Wm. M.	Perry	Wills A	1821-1855	36
Williams, William	Barbour	OCR 2	1842-1847	359
Williams, William	Lauderdale	Wills A	1835-1858	102
Williams, William	Morgan	OCR 12	1853-1855	380
Williams, William	Wilcox	Wills 2	1832-1850	246
Williams, Wilie	Wilcox	Wills 1	1821-1844	348
Williamson, Alex.	Sumter	Wills 2	1851-1872	252
Williamson, Arthur Fort	Lowndes	Wills C	1861-1899	147
Williamson, Benjamin	Wilcox	Wills 5	1855-1870	414
Williamson, Dorcas	Talladega	Wills C	1845-1853	280
Williamson, Eliza. W.	Lauderdale	Wills A	1835-1858	239
Williamson, George	Sumter	Wills 1	1828-1851	1
Williamson, Henry	Chambers	Wills 3	1856-1899	119
Williamson, Henry	Chambers	Wills 3	1856-1899	371
Williamson, Jason B.	Clarke	PR E	1840-1845	585
Williamson, Martha P.	Tuscaloosa	Wills 3	1858-1865	15
Williamson, Mary B.	Sumter	Wills 1	1828-1851	238
Williamson, Peter	Pike	Wills A	1845-1862	31
Williamson, Richard	Wilcox	Wills 1	1821-1844	360
Williamson, Robert	Mobile	Wills 2	1837-1857	88
Williamson, Samuel	Monroe	W&D A	1833-1841	205
Williamson, Stephen	Clarke	OCR F	1846-1850	67
Williamson, W. E.	Sumter	Wills 2	1851-1872	381
Williamson, William	Calhoun	Loose	Probated 1847	
Williamson, William	Talladega	Wills B	1839-1845	50
Willingham, Isaac	Coosa	W&OCR 2	1843-1883	185
Willis, Frances	Lauderdale	Wills 3	1821-1825	21
Willis, James	Montgomery	Wills 2	1820-1845	307
Willis, Maranda C.	Madison	Wills 1	1853-1875	56
Willis, Margaret E.	Etowah	Wills A	1866-1870	8
Willis, Moses P.	Pike	Wills B	1862-1879	92
Willis, Paul Tillman, Sr.	Chambers	Wills 3	1856-1899	10
Willman, Xavier	Talladega	W&I D	1867-1880	599
Wills, Williams B.	Greene	Wills B	1817-1841	249
Willsher, John D.	Marshall	FR 4	1850-1855	254
Willson, Robert	Madison	PR 3	1823-1826	364
Willson, William H.	Montgomery	Wills 4	1853-1869	79
Wilson, Alexander	Morgan	OCR 6	1831-1837	568
Wilson, Boyd H.	Sumter	Wills 1	1828-1851	74
Wilson, Cunningham	Talladega	W&I B	1858-1864	317
Wilson, Edward	Pike	Wills A	1845-1862	6
Wilson, Elizabeth	Clarke	PR L	1861-1864	108
Wilson, George G.	Limestone	Wills 9	1847-1850	127
Wilson, George S.	Madison	Wills 1	1853-1875	534

TESTATOR	COUNTY	WHERE FOUND		PAGE
Wilson, Hugh	Lowndes	Wills B	1830-1859	376
Wilson, J. R.	Lauderdale	Wills B	1859-1870	156
Wilson, James	Lauderdale	Wills B	1859-1870	11
Wilson, James M.	Perry	Wills A	1821-1855	104
Wilson, James W.	Lauderdale	Wills B	1859-1870	19
Wilson, Jesse	Dallas	Wills A	1821-1849	49
Wilson, John	Montgomery	Wills 4	1853-1869	259
Wilson, John S.	Lauderdale	Wills B	1859-1870	29
Wilson, Joseph	Baldwin	Wills A	1811-1881	2
Wilson, Joseph	Calhoun	Loose	Probated 1850	
Wilson, Joshua	Clarke	PR E	1840-1845	405
Wilson, Joshua	Clarke	PR L	1861-1864	106
Wilson, Margaret	Mobile	Wills 1	1813-1837	73
Wilson, Marvin	Wilcox	Wills 4	1847-1862	143
Wilson, Mary	Henry	OCR M	1861-1862	463
Wilson, Matthew	Lauderdale	Wills B	1859-1870	134
Wilson, Priscilla	Madison	Wills 1	1853-1875	444
Wilson, Rachel H.	Mobile	Wills 2	1837-1857	170
Wilson, Richard C.	Wilcox	Wills 3	1826-1858	321
Wilson, Sallie	Clarke	PR K	1858-1861	298
Wilson, Thomas	Monroe	W&D C	1845-1850	257
Wilson, William	Montgomery	Wills 2	1820-1845	270
Wilson, Woodman	Sumter	Wills 1	1828-1851	331
Wilton, Margaret	Coosa	W&OCR 2	1843-1883	224
Wimberly, Hardy	Jefferson	OCR	1831-1832	54
Wimbish, Frances	Chambers	Wills 3	1856-1899	25
Windfield, Freeman	Perry	Wills A	1821-1855	101
Windham, William	Montgomery	Wills 4	1853-1869	531
Wing, James M.	Baldwin	Wills A	1811-1881	107
Wingate, John M.	Sumter	Wills 1	1828-1851	274
Wingate, Walter	Monroe	W&D C	1845-1850	556
Winn, Abner	Tuscaloosa	Wills 3	1858-1865	35
Winn, Gallanus	Madison	PR 9	1839-1841	30
Winn, Jack	Tuscaloosa	Wills 4	1868-1897	66
Winn, Lemuel P.	Calhoun	Loose	Probated 1854	
Winn, Lucretia	Tuscaloosa	Wills 3	1858-1865	27
Winsett, Asa	Limestone	Wills 4	1831-1837	539
Winship, L.? (S.?) A.	Bibb	Admr.R I	1858-1865	465
Winslett, James	Tallapoosa	Wills 1	1838-1866	196
Winston, Lucy	Lauderdale	Wills 4	1821-1825	75
Winston, Lucy	Lauderdale	Wills B	1859-1870	20
Winston, Sallie Ann	Sumter	Wills 1	1828-1851	207
Winston, Thomas	Chambers	Wills 3	1856-1899	219
Winter, Charles	Tallapoosa	Wills 1	1838-1866	163
Wise, Jacob	Barbour	OCR 3	1847-1851	397
Wise, John	Chambers	Wills 3	1856-1899	61
Wiswall, Joseph	Mobile	Wills 3	1857-1870	209
Witherington, W. C.	Tuscaloosa	Wills 4	1868-1897	110
Withers, Augustine J.	Madison	Wills 1	1853-1875	407
Withers, John	Madison	PR 3	1823-1826	394
Withers, Mary H.	Madison	PR 14	1846-1850	138

TESTATOR	COUNTY	WHERE FOUND		PAGE
Witherspoon, R. F.	Greene	Wills B	1817-1841	278
Withrow, John	DeKalb	Wills A	1837-1863	21
Woody, ? Samuel	Chambers	Wills 3	1856-1899	131
Wofford, A. D.	Limestone	Wills 9	1847-1850	551
Wolff, Abraham	Mobile	Wills 3	1857-1870	81
Womac, Josiah	Calhoun	PR A-2	1856-1866	315
Womac, Josiah	Calhoun	Loose	Probated 1866	
Womack, John	Washington	Wills 1 ∅	1827-1888	137
Womack, John	Washington	Wills B	1827-	87
Womack, John B.	Lauderdale	Wills A	1835-1858	136
Womack, Kinchen	Monroe	W&D D	1850-1856	85
Womack, Mary Ann	Macon	Records 7	1857-1859	32
Womack, William	Tuscaloosa	Wills 3	1858-1865	93
Wood, Alexander H.	Lauderdale	Wills B	1859-1870	14
Wood, Callabel	Lauderdale	Wills B	1859-1870	275
Wood, Commodore D.	Coosa	W&OCR 2	1843-1883	109
Wood, E. B.	Greene	Wills B	1817-1841	179
Wood, Elizabeth	Montgomery	Wills 2	1820-1845	32
Wood, George	Calhoun	Loose	Probated 1859	
Wood, Green	Lowndes	Wills B	1830-1859	84
Wood, James	Calhoun	Loose	Probated 1841	
Wood, James	Pike	Wills B	1862-1879	42
Wood, Josiah	Lauderdale	Wills 3	1821-1825	36
Wood, Martha	Jefferson	Wills A	1856-1880	176
Wood, Mary	Lowndes	Wills B	1830-1859	148
Wood, Nancy	Lauderdale	Wills B	1859-1870	104
Wood, Nathan	Coosa	W&OCR 2	1843-1883	52
Wood, Rebecca	Madison	W&I	1810-1820	142
Wood, Sally B.	Shelby	Wills H	1847-1866	275
Wood, Sterling	Morgan	OCR 6	1831-1837	444
Wood, Susannah	Lauderdale	Wills 3	1821-1825	24
Wood, Thomas C.	Talladega	W&I B	1858-1864	273
Wood, William P.	Macon	Records 10	1863-1865	525
Woodard, Isham	Autauga	Reports F	1845-1850	257
Woodcock, Dr. John H.	Mobile	Wills 3	1857-1870	535
Woodfin, David	Perry	Wills B	1858-1873	184
Woodfin, James	Perry	Wills B	1858-1873	56
Woodruff, Daniel P.	Lowndes	Wills B	1830-1859	308
Woodruff, Lewis T.	Mobile	Wills 3	1857-1870	684
Woodruff, Luther D.	Mobile	Wills 2	1837-1857	3
Woodruff, Michael	Russell	Wills 2	1850-1873	422
Woodruff, Moses	Calhoun	Loose	Probated 1849	
Woodruff, Rosannah	Calhoun	Loose	Probated 1858	
Woods, Ashley	Dallas	Wills A	1821-1849	149
Woods, Bailey M.	Dallas	Wills A	1821-1849	60
Woods, C. A.	Lowndes	Wills B	1830-1859	99
Woods, Eliza	Lauderdale	Wills B	1859-1870	103
Woods, Martha	Chambers	Wills 1-2	1833-1856	468
Woods, Susana	Lauderdale	Wills A	1835-1858	40
Woods, Thomas, Sr.	Dallas	Wills A	1821-1849	108
Woods, William	Lauderdale	Wills A	1835-1858	217

TESTATOR	COUNTY	WHERE FOUND		PAGE
Woods, William C.	Dallas	Wills A	1821-1849	196
Woods, William H.	Sumter	Wills 1	1828-1851	288
Woodson, John G.	Russell	Wills 2	1850-1873	186
Woodward, Keziah	Tallapoosa	Wills 1	1838-1866	40
Woodward, Y. C.	Calhoun	Loose	Probated 1841	
Woody, Samuel	Chambers	Wills 3	1856-1899	131
Woodyard, Walter	Washington	Wills 1 ∅	1827-1888	129
Woodyard, Walter	Washington	Wills B	1827-	82
Woolard, Elizabeth	Mobile	Wills 2	1837-1857	267
Wooley, Columbus H.	Bibb	Admr.R I	1858-1865	745
Wooley, Pinkney	Bibb	Admr.R I	1858-1865	722
Woolf, Carlton	Calhoun	PR B	1856-1865	108
Woolf, Darius S. J.	Wilcox	Wills 4	1847-1862	72
Woolf, Henry	Marengo	Wills A	1820-1864	31
Woolf, Reading	Marengo	Wills A	1820-1864	24
Woolley, Andrew	Perry	Wills B	1858-1873	362
Wooten, Benjamin B.	Lauderdale	Wills B	1859-1870	184
Wooten, H. V.	Lowndes	Wills B	1830-1859	341
Wooten, James	Marengo	Wills A	1820-1864	312
Wooten, M. M. M.	Sumter	Wills 2	1851-1872	237
Wooten, William	Russell	Wills 1	1838-1849	147
Word, Charles	Madison	Wills 1	1853-1875	202
Worley, Adonijah	Dallas	Wills A	1821-1849	77
Worley, Cader	Clarke	GE&W	1832-1839	499
Worley, Francis	Madison	PR 15	1850-1853	609
Worrell, Richard	Marengo	Wills A	1820-1864	69
Worsham, J. B.	Washington	Wills 1 ∅	1827-1888	214
Worsham, J. B.	Washington	Wills B	1827-	129
Worthey, John S.	Montgomery	Wills 4	1853-1869	376
Worthington, George	Jefferson	OCR	1841-1844	420
Worthington, John	Jefferson	PM	1831-1832	42
Worthington, Juda	Jefferson	Wills A	1856-1880	4
Worthington, Judith	Jefferson	Wills A	1856-1880	4
Worthington, Robert	Jefferson	Wills A	1856-1880	300
Worthy, Thomas	Chambers	Wills 1-2	1833-1856	284
Wortley, Thomas R.	Macon	Records 3	1845-1850	701
Wray, Phillip	Montgomery	Wills 3	1840-1854	223
Wren, Robert L.	Marengo	Wills A	1820-1864	471
Wren, Samantha A.	Sumter	Wills 2	1851-1872	289
Wren, William	Dallas	Wills A	1821-1849	155
Wrenn, Sarah	Sumter	Wills 1	1828-1851	202
Wright, Benjamin	Autauga	Wills 1	1862-1925	30
Wright, Daviel, Sr.	Madison	PR 8	1831-1839	354
Wright, David	Montgomery	Wills 4	1853-1869	566
Wright, Elizabeth	Greene	Wills B	1817-1841	225
Wright, Francis	Chambers	Wills 1-2	1833-1856	226
Wright, G. W.	Butler	Wills 2	1864-1875	37
Wright, Henry	Chambers	Wills 1-2	1833-1856	298
Wright, James David	Madison	PR 2&5	1818-1826	368
Wright, John	Macon	Records 10	1863-1865	32
Wright, John	Montgomery	Wills 3	1840-1854	77

TESTATOR	COUNTY	WHERE FOUND		PAGE
Wright, Lancelot	Tallapoosa	Wills 1	1838-1866	161
Wright, Louis	Morgan	OCR 11	1850-1852	206
Wright, Meredith	Montgomery	Wills 4	1853-1869	319
Wright, Phillip	Lauderdale	Wills A	1835-1858	141
Wright, Rufus L.	Perry	Wills B	1858-1873	279
Wright, Thomas J.	Jefferson	Wills A	1856-1880	216
Wright, William C.	Mobile	Wills 3	1857-1870	379
Wyatt, Ann T. R.	Autauga	Reports F	1845-1850	570
Wyatt, Edwin H.	Chambers	Wills 3	1856-1899	215
Wyatt, Susanna E.	Madison	PR 8	1831-1839	165
Wyatt, Thomas M.	Coosa	W&OCR 2	1843-1883	311
Wyatt, William	Autauga	Reports K	1859-1861	125
Wyche, Mrs. Middleton	Madison	Wills 1	1853-1875	7
Wyche, Nathaniel	Madison	Deeds A	1810-1816	233
Wyche, William H.	Madison	PR 6	1832-1834	684
Wyckoff, Isaac B.	Chambers	Wills 3	1856-1899	233
Wynn, Eleanor	Greene	Wills C	1840-1864	203
Wyrosdick, Alex	Pike	Wills B	1862-1879	117
Yancey, Absalom	Russell	Wills 2	1850-1873	12
Yancy, Minus	Jefferson	Wills A	1856-1880	95
Yancy, William L.	Montgomery	Wills 4	1853-1869	425
Yarborough, Alfred	Sumter	Wills 2	1851-1872	143
Yarbrough, David	Perry	Wills A	1821-1855	129
Yarbrough, James W.	Coosa	W&PM A	1834-1842	296
Yarbrough, Mary A. B.	Limestone	Wills 12	1866-1872	629
Yarbrough, Manoah	St. Clair	Deeds B	1831-1849	313
Yeaman, William	Talladega	W&I B	1858-1864	413
Yeiser, Mary V.	Lauderdale	Wills B	1859-1870	176
Yeldell, Robert	Butler	Wills 2	1864-1875	148
York, Elizabeth	Clarke	PR L	1861-1864	78
York, Jabez	Clarke	PR H	1854-1856	365
York, Joseph	Madison	Deeds A	1810-1816	18 A
York, Uriah	Lauderdale	Wills A	1835-1858	9
Young, Bernard	Montgomery	Wills 4	1853-1869	293
Young, David	Lauderdale	Wills 3	1821-1825	105
Young, E.	Marengo	Wills A	1820-1864	304
Young, G. W.	Lowndes	Wills C	1861-1899	72
Young, Harrison	Tallapoosa	Wills 1	1838-1866	1
Young, Henry	Wilcox	Wills 5	1855-1870	143
Young, Henry, Sr.	Wilcox	Wills 4	1847-1862	200
Young, Isaac	Calhoun	Loose	Probated 1843	
Young, James	Marengo	Wills A	1820-1864	109
Young, James G.	Wilcox	Wills 3	1826-1858	447
Young, James W.	Mobile	Wills 3	1857-1870	738
Young, John	Coosa	W&OCR 2	1843-1883	126
Young, John	Lauderdale	Wills B	1859-1870	273
Young, John	Monroe	W&D A	1833-1841	80
Young, Robert J.	Mobile	Wills 3	1857-1870	672

TESTATOR	COUNTY	WHERE FOUND		PAGE
Young, Rebecca	Butler	Wills 2	1864-1875	16
Young, Samuel	Wilcox	Wills 3	1826-1858	356
Young, William	Marshall	FR 5	1855-1859	578
Young, William C.	Barbour	OCR 4	1850-1852	131
Young, William M.	Mobile	Wills 2	1837-1857	80
Youngblood, Thomas R.	Calhoun	Loose	Probated 1857	
Zeigler, Henry	Autauga	Reports C	1834-1838	675
Zeigler, Jacob	Autauga	Reports B	1829-1833	85
Zeigler, Nicholas	Autauga	Reports E-A	1838-1841	276
Zeigler, William	Autauga	Reports F	1845-1850	80
Zimmerman, Felix	Tallapoosa	Wills 1	1838-1866	135
Zimmerman, Irvin H.	Wilcox	Wills 4	1847-1862	18
Zimmerman, Thomas J.	Elmore	Wills A	1866-1906	17

www.ingramcontent.com/pod-product-compliance
Lightning Source LLC
Chambersburg PA
CBHW062045220426
43662CB00010B/1655